Designing
Things

To my Parents
To Paul

Designing
Things

A Critical Introduction to the
Culture of Objects

Prasad Boradkar

Oxford • New York

English edition
First published in 2010 by
Berg
Editorial offices:
First Floor, Angel Court, 81 St Clements Street, Oxford OX4 1AW, UK
175 Fifth Avenue, New York, NY 10010, USA

Berg is the imprint of Oxford International Publishers Ltd.

Library of Congress Cataloging-in-Publication Data

Boradkar, Prasad.
   Designing things: a critical introduction to the culture of objects / Prasad
Boradkar. — English ed.
      p. cm.
   Includes bibliographical references and index.
   ISBN 978-1-84520-427-3 (pbk.) — ISBN 978-1-84520-426-6 (cloth) 1. Design—
Philosophy. 2. Design—Social aspects. 3. Consumer goods—Social aspects.
4. Consumer goods—Psychological aspects. I. Title.
   NK1505.B67 2010
   745.401—dc22

                                                                          2010005520

British Library Cataloguing-in-Publication Data

A catalogue record for this book is available from the British Library.

ISBN   978 1 84520 426 6 (Cloth)
       978 1 84520 427 3 (Paper)

Typeset by JS Typesetting Ltd, Porthcawl, Mid Glamorgan
Printed in the UK by the MPG Books Group

www.bergpublishers.com

CONTENTS

ILLUSTRATIONS

INTRODUCTION

> The wealth of those societies in which the capitalist mode of production prevails, presents itself as "an immense accumulation of commodities," its unit being a single commodity.
>
> Karl Marx, *Capital*

> What is a thing? The question is quite old. What remains ever new about it is merely that it must be asked again and again.
>
> Martin Heidegger, *What is a Thing?*

> There is an extraordinary lack of academic discussion pertaining to artefacts as objects, despite their pervasive presence as the context for modern life.
>
> Daniel Miller, *Material Culture and Mass Consumption*

The study of things is also the study of culture. All things—big and small, mundane and extraordinary, simple and complex, expensive and cheap—are essential components of the culture of everyday life. The cities we live in, the buildings we occupy, the spaces we move through, the things we use and the images we gaze upon mediate our experience of the world. It is in the constant company of these things that we go about our daily rituals of work and play. These things shape our world. And a good number of them are products of our own making; they are of human design. Design's core mission is to fashion things so that we may have meaningful interactions with the world. Meanings are neither inherent properties of the things themselves, nor are they total fabrications of the human mind; they are suspended in the spaces between us and all that is around us. Meanings emerge and change continuously as people and things travel through their lives, constantly bumping into each other.

People and things together create networks or "webs of significance," as Clifford Geertz calls them. It is in these networks that the cultural meanings of things arise. Scholars in several disciplines including design, anthropology, philosophy, material culture studies, science and technology studies and cultural studies have developed critical theoretical positions in seeking to explain the significance of things in society. *Designing Things: A Critical Introduction to the Culture of Objects* offers insights into the ideological positions and methodologies adopted by these disciplines, and in this process, it attempts to make theoretical interpretations of objects more accessible to readers of design.

The relationship between people and things has endured through 2.5 million years, since the appearance of the first stone arrowheads made by members of the genus *Homo habilis*. This long-lasting bond has been symbiotic, and in order to recognize its significance, let us, for a moment, visualize two entirely different, improbable but potentially enlightening scenarios: a world without people and a world without things. In the first scenario, imagine that people have suddenly disappeared, leaving all things behind absolutely intact. Assume, for the second scenario, that all human-made artifacts have vanished leaving us in a world that can only be described as "natural." Such an exercise is, of course, riddled with the fundamental problem that making clear distinctions among these three entities—humans, natural things and artificial things—is not easy or even possible. However, for a moment, turn a blind eye to such boundary-defying hybrid entities as "frozen embryos, expert systems, digital machines, sensor-equipped robots, hybrid corn, data banks, psychotropic drugs, whales outfitted with radar sounding devices, gene synthesizers, audience analyzers, and so on" (Latour 1993: 49–50). In fact, doing so might actually serve to highlight how closely connected these concepts are.

Alan Weisman's *The World Without Us* (2007) is an example of the first scenario, a book in which he explains how nature, when left to its own devices, starts taking over all things artificial. Bit by bit, and with a determined force, unchecked natural forces start to demolish our products, buildings and entire cities, dismantling them with a slow and bewildering force. "On the day after humans disappear, nature takes over and immediately begins cleaning house—or houses, that is. Cleans them right off the face of the Earth. They all go... After we're gone, nature's revenge for our smug, mechanized superiority arrives waterborne" (Weisman 2007: 16). Water rusts metal, rots wood, dissolves chemicals, widens cracks and becomes the conduit for the destruction that unleashes itself on all human creation. Without people to clean, maintain and upgrade our air-conditioners, homes, roads, skyscrapers, bridges, subway systems and nuclear power plants, weeds would start sprouting from every available gap and fissure, and "gradually, the asphalt jungle will give way to a real one" (Weisman 2007: 28).

People and their things serve as a collective barricade, constantly pushing back the forces contained in plant growth, animal communities, weather systems and the ever-present gravitational tug. As shrubs, trees and eventually forests start to repossess all urban, suburban and exurban land, they bring with them wild animals. In the absence of humans, unprotected domesticated animals would quickly disappear, potentially leading to a surge in the populations of a variety of large mammals like elephants. All wilderness areas awkwardly trapped in between urban tracts would creep outwards into land left behind by humans.

However, not everything human-made falls apart. Noble metals like gold and silver used in our jewelry do not corrode and our electronics do not easily crumble; they will endure. So will bronze, an alloy of seemingly interminable durability. Ceramics and glass too possess the resilience to thwart nature's insistent proclivity for dismantling all it encounters. It is difficult to tell how long all our plastic products—bottles, packaging, bags, etc.—will survive, with or without our presence. We know how long it takes processes of biodegradation and photodegradation to decompose vegetable matter; what is not known is how long it will take to completely demolish plastics. Weisman discovers in his conversations with scientists that polymers have not been in existence long enough for microbes to develop enzymes with which to break them down. They could last for several thousand years before starting to degrade, but eventually they probably will. Weisman's detailed account of how nature eventually swallows up all human inventions makes it evident that things cannot survive without the continuous guardianship that people provide them. This first scenario proves that the durability of our products is very limited while nature's tenacity is boundless.

Imagine for a moment, the other extreme and our second scenario: a world entirely devoid of human-made things. People would be immediately stripped of their clothes, robbed of their means of transport and left homeless. Life as we know it would cease to exist; all habits of work and leisure that depend on our devices of communication, forms of shelter and systems of transportation would come to a grinding halt. We have designed cocoons (our homes and cars), personal devices (clothing and cell phones) and barriers (walls and fences) to help us manage the physical, social and cultural distance between us and other humans, and between us and nature. When the objects disappear, when the machine is taken out of the garden, will it signal an opportunity for us to fully experience an unrestrained natural world? Will it allow us enjoy what E. O. Wilson calls our biophilia: "the innate tendency to focus on life and lifelike processes" (Wilson 1984: 1)? Wilson suggests that "people react more quickly and fully to organisms than to machines. They will walk into nature, to explore, hunt, and garden, if given the chance" (Wilson 1984: 116). Does a world without things inspire a pastoral, idyllic image where humans (without any tools) would be seamlessly integrated into the natural ecosystem? Or will we be thrust into a harsh environment where survival would involve fierce struggle and staying on the top of the food chain would be neither guaranteed nor effortless. A reduction in the social, physical and cultural distance between us and the world around us would sharply redefine notions of privacy, ownership and status.

This imagined state of a world without things would not last for too long. Like our ancestors the *Homo habilis* who handcrafted their stone artifacts, tool-less modern humans would quickly begin populating the planet with new things. But in the meanwhile, an objectless world would be eerily quiet without the constant buzzing, whirring and creaking sounds of material friction. Nature's noisy machines rain and thunder, wind and tides will of course persist, but the incessant and often ignored clatter and hum of the engines of modern living would no longer be around. Our senses would have to adjust to sounds, sights, smells and textures that are not of our own making and have existed prior to us. In *Things That Talk*, Lorraine Daston too wonders what a world without things would be like. "It would be not so much an empty world as a blurry, frictionless one: no sharp outlines would separate one part of the uniform plenum from one another; there would be no resistance against which to stub a toe or test the theory or struggle stalwartly. Nor would there be anything to describe, or to explain, remark on, interpret, or complain about—just a kind of porridgy oneness. Without things, we would stop talking. We would become as mute as things are alleged to be" (Daston 2004: 9).

Both scenarios are improbable. And the goal of imagining them is not to suggest a contrast between the natural and the artificial, or reignite the conversation about the clash between nature and culture, or even suggest that these entities are distinctly different from one another. The purpose of these visualizations is to foreground the interdependence and dialog between people and things. Not only have we been creating, using, modifying and discarding things, but we have also been thinking and writing about them for a long time. Things, in turn, form the very material infrastructure on which our societies are built; they are inseparable from the activities of everyday life. In fact, "a key argument in science and technology studies has been that the nonhuman and the human are co-constitutive—together, constitute the world and each other" (Clarke 2005: 63). Human beings and things together possess *agency*, and they act in conjunction with each other in making the world. This idea is fundamental to the actor-network theory (ANT) developed by Michael Callon, Bruno Latour and John Law in the late 1980s as a social study of technology. According to Law (2003), one of the basic tenets of ANT is that "society, organisations, agents and machines are all effects generated in patterned networks of diverse (not simply human) materials." All actors in the network (people, things, institutions) possess agency and they are what they are because of the network within which they exist. For Latour, agency refers to the capacity of "making some difference to a state of affairs" (Latour 2005: 53). That *nonhumans possess agency* is possibly one of the more intriguing and unique propositions of ANT. Latour very simply explains how obvious this is. It is human agency that leads us to drive nails into walls, boil water or fetch provisions: actions generally performed with hammers, kettles and baskets. Accomplishing these tasks without these things is just not the same, and therefore he describes things as "*participants* in the course of action waiting to be given a figuration" (Latour 2005: 71). Figuration refers to the form or shape with which actors are endowed. As participants, things do not *cause* or *impose* the action; instead, they engage in a range of actions, some merely supportive or passive and others more vigorously active. In other words, the agency of things could take several forms; they might "authorize, allow, afford, encourage, permit, suggest, influence, block, render possible, forbid and so on" (Latour 2005: 72).

The title of this book, *Designing Things*, has two interpretations. In its more evident sense, *designing things* refers to the primary activity of making, i.e. the process of the design of products, buildings, graphics, interiors, services, systems, etc. Designers (and people in general for that matter) are constantly *designing things*. However, *designing things* can be read one other way. As things themselves have agency, they afford specific kinds of action, they encourage certain types of behavior and they can elicit particular forms of emotions. Therefore, in addition to being designed by us, things in turn design us. We are surrounded, not by an assemblage of passive things, but by a network of *designing things*. Winston Churchill famously said once, "we shape our buildings; thereafter they shape us." This astute observation can easily be extended beyond buildings to all things. *Designing Things*, therefore, refers to a *reciprocity of agency* and an ambiguity of design's locus of action. *People and things configure each other.* The word "configure," derived from Latin *con* ("together") and *figurare* ("to shape"), succinctly encapsulates the reciprocal form of the engagement between people and things. Indeed, this relationship directly influences how we produce our social structures and cultural forms. And it is this relationship that design seeks to "civilize" in all that it does.

Designing Things inhabits that space of inquiry where multiple academic disciplines overlap. And it does so as much out of joyous choice as out of sheer necessity. The scholarly conversation about things is as vast as it is deep, as diverse in theoretical inspiration as it is singular in purpose and as widely distributed across disciplines as focused in function. This book, in its attempt to nudge design discourse yet closer to the world of theoretical thinking about things, needs to inhabit this common ground of interdisciplinarity. In ecological studies, an "ecotone is the boundary between two natural communities where elements of both as well as transitional species intermingle in heightened richness" (Krall 1994: 4). Ecotones are rich habitats that demonstrate three key properties—a unique interaction between species, stunning biodiversity and organisms adapted to survive in these edge conditions. "To an ecologist, the 'edge effect' carries the connotation of complex play of life forces where plant communities, and the creatures they support, intermingle in mosaics or change abruptly" (Krall 1994: 4). This book is situated in a disciplinary ecotone, and hopes to enrich our understanding of things by taking advantage of the "edge effect." It seeks to build new insights upon the knowledge being developed in a broad range of disciplines, question and expand established points of views and present the seemingly mundane object as a complex network. Indeed, this is a position that material culture studies has adopted as well.

> The interstitial positions occupied by material culture studies provide a platform for a critical engagement with materiality for understanding issues facing us such as the fluidity of gender and body/object interfaces, recyclia, biotech, genetic engineering and the Internet—in short, those key materializing and transformative processes that shape new inclusions and exclusions as the critical focus of material culture studies such as new kinds of bodies, forms of 'nature' and political subjects. (Buchli 2002: 15)

Material culture studies serves as a vehicle by which to study a variety of systems of cultural production and consumption. This book also occupies the interstitial spaces among disciplines, drawing from several of them to create a mosaic understanding of things and develop new avenues for scholarly inquiry. It assumes that the boundaries circumscribing these disciplines are porous rather than impervious and elastic rather than rigid—conditions essential for a more informed understanding of things.

Behind interdisciplinarity, however, lurks danger. "The term *discipline* signifies the tools, methods, procedures, exempla, concepts, and theories that account coherently for a set of objects or subjects" (Klein 1990: 104). These elements, which define each discipline, become mixed, reappropriated and hybridized in interdisciplinary work. As Klein (1990) notes, in interdisciplinary research, the author carries the "burden of comprehension",[1] and needs to demonstrate an understanding of the primary context of the borrowed material. This burden multiplies as more disciplines are engaged, and creates a risk of a discourse scattered in content and style. This book will attempt to describe the primary context where possible, while recognizing that providing concentrated topical detail is neither the objective nor a possibility. Instead, through nine chapters, the book offers analytical perspectives on some of the most ordinary things inspired by the extraordinary vision some of the greatest critical thinkers of our time. Often, the scholarship produced by anthropologists, philosophers and theorists is inaccessible to readers of design. At times, the complexity of their thinking translates into specialized vocabularies and impenetrable writing. For a reader genuinely interested in theoretical examinations of material culture and design but unfamiliar with languages of the multiple disciplines engaged in this conversation, this poses a tremendous hurdle. *Designing Things* attempts to circumvent this obstacle in an effort to bring the worlds of object creation and object critique closer.

The surge in scholarship in material culture also raises the questions of whether things can and should be theorized. Such questions are certainly relevant, and one of the primary tasks of material culture studies (or any discipline, for that matter) is to establish its *raison d'être*, scope of study, objectives, methodologies and theoretical underpinnings. In his essay, *Thing Theory*, Bill Brown asks: "Do we really need anything like thing theory the way we need narrative theory or cultural theory, queer theory or discourse theory? Why not let things alone?" (Brown 2001: 1) The phrase "thing theory" does incite some skepticism. Is this cute alliteration an attempt to convert the corporeal into the ephemeral, the commonplace into the cerebral, the silly into the sublime? Is this a wasted/wasteful effort to try and theorize the trivial? There is a certain peculiarity to the juxtaposition of the word *thing* and the word *theory*; placed together, they exude an uneasy incongruity. They are like strangers who do not seem to have much to say to each other at a swanky party. Brown himself says that thing theory could sound like an oxymoron. But it is clear that critical, theoretical examination of things is a worthwhile study. The ubiquity of things in everyday life, their role in shaping identity, their critical presence in economic systems, their existence in art, their function as markers of history, all are qualities that make them socially and culturally significant. Theorizing things can help us determine the nature of how these processes unfold, and what things mean to people. However, it is also important to recognize that "there is not, and can never be, one 'correct' or 'right' theoretical position which we may choose to study material forms or to exhaust their potential for informing us about the constitution of culture and society" (Tilley *et al.* 2006: 10). It is therefore critical to draw upon multiple theoretical positions in order to develop a holistic understanding of things and their relationship to people.

Of late, the swelling interest in writing about material culture has led to a series of books that have taken on the analysis of paper clips, chairs, iPods, cars and a host of other everyday products. "Commodities have made a striking resurgence within the academy over the last decade after being relegated for a generation or more to a lower drawer in the dusty backrooms of economic geography" (Bridge and Smith 2003: 257). This scholarship is distributed across a variety of journals and books in a multitude of disciplines, pushing it beyond easy reach. With some exceptions, this increased academic interest has not necessarily resulted in a better understanding of the cultural meanings of things or the process of their manufacture and disposal. *Designing Things* strives to be an approachable text that provides access to some of this literature not only to design aficionados, but also to curious minds that possess an anthropological interest in all things material.

DESIGN AND THE CULTURE OF OBJECTS

As the title suggests, this book deals with design and the culture of objects. Subsequent chapters will explore the relationship among the three—design, culture and objects—through a series of thematic concepts. These ideas, when unpacked, reveal that they signify extraordinarily knotty concepts, and their meanings are rooted in networks of relationships. In addition to being under the scrutiny of a range of disciplines, each of these ideas also has entire areas of study devoted to their examination—design has design studies, culture has cultural studies, and objects have material culture studies. These three areas of study are themselves highly interdisciplinary; not only do they tap each other's scholarship but their purviews exhibit significant overlap as well. In order to develop a better understanding of design and the culture of objects, it is important to locate questions about the topic in the space shared by these three areas of study.

Of the three terms—design, culture and objects—it is culture that has been labeled by multiple accounts as one of the most complex words in the English language (Williams 1976; Eagleton 2000). In *The Idea of Culture*, Eagleton traces the history and evolution of the meaning of culture, and concludes that it is a concept that is at once too broad and too narrow, too imprecise and too specific. "Its anthropological meaning covers everything from hairstyles and drinking habits to how to address your husband's second cousin, while the aesthetic sense of the word includes Igor Stravinsky but not science fiction" (Eagleton 2000: 32). He explains that science fiction belongs to the arena of popular culture, which "floats ambiguously" somewhere between the aesthetic and the anthropological. All that design produces too flourishes in this space, at times hovering close to the aesthetic (with such artistic examples as original sketches drawn by Charles Eames or Frank Lloyd Wright) and at times close to the anthropological (with such everyday objects as the Oxo GoodGrips potato peeler). Clifford Geertz's (1973: 5) definition of culture as "webs of significance" within which human beings are suspended aligns itself closely to the anthropological sense, albeit with a semiotic twist to it. He explains these webs as "interworked systems of construable signs" and emphasizes that culture is a context rather than a power (Geertz 1973: 14). And it is within this context that "behaviors, institutions, or processes" can be described. Eagleton (2000: 34) defines culture "loosely" as "the complex of values, customs, beliefs and practices which constitute the way of life of a specific group." He adds, "culture is just everything which is not genetically transmissible" (Eagleton 2000: 34), i.e. all that is socially produced rather than hereditarily acquired. Eagleton also summarizes Raymond Williams' several definitions of culture "to mean a standard of perfection, a habit of mind, the arts, general intellectual development, a whole way of life, a signifying system, a structure of feeling, the interrelation of elements in a way of life, and everything from economic production and the family to political institutions" (Eagleton 2000: 36). To Williams

> a culture has two aspects: the known meanings and directions, which its members are trained to; the new observations and meanings, which are offered and tested. These are the ordinary processes of human societies and human minds, and we see through them the nature of a culture: that it is always both traditional and creative; that it is both the most ordinary common meanings and the finest individual meanings. (Williams 2001: 11)

In other words, everything from detective novels, Zunes, comic books, hip-hop, Hollywood blockbusters, and soap operas to literature, classical music, theater and the opera can be assumed to be "cultural." Design (in its role as the creative process of production, the results of which are concrete expressions of material culture) affects both aspects of culture—its known as well as new meanings. Everyday mundane things represent Williams' "ordinary common meanings" and the creative act of new design represents his "finest individual meanings" (Williams 2001: 11). Design and designers (along with use and users) are therefore active participants in the creation and consumption of culture. "Designers are immersed in this material culture, and draw upon it as the primary source of their thinking. Designers have the ability both to 'read' and 'write' in this culture: they understand what messages objects communicate, and they can create new objects which embody new messages" (Cross 2006: 9).

The culture of objects can best be described as a network of negotiated meanings. These meanings emerge and evolve as agentic things, humans and other participants interact with each other within a network that is distributed over time and space. These interactions among the actors are forms of social, political, economic, physical and environmental negotiations. And as Nigel Cross explains above, design's role, as one of the actors in the network, is to observe and direct these negotiations for common good.

THE SCOPE AND SOME THEMATIC APPROACHES

Designing Things has undertaken the task of introducing readers to the culture of objects. As the scholarship in design, anthropology, philosophy, material culture studies, science and technology studies and cultural studies indicates, the long history of our relationship to things has inspired significant thinking and writing on the topic. Therefore, the subject matter (or subject of matter, if you will) is as horizontally wide as it is vertically deep, and neither its sprawl nor its depth can be mapped in full or included in its entirety. However, it is possible to assemble the central themes from key scholastic traditions to start building a composite image of the critical thinking about objects. The task that this book undertakes is not unlike that of creating a large portrait in the technique of pointillism—an almost infinite number of dots have to be placed just so for a recognizable figure to emerge. It involves sketching out the entire image, adopting a specific approach/point of view, and finally moving in close to fill in the details. In a similar vein, *Designing Things* adopts three visual stances—the synoptic view, the point of view and the near view. An overview of the diversity visible in the disciplinary thinking of things will serve as the synoptic view. This synopsis will assist the reader in recognizing the diversity and difference of opinion in disciplinary positions. The book then adopts the position/point of view outlined in actor-network theory, which while embracing the complexity of the heterogeneous network in which things exist, bestows them with agency. All entities (people, things, institutions and so on) are *agentic actors* in this network, and it is the reciprocity of their respective agencies that shapes the interactions among them. As suggested earlier, people and things configure each other. The agency of actors is possible only because they are integral parts of the network; agency cannot be conceived as a property of either things or people.

ANT's pioneer John Law suggests, "in particular cases, social relations may shape machines, or machine relations shape their social counterparts" (2003: 3). That is, the relations among the various actors themselves exhibit agency and configure each other. Tony Fry traces the roots of this reciprocity to the earliest instances of design when tool-making began.

> While we have always been prefigured (that is designed) as soon as "we" started to modify our environment and make a world for ourselves via the use of tools, we began to form practices that were to structure what we were to become. Effectively, the designing of design and of our human being emerged out of the use of the most basic of tools. Not only did the use of tools facilitate prefigurative acts of world making and transformation that have brought us to the fabricated and damaged world we now occupy—they also acted back (in the sense of feedback within a cybernetic system) on the tool users— hence these proto-designer/makers themselves became designed. This process, while now infinitely more complex, remains the key to grasping the relation of humans to technology, science and the fabricated world. We are never just users; we are always equally the used. (Fry 2009: 24)

The tools we have been shaping over millennia have in turn been shaping our social structure, our design praxis, our material world and us. This thinking constitutes the point of view.

And finally, the near view that helps define the scope of this book is constructed around eight themes that highlight specific characteristics of the network of things. These themes, focal points in the network (or dots in our pointillist portrait), are organized as eight chapters in the book, and they address: (1) the value of things; (2) the human labor expended in their making; (3) the social process of their manufacture; (4) their aesthetic character; (5) obsolescence and the process of their aging; (6) the need we experience for them; (7) their presence as signs in society and, finally, (8) their fetish character. These focal themes, presented as individual chapters, together form a network of ideas that can help us understand some aspects of the culture of objects. While the brightest spotlight in this book is clearly focused on things, it is impossible to talk about them without a serious discussion of other actors in this network.

These thematic selections hover between production and consumption simultaneously, explicitly favoring neither. While some chapters may address processes of production more directly (labor, for example) and some focus more on consumption (fetishism, for example), the meanings of things depend on both, and therefore they cannot be truly cleaved from each other. Needs are truly felt and they are also manufactured; planning obsolescence into products is an act of production, while the generation of waste is a byproduct of consumption; objects exist as signs because designers pick their physical attributes (form, color, shape, texture...) that make them readable and meaning is generated as consumers interact with this manifest physicality. These attributes of things—their value, their life cycles, their role as signifiers, and so on—emerge in processes of production *and* consumption. Instead of the dialectical positions often assigned to these processes, in this book they will be treated as contiguous courses of action responsible for the creation of the meanings of things.

In summary, the approach adopted for this book includes a synoptic view that maps out the disciplinary diversity in thinking about things, a specific point of view inspired by actor-network theory and the reciprocity of agency, and the near view in the form of focal themes that help fill in details about the culture of objects.

DELIMITING THE STUDY

In order to maintain some sense of focus and ward off the temptation to make too many topical diversions, it was necessary to draw boundaries around three things—product, practice, and place. In most cases, the objects and things referred to in this book are not buildings, interior spaces, graphic systems, websites, or machines, but products of traditional industrial design (or product design) activity. And while it is true that industrial design practice today is by no means limited only to consumer electronics, tools, furniture, medical devices or transportation, this study will limit itself to these very things. *Designing Things* inhabits the world of mp3 players, water bottles, turntables, hammers, cars, etc. And while many of the concepts discussed here may be extended to spaces and buildings, the explicit focus is on products, and by extension, on the practice of industrial design. Yet another boundary marks the scholarly territory upon which the ideas in the book are built. The concepts and case studies are, for the most part, drawn from literature that has emerged in the West. The spotlight on design/products in/of Europe and North America is not, by any means, an act of ethnocentrism; it is merely an attempt to limit an unbounded topic.

CHAPTER OVERVIEWS

The following descriptions of the focal themes will offer an introduction to what follows in the subsequent pages of *Designing Things*.

Figure 0.1. The Thematic Approach to *Designing Things*. Illustration by Amethyst Saludo.

CHAPTER 1: THEORIZING THINGS: DISCIPLINARY DIVERSITY IN THINKING ABOUT OBJECTS

With some exceptions, design research has traditionally under-theorized the cultural meanings of objects, and Chapter 1 outlines some of the benefits of amending this situation. While there is significant research and publication in design history and methodology, and there is a growing body of work in sustainability, the cultural study of things could benefit from more attention. A greater academic interest in the cultural meanings of objects is witnessed in the social sciences and the humanities, and each of these examinations is structured around a specific set of concerns, theoretical positions and research methods. Chapter 1 outlines how, using these tools, these disciplines construct a social, cultural, political, environmental and economic conception of objects. This chapter offers an overview of theory and justifies the need for critical, theoretical portrayals of things. However, the sheer volume, diversity and ubiquity of things present considerable difficulty in generating overarching theories of things. These difficulties as well as the benefits of such research will be discussed in this chapter. Brief overviews of the disciplines of anthropology, cultural studies, material culture studies and science and technology studies will shape the synoptic view discussed earlier.

CHAPTER 2: VALUED POSSESSIONS: THE WORTH OF THINGS

Value may be understood in sociological, aesthetic, economic and symbolic terms, and Chapter 2 will critique the value of objects from these points of view. Objects mean different things to different people, and hence they are valued differently as well. Although the most common understanding of value typically refers to financial worth, it is clear that other forms of valuation need to be carefully examined too. Business literature often focuses its attention on consumer value, market value and shareholder value, but in anthropology and political economy, value is conceived primarily in terms of exchange, and generally determined socially and financially. In addition to the tangible value forms derived from commercial exchange, objects also possess tremendous value as signs in society. As objects go through their lifecycles, they accrue and shed several types of value (financial, functional, emotional, etc.). Therefore value will be explained as a fluid aggregate network, because the total value of a thing is a constantly changing relation that is influenced by the social network in which it exists. Chapter 2 offers a critical assessment of the types of value that things gain and discard in their journeys from raw materials to finished goods.

CHAPTER 3: MAKING THINGS: LABOR IN PRODUCTION

Manufacturing is a global activity and today it is not unusual for even simple products to be made up of components manufactured in one part of the world, assembled in another and sold in a third. Most of us have no idea exactly where or precisely how complex devices like laptop computers and mobile phones are made. Certainly labor is involved, but it is expended elsewhere, it is invisible. "In the finished product the labor by means of which it has acquired its useful qualities is not palpable, has apparently vanished" (Marx 1967: 183). This concealment can be seen as negation of human activity and likened to degradation of labor often found in sweatshops around the world. With robotic arms, stringent safety laws and more equitable trade agreements in place, manufacturing does not look like it did to Charles Dickens 150 years ago. But, exploitation continues in several forms. Labor is a global, social, political, moral and ethical issue. Chapter 3 will draw attention to some of the labor issues of alienation and gender inequity visible in the global manufacturing industry.

CHAPTER 4: PRODUCING THINGS: A HISTORY OF SYSTEMS OF MANUFACTURE

The human labor expended in the manufacture of goods occurs within well-defined production systems. While production in itself is rather messy, there have been many attempts in transforming it into a science. In this industry, people and machines have to make things cheaply, in large quantities and at breakneck speed. Mass production has been accompanied by several innovations such as the assembly line, Fordism, Taylorism, flexible manufacturing, etc., and the automotive industry has found extensive application for them ever since the first Ford Model T rumbled into the streets of early twentieth-century Detroit. Chapter 4 provides an overview of issues surrounding manufacturing labor in such industries as automotive, apparel and electronic products.

CHAPTER 5: BEAUTIFUL THINGS: THE AESTHETICS OF SURFACES

This chapter begins with a brief overview of the philosophy of aesthetics. One of design's fundamental tasks is to impart beauty to technology but aesthetic development is often seen as a mysterious, creative process. The external surfaces of objects serve as expressions of style and high design, stimulators of desire, blank canvases for designers and monetary gain for corporations. The creation of style, however, cannot be attributed to designers alone; style is as much a creative act of consumers as it is a result of the process of design. In consumption, style and form can serve as expressions of taste, identity and status for individuals and social groups. In production, style and form operate as mechanisms by which to satisfy the needs of a larger number of market segments, valorize capital and diversify a company's offerings. Just as the human skin protects the body while being its aesthetic front, the object surface operates as an interface between technology and the world, as a skin that shields components and becomes the location of beauty and seduction. This chapter offers an overview of the role of aesthetics in the lives of corporations and consumers.

CHAPTER 6: THE GREED IMPERATIVE: USER NEEDS IN PRODUCT DESIGN

As design methodology has evolved, the role of ethnographic research and observation of users has taken center stage. Designers routinely watch and study people to identify needs and find opportunities where a new product can be introduced. According to cultural theorists, as new products enter the market, they satisfy not only the needs of the consumers but also those of the system of production. Chapter 6 will present typologies of needs developed in philosophy, marketing, engineering and design, along with the problems in such classifications. Needs are dynamic in nature and they often grow over time as patterns of consumption change. This growth, however, is infinite, and the satisfaction that is expected never arrives. Often, needs are not satisfied; they are merely replaced with other needs. This chapter suggests that needs be conceived as forces in a network that have a ripple effect throughout the system. In other words, needs have to be imagined in more holistic rather than individual terms.

CHAPTER 7: PLANNED OBSOLESCENCE: UNSUSTAINABLE CONSUMPTION

Chapter 7 will introduce readers to the process by which obsolescence is built into designed products. The origins of "dynamic obsolescence" will be traced back to General Motors and the automotive industry, where this practice was promoted in the 1920s and 1930s as a means of maintaining a steady consumer interest in new cars and therefore a steady income for the company. The limited life spans of products have led to social, cultural and environmental problems and have been widely decried for being unsustainable. Arguments for and against obsolescence make it evident that it is not easy to find solutions that are economically viable, environmentally responsible and consumer friendly. The rapid acquisition and disposal of goods (whether caused by changes in technology, drop in quality or démodé appearance) are unique forms of consumption that lead to new forms of conspicuous waste. Discussions in this chapter will include commentary on the types of obsolescence, the culture of disposability, the economics of durability and the impact of these issues on individuals, corporations and design consultancies.

CHAPTER 8: OBJECTS AS SIGNS: WHAT DO THINGS MEAN?

"Semiotics is concerned with everything that can be taken as a sign. A sign is everything which can be taken as significantly substituting for something else" (Eco 1979: 7). Chapter 8 starts with a history of the discipline of semiotics and explains how this "doctrine of signs" has evolved over time into such forms as socio-semiotics. Semiotics is also concerned with meanings, which exist in a non-physical, non-psychical space between people and the material world. They are not fixed entities, but emergent structures that are heavily context-dependant. This chapter also includes a discussion of product semantics, a field of study dedicated to understanding the processes by which people make sense of things, and using that knowledge in doing design. Things are never what they seem and they have multiple hidden meanings. In its analysis, semiotics can help us discover some of these meanings.

CHAPTER 9: THE OBSESSION OF POSSESSION: FETISH OBJECTS

Chapter 9 examines the obsessive attachment and devotion we often exhibit towards certain possessions. Collecting and fetishism are two unique forms of possessing because, in these practices, it is sometimes not entirely clear who is the possessor and who the possessed. Both people and things have agency, and in these situations, where people invest significant resources into the acquisition and conservation of collectibles and fetish items, the agency of things gains tremendous power. Like fetish objects, collectibles possess symbolic meanings that replace or mask utilitarian meanings. In material culture studies, the concept of fetishism has been assigned positive as well as negative meanings, both of which are central to its discussion. Four key forms of fetishism—religious fetishism, commodity fetishism, sexual fetishism and semiotic fetishism—will be discussed in this chapter.

THE WORLD OF GOODS

Photographs of people with their favorite things like cars, trophies, stuffed animals and other collectibles are common. However, it is surprising to see an *average family with all of its possessions* in one photograph. This is one of many images of "average families" that photographer Peter Menzel has captured all over the world. The U.N. and the World Bank helped Menzel "determine what an average family actually is in a country according to location (urban, rural, suburban, small town, village), type of dwelling, family size, annual income, occupation and religion" (Menzel 1994: 11). The Cavin family seen here is

Figure 0.2. An Average Family with all its Material Possessions. Image courtesy of and © Peter Menzel, http://www.menzelphoto.com/.

completely dwarfed by the volume of what surrounds them. An invisible network connects all of these things to one another, to the Cavins, and to many other things Menzel's wide-angle lens could not capture.

Understanding this network of things requires recognizing and acknowledging its social, political, material, economic and environmental significance. Each and every thing in this world of goods is an active participant in a continually evolving material culture. Design praxis, knowingly or unwittingly, is itself an active participant in the creation of cultural materials. This book has undertaken the task of observing some of these cultural materials and unpacking them to reveal their stories. And it has relied on a rich and diverse assemblage of theories developed by scholars in an equally rich and diverse range of disciplines. The following stories of value, labor, beauty, need, obsolescence, semiotics and fetishism are meant to encourage broader thinking about *how* things mean what they do, and why it is important for us to think about them. An undertaking of this kind can by no means be considered to be comprehensive or complete. Things exist as actors in a network with far too many connections and far too many complexities to be easily and completely decipherable. This book is a small addition to the ongoing and infinite discourse about things and our relationship to them.

1 THEORIZING THINGS: DISCIPLINARY DIVERSITY IN THINKING ABOUT OBJECTS

Studies of the house do not have to be reduced to housing studies, nor studies of design to design studies.

Daniel Miller, *Material Cultures*

Despite our desperate, eternal attempt to separate, contain and mend, categories always leak.

Trinh Minh-Ha, *Women, Native, Other*

Things occupy central positions in our daily lives, but their presence in scholarly discourse is scattered across several academic departments. Disciplines and areas of study such as industrial design, art history, anthropology, material culture studies, marketing, architecture, engineering, science, technology and society (STS), philosophy, archaeology and cultural studies routinely examine and debate the significance of material objects but the symbolic meanings and values ascribed to them vary widely among these branches of learning. Each one of these disciplines, by examining the material world within which we live, creates a discourse about and around objects. And among these, material culture studies is quite possibly the only discipline that has expressly charged itself with the primary task of examining the social and cultural meanings of things.[1]

This chapter makes the case that things are under-theorized in design and their critical cultural examination could be a fruitful area of inquiry for design research. In order to clarify terminology, the differences in meanings of the several words used to describe things (products, objects, gadgets, devices, commodities, etc.) will be examined. This will be followed by a brief history of the philosophy of materiality, starting with the ideas of the Greek thinker Anaximander and leading up to contemporary philosophers Harman and Latour. After a brief introduction to what theory is, the discussion will shift to overviews of how several disciplines have theorized things. Finally, the chapter will end with a list of some of the problems and benefits of undertaking such critical examinations of things.

Each disciplinary lens sets its focus on things from a perspective that is shaped by the unique purpose of its inquiry. The questions asked, methodologies chosen and results sought are determined by disciplinary know-how, and therefore the critical knowledge generated is determined by the *situation* within which the analysis is conducted. However, it is important to note that while the disciplines bring to the study of objects their own unique theoretical underpinnings and specific methods of inquiry, they also share some ideological biases. In fact, interdisciplinary research is founded on the notion that there are productive areas of convergence (the ecotonal zones) among disciplines where new scholarship can emerge. While disciplinary analyses may foreground specific qualities of things, in interdisciplinary analyses they can inform each other while expanding the discourse of the cultural meanings of objects. Interdisciplinarity takes several forms, but the two most commonly discussed types are multidisciplinarity and transdisciplinarity. "Multidisciplinarity signifies the juxtaposition of disciplines. It is essentially *additive*, not *integrative*... The participating disciplines are neither changed nor enriched, and the lack of 'a well-defined matrix' of interactions means disciplinary relationships are likely to be limited and transitory" (Klein 1990: 56). Generally speaking, in multidisciplinary approaches experts from several disciplines are involved on a research project but their work may not always intersect. In such situations the problem may be segmented into smaller issues that can then be appropriately handled by single disciplines. On the other hand, transdisciplinarity refers to situations where the knowledge and tools of one discipline influence and redirect the results of another. Much more disruptive and difficult to manage, engagement of this nature typically signals a destruction of disciplinary boundaries with the hope of generating new knowledge that would be impossible to produce by a single discipline. "Transdisciplinary approaches are far more comprehensive in the scope and vision... Whereas 'interdisciplinary' signifies the synthesis of two or more disciplines, establishing a new method of discourse, 'transdisciplinarity' signifies the interconnectedness of all aspects of reality, transcending the dynamic of a dialectical synthesis to grasp the total dynamics of reality as a whole" (Klein 1990: 66). While multidisciplinarity may appear to be less desirable than transdisciplinarity, it offers unique benefits. On the other hand, transdisciplinarity is often expected to deliver much more than it easily can. In the case of such unbounded topics as the examination of the relationship between people and things (the subject at hand), being able to "grasp the total dynamics of reality as a whole" is practically impossible. This subject is large, unwieldy and fragmented (but also of great consequence, oft-ignored and thrilling), and creating boundaries within such unbounded topical geography demands a frame of reference and a position. In other words, it requires the adoption of a specific methodological approach that might be limiting and the construction of boundaries where they might be difficult to draw. As explained earlier in the Introduction, the methodological approach includes a synoptic overview, an ANT-inspired point of view and a theme-based near view. This chapter, in its multidisciplinary approach, offers a synoptic view of the diversity in thinking of things as manifest in a variety of disciplines.

Design, which has traditionally regarded objects in formal rather than social terms, can benefit by including within its systems of analysis a more socially and culturally rooted understanding of objects, which is germane to cultural studies. While philosophy, more specifically metaphysics, questions the nature of the very existence of things, scholars in STS perceive them as socially constructed technological events. Design discourse

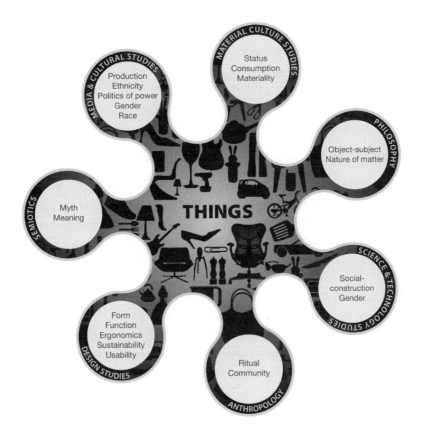

Figure 1.1. Disciplinary Diversity in Examining Things. Illustration by Amethyst Saludo.

expends more of its energies in analyzing processes, systems and methodologies of design construction, whereas cultural theory and media studies typically deconstruct materiality, drawing upon political, economic, and sociological approaches in their analysis. Anthropology views objects as artifacts and studies them as representatives of specific cultures, while engineering treats them as scientific entities subject to laws of physics and mathematics. An understanding of the politics of power, which is pivotal in cultural studies can inform designers of imperceptible social forces, just as comprehension of the design process can more fully educate cultural and social theorists about the role of design in fashioning objects.

The multiplicity of disciplines across which the critical thinking of objects is scattered makes it a daunting task to document but it holds benefits for research as well as teaching across these fields. Design may become less instrumentally pragmatic and shift its emphasis from predominantly formal and aesthetic to more social, political and economic readings of things central to the humanities and social sciences. Similarly, media and cultural studies might supplement its analysis of media, communications, institutions, audiences, and technologies with a deeper consideration of designed things and the processes of their evolution. A thorough comprehension of the processes of design might also inform anthropology's assessment of the role of designers in the creative, cultural production of artifacts. Locating things within theory locates the practices of design and production within a larger, social critique. An examination of the approaches central to disciplines engaged in object studies can trigger interdisciplinary learning, comparative studies and more holistic analyses. This discourse will arm design studies with a more inclusive and robust conception of things, thereby strengthening its presence, relevance and authority in object studies.

UNDERSTANDING THINGS THROUGH DESIGN RESEARCH/THEORY

The burgeoning interest in design research can play an important role in helping design to develop a critical knowledge of the meanings of objects. Through articles in journals, conference proceedings and books, design's history, theory and methodology are being mapped out at an international level. Over the last few decades, several articles have traced design's epistemological evolution (Roth 1999, Margolin 2002, Laurel 2003, Bayazit 2004, Cross 2006). It is clear from the surveys by these authors that though design research includes scholarship in several areas, a significant amount of intellectual energy has been focused on history and methodology. The classical definition of design research is traced to Bruce Archer, who presented it at a conference of the Design Research Society in 1980. According to Archer, "design research is systematic inquiry whose goal is knowledge of, or in, the embodiment of configuration, composition, structure, purpose, value, and meaning in man-made things and systems" (Bayazit 2004: 16). This definition is wonderfully expansive in its rendition and sweeps up a broad range of investigations surrounding design's process and product.

Bayazit (2004: 16) lists five major concerns of design research as they apply to design methodology and design science:

A. Design research is concerned with the physical embodiment of man-made things, how these things perform their jobs, and how they work.
B. Design research is concerned with construction as a human activity, how designers work, how they think, and how they carry out design activity.
C. Design research is concerned with what is achieved at the end of a purposeful design activity, how an artificial thing appears, and what it means.
D. Design research is concerned with the embodiment of configurations.
E. Design research is a systematic search and acquisition of knowledge related to design and design activity.

The first task of design research listed above emphasizes the examination of physical artifacts, but the focus is on physicality, utility and functionality. The third topic in the list above could include a concern for the social and cultural meanings of things but this is not explicit in design's conception as a science. The remainder of the concerns orbit around outlining design's praxis. Margolin (2002) advocates the use of the term *design studies* to serve as an envelope accommodating a wide range of research efforts within design. In addition to design methods research (understanding design's process) and project-oriented research (knowledge from practice), Margolin urges the examination of "design as a cultural practice," which requires "modes of thought that recognize design as a practice within culture and that bring to bear on its study the methods that have been used to understand other cultural practices and their resultant artifacts" (2002: 251). He lists four major areas of study that this research topic "design as cultural practice" may address: design practice, design products, design discourse, and metadiscourse. Research related to the theorization of things may be located under the category of design products, which Margolin explains as a "study ... that emphasizes the identity and interpretation of products" (2002: 253). Design practice relates to examinations of all aspects of product planning and execution, design discourse relates to the study of what design is and might be, and metadiscourse refers to the reflexive study of design itself. Though the theorization of things relates directly to the area Margolin refers to as design products, it borrows heavily from the other three as well. Objects are results of social practices of a large number of stakeholders (designers, engineers, marketers, reporters, consumers, etc.), and theories that attempt to explain their cultural meanings cannot do so without a lens wide enough to include several perspectives.

UNDER-THEORIZATION OF OBJECTS IN DESIGN RESEARCH

The relatively limited attention paid to the application of theory and criticism toward the analysis and interpretation of objects opens up a significant arena of opportunity for design research. Within this steadily growing body of knowledge, scholars have begun to devote attention to theorizing the products of design. Increasingly prevalent in their work is the notion that the meanings of objects should be situated not only within the context of design and manufacturing activity but also within the circumstance of individual and social activity. This understanding is particularly evident in the work of several design historians who have addressed the narratives of objects from perspectives that transcend the aesthetic and technological.[2] In these publications, the examination of designed objects often reveals the influence of the social sciences—specifically the discourse from anthropology and cultural studies.

For several reasons, a large volume of the discourse around objects exists in disciplines outside design. First, as a formal discipline, design is relatively young and the comprehensive theoretical foundations that organically evolve to serve as pillars of the profession are yet to acquire the sturdy proportions of more established disciplines. By contrast, some allied disciplines such as architecture have a reasonably long history, as do others like engineering and archaeology. Second, design's traditional role has been the production rather than the critical interpretation of things. Industrial design programs in educational institutions have a commandingly larger number of skill-based studio courses than critical/analytical ones. This emphasis on the teaching of design ability and skill has created the situation where students at the undergraduate level are mostly unfamiliar with the theories that could be used in the analysis of objects.[3] Third, being a "professional" discipline, a large percentage of design practitioners and educators tend to focus on praxis rather than theory, a condition that directly contributes to the relative scarcity of published research within the discipline.

Though current research in design history and design studies reveals an increasing recognition of theories, methods, and perspectives from the social sciences (as evidenced in several books and such journals as *Design Issues*, *Design and Culture*, *Journal of Design History*, *Design Philosophy Papers*), disciplinary boundaries are far from permeable. In design, our present understanding of objects is only partial; it continues to be predominated more by aesthetic and technological concerns rather than social and cultural ones. However, the deficiency in our knowledge of things cannot be entirely attributed to the divisions among disciplines. The very multiplicity of the meanings of things that engenders such a diversity of reading also makes it difficult to create an inherently cohesive theoretical model for their interpretation and analysis.

WHAT IS THEORY?

In generic, non-discipline specific terms, a theory may be described as a set of general principles employed to explain specific phenomena. These general principles may be laws or facts developed through research in order to describe and clarify natural events, human behavior or properties of things. In common language, the word theory may signify a hypothesis, a belief, a hunch or even a guess, but neither one of these terms truly conveys the meaning of the definition above. A theory is built around evidence and is supported through the scholarship of not a single individual but several scholars. In addition to the abundant generic definitions, there exist several specialized characterizations of theory developed by individual disciplines. In sociology, for example, theory is defined as "an integrated set of concepts formed into propositions that explains particular conditions or events in the world around us" (Schneider 2006: 2). Schneider explains concepts as abstract terms that refer to phenomena, events, things, etc. However, the concepts by themselves are not sufficient in the formulation of theories; relationships among them have to be formalized into propositions, which then take shape as theories. For example, germ theory proposes that invasions of microorganisms such as bacteria, viruses and algae cause human and animal diseases. Here, disease, the human body and bacteria represent the fundamental concepts while mechanisms of infection and viral invasions represent relationships. Repeated observations and lab testing then led to the formulation of the theory. The natural sciences expect mathematical proofs and formulae in their construction of theories. The National Academy of Sciences defines theory in science as "a well-substantiated explanation of some aspect of the natural world that can incorporate facts, laws, inferences, and tested hypotheses. They are understandings that develop from extensive observation, experimentation, and creative reflection."[4] Within the natural sciences, biologists hold that "theory is critical to understanding what is observed in the natural world; it also enables biologists to make predictions, develop new approaches, and translate biological research into practical applications."[5] A theoretician, therefore, identifies phenomena in the world, studies them and makes assertions about their underlying structure. Color theory, probability theory, the theory of relativity and Big Bang are all examples of theories.

THEORIES FOR DESIGN AND FOR THINGS

"The notion of design theory may seem wooly-headed and irrelevant but it has a place: theory can provide a structure for understanding problems and help generate methods for solving them" (Doblin 1988: 6). If we accept that understanding the culture of objects presents itself as a problem to be solved, and that methods to do so are in need, developing means by which to theorize things is critical. Ken Friedman develops a framework for a general theory of design in order to shift the discipline "from a rough, ambiguous territory to an arena of reasoned inquiry" (Friedman 2003: 507). Drawing upon ideas from such disparate disciplines and sources as cybernetics, systems theory, management science, philosophy as well as dictionaries of languages and ideas, Friedman recommends the development of a *grounded theory based on practice*.[6] In other words, design theory should emerge from empirical information gathered by observing design practice.

For an examination of the cultural import of things, theories developed within the social sciences and humanities hold more promise than those utilized in the natural sciences. The nature of the problems identified in design, the character of evidence gathered by designers and critics and the types of theoretical propositions made in design research specifically regarding the social and cultural meanings of objects are well suited for examination through the lenses of critical and cultural theory. Critical theory could be described as "a rigorous critical engagement with social and philosophical issues which [is] aimed at the cross-fertilization of research methods derived from the social sciences with a Marxist theoretical framework for conceptualizing social relations" (Edgar and Sedgwick 2008: 72–73). Since the 1980s, critical theory has been most actively used in analyzing literature but of late, it has found more application in the social examination of such diverse phenomena and entities as music, television, the city, Disneyland, technology and products. Critical theory serves as an overarching domain for several other theories (such as structuralism, post-structuralism and post-modernism), a large number of which have been developed by Marxist thinkers.

Max Horkheimer, regarded as the pioneer of critical theory, also offers several suggestions about the fundamentals of theory construction.

- Theory is "the sum-total of propositions about a subject, the propositions being so linked with each other that a few are basic and the rest derive from these."
- "The smaller the number of primary principles in comparison with the derivations, the more perfect the theory."
- "The real validity of the theory depends on the derived propositions being consonant with the actual facts. If experience and theory contradict each other, one of the two must be reexamined" (Horkheimer 1972: 188).

As the fundamental principles of critical theory have found application outside literature it is transforming into an interdisciplinary *cultural theory* with roots not in one but several disciplines. Cultural theory texts cover a staggeringly wide array of topics including Marxism, semiotics, structuralism, post-structuralism, hermeneutics, feminism, psychoanalysis and postmodernism. Cultural theory can be defined as a literature that aims to develop a systematically ordered model of the empirical world to explain the nature of culture and its implications for social life (Smith 2001). Since the 1980s, cultural studies has emerged to take center stage as a movement and a discipline, and has gained significant ground in universities all over the world.

ON THINGS, OBJECTS, GADGETS...

The terminology used to talk about things is almost as varied as things are themselves. What are things? And how do they differ from objects, artifacts, products, devices, gadgets, goods and commodities? May these terms be used interchangeably as they all embody and express the matter of materiality? Though in common parlance they may be often employed to convey similar meanings, they may be distinguished on the basis of specific attributes and disciplinary approaches. Quick examinations and brief etymologies of some of these terms will help differentiate them from one another.[7]

The term "artifact," (or artefact) often used in art and design and derived from Latin roots *arte* (by skill) and *factum* (thing made), refers to something that is a result of human labor (often artistic). In archaeology, the term "artifacts" may be used to refer to products of prehistoric or aboriginal craft to differentiate them from naturally produced ones. This may be contrasted with the term "product", derived from Latin *productum*, which also refers to something produced; a product is the end result of a process. Product is a term primarily employed in design and engineering. As an artistic good, an artifact may often be produced by craft, while products, in most cases, rely on mechanized modes of manufacture. Inherent in this definition of products is the understanding that they exist in identical, multiple copies as they are manufactured in large quantities. A "device" has its etymological roots in the Old French word *devis*, and signifies a thing created or adapted for a specific purpose. This term makes a reference to the technology embedded within it (mechanical, electronic, etc.), which allows it to perform the particular tasks for which it is designed. "Gadgets" are small devices or tools that often possess an ingenious quality. This word is derived from sailors' slang for mechanical parts of ships for which they lacked or forgot the name. Here too, the presence of technology is foregrounded as a defining aspect of devices. The term "goods" finds usage largely in a commercial sense, and refers to property or merchandise, things that may be bought and sold, mostly in large quantities. The "commodity" owes its linguistic roots to Middle French *commodité* and Latin *commoditas*, which mean benefit or profit, and their usage often amplifies not only their mercantile existence and economic function but their presence in Marxist analysis as well. For Borgmann, commodities are "highly reduced entities and abstract in the sense that within the overall framework of technology they are free of local and historical ties. Thus they are sharply defined and easily measured" (1987: 81). The word "thing" has a wide range of meanings that can be traced back to the fourth century to several languages including Old English, Old High German, Old Dutch and Classic Latin. The primary meanings that relate to contemporary usage are entity, being, matter or body. "Object" is derived from Medieval Latin *objectum*, which means "thing put before" and it is sometimes explained in binary terms as it stands in opposition to the subject.

Heidegger makes a clear distinction between 'things' and 'objects'. Things, to him, are self-supporting and independent, while objects exist in opposition to subjects. The favored term in design is "product" while in political economy and Marxist analysis it is "commodity." While commodities for Borgmann are measurable, "things engage us in so many and subtle ways that no quantification can capture them" (1987: 81). "Objects" and "things" are possibly the most non-discipline specific and semantically expansive terms, and are often used in philosophy and anthropology. Their labels do not amplify any one of their attributes, thereby facilitating multiple interpretations of equal value. "Things are objects available to our senses as discrete and distinct entities which do not count as other beings or other objects" (Dant 1999: 11). The interchangeability of usage of the terms "things" and "objects" is obvious in Dant's definition. Confessing that things have effectively dodged an exacting definition in spite of the attention of philosophers, Attfield defines them as "objects of human production and exchange with and through which people live their everyday existence" (2000: 11). While recognizing the philosophical difference among the terms, "things" and "objects" will both be employed in this book to refer to all physical entities created by human labor that acquire cultural meanings as they circulate through the socioeconomic processes of production, distribution and consumption.

UNDERSTANDING OBJECTS AS A MEANS OF UNDERSTANDING CULTURE

People employ an extraordinary quantity and diversity of material things in their daily lives to signify identity, social relations, history, ritual, power, resistance, economic standing and politics. For designers, anthropologists, sociologists, philosophers and all students of culture, an understanding of how objects are theorized in multiple disciplines can aid in the development of a comprehensive and potentially holistic reading of the cultural meanings of objects. This can help designers develop a higher awareness of the role of objects as mediators of human relations, and assist cultural studies scholars understand the social and cultural impact of design activity.

Through their ubiquitous presence in our material landscape, things press on us. They are present not only as visual and material elements of our environments—they also serve as the basic components of our cultural lives. Inherently polysemic,[8] they are utilitarian gadgets as much as they are frivolous excesses; they play a significant role in the formation of identity, style, status, and they are material embodiments of cultural practices. Just as archaeologists read ancient cultural practices in excavated artifacts, we can understand contemporary popular material culture by analyzing and interpreting everyday things. If one traces the trajectory of designed objects through their existence, it is evident that they make incredibly complex journeys from their origins as immaterial concepts in the minds of designers, inventors and engineers to their disposal into rubbish bins or dispersal into recycling containers. As they interact with several stakeholders through this trajectory of production, distribution and consumption, they acquire and discard multiple meanings. Each one of the activities of making, circulating, using and discarding signifies a unique culture: that of design and manufacturing, of sharing and exchange, of possession and use, and of waste and abandonment. "Biographies of things can make salient what might otherwise remain obscure" (Kopytoff 1986: 67). Kopytoff suggests that asking the same questions of things (where does a thing come from, who made it, what has happened in its life so far, etc.) as one would of people, can lead to the discovery of critical cultural meanings. As Daniel Miller (eloquently) writes in his seminal essay *Why Some Things Matter*, such studies are a "highly effective means to enquire into the fundamental questions of what it is to be human within the diversity of culture" (1998: 20).

The study of objects remains diverse in approach and "eclectic in its methods. Approaches from history, archaeology, geography, design and literature are all equally acceptable contributions" (Miller 1998: 19). This diversity adds richness to the discourse, but also means that the scholarship in the field tends to be scattered across disciplines. This situation has prohibited the development of a comprehensively coherent model for studying things grounded in a specific array of theories, methods, and approaches. However, considering the nature of the material world and culture, it is neither possible nor desirable to develop a singular model or theory of things. Instead, analytical frameworks that allow incorporation of multiple approaches representing several disciplines might offer more promise.

A VERY BRIEF HISTORY OF THE PHILOSOPHY OF THINGS

Philosophy, arguably the oldest discipline of academe, has pondered the existence of physical things—matter, substance, objects—for centuries. Questions about the nature of physical reality, the meaning of matter and its relation to the human mind have engaged and perplexed philosophers since Greek antiquity. The core topic of this book does not permit a lengthy discussion of the history of philosophy of matter and things, but a quick peek into the minds of some of the important Western philosophers will help supplement the synoptical view of things. This synopsis was complied by poring over several seminal texts but much of it is indebted to a few wonderfully lucid histories of philosophy (Durant 1961, Wedberg 1982, Shand 1993, Solomon & Higgins 1996, Kenny 2006).

In the Western ancient philosophical tradition, the contemplation of all things physical can be traced back to pre-Socratic philosophers Thales (625?–547? B.C.E.), Anaximander (610 ca.–545 B.C.E.) and Anaximenes (fl.ca. 540 B.C.E.)—the materialists—who shared the conviction that the world was made up of some type of basic matter. For Thales this fundamental substance was water; for Anaximander it was *apeiron* (loosely translated from the Greek as basic stuff), and for Anaximenes it was air. They believed that there was a singular element of which everything was composed, and their thinking was important because it signaled a move away from mythological explanations of the universe. Following and turning away from the materialists, Pythagoras (ca. 581–ca. 507 B.C.E.) suggested that the elements of which the world was composed were not material entities but numbers and proportions. In mathematics, he found a universal truth that was not dependent on context of location or time of day. Equations and formulae were constant regardless of where they were encountered, and were therefore suitable for explaining the fundamentals of matter. For another Greek philosopher Heraclitus (ca.428–348 or 347 B.C.E.) fire was primary matter, its unsteady and dynamic state a metaphor for the constantly changing world. Parmenides (ca.535–475 B.C.E.), on the other hand, did not seek to explain materiality (and reality) through the elements (air, water, fire…). Instead, he suggested, often through convoluted and dense argumentation, that reality was ultimately unknowable and all that we saw around us was nothing more than an illusion.

While these philosophers sought out single, perceivable elements to unify and connect all reality, the philosophers referred to as the pluralists constructed the world using multiple elements. Anaxagoras (ca. 500–428 B.C.E.) rejected the notion of oneness for a pluralistic position, and announced that things were composed, not of such primary matter as air or fire, but of a combination of materials. There was, for him, an innumerable list of materials such as marble and copper, skin and hair of which things were made. The notion that things could be composed of (and therefore divided into) multiple parts instead of a singular entity inspired Democritus (ca.460–ca. 370 B.C.E.) to push the concept of divisibility until he arrived at the idea of the atom—that which can no longer be split into its elements. The atom became the new primary matter of reality; it was in everything, including for Democritus, the soul. Early Greek philosophy—physical philosophy—"looked out upon the material world and asked what was the final and irreducible constituent of things" (Durant 1961: 3).

Plato (ca.428–348 or 347 B.C.E.) presented a vision of cosmology composed of two elements: the World of Becoming, the gritty, impermanent reality we know and see around us, and the World of Being, a perfect, unchanging world of ideal forms. In *Republic*, Plato explains this duality using the metaphor of shadows; the World of Becoming—the shadow— is a real but flitting representation of the *real* reality, the World of Being. Aristotle, Plato's pupil and regarded as the philosopher's philosopher, collapsed this duality by disputing Plato's vision of one ideal, unchanging form for many discrete and changing objects. For Aristotle, only individual things existed. "There is no superreality, no world of forms insisted Aristotle, but only the individual things in the world" (Solomon and Higgins 1996: 59). These, to Aristotle, were substances, each with a set of essential and non-essential properties. The essential properties of things defined their unchanging essence. And, the non-essential properties could and would change without altering their essence. Essential properties gave things their permanence, while non-essential properties gave them their individuality.

Things also had purpose or function that served as guiding principles. Substance gave things presence, while function gave them their means of change and growth.

In the history of Western philosophy, Bertrand Russell refers to the time between 400 and 1400 as the age of Catholic philosophy. Roughly coinciding with the Middle Ages (from the fourth through the sixteenth century, from the fall of the Roman Empire to the Renaissance) this was a time when the Church exercised a greater influence on the minds of philosophers. However, this started changing with the emerging significance of science, leading to the era now referred to as the age of modern philosophy (between the seventeenth and twentieth centuries). Frenchman René Descartes (1596–1650), considered one of the rationalist philosophers and a founder of modern philosophy, sought an objective explanation of reality which is not dependant on human senses. Mathematical concepts, he believed, were sense-independent, and they could be employed in formulating an explanation of the material world. For Descartes, mathematics could be trusted where the senses were deceptive. For instance, a white object may appear pink if viewed in red light, just as a spoon may appear distorted if seen in a glass half-filled with water. He believed that all essential properties of matter were derived from geometry. For Descartes, the properties of extension, motion and shape represented those dimensions of matter that were essential to its existence. (Extension referred to anything that had length, breadth and depth.) These properties could not be separated from things and therefore were critical to our perception of their presence. "There are three substances according to Descartes: matter, whose essential property is extension; mind, whose essential property is thought; and God, whose essential properties are perfection, omnipotence, benevolence, infiniteness, and existence" (Shand 1993: 82). Soul and body, mind and matter were separate entities and our intellect, not our senses, perceived their essential properties. For Descartes, the external world could only be known through the mind. In fact, he suggested that human existence itself could be justified in its thinking, a notion that that led to his now legendary dictum *Cogito, ergo sum* (I think, therefore I am). Descartes was truly influential in shifting "the locus of scientific enquiry from things themselves to the ideas we have of them" (Moyal 1991: 2).

Benedict (Baruch) de Spinoza (1632–1677) accepted Descartes' notion of the fundamental separation between things and ideas, and suggested a one-to-one relationship between them called the theory of parallelism. The mental process corresponds to the material process. However, Spinoza also believed that everything was made of one substance: God or the totality of nature. All things, therefore, were different forms of this one substance and he referred to them as modes. Substance could not be divided into parts; it was self-caused and self-explanatory. Descartes' mind (thought) and matter (extension) for Spinoza were only attributes of the same substance, two sides of the same coin.

John Locke (1632–1704), referred to as an empiricist philosopher, rejected Descartes' reliance on reason and methodical doubt as a means of understanding the world and instead suggested that knowledge was derived from experience through our senses. He assumed the mind to be a *tabula rasa*, a blank slate on which our experiences of the world are written.

Therefore our perception of things was entirely dependent on how we experienced their "sensible" properties. Locke attributed some of these properties to the things themselves (such as mass) and some (such as color) to us. This, however, was an unresolved explanation by Locke's own hypothesis. If all we know is what our senses gather through experience, where properties of things lie has little consequence to their existence. If all matter is purely sensation, it exists only as a form of mind.

German philosopher and mathematician Gottfried Wilhelm Leibniz (1646–1716) took Spinoza's doctrine of substance in a wholly new direction with his theory of monadology. He created a new vision for a material world that was composed of monads, which were invisible but omnipresent spiritual entities (not physical atoms). Substance, the ultimate, unchanging and indivisible constituent of reality, was composed of monads. Leibniz believed that the diverse and continually changing world around us can only be explained and understood by something constant. "Things appear to change in the world; the explanation of these changes comes to an end at something that remains the same, otherwise the explanation would go on forever" (Shand 1993: 105). Monads were not atoms and they had no quantitative dimensions (length, mass, weight). The world that we perceived was secondary and derived from an infinity of monads. Created by god, monads were self-contained, self-explanatory and utterly independent, and therefore there was no interaction among them. Leibniz tackled the Cartesian dualism of mind and matter by proposing the principle of pre-determined harmony. By his explanation, the physical world and the mental world were structured *a priori* to be in harmony in spite of being independent of each other. Leibnitz's metaphysics (evidenced in monads and pre-determined harmonies) displayed a certain level of mysticism that traced all explanation (such as monads and harmony) back to the idea of a perfect god.

Immanuel Kant (1724–1804), in developing his vision of knowledge, was successful in drawing from both, rationalists like Descartes as well as empiricists like Locke. He rejected Locke's hypothesis that our knowledge of the world was limited to what our senses gathered. "Though all our knowledge begins with experience, it by no means follows that all arises out of experience" (Kant 1902: 43). He suggested that some of our concepts are not derived empirically by experiencing the world but are "independent of experience... Knowledge of this kind is called *a priori*" (Kant 1902: 43). This form of knowing transcended our sensations. For Kant, our knowledge of the thing in the world involved a series of processes that engaged sensations and perceptions, collected by experience and structured by *a priori* concepts. The sensation of a thing—say, a chair, for example—starts with sensory stimuli. We see its color, feel the pressure of the material against our skin and we might hear it creak as we settle into it. These sensations, however, do not constitute our perception of the complete chair as it exists in its context, unless they are organized and grouped in our mind. It is here that *a priori* knowledge of space and time step in. These perceptions are categorized by the mind (and coordinated) to become knowledge. "Just as perceptions arrange sensations around objects in space and time, so conceptions arrange perceptions (objects and events) about the ideas of cause, unity, reciprocal relations, necessity, contingency, etc.; these and other "categories" are the structure into which perceptions are received, and by which they are classified and moulded into the ordered concepts of thought. These are the very essence and character of the mind; mind is the coordination of experience" (Durant 1961: 270–1). These categories organize our experiences into what we understand as objects. Kant also made a distinction between the noumenal world (that which exists beyond our experience, the thing-in-itself) and the phenomenal world (the one that we are able to experience) and in doing so clearly established the limits of our knowledge.

> The object as it appears to us is a phenomenon, an appearance, perhaps very different from the external object before it came into the ken of our senses; what that original object was we can never know; the "thing-in-itself" may be an object of thought or inference (a "noumenon"), but it cannot be experienced-for in being experienced it would be changed by its passage through sense and thought. (Durant 1961: 272).

German philosopher Georg Wilhelm Friedrich Hegel (1770–1831) faulted Kant for setting up a dichotomy between what we see and what exists behind it, between appearance and essence, between the phenomenon and noumenon, between the subject and the object. For him, the notion of a dialectical logic created a unity between the two artificial entities. He suggested that there was nothing beyond appearances that needs to be revealed. "[Hegel] maintains, rather, that if it is claimed that reality is unknown to us, that there are unknowable things-in-themselves, then this can only be because there is no more to things-in-themselves than is contained in the statement that they exist, that there is, as it were, no more to the iceberg than its tip" (Inwood 1983: 120). To Hegel, the knowledge that we possess of things is in fact knowledge of their properties such as their color, taste, or weight. Our knowledge is of a *thing with properties*; we never know the bearer of those properties. "He points out that the thing-in-itself in this sense is unknowable simply because there is nothing to be known. Whatever knowledge we have about a lump of sugar [for example] counts as knowledge of its properties and not of it, the bearer of those properties" (Inwood 1983: 121). These properties are determined by the relationships a thing has with other things. To Hegel, our process of knowing could not be separate from absolute reality, but needed to be a part of it. The separation of knowing from the absolute was unjustifiable and incoherent. Hegel's dialectic is often explained as a triadic relationship among thesis, antithesis and synthesis. Though he did not expressly use these terms himself, he believed that things and ideas have their opposites inherent in them. "The living die, simply because as living they bear in themselves the germ of death" (Hegel 2009). In a sense, the notion of planned obsolescence refers to that very idea, when the total life and ultimate death of products are designed into their form, technology and use. These two states of things and their inner contradictions can be compared to thesis and antithesis. To Hegel, the dialectical moment represents a form of unification of the opposites, a condition that may be referred to as synthesis.

Viennese philosopher Ludwig Wittgenstein (1889–1951) in *Tractatus Logico-Philosophicus* presented the world as "the totality of facts not of things" (Wittgenstein 1998: 29). He further explained facts as states of affairs, which, in turn were combinations of objects. "Just as we cannot think of spatial objects apart from space, or temporal objects apart from time, so we cannot think of any object apart from the possibility of its connection with other things" (Wittgenstein 1998: 30). To Wittgenstein, objects linked together as if on a chain, creating a state of affairs, and reality was essentially all possible states of affairs. It was the properties of objects that determined the relation among them; in other words, objects were inseparable from context. Wittgenstein suggested that objects had internal and external properties; the internal properties determined how they combined with other objects and the external properties situated them within specific states of affairs.

It is in the work of German philosopher Martin Heidegger (1889–1976) that we find the most extensive discussion of things. In his essay *The Thing* (1971), Heidegger uses the example of a jug as the means to explain what a *thing* is and how it differentiates itself from an *object*. While the thing is an independent, self-supporting entity, an object exists as something against us, something that "stands forth" opposite to the subject. He describes the jug through its principal attributes—it is a vessel for "holding" wine, it appears out of the potter's "making," it facilities "outpouring" wine as gift, etc. Heidegger uses the term "presencing" to denote these properties of the jug. In the poured gift, the jug "presences" as jug (Heidegger 1971: 173). Heidegger traces the etymology of the word "thing" and its German form *Ding* to one of its more ancient meanings—assembly or gathering. "A jug 'things' insofar as it holds the 'gift' of wine, and thereby gathers the sky's water, the earth's grape, humanity's production of wine, and the presence of gods when wine is used in religious ceremonies (libation)" (Economides 2007). Heidegger referred to these four—earth, sky, divinity and mortals—as the fourfold within which the thing stays united; it is here that "the thing things" or presences (Heidegger 1971: 181). Heidegger also explains a category of things he calls useful things. These are things that allow us to perform tasks such as writing, reading, driving, etc.; they are tools. His famous analysis of tools suggests that these things are invisible to us as long as they function in a manner that we expect them to; however, it is when they are unusable that they spring into our consciousness. Using these objects reveals their particular "handiness," a quality that is dormant until the thing is picked up and put to task. "What is peculiar to what is initially at hand is that it withdraws, so to speak, in its character of handiness in order to be really handy" (Heidegger 1996: 65). Tools exist in two states: *ready-to-hand* when they are in this withdrawn state but ready to be used, and *present-at-hand* when they are conspicuous. These withdrawn things can be compared to Braun designer Dieter Rams' conceptions of products as "silent butlers" available to serve when needed and quick to fade into the background when not in use. While Heidegger's things withdraw in a phenomenological sense, Rams' things do so in a direct physical way "[as] silent butlers: invisible and subservient, and there simply to make living easier and more comfortable. They were to be as self-effacing as possible..." (Sparke 1998: 184). However, these disappearing acts of things come to a halt when they break down. "When we discover its unusability, the thing becomes conspicuous" (Heidegger 1996: 68). In fact, Heidegger finds these things not only conspicuous but obtrusive and obstinate. Useful things are those which we use and take care of without paying "specific attention" to; unusable things are those we keep "bumping into," obstinate things that refuse to work for us.

Edmund Husserl (1859–1938), author of *Logical Investigations* often credited as being the inventor of phenomenology, was interested in analyzing the phenomena that appear in acts of consciousness. One of the key ideas presented in phenomenology is that of intentionality or directedness. All consciousness is consciousness of something, and our experiences are directed towards things through images, ideas, concepts, etc. Husserl referred to the consciousness of objects as the intentional object. He rejected the subjective notion that things can never be known to us because of the limitations of our perceptions. Instead, "phenomenologists claimed that both the traditional concepts of subject and of object were philosophical constructs which in fact distorted the true nature of human experience of the world" (Moran 2000: 13). Therefore, phenomenology focuses on how objects appear to us in our consciousness through experience. Husserl introduced the notion of *Lebenswelt* or life-world, as a world of objects, people and relationships that subjects can experience collectively. It is in this life-world that experiences unfold; it serves as an ever-changing backdrop where things become meaningful to people.

Contemporary philosopher Graham Harman has developed Heidegger's tool analysis in an exciting new direction he calls object-oriented philosophy. Harman highlights two critical concepts from Heidegger's analysis of tools—invisibility and totality. Ready-to-hand things are invisible; they disappear into a world Harman calls subterranean (2002). This invisibility is not merely a lack of human awareness of the presence of the object; it refers to a "kingdom," a conceptual condition where the function of the tool withdraws. The second concept, that of totality refers to the fact that nothing (no thing) exists in isolation from other things. All things are inseparable components of a larger network. "The totality of equipment means that each tool occupies a thoroughly specific position in the system of forces that makes up the world" (Harman 2002: 23). It is important to note that Harman constructs a much more expansive meaning for the word "tool" than is held in common perception; he refers not only to hammers, chain saws and knives, but all things of this world, natural and artificial. "The world of tools is an invisible realm from which the visible structure of the universe emerges" (Harman 2002: 24).

For Harman, Heidegger's unusable products—things that suddenly appear in the visible realm when they stop working—are broken tools. This dualism between tool and broken tool constitutes one of the foundations of his object-oriented philosophy. "Before any object is present-at-hand, it is ready-to-hand: sincerely engaged in executing itself, inaugurating a reality in which its characteristic style is unleashed. The tool-being of the object lives as if *beneath* the manifest presence of the object" (Harman 2002: 220). Harman offers an entirely new perspective on the tool/broken tool dualism by suggesting that the two are not sides of the same coin, but are different entities altogether. The tool-being is a relational system that includes the thing and the human being using it. "Not only does tool-being withdraw from all relation; it itself turns out to be a relational system (Harman 2002: 267). In developing this object-oriented philosophy, he advocates a restoration of the primacy of things, not necessarily as parts of wholes or contexts, but as individual items. A new theory of objects should "retrieve the integrity and isolation of discrete substances without positing them as a limited set of privileged discrete units" (Harman 2002: 276). While this may seem contradictory, Harman suggests that all entities are simultaneously relational and isolated. In fact, for him, relations themselves are entities. This is the fundamental duality of the world (not the duality of noumenon and phenomenon). All things are forms of a composite reality—a reality that includes tool and broken tool.

While in *Tool-Being* (2002) Harman lays out a proposition that objects exist in independence and isolation, in *Guerilla Metaphysics* (2005), the sequel, he offers the other half of this object-oriented philosophy by showing how objects relate to one another. Things exist in a private world where they live their individual lives, and they also participate in a public world in which they rub shoulders with all other things. Harman rejects the notion of universal building blocks or elements of which these objects are mere sums; objects are much more. The relations in which all objects engage are structured around qualities and occur in a medium. "A medium is any space in which two objects interact, whether the human mind is one of these objects or not" (Harman 2005: 91). This medium facilitates relations among objects, and this is where worldly events unfold.

Bruno Latour, French sociologist and eminent scholar in science and technology studies, suggests that things be considered not merely as matters of fact, but *also* as matters of concern:

> For too long, objects have been wrongly portrayed as matters-of-fact. This is unfair to them, unfair to science, unfair to objectivity, unfair to experience. They are much more interesting, variegated, uncertain, complicated, far reaching, heterogeneous, risky, historical, local, material and networky than the pathetic version offered for too long by philosophers. Rocks are not simply there to be kicked at, desks to be thumped at. (Latour 2005: 21)

He urges us to consider objects critically "with the tools of anthropology, philosophy, metaphysics, history, sociology to detect *how many participants* are gathered in a *thing* to make it exist and to maintain its existence" (Latour 2004: 246). Latour picks up Heidegger's use of the word "gathering" and suggests that it might be a promising direction to explore matters of concern. "A thing is, in one sense, an object out there and, in another sense, an *issue* very much *in here*, at any rate, a *gathering*" (Latour 2004: 233). A thing, when imagined as a gathering, reveals all that it can hold within it; it foregrounds all the connections and relations that it exists because of and within. Latour also extends Heidegger's fourfold (earth, sky, divinity and mortals) within which things are united to "thousands of folds." In other words, Latour seems to suggest that while objects do exist as individuals, they *gather* their meanings from the large network in which they exist. These ideas are central to his actor-network theory (ANT).

Objects are what they are because of the relationships in which they exist. They exist in large dynamic networks of people, other objects, institutions, events, etc., and should be treated as having equal weight and interest as everything else in the network. According to ANT, objects are not seen as types of substance with varying properties; neither are they seen as representations of other, unknowable realities. Actor network theory pioneer Law suggests that there is an inherent dynamic tension between the centered actor and the distributed network that is critical to the way ANT works (Law 2003). When all the actors within a network are aligned to a certain goal, there is stability in the network. Actor network theory scholars prefer to use the term *actant* rather than actor and they mean it to refer to all things human and non-human, material and ephemeral, large and small. Urban transportation, for example, involves such actants as trains, buses, cars, highways, departments of transportation, advertising, federal funding, transportation policy, commuters, electricity, gasoline, pollution, specific bodies of transportation knowledge, university research, and so on. All these actants exist within a large strong network, and they derive their form and their properties from their specific locations in this network. A network is formed through multiple processes of translation (Callon 1986), where actants set agendas, establish connections with other actants, define roles and mobilize actions. These networks are dynamic, in a continuous state of evolution (and often dissolution) and therefore constantly in need of maintenance. Actor network theory has received significant attention in science and technology studies and has found application in a large number of disciplines.

Verbeek, another contemporary philosopher, who has turned his attention to things, like Harman, also asks for a philosophy of artifacts that is different from a philosophy of technology. He suggests that the philosophy of technology has itself ignored artifacts. Verbeek objects to the classical view of technology as a dominating power that can bring nothing but alienation and mass rule. Technology should not be considered in terms of possibilities, he says, but "in terms of its concrete presence and reality in human experience and practices" (Verbeek 2005: 9). Verbeek's philosophy of artifacts is grounded in the notion of mediation. Things mediate relations between people, between people and technology and between people and the world. "Artifacts can only be understood in terms of the relation that human beings have to them" (Verbeek 2005: 117). It is the process of mediation by which technological artifacts enter our lives, shape our experiences and make reality present to us. Verbeek points out that this mediation is ambivalent, as it can in some cases strengthen the presence of reality but can also weaken it. One of the few philosophers to extend his work explicitly and directly to the profession of industrial design, Verbeek attaches two moral dimensions to design activity. "First, designed products play a mediated role in the moral considerations of people, and second, the design process can involve moral choices with reference to this mediating role" (Verbeek 2005: 217). People make choices with their products; they use them in certain ways and these actions often have moral dimensions. They may save someone's life (using a defibrillator), damage the environment (using a polluting car), hurt animals (using a gun) or nurture a child (using a stroller). Therefore, in the process of design, as Verbeek's second moral dimension notes, designers themselves have to make choices about the kinds of actions the artifacts will allow and encourage or prevent and forbid. Designers have to anticipate the potential mediating roles that artifacts *will* play and use those in shaping their own design choices.

This philosophical discussion of things from Thales to Verbeek demonstrates that a few key concerns continue to re-emerge throughout the history of this topic. The nature of substance and the primary constituent of matter is one such concern. Philosophers have wondered what things are actually made of (whether fire, water, the atom, a monad or strings). Another concern is the obsession with duality (between matter and mind, object and subject, noumenon and phenomenon, World of Becoming and World of Being, ready-to-hand and present-at-hand, tool and broken tool, and so on). And finally, the third concern deals with the human-object relation. The question is whether things exist only in the minds of people or whether they exist with people in a complex network. For this study, things will be treated as inseparable from the networks to which they belong.

DISCIPLINING THINGS

Each academic tradition examines specific aspects of the existence of things and therefore the key concerns and methods used by scholars in the disciplines vary as well. However, scholars do share some theories and methods (such as Marxism, psychoanalysis, semiotics, etc.) regardless of their designated academic departments. The following pages offer brief overviews of a few disciplines engaged in object studies.

Each discipline adopts its own ideological position(s), uses specific methods and seeks specific kinds of results. Topical boundaries among these disciplines are permeable and elastic—the same texts and scholars are often cross-referenced, modes of criticism (such as Marxist, rhetorical or semiotic analysis) are often shared, and so are emphases and viewpoints (consumption rather than production). The similarities and differences can be attributed to disciplinary traditions and the increasing interest in multidisciplinary work.

ANTHROPOLOGY

According to the Royal Anthropological Institute, "anthropology concerns itself with humans as complex social beings with a capacity for language, thought and culture" and its study "is about understanding biological and cultural aspects of life among peoples throughout the world."[9] In the U.S., anthropology is often divided into four subfields—biological or physical anthropology, socio-cultural anthropology, linguistic anthropology and archaeology. While biological/physical anthropology focuses its attention on such biological issues as evolution, genetics, primatology, etc., linguistic anthropology examines the social and cultural meanings of language in human communication. The other two branches of

TYPICAL ISSUES & CONCERNS	METHODS	EXAMPLES OF OBJECTS ANALYZED
Anthropology		
Artifacts as cultural forms, Social practices, Cultural perceptions, Objects in myths & rituals	Photography, Visual analysis, Chemical analysis, Ethnography, Extensive field observation, Informant interviewing, Theoretical analysis	Tools, Pottery, Baskets
Cultural Studies		
Relationship between material and cultural forms, Politics of power, Race, Gender, Structuralism, Sexuality, Style & subculture	Critical theory, Marxist analysis, Participant observation, Interviewing, Ethnography	Walkman, Television, Vespa scooters
Industrial Design		
Aesthetics, Functionality, Human interaction, Materials selection, Sustainability, Manufacturing technology, History analysis	Prototyping, Observation, User testing, Interviewing	Domestic appliances, Furniture, Transportation, Toys
Material Culture Studies		
Object-subject relationships, Study of consumption, Social role of commodities	Critical theory, Philosophical analysis, Interviewing, Ethnography	Cars, Coca-Cola, Barbie dolls, Radio
Science & Technology Studies		
Social shaping of technology, Gender roles in production and use	Theoretical analysis, Systems theory, Actor-network theory, Philosophical analysis, Participant observation, Ethnography	Bicycles, Refrigerators, Electric ovens, Microwave ovens

Figure 1.2.   Disciplinary Concerns, Methods and Case Studies. Illustration by Amethyst Saludo.

anthropology, archaeology and socio-cultural anthropology are the most directly involved in the interpretation of artifacts and cultures. Archaeology may be defined as the study of human cultures and the natural, social, ideological, economic, and political environments in which they operated in the recent and distant past. Socio-cultural anthropology, on the other hand, concerns itself with in-depth examinations of the culture and social systems of people, and the human capacities that enable them. Socio-cultural anthropologists are interested in matters of everyday life and they conduct ethnographic studies to understand common rituals, gender relationships, family structures, mythologies, religion, etc. of societies.[10]

Although traditionally associated with cultures and objects of ancient civilizations, many socio-cultural anthropologists have turned their attention in recent years to the study of consumption and the social meanings of mass-produced, everyday objects. Exploratory and inductive in nature, socio-cultural anthropology possesses the conceptual flexibility to study complex situations involving people, the environment and cultures in dynamic and constantly evolving societies. According to Berger, "the task of the anthropological analyst of material culture is to see the role that various objects play in the most important myths and rituals of specific cultures and subcultures and the manner in which all of these relate to dominant values and beliefs" (1992: 47). By viewing objects as cultural data, socio-cultural anthropologists are better able to comprehend their meanings. They gather information over reasonably long periods of time using ethnographic research methods such as field observation and key informant interviewing.

Archaeology may be defined as the scientific study of ancient cultures (typically preliterate) through the scrutiny of the artifacts left behind. In general, archaeologists use methodologies such as excavating, sampling, aerial photography, chemical and visual analysis, nuclear dating, etc. in order to understand the artifacts of their scrutiny. For example, if found at an archaeological site, artifacts made of stone (lithics) can reveal invaluable information about how past cultures managed their natural resources. Other artifacts such as projectile points used in spears can be analyzed to understand the hunting habits and skill levels of toolmakers, and chronologically date the civilizations. Therefore, pottery, jewelry, baskets, or their broken bits, become repositories of the practices of entire civilizations.

Using a wide array of research methods, contemporary anthropologists have undertaken the examination of a dynamically growing variety of artifacts including interiors of barber shops, magazines, food, military vehicles, chairs, toys, etc.

CULTURAL STUDIES

Cultural studies is inherently multidisciplinary; it absorbs methodologies from various disciplines and in its analysis situates a wide range of cultural products within social issues such as race, gender, ethnicity, and sexuality. The following quotation aptly reflects the complexity of this approach:

> While the term cultural studies may be used broadly, to refer to all aspects of the study of culture, and as such may be taken to encompass the diverse ways in which culture is understood and analyzed, for example, in sociology, history, ethnography and literary criticism, and even sociobiology, it may also, more precisely, be taken to refer to a distinctive field of academic enquiry. (Edgar and Sedgwick 2008: 81)

Recognition of the politics of power is central to cultural studies discourse, and its critique is often inspired by Marxism, feminism, structuralism, post-colonial studies, queer theory, etc. Apart from the investigation of products, scholars in this field have also critiqued music, sports, pornography, technology, advertising, and many other forms of cultural production.

Cultural studies scholars often derive their ideologies and interpretive tools from cultural theory and examine contemporary issues of power, identity, history, gender, etc. in various forms of cultural production and cultural consumption (Cavallaro 2001). Critical theory "traverses and undermines boundaries between competing disciplines, and stresses interconnections between philosophy, economics and politics, and culture and society…" (Kellner 1989a: 7). Indeed, it is the very existence of the complexity and multiplicity of meanings of things that necessitates the kind of multidisciplinary approach central to cultural studies. A good example of the cultural studies approach in the analysis of technological objects is a study of the Walkman introduced by Sony Corporation in 1979. In performing its "cultural study," du Gay *et al.* refer to it as "a typical cultural artefact and medium of modern culture" (1997: 2). They suggest that "through studying its 'story' or 'biography' one can learn a great deal about the ways in which culture works in late-modern societies such as our own" (du Gay *et al.* 1997: 2). The authors narrate the story of the Walkman through five cultural processes: its production (cultural and technological), consumption (meaning-making by consumers), representation (in verbal and visual language), identity (of the corporation, people and the product), and regulation (institutional control of the use of objects).

Michael Bull furthers the cultural study of the Walkman by providing an account that "draws Critical Theory together with a more ethnographic approach tied to an empirically

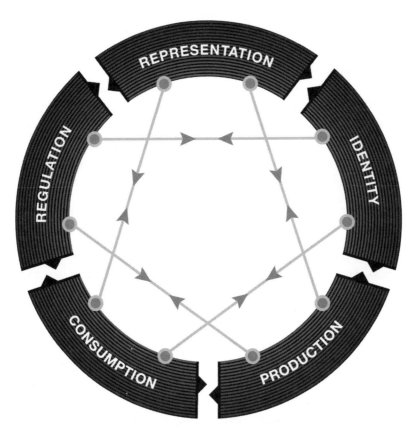

Figure 1.3.   Circuit of Culture. Adapted from Du Gay *et al.* (1997), illustration by Amethyst Saludo.

orientated phenomenological methodology" (2000: 10). By studying the social practices associated with the Walkman, he is able to explain how people use products to manage everyday life. Both studies situate the object within structures of society and draw from theories that contend with everyday life, urban environments, technology and consumption. These cultural studies analyses demonstrate that the Walkman has multiple meanings generated through design, advertising, use and regulation. It also shows how the product serves as an identity marker, especially for youth.

Several other cultural theorists have examined the role of objects in society using specific case studies. In his work with subcultural groups in postwar Britain, Dick Hebdige (1988) provides an in-depth analysis of the Mods and their fascination with the Italian motor scooters—the Vespas, manufactured by Piaggio. Raymond Williams has written a sociological critique of television, which includes its social history, its role as technology and as cultural form, and its dependence on institutions of public service (such as the government) and those of commerce (media corporations). Williams' (1975) analysis reveals that television was successful in its early days because its cultural form suited prevalent models of private consumption while its physical form was designed like furniture and therefore fit the domestic environment. In general, these and other cultural studies of things heavily emphasize the importance of considering the meanings of objects within the social processes of consumption and production.

MATERIAL CULTURE STUDIES

Born out of anthropology, material culture studies is recognized today as the one field of study that is wholly engaged with materiality and its significance in the social world. Scholars in this area have established that though objects were largely ignored by the social sciences in the past as inconsequential to the concept of culture, they are now recognized as integral components of the culture of everyday life. In fact, all that was material was often regarded to exist in opposition to all that was cultural; matter was seen as subservient to mind; the thing trivial in relation to thought. Material culture studies has played a significant role in changing this view; objects are now deemed worthy of study and it is generally accepted that their examination can help us understand the significance of materiality in human life. "This field of study centres on the idea that materiality is an integral dimension of culture, and that there are dimensions of social existence that cannot be fully understood without it" (Tilley et al. 2006: 1). Tilley et al. (2006) refer to this field of study as eclectic and uncharted and undisciplined; and in this sense, they view it as a manifestation of the culture of postmodernity involving plurality and ambiguity.

In the seminal, introductory chapter to *The Social Life of Things*, Appadurai suggests that we should "approach commodities as things in a certain situation, a situation that can characterize many different kinds of thing, at different points in their social lives" (1988: 13). He argues, as do cultural studies scholars, that one should take into account all the stages of the object's journey through its life: production, distribution, and consumption.

Historically, scholars in the Marxist tradition have focused primarily on forces of production, describing them as instrumental in coercing people to consume. This treatment of people as dupes operating under corporate manipulation has been losing ground in more recent work, such as Miller's *Material Culture and Mass Consumption* (1994), in which he develops the idea of consumption as a positive force in the development of identity. It is also suggested through these and other more recent texts that our culture is progressively becoming a more material one, and the study of consumption is particularly necessary to adjust the imbalance caused by the historical emphasis on production. These approaches do not view objects as signifiers of the alienation caused by modern life, but as markers of the processes by which we understand society and ourselves.

As the examination of all things material—indeed all of materiality—falls within the general purview of material culture studies, its analytical reach has included a staggering variety of objects. Scholars have examined architecture, landscapes, cities, food, clothing, cars, scooters, signage, furniture, art and technology in a variety of cultural contexts, in contemporary and past societies. And as the field grows, its repertoire of material entities expands exponentially. In this analysis, scholars employ theoretical models (often from cultural theory) as well as ethnography (often field observations and interviews).

The automobile, aptly referred to as the "machine that changed the world" (Womack, Jones and Roos 1990) is the object for study in Daniel Miller's edited volume *Car Cultures* (2001). Miller and other authors follow the journey of the automobile in societies all over the world and demonstrate its role as an agent of oppression and class differentiation, a signifier of urbanism, a refuge, artistic production, and so on. The essays are a testimony to the multiple meanings of the car as a culturally embedded object in society. Another example of the study of material culture is seen in Attfield's *Wild Things* (2000), in which she uses furniture as a case to examine concepts of tradition, Modernism and design. Her analysis reveals that original antique chairs are perceived to be more valuable than reproductions and fakes because they objectify the notion of authenticity. Other instances of material culture studies include the critical examination of such electronic goods as the iPod, fashion items such as blue jeans/denim, entertainment venues such as Disneyland and food items such as Coca-Cola. Material culture remains eclectic in approach, and embraces various combinations of philosophical analysis, critical theory as well as ethnography.

SCIENCE AND TECHNOLOGY STUDIES (STS)

An emerging group of scholars interested in the origins, nature and social significance of science and technology has suggested that technology shapes society as much as it is shaped by it. One of their goals is to upend the popular notion of technology as the sole driver of progress in society and replace with a socially informed reading which suggests that "what matters is not technology itself but the social or economic system in which it is embedded" (Winner 1980: 122). Science and technology studies insists that technology is not an independent force driving societal change, but one of several factors (cultural, economic, political) that leads to change. In other words, they urge us to avoid technological determinism and consider the social construction of technology (SCOT). "The technological, instead of being a sphere separate from society, is part of what makes society possible- in other words, it is constitutive of society" (Mackenzie and Wajcman 1999: 23). The study of science and technology has also engaged with feminism to show that gender identities should be taken into account for a full understanding of the social aspects of technology. In her analysis, Cockburn (1985) points out that women have been distanced from science and technology on account of male dominance not only in society in general but in the working trades as well. These perspectives have led to the development of a more holistic understanding of domestic technologies and products such as ovens, microwaves, refrigerators and shavers.[11]

Researchers often conduct extensive observations and use surveys, interviews and questionnaires in the homes of people to comprehend fully the relationship between the domestic and the technological. The actor-network theory (ANT) developed by Callon, Latour and Law emerged from STS, and in its examination of technology, it considers the material and non-material world as a network inhabited by human and non-human agents. Law suggests that "society, organisations, agents and machines are all effects generated in patterned networks of diverse (not simply human) materials" (Law 2003). ANT, therefore, may be described as a sociology of interactive effects. Objects and people together shape the interactions in any given situation. While ANT emerged from a social study of technology, its model can be fruitfully used in the examination of all phenomena of the world.

Not unlike material culture studies, STS literature includes a diverse range of objects from pencils to nuclear missiles, analyzed from the perspective of social construction of technology. The high-wheeled bicycle from the 1870s (Bijker 1995), Edison's electric light (Hughes 1999), open-hearth stoves and microwaves (Schwartz-Cowan 1983) are some products featured in this discourse. Cipolla's discussion of the significance of armed, ocean-worthy sailing ships in the development of the European empire, as well as Mackenzie's discussion of nuclear missile guidance systems are examples that document STS's concerns regarding the relationship between military technology, politics and the shaping of empires. This field of study highlights the fact that technological determinism can lead to an incomplete recognition of the forces that shape human civilizations.

Multidisciplinary approaches to the analysis of things can reveal a variety of meanings as is evidenced in the example of Apple's iPhone. An anthropological analysis can expose the process of mythification of Apple and its products; a cultural studies analysis can explain how issues of style influence processes of consumption; and an analysis inspired by principles of STS can better explain the role of gender in iPhone design and use.

THE PROBLEMS AND BENEFITS OF THEORIZING THINGS

It is clear that in order to develop an understanding of the cultural meanings of things, it is imperative to create a discourse around them by drawing upon the theoretical developments in a variety of disciplines. It is through theoretical analysis that the Gordian task of mapping

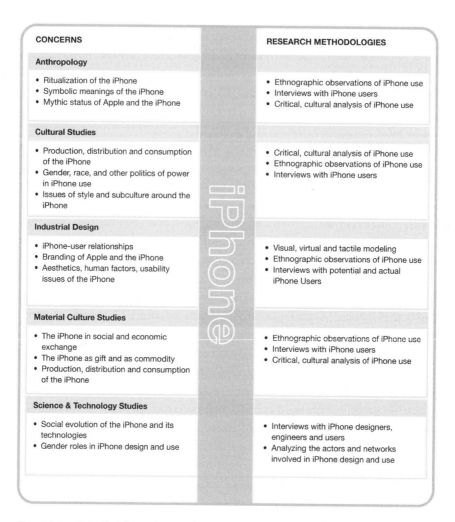

Figure 1.4.   Multidisciplinary Approaches to the Cultural Analysis of Apple's iPhone. Illustration by Amethyst Saludo.

the intersection between the world of things and the world of people can be undertaken. But, the process of theorizing things is confronted with a series of challenges. The enormous quantity and staggering variety of objects represents the first challenge. Can theoretical construction be expansive enough to be applicable to such magnitude? Second, is it possible to chart all possible meanings and interpretations of objects? And third, does this form of theorization amount to a form of fetishism?

The material world presents a prodigious diversity of things, which includes everything from toothpicks to computers. If, in the process of theorizing, this diversity is categorized into product types such as chairs, computers, mp3 players, etc., it is equally important that the specific products contained within each of the categories such as Herman Miller's Aeron

Chair, the Sony Vaio, the 80 GB iPod, etc. are accommodated as well. As Miller suggests, "the generality of materiality, that is any attempt to construct general theories of the material quality of artefacts, commodities, aesthetic forms and so forth, must be complemented by another strategy that looks to the specificity of material domains and the way form itself is employed to become the fabric of cultural worlds" (1994: 6). On one hand, theory must be able to explain the meanings of all bottle openers (the category that represents diversity) as well as the Alessi Diabolix (a specific example). Though the iPod from Apple can be situated within the category of all mp3 players, it also stands apart as a significant, iconic product with unique meanings outside the general category. Any theoretical explanation should be able to highlight the meanings that parallel all similar products as well as those that differentiate it from the rest.

In constructing a discourse of objects it is also important to ensure that it accommodates their polysemic nature—that it accounts for all their possible meanings. Meanings of objects are context dependent and they change with changes in spatio-temporal location, frame of reference, cultural environment, etc. To be effective, theorization should address all attributes of things that influence their existence and meaning in relation to people, other things and the environment. These attributes may be corporeal, ephemeral, economic, social, technological, cultural or political.

Material culture scholars warn of the theorization of objects as a form of fetishism. Fetishism has several meanings, one of which describes it as a process in which people attribute human qualities to objects and develop obsessive attachments to them. Can the study of materiality itself be a form of fetishism? Are we, through this process of analysis and theorization truly able to understand our culture and ourselves more clearly, or are we ultimately converting objects into fetishes? "The blatant contemplation of the material presence of things, with no alibi that transfers the object into cultural identity or social relation, runs the serious risk of being accused of fetishism" (Attfield 2000: 34). According to Marx, fetishism turns commodities into strange things, and leads to a situation where "things are personified and persons objectified" (Edgar and Sedgwick 2008: 56). Subjecting things simply to the gaze, or reducing them so they may be read as text, art or sign, and not as cultural forms may amount to fetishism. Any study of material culture, therefore should recognize objects as socially and culturally embedded. Newer consumption-based approaches treat objects as integral elements of cultural life and emphasize that their values surpass mere use and exchange. This perspective validates the study of consumption and the theorization of objects as a necessary interpretive activity aimed towards creating a more holistic understanding of people, society and culture.

The response to under-theorization cannot be a singular, comprehensive, reductive theory. It has to be an interdisciplinary endeavor that locates things within a larger social critique and expands the discourse of design. Despite the impediments that may face this task, it is a worthy exercise with several benefits to design. Locating objects within theory can not only advance design's understanding of the material world but it can galvanize its self-reflexivity.

Should industrial designers inform their practice with a critical knowledge of things and initiate their creative efforts by questioning social and cultural meanings of objects, processes of their production, their risk of becoming fetishes, etc., they may recognize more clearly the impact of their design actions. This knowledge may be used in the conceptualization of a new product to steer the design or after its launch to study its actual impact. Its application also extends toward the redesign of products that may be due for a new version, or for those that may have failed after introduction. The theoretical construction of things can perform an invaluable pedagogical function. As students learn about the design process in undergraduate industrial design programs, theoretical approaches can provide them with a vantage point from which to understand the social and cultural role of objects in society. In a highly studio-based educational environment, the introduction of critical concepts from cultural theory can cast objects in a new light, and serve the function of encouraging students to reflect on the societal significance of the built environment.

Just as the process of theorizing things needs to draw from several disciplines, its benefits can extend across disciplines as well. Media and cultural studies can supplement their analyses of the production of media forms with knowledge of design processes. Anthropology and material culture, in their study of everyday life and culture, can gain a better understanding of the role played by design and designed goods in processes of fetishization, exchange and consumption. Theories of things generated within design studies can complement and build upon those in science and technology studies such as ANT and social construction of technology (SCOT), further advancing the increasing engagement between S&TS and design. The growing literature in design, evidenced by the increasing number of journals and critical texts, signifies a maturing of the discipline. Scholarly endeavors directed toward the theoretical interpretation of material things can only advance this process. The several benefits listed of theorizing things will contribute to the richness, robustness, diversity and growth of the field of design studies.

2 VALUED POSSESSIONS: THE WORTH OF THINGS

Value does not designate that which is desired, but that which is desirable...

Ludwig Grünberg, *Mystery of Values*

A Coke is a Coke and no amount of money can get you a better Coke than the one the bum on the corner is drinking. All the Cokes are the same and all the Cokes are good. Liz Taylor knows it, the President knows it, the bum knows it, and you know it...

Andy Warhol, *The Philosophy of Andy Warhol (From A to B & Back Again)*

We believe customers just don't buy a product; they buy value in the form of entertainment, experience and self-identity.

Hartmut Esslinger, *Frog: Form Follows Emotion*

Thinking about the value of our material possessions instantly raises a series of complicated questions. What is the true worth of the things that surround us and fill up our spaces as well as our lives? Do we really value everything we buy and own? How do we develop value judgments? Clearly, we have come to depend upon large numbers of products for almost all of our routine work and leisure tasks. We need things to extend our physical and mental capabilities; we use them to express our personal as well as group identities and we are utterly lost without their constant presence. Can the value of things therefore be measured in terms of the level of our reliance on them; can it be measured in terms of how their absence incapacitates us; or can it be treated as a measure of how tightly we wrap our identities with them? Is value designed into objects as an intrinsic property through processes of production, is it what advertising tell us it is, or is it something we construct actively as we consume? In other words, is value a quality of the object or of the subject? And, how long do these values endure? The statistics of daily waste generation in the Western world sadly suggest that we often discard things with as much ease as we acquire them, and if that is the case, how much do we really value our goods? Such questions are fundamental to understanding the value of things.

In this chapter, value will first be introduced as a *fluid aggregate relation*, i.e. not as a fixed ✳ property attached to things, but instead as a multidimensional, constantly changing relation between people and things. Scholars in a variety of disciplines have proposed the notion of value as a relation, and brief summaries of their points of view will demonstrate the advantages of this approach. Although the most common understanding of value typically refers to financial worth, it is clear that other forms of valuation also need to be carefully examined. This chapter explores some of the questions of value as they are discussed in axiology, political economy, anthropology, business and design. The discussion of value in political economy will focus on use-value, exchange value and sign-value of commodities as proposed by Marx and Baudrillard. In business literature value is often construed in financial terms, and typically refers to consumer value, market value and shareholder value. In anthropological literature, value is imagined as a relation that appears in the exchange of goods. In design and engineering, value is often treated as a goal to be achieved by corporations for the products they create for consumers. Objects are polysemic (they have multiple meanings), and therefore the value attached to them takes several forms. In order to demonstrate the multidimensional quality of value, a taxonomy, which includes its economic, functional, cultural, social, aesthetic, brand, emotional, historical, environmental, political and symbolic forms will be developed in this chapter. These multiple dimensions make "aggregate" an appropriate term to describe value. Finally, the chapter will end with a discussion about the difference between value and values. While value may be the worth of something, values refer to ethics and moral codes. If design redirects its attention from value to values, it might present itself as a new strategy for sustainable development.

VALUE AS A FLUID AGGREGATE RELATION

"All value is radically contingent, being neither a fixed attribute, an inherent quality, or an objective property of things but, rather, an effect of multiple, constantly changing, and continuously interacting variables or, to put this another way, the product of the dynamics of a system, specifically an *economic* system" (Hernstein Smith 1988: 30). Value, as Hernstein Smith explains, is fluid; what something means to someone at any given time is dependent on a range of factors like personal needs, individual preference, available resources, market conditions, branding, profit margins, etc. Hernstein Smith suggests that there are two kinds of interrelated economic systems that rely on and drive each other—a personal economy and the market economy. Both these systems are constantly mutating; global markets are known to be volatile and they shift directions by the second, and our personal value systems are given to changes as well. In addition, these systems are integrally linked to each other because "part of our environment is the market economy, and the market economy is composed, in part, of the diverse personal economies of individual producers, distributors, consumers, and so forth" (Hernstein Smith 1988: 31). Through their lives, things are tossed among people and between these economic systems, and therefore their value is in a state of constant flux. The value of things is established in their dynamic interaction with people within specific contexts.

Value can be conceived as a *fluid aggregate relation*, continuously in flux through processes of production, distribution and consumption involving the engagement of numerous stakeholders. The fluid aggregate value of things depends upon a large array of motivations and forces, many of which are socially, economically and politically constructed. It is not unusual to discover that certain things that an individual may consider invaluable may possess no market value whatsoever, and things that sell on the market for significant sums may seem utterly worthless to an individual. Value is dynamic; it changes over space and over time. Removed from its usual spatiotemporal context, a thing may lose its utilitarian value entirely and in its new location gain other unexpected symbolic value as an exotic object. The value aggregate is constantly shifting, its fluctuations determined by changes in meaning.

THE FLUID AGGREGATE OF VALUE: A SUBJECT-OBJECT RELATION

Axiology is one of the three most general philosophical sciences besides epistemology (inquiry into knowledge) and metaphysics (inquiry into existence), and its fundamental charge is the examination of human/personal values as well as the value of goods. "While metaphysics and ethics flourished in Ancient Greece, and theory of knowledge started in the seventeenth century, value theory, also called axiology, was not formulated until the end of the nineteenth century" (Frondizi 1971: 3). And, since its inception, axiology has grappled with the same fundamental and somewhat intractable problem that has doggedly flustered thinkers in other branches of philosophy—the object-subject dichotomy. Does reality exist outside and in spite of our existence (the objective stance) or is reality purely a construction of the human mind (the subjective position)? Is life meaningful because we think it is, or would it be meaningful regardless of our existence? Are goodness and beauty inherent to things or are they fabrications of the human mind? Grünberg explains this dilemma in the form of the question: "are some things, works, deeds valuable because we assign value to them, or do we assign value to them because they are valuable?" (2005: 5). This question reveals one of the key issues of contention about how value is determined—subjectively or objectively. In other words, is value a natural property of things, or of the beholder's eye? Does value inhabit things, or us? The difficulty of answering this question is further complicated by two other questions. If there was nothing to evaluate, would values exist? And, if values did not exist, how would we evaluate things? Philosophers have taken up positions for and against the subjectivity and objectivity of value, with few attempting to bridge this fundamental theoretical chasm.

"In whatever empirical or transcendental sense the difference between objects and subjects is conceived, value is never a 'quality' of the objects, but a judgment upon them which remains inherent in the subject" (Simmel 2001: 63). Simmel therefore posits value in subjective terms, as an appraisal of the object by the subject, not as a property of things. Further along in the discussion though, adopting a highly objective position he suggests that objects "are not only appreciated as valuable by us, but would still be valuable if no one appreciated them" (Simmel 2001: 67). Simmel (the subject) appears to want his (objective) cake and eat it too, but it is when he refers to value as "attributed to the objects of subjective desire" that his somewhat difficult and ambiguous position becomes partially clear (2001: 67). He clarifies by proposing that in order to truly comprehend the meaning and significance of the concept of value, the subject-object distinction is not critical, and the human mind is able to negotiate the contrast and distance between them. He cites the example of thorough enjoyment of objects when one is so fully immersed and engaged in the experience that it is utterly possible to forget the distance between oneself (subject) and the focus of one's attention (object). In such situations, the subject-object dichotomy is blurred if not erased. Yet, in the empirical world, he says, objects do exist as separate from us, and it is in this contrast that value resides. "The moment of enjoyment itself, when the opposition between subject and object is effaced, consumes the value" (Simmel 2001: 66). Value, to Simmel, transcends object and subject into a third form that he calls demand. In situations where a certain need can be met by any one of a number of object choices, value is determined subjectively by the individual rather than the object that satisfies the need. However, when the need is such that it can only be met by a specific object that differentiates itself from the rest, value is determined more objectively. Simmel, in grappling with value, positions it as a bridge that spans the gap between us and the things that surround us, as something that transcends the object-subject divide in a third form called demand, and as a judgment that could be both determined by the nature of things and the type of our impulse.

Frondizi, too, recognizes the theoretical impasse produced by the subjective and objective ideological positions adopted by philosophers. "The difficulty springs from an 'either-or' way of thinking, that value has to be an empirical, natural quality *or* that it has nothing to do with empirical qualities and is a nonnatural quality grasped by intuition" (Frondizi 1971: 159). He dismisses the object-subject dichotomy by suggesting that value represents a tension between the subject and the object, and therefore stands for both. Rejecting both radical objectivism and subjectivism, he suggests that values are neither projected on things (properties of objects) nor are they reflected in things (as properties of people); they are a result of the relation between objects and subjects. And these relations depend upon the physical environment, cultural environment, social environment, the space-time factor and human needs (Frondizi 1971). Presenting value as a Gestalt quality, he suggests that it should be understood as a complex whole that is irreducible to its parts. For example, the aesthetic value of a beautiful chair does not depend on its individual components and parts (back, seat, armrest, support, etc.), nor on the characteristics of these components (color, texture, form, material, personality, etc.); instead, its value depends on how these parts behave as a whole to provide the experience of beauty. "Value is a Gestalt quality, the synthesis of objective and subjective contribution, and which exists and has meaning only in concrete human situations" (Frondizi 1971: 160). Collapsing the subjective and objective interpretations into one Gestalt may be seen as a form of intellectual sidestepping, a maneuver that grants escape from having to confront the dichotomy. However, this seems to be the only mechanism by which to make sense of the divergent positions. In describing the conditions of postmodern architecture, Venturi (1977) uses the terms "either-and", "black and white", over "either-or" and "black or white" to refer to a more contemporary, non-exclusive form of building that negotiates its popular and elitist meanings. Similarly, a concept of value that embraces these divergent points of view is more meaningful in making sense of the value of things.[1]

Value exists because it is generated by a relational act between an object (a thing) that is being evaluated, and a subject (a person) engaged in the process of evaluation. Therefore, the fluid aggregate of value is not an intrinsic quality of an object; it is a relation. According to Grünberg, within the notion of value is tied up the idea of relativity and polarity, of good and bad, valuable and valueless, positive and negative. Objects are judged in relation to other objects and to standards. "Once value is assigned to an object, indifference is impossible. Axiological temperature never reads zero" (Grünberg 2000: 17). If true, this would mean that value exists on a continuum between two poles without the availability of a midpoint. To Grünberg, therefore, this would be tantamount to suggesting that you either like something or you do not; you cannot be neutral to it. This philosophical position does not necessarily hold true in case of things, for it is indeed possible to be utterly disinterested in certain products and not have a value opinion about them. The neutral position is not that of valuelessness; it merely indicates a different form of valuation, one that is neither positive nor negative. There is value in neutrality; neutrality is value.

NATURE AND ATTRIBUTES OF THE VALUE AGGREGATE

Things gain and lose value (value accretion and value depletion) throughout their existence. These processes span the entire lifecycle of the product including the stages of production (design and manufacturing), distribution (transportation and advertising), consumption (acquisition and use) and disposal (landfilling and recycling). In product development, design is perceived as a service that can provide tangible and intangible value to goods if it addresses the unique needs of all the stakeholders—manufacturers, marketing personnel, distributors, regulators and users. For example, while an eco-friendly product may be more valuable to an environmentally conscious consumer, profitability may be more valuable to the manufacturer and shelf life more valuable to the retailer. Therefore, the fluid aggregate of value is constructed by the individual perceptions of all stakeholders who, in some fashion, engage the object.

The value attributed to things changes constantly with context, and as social norms and practices evolve, as economic contexts change, as new technologies emerge and as objects move through their life cycles, they gain or lose value. As people grow older, become educated professionals, travel to new places, develop political alliances or move up or down the socioeconomic ladder, they adjust the value they attach to things. In other words, value is determined in socio-economic settings and on individual terms. The qualities of things that make them valuable often include such properties as affordability, beauty, authenticity, durability, rarity, status, usability, identity, emotional connection and so on. These characteristics might possess universal appeal, but the creation of a classification system for value presents challenges. A general taxonomy of value attributes can be used to map some of the fundamental drivers people use to evaluate the worth of things. However, while classification has heuristic value and can help understand complex concepts, the taxonomy itself should not be assumed to be a refutation of the complexity or an act of reduction.

Though each distinct type has a label and appears as a unique entity, there is conceptual overlap among them. An heirloom object, for instance, may have significant emotional value to the owner while being of historical value to the family. In March 2009, a few personal belongings of Mahatma Gandhi were auctioned in New York City. The items—Gandhi's eyeglasses, a pair of sandals, a watch and other effects—were sold for 1.8 million U.S. dollars. The Gandhi family found it "reprehensible" that these "priceless" items could be exchanged for money. The Indian government attempted to stop the auction and demanded the return of these "national treasures." It is clear that in this case the emotional, symbolic, political and historical values embodied in the artifacts are inseparable from each other. In fact, things acquire symbolic value because they possess other forms of value such as brand value or cultural value. The following value types should therefore be treated as means of acknowledging rather than reducing the complexity of the notion of value.

- *Financial/economic value.* This form of value generally is linked to the price of objects and their affordability. While price is fixed by profit margins and market conditions, affordability is determined by salary, amount of disposable income, measure of how parsimonious or spendthrift a consumer is, and so on. Profit, a form of economic value that is of extreme significance to corporations almost always stands in opposition to affordability.
- *Aesthetic value.* Style plays a significant role in the purchase of goods, especially for such fashion accessories as clothing, shoes, jewelry, watches and some personal consumer electronics. Highly contextual, aesthetic value depends upon the physical characteristics of things as well as the cultural, historical and social milieu in which they exist.
- *Functional/utilitarian value.* Largely determined on the basis of how well something works, utilitarian value is a function of engineering and design.
- *Brand value.* A product's brand is composed of a series of tangible and intangible qualities perceived by consumers. Corporations like Apple, Louis Vuitton and Prada possess high brand value and inspire significant consumer loyalty. In such cases, functional and economic values of the products are often ignored for brand value.
- *Emotional value.* Material goods often become repositories as well as triggers of memories and emotions. In such cases, their value lies not directly in form, function or other immediate properties, but on their ability to inspire specific emotions and feelings in people.
- *Historical value.* Design classics, limited edition products, archeological artifacts and other goods that signify histories of designers, specific designs, or civilizations possess unique historical value.
- *Environmental value.* Products designed and manufactured around principles of eco-design (green goods) possess environmental value as they represent sensitivity to the natural world. These products also possess emotional, social, cultural, political and economic value derived from their greenness.

- *Social value.* Difficult to measure and quantify, this form of value is generally found in products that demonstrate positive societal impact. Products manufactured by corporations that employ fair-trade principles to minimize labor exploitation, provide fair living wages and maximize opportunity for workers, possess positive social value. While this reading of "social" is very limited, it helps focus on an aspect of designed objects that deserves critical attention.

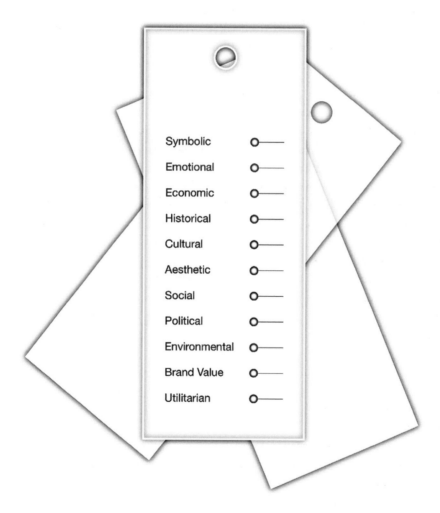

Figure 2.1. Value Types in the Aggregate. Illustration by Amethyst Saludo.

- *Cultural value.* Things that are central to the lifestyles, behaviors, rituals and practices of individuals and groups possess high cultural value. These values may be unique to specific populations, but with the global flows of goods and services and the worldwide presence of multinational corporations, some products achieve multicultural value.
- *Political value.* Things that influence the relationships of power and authority between social groups possess political value. Such objects as political badges and seals of approvals are obvious carriers of political value. But all material goods emerge from structures of power and therefore possess political value.
- *Symbolic value.* Objects often serve as signs and symbols of something else; at times they may not have any utilitarian or aesthetic value but may possess special symbolic significance. The status derived from the possession of certain products (inalienable goods or very expensive products) is attributed to its symbolic value. This form of value is broad in its definition and can include several other types in it.

In varying degrees, all things possess some degree of the types of values listed above. These value attributes are not discrete, unconnected or independent elements but are inseparably intertwined with each other. An inalienable possession such as an heirloom wedding ring that has been handed down several generations has high historical value. A unique symbol of the bond between two individuals, the ring has special memories and connotative meanings and therefore also has high symbolic and emotional value. If antique and made from precious materials it may also have high economic and aesthetic value. The environmental value of the ring may be evaluated in terms of the type of mining involved in

Figure 2.2. Value Aggregate for an Heirloom Wedding Ring. Illustration by Amethyst Saludo.

the extraction of the materials of which it is made. And, should it contain a precious stone that is a blood diamond, it holds political value as well. Its political value also resides in the power relations that may exist between the individuals of the couple. The ring has cultural value because it is a widely recognized signifier of the social ritual of marriage. For queer couples living in states/countries that define marriage purely in heteronormative terms, the ring can assume a discriminatory meaning and gain negative political value.

MAPPING VALUE

Value takes on different disciplinary meanings as it is discussed in the social sciences, philosophy, business and design. While axiology approaches value from a philosophical perspective, business generally adopts a financial perspective, and anthropology, for the most part, assumes a socio-cultural perspective. Anthropologists ask how society and individuals find/construct value in materiality, financial managers ask how a corporation can maximize the market value of its products, while philosophers often approach value from an ethical perspective with questions about value and goodness. According to Mitcham, in science and technology studies, scholars are concerned with three key questions: "What sort of property is involved with having a value or being valuable? (That is, are values primarily aspects of things or of knowers and users?) Is this property subjective or objective? (That is, to what extent is value subject to scientific study?) How might this property be designed into products, processes, or systems? (That is, can values be part of engineering design and technological invention?)" (Mitcham 2005: 20–3). Each discipline/area of study foregrounds those aspects of value that further its fundamental inquiry. A closer examination of some of these disciplinary approaches will demonstrate that while some questions regarding value are shared, the form of value (economic, social, material, etc.) emphasized by each discipline is different.

THE BUSINESS APPROACH TO VALUE

"The difference between value, that is, what buyers are willing to pay for a product or service, and the cost of performing the activities involved in creating it, determines profits" (Porter 1998: xvi). Business practice generally achieves its goal of the maximization of profit by increasing value to the consumer and reducing cost to the manufacturer. Porter introduces the concept of the "value chain" as a series of activities performed by workers on a product (and/or service) that incrementally add to its value. The raw materials for a product (polymer pellets, a printed circuit board, buttons, batteries, and so forth) possess little to no value to a consumer. However, it is the process of assembly that transforms those materials and components into a finished product, generating value for consumers and profit for the corporation. Porter's value chain includes a series of steps that starts with receiving and warehousing of materials and ends with customer service and repair of finished products. The value chain of any given company exists within a "value system" that includes the value chains of all the suppliers and buyers economically tied to the corporation.

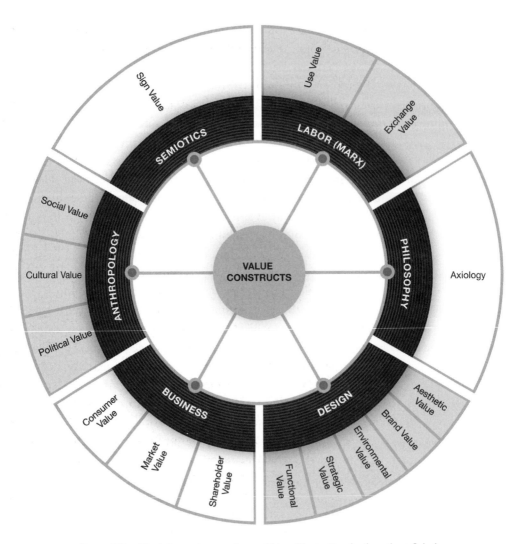

Figure 2.3.   Disciplinary Approaches to Value. Illustration by Amethyst Saludo.

Value can also be examined on the basis of all the participants who play a key role in the economic engine that drives all industry. Consumer value, market value and shareholder value are the three essential forms of value discussed in business literature.

CONSUMER VALUE

A term commonly used in business scholarship, consumer value generally and very simply refers to the worth people attach to products and services. In recent years, corporations have placed a larger emphasis on understanding people's needs and wants instead of focusing on internal resources and capabilities for new product development, and have therefore developed strategies and tactics to better understand and respond to what people want and value. It is clear that the value consumers see in products depends not only on the product itself, but also on the company, its service strategy, its advertising, and so on.

Corporations may use checklists to evaluate their value-providing capabilities:

> Do your goods and services really perform? Do your company and its people give more than what is expected? Does your firm stand behind its work with service warranties? Are your pricing policies realistic? Do your advertising and promotional materials give customers the necessary facts? Do you use frequent-buyer programs, toll-free numbers, and membership clubs to build customer relationships? (Johnson and Weinstein 2004: 9)

To Johnson and Weinstein (2004), these questions embody the four elements that make up the fundamentals of customer value- service, quality, image and price. Though these four capture the key components of the value of goods and services, several more comprehensive lists have been developed in academia as well as the corporate world. For example, research and consulting firm Social Technologies (2009) has created a list of twelve values, extracted from a list of 150, which consumers will look for in technology products. These are user creativity, appropriateness, intelligence, personalization, convenience, protection, simplicity, connectedness, health, assistance, efficiency and sustainability. The firm uses these to help companies develop market strategies and product solutions that possess these value attributes.

Morris Holbrook (1999: 183) defines consumer value as "an interactive relativistic preference experience," emphasizing that it is heavily context dependent. "We mean that the relationship of consumers to products (subjects to objects) operates relativistically (depending on relevant comparisons, varying between people, changing among situations) to determine preferences that lie at the heart of the consumption experience" (Holbrook 1999: 9). Holbrook creates a typology of consumer values that includes eight categories— efficiency, excellence, status, esteem, play, aesthetics, ethics and spirituality—that can be used to determine the ways in which consumers evaluate products and make buying decisions. In contrast to the more economically constructed drivers such as exchange value or the more pragmatically constructed drivers such as use value or utility, these descriptors are constructed around people's expectations and desires.

MARKET VALUE

In the simplest terms, market value may be defined as the price at which sellers and buyers trade any given item in an open marketplace. The International Valuation Standards Committee defines value as "a representation of value in exchange," or "the estimated amount for which a property should exchange on the date of valuation between a willing buyer and a willing seller in an arm's-length transaction after proper marketing wherein the parties had each acted knowledgeably, prudently, and without compulsion" (2003: 95–96). Though the term "property" in this definition refers to real estate, the central ideas expressed here hold true for products as well. It is clear from the definition that market value is an estimation rather than predetermined amount; it is not the sales price. Market value also fluctuates constantly as it depends rather heavily on political and economic conditions. Equally important in this definition are the assumptions of willingness, knowledge and prudence. It would be easy to presume (and the world of finance operates on these suppositions) that corporations sell to willing, prudent and knowledgeable consumers and that we are not physically dragged against our wishes to shopping malls and forced to dispense of our money in exchange for goods. However, the pressures to keep up with one's neighbor's possessions so as to gain or maintain social status, the persuasive power of advertisements and promotional materials and the difficulty of being conversant with the pros and cons of all the product choices in the market make it rather difficult for consumers to be perfectly willing, knowledgeable and prudent. Generally speaking, though, corporations determine market value on the basis of the cost of manufacturing and marketing the product, its uniqueness in the marketplace, the degree of its need in people's minds, its replacement cost, its durability and longevity, the presumed loyalty of the consumer and in relation to competitors' products. The significance of market value extends beyond the corporation's account books and its profit margins, and has much broader impact in the economic world. The gross domestic product (GDP) is the total market value of all the goods and services produced by a country over a specific time frame, generally the span of one year. Gross domestic product is the most frequently used indicator of a nation's economic health as well as its standard of living. There are several arguments against linking GDP to standard of living because it does not account for several non-economic factors responsible for general well-being, it continues to be used internationally as one of the prime indicators of welfare and growth.

SHAREHOLDER VALUE

Shareholder value, introduced in the U.S. by business consultants in the 1980s, is the financial value investors (shareholders) can obtain based upon their investment in a company, and generally refers to the future worth or expected cash flows of the company rather than its present value. This form of value therefore alludes not to individual products but to the worth of the corporation itself. Shareholder value takes the form of capital gains, dividend payments, proceeds from buyback programs and any other types of disbursements investors receive from the corporation. Financial consultants often believe that "maximizing shareholder value is or ought to be the fundamental goal of all businesses" (Copeland *et al.* 1995). However, this single-minded focus on the shareholders has been critiqued as overly protective of the financial gains of the owners and investors at the cost of the employees, society, environment and ethics. The practice of emphasizing shareholder value above everything else can lead to corporations sacrificing intangible and qualitative values such as labor welfare and sustainability in favor of quantifiable economic ones. The weight attached to shareholder value highlights the core of Marx's critique of capitalism, where the production of wealth for the owners becomes the central mission of the enterprise, often at the expense of all else.[2] In the recent years, though, corporations and consultants are embracing the notion of stakeholder value, and in the process, expanding the circle of concern to include employees and suppliers (Prahalad 1994). However, this too has a financial goal and is constructed around a limited view of who the stakeholders are. A broader definition of stakeholders includes not only the employees and suppliers, but society and the environment as well. Walker and Marr (2001) provide a list of "extended stakeholders" that also includes such groups as labor unions, environmental groups, governmental regulatory bodies, N.G.O.s, the media, education leaders, competitors, the community, etc. According to Laszlo (2008), focusing on stakeholder and shareholder value can create "sustainable value" for the corporation that benefits people, society and the planet. For him, stakeholder value is based on the "economic, ecological and social impacts a company has on its diverse constituents" (Laszlo 2008: 21). In Laszlo's map below, sustainable value emerges when business processes do not sacrifice stakeholder value for shareholder value and both groups experience positive value. This is demonstrated in the upper right quadrant in the diagram. While locating shareholders and stakeholders on the two axes highlights the tensions that exist between them, this model also pitches them against one another, creating three unsuccessful, unsustainable scenarios, and only one positive one.

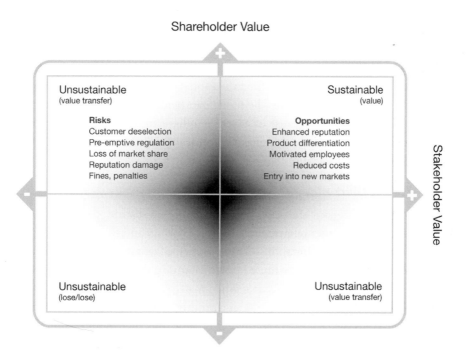

Figure 2.4. Sustainable Value Map. Adapted from Laszlo (2008), illustration by Amethyst Saludo.

A non-hierarchical model in which the shareholders are included within the stakeholder group, along with employees, vendors, labor unions, environmental groups, governmental regulatory bodies, N.G.O.s, etc. will promise better equity for all involved with the corporation.

THE POLITICAL ECONOMY OF VALUE

Marx's political economy was fashioned during the upheavals of the Industrial Revolution. This was a time when the production of commodities was shifting from craft to mechanical systems, cottage industries were being replaced by factories, the quality of goods was often being compromised by their quantity, and control of labor power was shifting from the hands of the workers to those of factory owners. Factory workers toiled long, hard hours for meager wages and most of the benefit of their labor went to the factory owners, the capitalists. The nature of the work was tedious and mechanical, and rarely were the workers able to buy the things they made. It was under these conditions that Marx started formulating his theory of value, and it is because of these conditions that he so closely linked it to labor. "As values, all commodities are only definite masses of congealed labour-time" (Marx in Tucker 1972: 203). Marx theorized commodities as embodiments of the social substance of labor, and sought to equate their value to the duration of labor expended in their production. He asks, "How then, is the magnitude of this value to be measured? Plainly, by the quantity of the value-creating substance, the labour contained in the article" (Marx in Tucker 1972: 202). It is through the efforts of workers manipulating raw materials in the production of goods that the value of commodities is realized. Marx's goal in writing *Capital* was to demonstrate the social exploitation that resulted from the factory system of nineteenth century England. And in constructing a notion of value around labor, he attempted to show that though increased value of the commodity benefited the capitalist, it did not translate into increased wages for the workers. In this section, the term "commodity" will be used more frequently instead of "thing" or "object" because of Marx's emphasis on their economic function. Of course, the economic function of things is by no means delinked from social function; in fact, it unfolds within the social system.

USE AND EXCHANGE VALUES

In *Capital,* Marx writes about the value of goods from two distinct perspectives, *use-value* and *exchange-value*, the former referring to the object's utility and the latter to its tradability. For him, use-values were combinations of two elements—matter and labor. "A use-value, or useful article ... has value only because human labour in the abstract has been embodied or materialised in it" (Marx 2001: 57). It is when matter is worked on by human labor that use-value is generated and the object becomes a product of utility. "Nothing can have value, without being an object of utility. If the thing is useless, so is the labour contained in it; the labour does not count as labour, and therefore creates no value" (Marx 2001: 60). The value of a commodity, therefore, is dependant upon its utility, which in turn depends upon the labor expended in its making. Use-value is inextricably linked to the commodity and to the process of consumption. It cannot exist without the material body of the commodity that it inhabits, and it does not become a reality until the commodity is consumed. Marx explains this through the example of linen and a coat, the material and the commodity. Both the linen and the coat have use-value because labor has been expended in their making—the linen woven from yarn, and the coat stitched from the linen. "The linen expresses its value in the coat; the coat serves as the material in which that value is expressed. The former plays an active, the latter a passive, part" (Marx 2001: 71). The product, therefore, serves as a receptacle for raw materials to express value; both matter and labor are essential in the creation of value.

Marx explains exchange-value as a "quantitative relation, as the proportion in which values in use of one sort are exchanged for those of another sort, a relation constantly changing with time and place" (Marx in Tucker 1972: 200). Exchange-value is what allows commodities to be bartered with other commodities or traded for money. Marx severed the link between these two forms of value by postulating that when commodities are traded, their exchange-value manifests itself as entirely independent of their use-value. While use-value is negotiated between people and things, exchange-value is realized only through the socio-economic processes of trade. Marx perceived exchange-value as a property of commodities themselves, but use-value as not. Exchange-value is sometimes described as the quantitative aspect, while use-value as the qualitative aspect of the value of commodities, or as the proportion in which the use-value of one kind can be exchanged for the use-value of another kind.[3] Marx explained exchange-value as being equal to the quantity of labor contained in it. In barter economies, the exchange-value of a commodity equated to the certain amount (or number) of another commodity, for which it could be traded. However, in an economy where the unit of exchange is money, exchange-value is often expressed as price. To Marx, exchange-value was essentially the vehicle by which value of a commodity could be perceived. "Value ... is not something that is observed directly, but manifests itself only when commodities enter into relations of exchange with one another. Exchange-value, then, is the expression, or phenomenal form, of value" (Fox and Johnston 1978: 90).

SURPLUS-VALUE

Marx explains two distinct processes of the circulation of commodities and money—selling in order to buy and buying in order to sell. C-M-C (commodity-money-commodity) refers to the process of selling a commodity for a certain sum of money and then using that money to buy more commodities. M-C-M (money-commodity-money), on the other hand, refers to the process of buying in order to sell, or converting money into commodities only to transform them back into money. It is in the second form of exchange that Marx explains surplus-value. If a trader buys a commodity for a certain amount of money ($X) with the pure intention of selling it back into the market, he or she will only do so for a sum of money higher than the original amount ($X+\Delta X$). The additional ΔX is surplus-value.

Marx argues that the goal of the capitalist is to produce use-value through the production of commodities. But, it is also imperative that the commodities produced have some exchange-value so that they may be traded. And, in addition, in the process of exchange, the commodities also should produce surplus-value. The reason the capitalist is able to sell commodities is because the process of labor is the process of creation of value, and the worker is able to produce surplus-value for the capitalist. When workers produce just enough for themselves, the commodities that result from their labor have use-value but no exchange-value. However, when they produce more than what they need, that is owned by the capitalist as surplus-value. The capitalist needs this to increase the amount of capital, a process known as valorization. In fact, Marx presents surplus-value as the very basis of capitalism. "Capitalist production is not merely the production of commodities, it is essentially the production of surplus-value. The labourer produces, not for himself, but for capital. It no longer suffices, therefore, that he should simply produce, he must produce surplus-value" (Marx in Tucker 1972: 304). The capitalist extracts this surplus-value from the worker either by lengthening the work day, increasing the intensity of the work or changing productivity levels. It is this surplus-value that leads to accumulation of capital for the factory owners at the expense of the workers. "Accumulation of wealth at one pole is, therefore, at the same time accumulation of misery, agony of toil, slavery, ignorance, brutality, mental degradation, at the opposite pole" (Marx in Tucker 1972: 311).

SIGN-VALUE

Baudrillard extends Marx's ideas of use- and exchange-value into the realm of semiotics by adding the notion of sign-value, and in doing so he attempts to conjoin some of the fundamental principles of semiotics with Marxist notions of commodity value:

> Baudrillard believes that, without a theory of sign value, political economy cannot explain *why* commodities become such objects of desire and fascination, why certain types of consumption take place (as, for example, conspicuous consumption), why certain commodities are preferred to others, and why consumption can take on such an important function in contemporary capitalist societies. (Kellner 1989b: 24–25)

For Baudrillard, commodities exist within a cultural system of consumption as signs and symbols, and that is what we consume. "In the logic of signs, as in the logic of symbols, objects are no longer tied to a function or to a defined need" (Baudrillard 2001: 47). Instead of presenting commodities as satisfiers of human need, he suggests that they are sign-values that provide status, social standing and prestige to consumers. Expensive cars and big mansions possess high standing in the realm of sign-values, lending higher social rank to their owners. "Through objects, each individual and each group searches out her/his place in an order, all the while trying to jostle this order according to a personal trajectory" (Baudrillard 1981: 38). The search for prestige and higher sign-values, a form of conspicuous consumption and display, creates a new social order constructed and managed around possessions. Consumer society operates on an established and shared code of sign-values, and is captive to its hierarchy of status and prestige.

Baudrillard suggests that needs and use-values are created purely for the benefit of the capitalist system and not for people. In fact, he argues that the process of consumption *reduces* people to being consumers, who are then forced to adopt the role of maintaining and promoting the system of mass production. By Baudrillard's account, capitalism, through its system of sign-values, uses commodities as vehicles to impose a form of social and class domination. However, this position has been contested as being too production-centric and one that does not recognize human agency and individual choice. In an analysis of Baudrillard's work, Douglas Kellner argues that "commodities have various uses, some defined by the system of political economy and some created by consumers or users" (2001: 37). In other words, meanings are generated in production and consumption, and the reciprocal agency of people and things plays a significant role here.

One Piece At A Time, a song written by Wayne Kemp and performed by Johnny Cash, narrates the tragicomic story of an automobile worker who knows he cannot afford to ever buy the Cadillacs he builds, and decides to assemble one in his garage by smuggling components from the factory one by one in his lunchbox until he has the complete vehicle. With parts from the year 1949 through 1968, the car ends up with mismatched headlamps, one tailfin, three doors and other oddities—a bizarre-looking victim of the annual model change. The song demonstrates one man's creative strategy to acquire a highly desirable object that he can never afford to buy. The value of this Cadillac lies clearly in the pride of its possession and its rarity for being, as the song says, "the only one there is around."

In 1976, Johnny Cash's producers approached Bruce Fitzpatrick of Abernathy Auto Parts in Nashville with a request to actually build a *One Piece at a Time* Cadillac to promote the song. In a recent conversation with Fitzpatrick (personal interview, 2009), he mentioned that he started with a broken-down 1960 convertible Cadillac, and "started getting parts off different vehicles and sticking them on there!" The car did not run and it had to be towed to the House of Cash (Johnny Cash's estate and museum) for the photograph in Figure 2.5. When asked what eventually happened to the car, Fitzpatrick, a man with a sense of humor, chuckled and said, "In my infinite wisdom, I had it crushed... This was not a big deal at that time... I don't know how much the car would be worth today; I'd be shocked."

In the song, the Cadillac does have use-value as the protagonist is able to drive his wife uptown for a spin (amidst laughter in the streets). However, its strange asymmetry of mismatched parts gives it little exchange-value; it is not a car that might have interested buyers. In spite of its patchwork origins, it has tremendous sign-value; it is after all, a Cadillac—an improbable possession of an assembly line autoworker. Fitzpatrik's *One Piece at a Time* Cadillac also had little use- or exchange-value for him at that time. Though crushed into scrap and no longer in existence, its sign-value lives on.

"One Piece at a Time" April 1976

Figure 2.5. The *One Piece at a Time* Cadillac built by Bruce Fitzpatrick. Image courtesy of Bruce Fitzpatrick, Abernathy Auto Parts.

THE ANTHROPOLOGICAL CONCEPT OF VALUE

Marx presented labor as an abstract human power rather than a cultural phenomenon. And as his theory of value is grounded in the idea of generic human labor, it presents itself as a universal and absolute system. In contrast, if value is explained in anthropological (and more specifically in ethnographic) terms, it automatically becomes culturally dependent and therefore relative to specific populations rather than universally absolute. In recognizing this, anthropologists have expanded the meaning of value beyond labor and production to include consumption and use as means of value creation.

The value of goods, anthropology reminds us, should not be measured in purely economic terms, and its discussion should include the social, symbolic, aesthetic and functional dimensions as well. While functional value may be potentially objectively determined, symbolic value may not. If Frondizi's notion of value as tension between subjective and objective elements is extended to designed objects, it means that value is determined during processes of production and consumption *both*, as a form of negotiation between the producers and the consumers. Simmel too, like Grünberg and Frondizi, perceives value as relation rather than an inherent property of things. "We desire objects only if they are not immediately given to us for our use and enjoyment; that is, to the extent that they resist our desire... We call those objects valuable that resist our desire to possess them" (Simmel 2001: 66–67). He explains value as the relational distance between desire and possession, and the more desirable an object, the farther it stands from possession, and the greater its value. It is through economic exchange—shopping—that people traverse this distance and transform commodities into possessions. However, does desire (and therefore value) exist only when the object and subject are distanced from each other, and therefore, is value expended when this separation no longer exists? For Simmel, the root of value is exchange, and the value of an object is established as it is exchanged for another object or for money. The process of exchange involves acquisition and sacrifice; in order to buy a thing, another thing has to be forfeited. Therefore, when the "resistance" of a specific instance of a commodity is overcome and it becomes yet another possession, by Simmel's analysis, its value should evaporate. However, that is not the case; its value changes as it makes its way from the store shelf to the home and although the level of desire it induces may drop, it continues to hold value, albeit in different form. The acquisition of a specific thing in no way reduces a general craving for things, and neither does the purchase of a larger and larger number of goods lead to satiation of desire.

In one of the most influential discussions of commodities and the politics of value, Appadurai (1988) suggests that things, like people, have social lives and therefore have biographies. Their value is largely dependant upon relations between people, and it changes throughout their life history. Appadurai extends the value of things beyond utility, exchange or signs into the realm of relationships, and suggests that commodities travel between several worlds and "regimes of value" in space and time (1988: 4). Value is constructed socially by human agency through exchange and interaction. In anthropological literature, there exists a tradition of contrasting the exchange of the *commodity* with the exchange of the *gift*; the former regarded as primarily economically driven, capitalist, alienating and calculating; while the latter as reciprocal, non-capitalist, social and human. These viewpoints can be traced back to the hugely significant analyses of Marx (2001, original 1867) of the commodity and Mauss (2000, original 1923–1924) of the gift, which were followed and developed by countless material culture scholars. Suggesting that this distinction between gifts and commodities is oversimplified and that the conditions under which they are exchanged are not as distinct as they may seem, Appadurai takes a closer look at them through the lens of the "politics of value". Politics—broadly construed as the interrelationships of power, authority and manipulation—signifies struggle, and in case of commodities, it is the push and pull between those in power who control exchange and those who try to defy that control. According to Appadurai, powerful commercial, governmental and other forces try to regulate exchange and consumption to their benefit, while popular forces attempt to surmount it to theirs, and it is the result of this struggle that he refers to as "regimes of value." Graeber explains it as "the degree to which these elites [those in power] have succeeded in channeling the free flow of exchange, or, alternately, to which existing cultural standards limit the possibilities of what can be exchanged for what" (2001: 32).

Mauss (2000) referred to gifts as "inalienable" because even after being gifted they continue to retain a shred of the gift giver's personality. To Weiner (1992), therefore, such gifts as heirlooms are valuable because they are repositories of histories and personal memories. Owners of these possessions guard them closely, hand them down generations, and generally try to keep them beyond economic circulation. "Whereas other alienable properties are exchanged against each other, inalienable possessions are symbolic repositories of genealogies and historical events, their unique, subjective identity gives them absolute value placing them above the exchangeability of one thing for another" (Weiner 1992: 33). Weiner refers to this as absolute value, a form that is far removed from exchange-value.

In a comprehensive study of the concept of value from an anthropological perspective, Graeber begins to develop a theory that recasts value not as a static entity but as something in motion within a social totality. "Value emerges in action; it is the process by which a person's invisible "potency"—their capacity to act— is transformed into concrete, perceptible forms" (Graeber 2001: 59). Value is not what something is, but what it could be within the context of a specific social structure. "Value is the way actions become meaningful to the actors by being placed in some larger social whole, real or imaginary" (Graeber 2001: 254). Graeber outlines a promising new direction but does not develop these notions of "action" and "totality" fully in his book. These concepts could serve well in determining the value of things because it is indeed in the action of use and totality of context that meaning is developed.

VALUE OF AND BY DESIGN

The conversation about value in design can be structured around the value of the things of design and the value of the design of things, the former referring to the products and the latter to the process of design. Traditionally, designers have defined the value of things from perspectives of form and function. However, as design redefines its objective to be the creation of engaging experiences rather than physical products, value too gets redefined in broader terms. "Since products enable an experience for the users, the better the experience, the greater the value of the product to the consumer" (Cagan and Vogel 2002: 62). A valuable experience depends not only on the object but also on the environment within which it is experienced. Beauty, utility, sustainability, affordability, durability, identity, brand recognition, emotional connection, symbolic meaning, etc. are some of the characteristics that are often used in measuring the value that design is capable of imparting to the product experience. Value is therefore perceived as the capability of things to satisfy the physiological, cognitive and emotional expectations (or needs) of people. And, the more things are successful in exceeding these expectations, the higher their value.

In the business community, there is a growing awareness of the role that the design of products can play in enhancing a company's financial standing. In current popular literature, design is presented less as the process of aesthetic manipulation that enhances the appearance of things and more as a strategic tool that can augment profits for the corporation. "Good design is serious business" says A. G. Lafley, chief executive of Procter & Gamble (Canabou 2004). Design's history reveals that this is by no means a novel concept;

designers themselves have always believed in the power of design in boosting the bottom line. Raymond Loewy, one of the legends of industrial design in the U.S., is known to have said: "Industrial design keeps the customer happy, his client in the black and the designer busy" (Greenhalgh 1993: 117). In order to gain market share and increase shareholder value, corporations are always seeking methods by which to distinguish their products from the rest in the cluttered retail environment, and design has served as one of the tools by which to achieve this differentiation. In fact, it may be argued that design's very existence can be traced back to the first few decades of the twentieth century when corporations, struggling in a market crowded with unsold goods, turned to design to distinguish their products from the rest and increase sales. "Industrial design was born of a lucky conjunction of a saturated market, which forced manufacturers to distinguish their products from others, and a new machine style, which provided motifs easily applied by designers and recognized by a sensitized public as 'modern'" (Meikle 1976: 39).

In a publication titled *Better by Design*, Heskett (2008) makes a distinction between the addition and creation of value. While adding value refers to the design of products within existing markets, creating value refers to the process of entering new markets with new product offerings that "people never thought they could have or never knew they wanted" (Heskett 2008). Heskett suggests that when design holds a strategic role within corporations, it is in a better position to create value by identifying new market opportunities, but if it is considered mostly as a service, it tends to simply add value through the redesign of single products. While economic value is of critical significance to industry, Heskett also points out that the value of things is determined by users, and suggests one of the central roles that design has to play is the negotiation and management of these forms of value. "Designers need to comprehend two distinct contexts: of production where profitability in monetary terms is the main index of success; and of use, where people establish whether something has value or not. Reconciling these two successfully through the concept of interface is a primary function of design" (Heskett 2005: 74). Design, therefore, straddles the worlds of production and consumption; its practice has to ascertain economic value for corporations, while creating the kinds of goods people will find valuable.

The Sirius Stiletto 2 satellite radio was created by Ziba Design of Portland, Oregon. In a recent conversation, Steve McCallion, Creative Director at Ziba explains that "one of their goals with this portable device was to make it reminiscent of devices such as transistor radios. The circular dial on the product was designed with that very purpose. In addition, the bump on the top edge was designed for two reasons… From a functional point of view, it created room for the patch antenna that allowed for better reception, and the second thing it did was that it communicated the idea that this product is alive" (personal interview, 2009). In other words, the radio is constantly in communication with a satellite and is therefore not a dead device but one that is constantly connected and alive. These features, according to McCallion, are the kinds of details that offer "emotional reminiscent benefit" to the user. For McCallion, "design delivers value at several levels—functional, emotional,

Figure 2.6.   Sirius Stiletto 2 Satellite Radio, by Ziba Design. Image courtesy of Ziba Design.

and also at a deeper level by helping you understand your relationship to the things around you."

VALUE ENGINEERING

During the Second World War, in order to extract the most advantage from limited human labor and natural resources, General Electric Co. introduced the methodology of value engineering. "Value engineering (V.E.) is an organized effort directed at analyzing the function of goods and services for the purposes of achieving basic functions at the lowest overall cost, consistent with achieving essential characteristics" (Younker 2003: 22). Value engineers examine all functions surrounding the manufacture of a product or delivery of a service, identify those that bear a high cost, and redesign them to minimize the cost without sacrificing quality, safety, utility, aesthetics and other features of the product. The Society of

Value Engineering International (SAVE International), a professional organization formed to promote value engineering defines value as "a fair return or equivalent in goods, services, or money for something exchanged" and is represented by the equation,

Value = function/resources (Kolano *et al.* 2007)

In this equation, "function is measured by the performance requirements of the customer and resources are measured in materials, labor, price, time, etc. required to accomplish that function" (Younker 2003: 8). The resources in the equation and definition above are generally measured in terms of cost and therefore, in some V.E. literature, value is defined as a ratio of function to cost:

Value = function/cost

The SAVE International value engineering process involves a series of six major steps referred to as the job plan. After these are completed, it is the task of the general management to decide mechanisms of implementation:

1. Information Phase
2. Function Analysis Phase
3. Creative Phase
4. Evaluation Phase
5. Development Phase
6. Presentation Phase

The first phase involves the gathering of relevant research material for the specific product, process, or service that has been picked for value improvement. In the second phase, all the functions performed by product/service system are listed to identify ones that are the most resource intensive. This list is written up in a verb-noun sentence form to highlight the function and its location. For example, a value engineering exercise around a chair would list all functions in as "support the human body," "minimize feeling of entrapment," "move easily across various floor surfaces," and so on. The Creative Phase is a brainstorming exercise in which the team is encouraged to think outside the box and is charged with the goal of finding unique ways to perform the functions generated in Phase 2. These ideas are then evaluated in Phase 4, developed in Phase 5, and a select few that have the potential of increasing value are then presented to the decision-making group in the last phase of the process. It should be noted that two activities—the initial planning before the job plan starts and the implementation of the ideas—are not included in this process explanation.

In new product development, value engineering can be implemented at any stage of the project, from the early conceptual phase of a new product design to the redesign of existing products.

V.E. helps your organization:

- Increase bottom-line profits
- Solve problems
- Use resources more effectively
- Improve costs
- Save time
- Increase market share
- Compete more successfully in national/international markets
- Improve resource efficiency
- Improve quality
- Reduce risk
- Manage value objectives
- Resolve issues
- Increase potential for improved return on investments
- Recover schedule delays. (Younker 2003: 23–4)

An examination of the benefits of value methodology listed above makes it evident that in most situations (including the early uses of V.E. practice at GE), value engineering focuses on maximizing financial benefit to the corporation.

VALUE OVER LIFETIME

The value of an object can be assessed over the following six major phases of its life.[4] These stages can be named *need recognition, planning, materialization, distribution, possession* and *divestiture*. These six phases refer to the following processes: the realization of a need or desire that could be met with certain products, the appropriation of design and manufacturing resources, transformation of these resources into components and eventually into usable goods, the regional, national or global distribution of the goods from the factory floors to retail outlets and people's homes, the use of the products as long as they last or are able to sustain people's interest, and finally, the relocation of the products into storage, locations of decomposition or destruction, or regeneration by downcycling or recycling.

As things travel through the various stages of their lives, they encounter multiple actors—financiers, designers, marketing professionals, engineers, manufacturing laborers, packers, shippers, drivers, users, critics and others. As we have seen earlier, value is best described as a fluid aggregate relation, and therefore the value of a thing depends on the actors it interacts with as it traverses the network. These actors associate with things differently throughout these phases, and they evaluate them differently as well. For example, during the distribution phase, a user might evaluate a product on the basis of its intact and safe delivery, a supply chain manager may evaluate it on the basis of how quickly he or she can move it down the chain, and a warehouse worker may evaluate it for its overall weight and size. These evaluation criteria are driven by individual needs of the people involved in the new product development process.

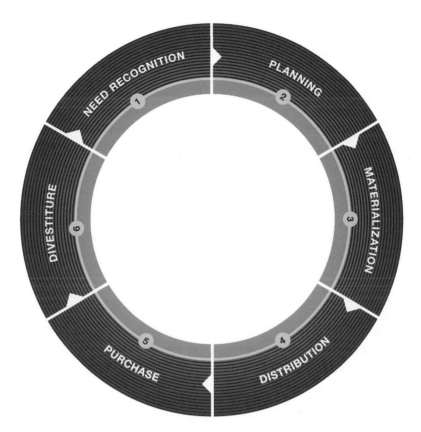

Figure 2.7. Value Phases over an Object's Lifetime. Illustration by Amethyst Saludo.

NEED RECOGNITION/DESIRE

For a corporation, one of the first stages in the design of a new product is often the recognition of an unmet user need, or at times the recognition of an opportunity to create a new desire. For a consumer, on the other hand, one of the earliest pre-purchase activities is the realization of a desire or need for a product. For both, the product does not exist as a thing yet; for the designer and the corporation it exists as research and development effort—it is information; for the user it exists as fantasy—an eventual possession. Its value in both cases is that of unrealized potential. Corporations invest significant amounts of human and financial capital in trying to understand and predict people's needs and desires, and the knowledge of these needs is of immense value. New product development relies on market research, consumer behavior studies, future studies and trend analyses to uncover the existing, unmet, latent and future needs of potential consumers. Design's primary goal is to translate these needs into products.

PLANNING

During the planning stage things start to take form and materiality. For the designer, plans are represented through sketches, renderings, computer simulations, models and other physical/virtual expressions of the design. At this stage in the design process value is scattered across multiple product design solutions. In the consumption cycle, users in the planning stage may not have identified a singular product but several possible options to pick from, each holding a certain amount of positive, neutral or negative value. For corporations, the research and development revenue expended in this stage of the project holds negative financial value, to be recuperated at a later date through sales.

MATERIALIZATION

This stage represents the materialization of a singular thing in tangible form. For a new product being developed in a corporation, a decision making group—that may involve designers, engineers, marketing personnel and other executive officials—selects one out of several options having found it to have the most value return on investment. Subsequently, it goes through the rigors of redesign, engineering, prototyping, testing, evaluation, re-evaluation, redesign and manufacturing. The new product now has significant resources embedded in it and therefore holds tremendous financial value and brand value for the corporation. The consumer, typically after the evaluation of a number of options, finds one product as the most valuable, and makes the decision to buy.

DISTRIBUTION

The distribution of a product depends upon a wide network of people, storage facilities, transportation equipment, software programs and a host of other infrastructural devices that constitute the supply chain. Things possess negative as well as positive value in this phase depending upon their location in space and time. When stored in a warehouse as inventory waiting to be shipped to a retail outlet, a product may signify lost revenue or negative value. For a consumer who is awaiting delivery of a new product, this stage signifies anticipation, which for a certain length of time is positive but can quickly turn negative if the waiting time is perceived as inordinately long. Apple uses this anticipation very effectively as marketing strategy to build an aura around its products. C.E.O. Steve Jobs first introduced the iPhone at MacWorld on 9 January 2007, but the device was not actually available till 29 June, almost six months later. "Mr. Jobs succeeded in building expectations for what some have called 'the God machine.' The bar-of-soap-size phone is being coveted as a talisman for a digital age, and iPhone hysteria is beginning to reach levels usually reserved for video-game machines at Christmas" (Markoff 2007). Such anticipation intensifies desire for the product, increases demand and therefore enhances its perceived value.

PURCHASE AND USE

Our personal possessions elicit a panoply of experiences and emotions ranging from highly positive and pleasurable, to utterly disappointing and negative. If, while interacting with an object, the owner experiences beauty, utility, affordability, durability, sustainability and so on, the value relation is positive. However, if the experience leads to failed tasks, disappointment, anger and so on, the value relation is negative. It is important to note that beauty, durability, sustainability, etc., are fluid concepts; their meanings shift constantly in response to personal as well as market changes. To the designer, the value that people see in their possessions serves as research for future design and development. For a corporation, positive values of things translate directly into sales volumes and therefore positive cash flow.

DIVESTITURE

Unless antique, vintage or imbued with other forms of nostalgic value, most things that have lived their lives of utility go through a process of rapid devaluation and end up as rubbish in landfills. In some cases, as with automobiles in the U.S., objects often experience a dramatic drop in financial value moments after purchase. However, used goods and objects that may have second lives as hand-me-downs do possess a certain amount of value after dispossession. In the case of recyclable goods, the value of a divested object lies in its new life as raw material. For designers, the second life value holds tremendous importance in making objects more sustainable and better for the environment. However, objects that do not get recycled and that end up on landfill heaps possess negative value as rubbish, environmental burden and blights on the landscape.

The value aggregate can be mapped out on two dimensions: the various forms of value that are relevant to the object (economic, symbolic, historical, etc.) and the phases of the life of the object (need recognition, planning, materialization, etc.). This can be used as a descriptive and an analytical tool to track value fluctuations over the lifecycles of things.

AGE AND DEVALUING

Sadly, most things devalue as they age. Some devalue rapidly and are discarded; a few maintain steady value throughout their lives and fewer still accrue value. Most kitchen appliances, cars, toys, electronic gadgets and other objects of everyday life deteriorate in value rapidly either due to malfunctioning, breaking down and becoming technologically obsolete, or losing their initial aura of novelty. People's homes, garages, attics, basements and offices are crammed with things that have eroded in value to an extent that they are no longer used, but have still retained just enough worth to be held in material purgatory.

The meteoric growth of self-storage units in the U.S. demonstrates that millions of objects of little immediate utility continue to be held in remote, human-less concrete cells like prisoners awaiting the freedom of an open landfill. According the Self-Storage Association, a not-for-profit trade organization, "nearly 1 in 10 U.S. households (HH), or

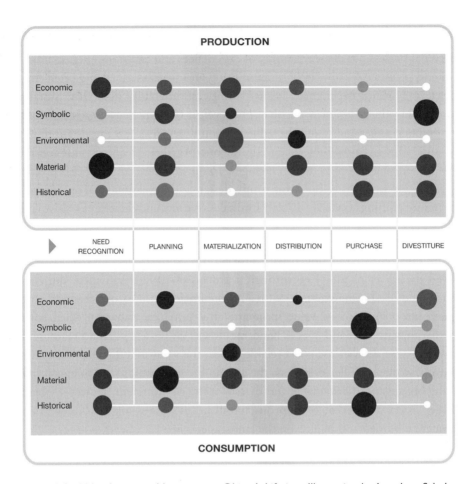

Figure 2.8.   Value Aggregate Maps over an Object's Lifetime. Illustration by Amethyst Saludo.

10% (10.8 million of the 113.3 million U.S. HH in 2007) currently [January 2008] rent a self storage unit; that has increased from 1 in 17 U.S. HHs (6%) in 1995—or an increase of approximately 65 percent in the last 12 years."[5] These things are not valueless; they have merely degraded in value to be banished from everyday life. In many cases, the storage units are used by people who might be moving, but often they are used when there is simply no more garage, attic or basement space for all their material possessions.

Durable items like heavy furniture, nostalgic items such as photographs and things of artistic worth often tend to maintain their value through their lives. A few things, often those things that are made from materials that age well, or have a higher symbolic value than economic value, tend to accrue value with age. A leather jacket that bears the scars of use and therefore holds cherished narratives of life, a car that has toiled away for years and has personal value, a rare book that has become rarer over time, a cast-iron skillet that has developed an oily patina over decades, are examples of value accreting products.

Although value depends primarily on the kinds of meanings people generate for their products in use, designers can create products that retain a better chance of gaining value with age. The simplest and most obvious design strategy is the use of material. If the material of which the object is made ages gracefully, if it changes to show its past, it can lead to value-accretion. The same can happen if the object is so designed that it invites stories and it easily becomes a receptacle for memory. If things are designed to invoke "deep archetypes" we carry with us, they have a better possibility of having enduring lives (McCoy 1998). However design can only play a partial role in this process; the well-designed object can offer itself as a location for life's narratives, the creation of stories and memories depends on people. This in no means absolves design of any responsibility; it merely acknowledges its limitations.

THINGS OF VALUE AND THINGS WITH VALUES

The discussion in this chapter has focused more on *value* than on *values*, a distinction by no means trivial. While value refers to what something is worth (in financial and other terms), values refer to moral codes, ethics and standards of behavior adopted by individuals or groups. In fact, material culture scholar Daniel Miller uses these terms to refer to two extremes, and suggests that "values are not the plurality of value, but refers to inalienable as opposed to alienable value" (2008: 1123). The literature in anthropology refers to alienable goods as commodities; they have exchange value and are therefore traded among people for other goods or money. In contrast, inalienable possessions have unique qualities that symbolize the identity of the owner and, therefore, instead of being exchanged, these goods (such as family heirlooms, crowns) are guarded within the family/community and passed on from generation to generation (Weiner 1992). According to Miller's explanation, inalienable values are those that people do not "reduce" to monetary appraisals (family, religion, etc.) and alienable value is that which refers to financial worth. In other words, the colloquial distinction between value and values represents the gap between the economic and all other forms of valuation, or that value is price and values are priceless (Miller 2008). Miller critiques the "bottom-line approaches" to value as being reductionist and quantitative because they diminish value to singular elements (such as shareholder value or price or labor) and seek numerical mechanisms of evaluation. Therefore, when the value of a company is measured purely in terms of the financial worth of its shares at the stock exchange, or the value of an object is considered purely in terms of its cost, it drives a wedge between value and values. Instead, a broader conception of value made up of qualitative, moral and ethical constituents will nudge value closer to the notion of human values.

In 1997, John Elkington defined "sustainability" as development that includes social equity, environmental responsibility and economic prosperity. This reigning definition, which includes environmental quality and social justice in addition to profitability, is often referred to as the triple bottom line for the very reason outlined by Miller above. Concerns of ecological sensitivity and social equity when added to the economic bottom line indeed shift the notion of value towards human values. While it is clear that things possess *value,* can things have *values?* We can say that sustainable design, with its environmental and social emphasis, attempts to create *things with values*: things that create no negative environmental impact, improve social conditions, assist disadvantaged individuals, are affordable and benefit society.

Design stands to benefit tremendously by bridging the semantic chasm between *value* and *values*. The design of *things with values* can only improve the value that things already possess.

3 MAKING THINGS: LABOR IN PRODUCTION

Infamous sign on the factory door: If you don't come in on Sunday, don't come in on Monday.

Alan Howard, "Labor, History, and Sweatshops in the New Global Economy"

A thing is objectified labor.

Few of us question the origins of our products or inquire about the processes that make them what they are. It may be easy to decipher how, for instance, a handcrafted kite is made and what kinds of paper, bamboo and glue were used in its construction, but such questions are not easy to answer for products like cars and mobile phones. Their manufacture often involves thousands of components, complex automated systems and infinite assembly lines. This chapter deals with labor, an issue practically ignored in design discourse. Some of the primary activities in which we involve technology in the making process are "crafting, inventing, designing, manufacturing, working, operating, and maintaining" (Mitcham 1994: 210). While all these activities are central to the production of things, the focus here will be primarily on manufacturing labor involved in the making of things—forging, molding, machining, assembling types of work. In these conditions, human agency is executed through the bodies of the workers in the most visceral ways. It was this type of labor that inspired Marx's critique of the socioeconomics of capitalism. This chapter will devote some attention to Marx's theory of alienation, which will be explained in the context of the kinds of working conditions that he observed in factories in England. The issue of human exploitation is nowhere more pronounced than in circumstances of sweated labor. While those conditions have improved significantly today, alienation has taken a few different forms; in some ways, it has shifted from the arena of production to that of consumption. This situation will be discussed through the analysis of a commodity that opens up the world of all other commodities—the credit card. A case study of the soccer ball will demonstrate how activists, labor organizations, corporations and governments have worked together to minimize exploitation and promote the concepts of humane labor practices through fair trade agreements. The volume of the global flow of capital, people and things today has made fair trade more critical than ever before. This chapter will also examine the economics of outsourcing and offshoring. While some economists argue that low-cost outsourced labor serves a critical function and is essential to global economic development, others describe it as a form of exploitation that can and should be avoided. In these types of labor situations, it is common for women to be unduly and disproportionately affected. A discussion of factories in China and Mexico will unpack some of these concerns of gender, technology and the factory. It is clear that things conceal the labor expended in their making. This chapter offers a closer look at the network of factories, labor organizations, workers and goods that is set into motion through the human agency of labor.

Economists generally define labor as the measure of work done by human beings, and along with land and capital, it is one of the prime movers of processes of production. However, labor should not be defined purely in economic terms; it has a social dimension that involves the mental and physical exertions of individuals and groups in society. The new product development process involves labor of various kinds—design, engineering, advertising, manufacturing, selling, maintenance, repair, recycling, etc. This type of work involves physical (blue collar) and mental labor (white collar) but most of this chapter will focus on manufacturing labor in such industries as automotive, apparel and electronic products, where workers often face the largest challenges of alienation. A significant amount of the manufacturing industry has moved from richer to poorer nations[1] over the last few decades (primarily from North America and Western Europe to Asia, Eastern Europe and Central/South America) through processes of outsourcing. This has given rise to a host of ethical issues regarding working conditions, fairness of wages, child labor, etc. The individual narratives of the workers are a part of the things they create. The culture of these objects is formed in their stories of labor.

TYPES OF LABOR

Through their lifecycles, things travel through three realms—production, distribution and consumption—that involve large numbers of actors operating within a complex network. Human actors include designers, investors, manufacturers, transporters, users and recyclers. The network also includes such non-human actors as manufacturing facilities, regulatory bodies, machines, governments and the things themselves. This chapter will focus specifically on manufacturing labor, a critical segment of the making of things.

The type of labor performed can be classified in multiple ways: by nature of work (color of collar), by level of skill, by industry, by earnings, by title, and so forth. "Classifications of workers, however, are neither 'natural' nor self-evident, nor is the degree of skill a self-evident quality which can simply be read from the labels given to various such classifications" (Braverman 1974: 428). Occupational classification dates back to 1897 when the U.S. Census Bureau created four groups of workers—proprietors, clerical employees, skilled workers and laborers. In the 1930s, workers were further sub-grouped as operatives and laborers. Operatives were those who operated mechanical equipment and laborers were the rest. Braverman points out that "laborer" continued to be the residual category, a catch-all group that included all those who did manual work and were not recognized to possess any skill. The classification of skilled, semi-skilled and unskilled labor came into being at this time as a hierarchy with skilled workers at the top, operatives in the middle and laborers at the bottom.

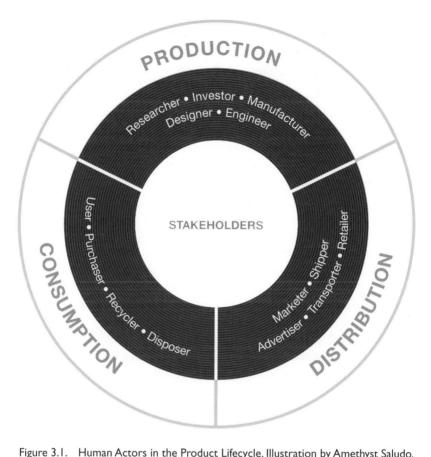

Figure 3.1. Human Actors in the Product Lifecycle. Illustration by Amethyst Saludo.

The International Labour Organization's (I.L.O.) website provides the International Standard Classification of Occupations, "a tool for organising jobs into a clearly defined set of groups according to the tasks and duties undertaken in the job." The I.L.O. has created major, sub-major, minor and unit categories for labor based upon the type of work performed and skill levels. The major categories include the following:

1. Legislators, senior officials and managers
2. Professionals
3. Technicians and associate professionals
4. Clerks
5. Service workers and shop and market sales workers
6. Skilled agricultural and fishery workers
7. Craft and related workers
8. Plant and machine operators and assemblers
9. Elementary occupations
10. Armed forces

These major categories are further subdivided into 28 sub-major, 116 minor and 390 unit groups. The definition of the first major category demonstrates its reach and impact potential as well as the intellectual nature of the work.

> Legislators, senior officials and managers determine, formulate, direct or advise on government policies, as well as those of special-interest organisations, formulate laws, public rules and regulations, represent governments and act on their behalf, oversee the interpretation and implementation of government policies and legislation, or plan, direct, and coordinate the policies and activities of enterprises or organisations, or their internal departments or sections. (I.L.O. 2008)

On the other hand, the last category of elemental occupations includes labor of several kinds:

> Labourers in mining, construction, manufacturing and transport mainly perform simple and routine tasks in connection with mining, construction, manufacturing and transport, requiring the use of simple hand-held tools and very often considerable physical effort. Tasks performed by labourers in this sub-major group usually include: digging, shovelling, lifting, moving, carrying, clearing, loading, unloading; cleaning disused workings in mines and quarries; spreading gravel, carrying bricks, and performing similar tasks in the construction of roads, dams, or buildings; working on demolition sites; carrying out simple tasks in manufacturing, including product-sorting and simple hand-assembling of components, where it is not necessary to follow strictly laid-down rules; packing by hand; freight handling: pedalling or hand-guiding vehicles to transport passengers and goods. (I.L.O. 2008)

In highlighting the essential duties of these two classes of workers, the two definitions foreground the power disparity between the corner office C.E.O. and the factory floor assembler. Evident in these work descriptions is the segregation of labor, the labor-based class structure inherent to organizations and the hierarchy of power of white-collar over blue-collar work. The classifications of skilled, semi-skilled and unskilled are no longer used by the I.L.O. or the U.S. Department of Labor but actively employed in industry. This system limits options for the elemental occupations. Unless they have an education in science and engineering, their prospects for moving out of the elemental quality of work are dismal. Braverman (1974: 445) summarizes this condition brilliantly.

> For the worker, the concept of skill is traditionally bound up with craft mastery—that is to say, the combination of knowledge of materials and processes with the practiced manual dexterities required to carry on a specific branch of production. The breakup of craft skills and the reconstruction of production as a collective or social process have destroyed the traditional concept of skill and opened up only one way for mastery over labor processes to develop: in and through scientific, technical, and engineering knowledge. But the extreme concentration of this knowledge in the hands of management and its closely associated staff organizations have closed this avenue to the working population. What is left to workers is a reinterpreted and woefully inadequate concept of skill: a specific dexterity, a limited and repetitious operation, 'speed as skill,' etc.

Braverman also exposes the myth and problematic use of terms white and blue-collar work. Both collars serve as signifiers of work: the white of clerical, office-administrative and managerial work, and the blue of manual labor that requires the wearing of a mandated uniform. The blue-collar is a sign of a life of physical toil, alienating work and a lower socio-economic class. The white-collar, as a sign, may stand in for work that is more privileged in terms of pay and authority, when in fact the conditions in the office may not be so. In a study of the American middle class, C. Wright Mills (1951) discovered that white-collar workers suffered similarly from the alienating effects of industrialization as the blue-collar workers. As a potent signifier of office work, and by sending an incorrect signal, the white-collar is a sign that lies by hiding its wearer's alienation (Eco 1979).

MARX'S VIEWS ON LABOR

Karl Marx's first volume of the immensely influential *Capital* was published in 1867 while he was in England, having fled Germany after participating in a failed democratic revolution. It was in London, working mostly at the British Museum, where he created the phenomenal oeuvres in which he relates social conditions to economic theories and capitalist modes of production. His writing responded to the changing economic landscape brought on by the Industrial Revolution. When Marx wrote *Capital*, production was largely controlled by independent farmers and craftspeople through most of the world, except for a few Western European capitalist nations. The situation today, as we know, has more than reversed, and a significant amount of the world's wealth is owned by a small number of large private, industrial and financial corporate entities. England was in the throes of the Industrial Revolution during the time of his writing. In the early 1700s, England's economy depended largely on the cottage industry. Merchants sold raw material to workers, who would transform it into products that were then managed and sold (in most cases) by a few people close to the workers. Production volumes were low, products were far simpler in construction, speeds were very slow and prices were high. As with traditional craft industries, the longer it took a worker to produce an artifact, the higher was its price. Therefore, only the wealthy had access to a large number of the goods available on the market. In the 1730s, demands for more cotton fabric started rising in England and elsewhere, and workers in the cottage industry were unable to keep up with the increased volumes and speeds requested of them. It was during this time that John Kay invented the flying shuttle, a device that mechanized and speeded up the process of running the weft thread through the warp threads, helping workers weave twice as much cloth in the same amount of time. This invention led to many more, not just in the garment industry but others as well, and soon mechanization of work was starting to transform social and economic systems in England.

In the cottage industries, workers generally owned their own tools and were in control of their production schedules, volumes and speed. With the advent of machines, capitalist-owned factories equipped with mechanisms of mass production started replacing these cottage industries, and production was no more in control of the hands of individual workers. With increased volumes prices started dropping, and commodities that were too expensive for lower income groups earlier were now within their reach. Working conditions in early factories, however, were dismal and were largely defined by child labor, grueling hours, unclean conditions, utter lack of safety systems, poor pay and cramped quarters. Between September 1844 and March 1845, Frederich Engels, Marx's friend and closest collaborator, wrote *The Condition of the Working Class in England*, in which he documented the "social misery" that was brought on by the rapid industrialization of the textile industry (Engels 1973). With two years of intense research that involved personal observations, interactions with the proletariat and the examination of several reports, Engels showed that workers toiled and lived in wretched conditions, they were paid poor wages and the rates of mortality in the farming, textile and mining industries were high.

In *Capital*, Marx defines labor in general terms (outside capitalism) as follows. "Labour is, first of all, a process between man and nature, a process by which man, through his own actions, mediates, regulates and controls the metabolism between himself and nature. He confronts the materials of nature as a force of nature" (Marx 1990: 284). This definition highlights the corporeal and material elements essential to this physical activity of humans exercising force against nature's resistance. He further divides this process into three key components: "(1) purposeful activity, (2) the object on which that work is performed, and (3) the instruments of that work" (Marx 1990: 284); in other words, labor involves action, a product and some tools. This is activity that is directed towards the creation of use-values. Marx also defines labor as "productive consumption" because in the process of making something, a worker "uses up" materials and tools. In order to make products, it is essential to consume others. Having defined labor in these general terms, he describes two unique peculiarities of labor in capitalist systems. First, workers no longer work for themselves; they are under the control of the factory owner who carefully monitors the three components listed above. The capitalist ensures that the workers' activities are indeed purposeful, that materials are used appropriately without waste, and that the tools show suitable wear. In pre-capitalist systems, workers exercised a much greater control on all three elements. Second, the commodities created by the workers belong solely to the capitalist. Workers are engaged to provide labor-power in exchange for wages. Labor has a use-value for the capitalist, and within the confines of the factory, every worker's use-value belongs to the capitalist. "In the labour process, therefore, man's activity, via the instruments of labour, effects an alteration in the object of labour which was intended from the outset. The process is extinguished in the product. The product of the process is a use-value, a piece of natural material adapted to human needs by means of a change in its form" (Marx 1990: 287). Because workers are required to divest all control of the work as well as the results of the work, their labor disappears into the commodity produced. For the capitalist, labor is essential in creating value, because the value of each commodity depends upon the amount of labor that has been expended in creating its use-value. "During the labour process, the worker's labour constantly undergoes a transformation, from the form of unrest [*Unruhe*] into that of being [*Sein*], from the form of motion [*Bewegung*] into that of objectivity [*Gegenständlichkeit*]"

(Marx 1990: 296). Raw materials absorb the labor expended on them, without which they have potential, but not real use-values. Living labor transforms them into use-value, but in process itself ossifies into the commodity.

WORKING CONDITIONS

Marx provides accounts of the heinous conditions found on factory floors and the severe overwork that workers were subjected to in the mid to late 1800s. "The Factory Act of 1850 now in force (1867) allows 10 hours for the average working day, i.e. for the first five days 12 hours from 6 a.m. to 6 p.m., including half an hour for breakfast, and an hour for dinner, thus leaving 10½ working hours, and 8 hours for Saturday, from 6 a.m. to 2 p.m., of which half an hour is subtracted for breakfast" (Marx 1990: 349). In addition to the long working hours, child labor was rampant. Plaintive narratives from children between ages 7 to 10 are poignant testimonies to the wretched conditions within which they worked. Marx quotes them from the first report of the Children's Employment Commission released in 1863:

> William Wood, 9 years old, "was 7 years 10 months old when he began to work". He "ran moulds" (carried ready-moulded articles into the drying-room, afterwards bringing back the empty mould) from the very beginning. He came to work every day in the week at 6 a.m., and let off at about 9 p.m. "I work till 9 o'clock at night six days in the week. I have done so for the last seven or eight weeks." Fifteen hours of labour for a child of 7! J. Murray, 12 years of age says: "I run the jigger and run moulds. I come at 6. Sometimes I come at 4. I worked all night last night, till 6 o'clock this morning. I have not been in bed since the night before last. There were eight or nine other boys working last night. All but one have come this morning. I get 3 shillings and sixpence. I do not get any more for working at night. I worked two nights last week." Fernyhough, a boy of 10: "I have not always an hour (for dinner). I have only half an hour sometimes: on Thursday, Friday, and Saturday." (Marx 1990: 354)

Though working conditions were poor in most of the industries, they were outright dangerous in some. For example, the match-making industry was notorious because of the use of the highly combustible and poisonous phosphorus that was essential for the tips of the matches. Mill owners were able to find laborers, who, driven by desperation and economic distress accepted work in spite of the dangerous conditions. "The manufacture of matches, on account of its unhealthiness and unpleasantness, had such a bad reputation that only the most miserable part of the working class, half-starved widows and so forth, deliver up their children to it" (Marx 1990: 358). These conditions of labor in England in the late 1800s moved Marx to examine the economic system critically and uncover its appalling disregard for human life. With the advent of the factory and its mechanized systems of production, labor became subordinate to capital. The more production relied on machinery, the more it demanded workers to submit to the needs of the machine. For Marx, this led to a form of alienation between the workers and their products, and between workers and work itself.

ALIENATION

It was when Marx observed and uncovered research about factory conditions, human suffering and weak labor laws that he started outlining his theory of alienation (also sometimes referred to as estrangement), explained in *Economic and Philosophical Manuscripts of 1844* (Marx 1968). Though philosophers Hegel and Feuerbach had developed the concept of alienation before him, for Marx, alienation was signified by loss of control over one's own labor, and therefore it was, for him, a social phenomenon closely tied to the materiality of commodities. Marx attributes several causes to the condition of alienation, but one in particular —division of labor—is significant. Division of labor is a function of demand, which clamors for high speeds and high volumes of production. Dividing the process of production into steps and distributing it among the workers is one mechanism by which to achieve speed. Instead of making one product, each worker repeatedly performs only one step in the overall operation of the manufacture of the product and is required to specialize in that task. In addition to the drudgery of having to perform the same task *ad infinitum, ad nauseam* and to the utter lack of opportunity for advancement through skill development, this deprives the worker of a sense of completion or satisfaction as no worker individually produces a complete object.

Marx identified four forms of alienation faced by workers in capitalist systems of production: alienation from the product of labor, process of labor, fellow humans and human nature.

1. ALIENATION FROM THE END PRODUCT OF LABOR

"The alienation of the worker in his product means not only that his labor becomes an object, an external existence, but that it exists outside him, independently, as something alien to him, and that it becomes a power of its own confronting him" (Marx 1968: 72). Here, the agency of things acts against the very people who bring it into being. As the workers do not own the products of their labor, they are distanced from the use-value they create. The object of the labor is alienated from the worker. This use-value is owned by the capitalist, as is the exchange-value of the commodity on the market. The division of labor, in fettering individuals to components of the product and fragments of the process, further separates the workers from the result of their work. This situation is painfully evident today in several luxury goods. People involved in the manufacture of expensive clothes, high-end electronic products, fast cars or big mansions rarely can afford to buy them. As wage laborers, they are paid in money, but never enough so that they may afford to wear, own, drive or live in many of these objects of their creation.

2. ALIENATION FROM THE PROCESS OF LABOR

Working in a factory signifies working not for oneself but for the mill owner, the employer, the capitalist. Workers have to divest control of the process that they have to routinely perform day after day. Manufacturing processes are designed and fine tuned to guarantee predetermined performance standards, specific productivity levels, high production volumes and target assembly times, and any deviation from these disrupts the system. In following these rigid guidelines, workers operate in submission to the process and to the machines. The process of labor is external to the workers and therefore alienated from them. "In his work, therefore, he does not affirm himself but denies himself, does not feel content but unhappy, does not develop freely his physical and mental energy but mortifies his body and ruins his mind" (Marx 1968: 74). Factory conditions and labor laws have changed significantly since Marx's times but work in heavy industries and chemical plants on assembly lines, especially in poorer nations of the world, needs significant improvement. Blue-collar workers (and to a certain extent, white-collar workers as well) have limited control on their workdays and face the effects of alienation on a regular basis. With the ubiquity and increasing capabilities of personal digital assistants and smart phones, people today have even lesser control on their hours of work.

3. ALIENATION FROM HUMAN NATURE (SPECIES-BEING)

Marx conceived of labor as a uniquely human characteristic and defined it as a process between humans and nature that changes not only nature but also the workers themselves. "Man not only effects a change of form in the materials of nature; he also realizes [*Verwirklicht*] his own purposes in those materials" (Marx 1968: 284). It is through work, believed Marx, that human beings prove their human nature, their "species-being." However, if the process of labor and the product of this work are not owned anymore by the workers, they are alienated not only from the activity and the end result, but from human nature itself. The capitalist owns the labor that the worker performs in the factory and therefore it does not serve the worker, and its use-value only profits the capitalist. This, to Marx, was forced labor that did not bear the potential to change the worker in positive ways. Instead, it alienated.

4. ALIENATION FROM FELLOW HUMANS

"Within the relationship of estranged labor each man views the other in accordance with the standard and the relationship in which he finds himself as a worker" (Marx 1968: 115). Workers alienated from their work view other workers as alienated from their work and therefore find themselves in a condition where they feel alienated from each other. In addition, Marx saw the class struggle existing in capitalist systems of production as another cause of alienation:

> The extortion of surplus-value from living labour means a struggle by the capitalists to lengthen the working day, to increase the work-load of the workers without increasing wages, to appropriate for capital all the benefits of increased productivity of labour. Conversely, the struggle against capitalist exploitation means, for the workers, a struggle to reduce the working day without any reduction of wages, a struggle for cuts in the workload, a struggle for increased real wages. (Marx 1990: 35)

This class struggle leads to rancor between the working class and the capitalist class and hence to alienation. In addition to the struggles created by conditions of production, processes of consumption too can lead to situations of social hierarchies and isolation. Practices of consumption (where, how, when and why we buy) and objects of consumption (what we buy) are active agents in the construction of identity. Our possessions help define who we are and also who we are not. In hyper-consumptive societies, consumers become competitors, and see themselves as inferior or superior to each other. This type of division too leads to alienation.

ALIENATION TODAY

The concept of alienation was further developed by several other authors including Durkheim, Weber and others who criticized technology as a force "separating humanity from nature and the affective life" (Mitcham 1994: 243). Marx's view of alienation was shaped largely by the conditions he observed. Do his concepts hold true in contemporary society? Certainly processes of production have evolved significantly, patterns of consumption have changed and mechanisms of commerce have changed radically since Marx's time but has that led to a reduction in the alienation experienced by workers? According to Mitcham, a certain kind of alienation might be, very simply, a part of any making process. Using the analogy of thinking, he explains—just as the act of thinking can present puzzles or unsolvable situations, the process of making "involves a moment of alienation or estrangement" (Mitcham 1994: 242). In addition, Mitcham also suggests that alienation cannot be restricted (as C. Wright Mills too suggested earlier, albeit for a different reason) to manufacturing processes only; it is also present in design and engineering activity. In the past, traditional design, engineering and production was driven by *unaltered* natural resources, it was not possible to create things alien to us. However, with the advent of new forms of energy such as electricity, internal combustion engines, chemical energy, nuclear power, etc., we are able to create more things that are alien to us (Mitcham 1994: 243).

Other forms of alienation can be found in the arena of consumption. Padgett (2007) draws attention to the credit card as one of the key expressions of alienation in contemporary society, and shows how it has alienated workers from the products of their labor. The use of credit cards is commonplace in rich nations and is rapidly finding acceptance in poorer nations. According to the *New York Times* (2007), credit card usage per capita in the adult population averaged at 5.35 in the U.S., 1.36 in Britain and significantly lower in poorer nations. However, numbers in such countries as India, China and South Korea are rising rapidly with a burgeoning middle class.

In the U.S., according to a Federal Reserve Statistical Release (2008), outstanding consumer credit in April 2008 reached 2,550.8 billion U.S. dollars. (The Federal Reserve Bulletin classifies lower income households as families that earn less than $10,000 a year, moderate income households those that earn between $10,000 to $25,000 and middle income households those earning $25,000 to $50,000 a year.) "The commodity which

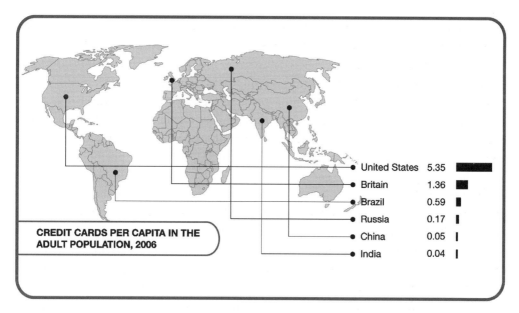

Figure 3.2. Credit Card Use per Capita. Data from the *New York Times,* 2 June 2007.
Source: Lafferty Group, illustration by Amethyst Saludo.

functions as a measure of value and therefore also as the medium of circulation, either in its own body or through representative, is money" (Marx 1990: 227). To Marx therefore, money performed two functions: it served as a mechanism to gauge value and as a medium for circulation. The shift from paper and metal (bills and coins) to plastic (credit cards) signaled more than just a new material for financial transactions. It dematerialized money, allowed consumers to defer payments, created a sense of false wealth, increased consumer debt and made credit card companies omnipotent and extremely wealthy.

Credit cards are being used more than ever before for the purchase of necessities such as essential goods and services and for medical bills. Therefore it is incorrect to suggest that credit card purchases are predominantly desires turned into needs. The high cost of education, increasing unemployment, growing inflation and higher healthcare costs are some of the factors that lead to higher credit card debts. It is also important to note that credit cards can be of help in situations where households may not have available cash but are on a trajectory of additional wealth acquisition. Credit card companies often create categories of consumers with such labels as "deadbeats," "revolvers," and "rate surfers" based upon patterns of card usage (PBS.org 2004). Consumers who pay their entire bill each month and do not carry over balances are deadbeats as they bring no profit to the card companies. Rate surfers rapidly change cards and are able to maintain debt at low interest rates; they are not much help to card companies either. Revolvers are those who are able to pay only fractions of what they owe and therefore carry over monthly balances for years.

Revolvers really help boost corporate revenues because they pay high interest rates over long periods of time. As an alienating force, the credit card pushes consumers (especially lower-income groups) deeper into a world of debt over time. And in stacking up debts, consumers "are agreeing to sell their future labor at a discount rate" (Padgett 2007: 37).

The constant design and production of new things creates desire, and over time luxury items become necessities. And when workers do not have available money to satisfy these needs, they turn to available credit, which is made "affordable" by banks and other financial institutions. Should they be classified as high-risk accounts for their potential inability to make the minimum payments, consumers are charged an inordinately high interest rate, which creates surplus-value for the banks. In sinking deeper into debt, in becoming poorer, the worker creates a higher surplus-value and additional profit for the bank. The option of minimum payment allows credit-card users to pay only a portion of the value and yet be able to possess the commodities in entirety. The instant ownership for payment over time is what makes credit cards so attractive as mediums of circulation. "Credit cards ... mediate in a manner that incorporates and manipulates the element of time; their use merely initiates a mediation event that continues far beyond the point of sale" (Padgett 2007: 24). Padgett refers to the purchasing power of the credit card as "alien" power or a false power that gives users an illusory a sense of freedom. In the long run, they pay significantly higher sums of money for the commodity because of interest rates, and therefore the credit card serves as an "invitation of the capitalists for common persons—wage-laborers—to live beyond their actual means" (Padgett 2007: 26).

THE CONCEPT OF FAIR TRADE

In manufacturing facilities, often when outsourcing and offshoring are involved, weak regulations, inadequate education, financial desperation, profit maximization, corporate opportunism and poor ethics have led to situations of worker alienation, global exploitation, consumer apathy and income inequality. Fair trade aims to minimize these conditions by pressing for rights of the anonymous workers in unknown countries all over the world toiling over consumer goods that they produce and almost never use.

> "Fair Trade is a trading partnership, based on dialogue, transparency and respect, that seeks greater equity in international trade. It contributes to sustainable development by offering better trading conditions to, and securing their rights of, disadvantaged producers and workers—especially in the South." (Fairtrade.net)

The concept of fair trade can be traced back to the 1940s when enterprises like Ten Thousand Villages and Sales Exchange for Refugee Rehabilitation and Vocation (S.E.R.R.V.) started importing goods from artisan communities from poor nations at fair prices to improve their financial condition. Since then, in addition to crafts, fair trade has expanded to other industry sectors to include clothing and textiles, coffee, tea, chocolate and sports goods. The International Fair Trade Association (I.F.T.A.) prescribes 10 standards that have to be met for corporations to classify their products as fairly traded. The following are condensed versions of those available at the I.F.T.A. (2008) website:

- Creating opportunities for economically disadvantaged producers, and helping alleviate poverty through sustainable development.
- Transparency and accountability in trade partnerships to ensure fairness.
- Assisting in capacity building for the producers so that they may become independent.
- Promoting fair trade by providing information to customers and raising general awareness.
- Payment of a fair price within the local context that is gender equitable, assists with pre-production (or pre-harvest) financing, and timely payments.
- Promoting gender equity and rights to women by work and not gender-based compensation.
- Working conditions that are safe, clean and healthy
- Child labor in accordance with the UN Convention on the Rights of the Child that does not adversely affect their well-being, security, educational requirements and need for play.
- Encouraging better environmental practices.
- Developing and maintaining trade relations that assist the manufacturers socially, financially and environmentally.

One of the best-known examples of products that kicked the complex issues surrounding fair trade into the air is the hand-stitched soccer ball. In June 1996, *Life* magazine reporter Sydney Schanberg traveled to Pakistan to several soccer-manufacturing facilities and wrote a heart-wrenching article about the child labor involved in the sewing of the hexagonal leather patches into soccer balls for Nike, Reebok and others. At this time, 75 percent of the world's hand-stitched soccer balls were made by "close to 10,000 Pakistani children under the age of 14 work[ing] up to 10 hours a day stitching the leather balls, often for the equivalent of $1.20 a day" (Schanberg 1996). The center of this manufacturing activity was the city of Sialkot, where factories handled mechanical work of die cutting and creating components for the balls. The hand-stitching was then outsourced to middlemen who subcontracted the work to adults and children, who completed the work not on the factory premises, but in their homes in villages. Later that year, in response to the international outcry against these practices, the Sialkot Chamber of Commerce and Industry (S.C.C.I.), the United Nations Children's Fund (U.N.I.C.E.F.) and the I.L.O. joined forces to create the International Partners Agreement to Eliminate Child Labour in the Football Industry in Pakistan, also known as the Atlanta Agreement. Manufacturers were invited to register with the International Programme for the Elimination of Child Labour (I.P.E.C.), a monitoring body that conducted unannounced visits to factories and stitching centers. The program slowly started getting recognition and by 2005, most of the manufacturers had registered with I.P.E.C., accounting for 95 percent of production of soccer balls.

Figure 3.3. Women Hand-stitching Soccer Balls in Sialkot, Pakistan. Image courtesy of Sebastian Lasse.

The results of this effort are mixed. According to one report (Hussain-Khaliq 2004), it has led manufacturers like Sialkot's Saga Sports, one of Nike's largest suppliers, to establish stitching centers in the factory to monitor the work force and completely eliminate child labor. Saga Sports also established a higher pay structure, provided medical, life and partial disability insurance, arranged transportation between villages and the factory and invested in community development. However, in 2006, the *Christian Science Monitor* reported that Nike had severed its contract with Saga Sports due to labor violations, after discovering that children were still being employed in spite of the I.P.E.C. recommendations (csmonitor. com 2006). Though child stitching has been reduced by significant amounts, it has led to a series of other problems. The Clean Clothes Campaign (C.C.C.) reported in 2002 that children not working in ball stitching are often found doing nothing or working in other industries where conditions might be worse (cleanclothes.org 2002). More children are found going to school, but in some cases household incomes have dropped by almost 50 percent, leading to fewer meals for families. Women workers who are unable to travel to the stitching centers still work at home, but are paid less. This has continued the practice of a gender-based payment system and has widened the income gap between men and women. The Atlanta Agreement has affected 6,000 to 7,000 children in the Sialkot area, but the

Figure 3.4. The Hand-Stitching of Soccer Balls in Sialkot Pakistan. Image courtesy Sebastian Lasse

C.C.C. estimates that there are 3.5 million working children in Pakistan for whom this has meant nothing. The soccer ball, manufactured for a mere fraction of its final sales price is a repository of tales of the complex conditions under which it is manufactured. Stories of greedy capitalism, opportunistic outsourcing, abusive exploitation, exorbitant marketing and price markups are stitched into the seams of the soccer ball. Similarly, narratives of international indignation, labor negotiation, corporate codes of conduct and improved factory conditions also co-exist within the same ball. International labor markets today are replete with contradictions and the soccer ball is just one such repository where the tensions between exploitation and fairness are played out.

SWEATSHOPS

Labels on clothing are being inspected by consumers more closely today than ever before, and not necessarily to learn whether the fabric is cotton or polyester and how to care for it, but to know where the garment is made. The growing reliance of corporations on labor in foreign nations, the increasing scrutiny of labor practices by the government and more frequent media coverage of tales of exploitation have finally filtered to the consumer level and has piqued interest as well as reaction. Photographs of women toiling over sewing machines and men working in cramped quarters circulate widely over the Internet, television and magazines and they have left an impression on consumers. Though a significant number of clothing labels still say "Made in Honduras," "Made in the Dominican Republic" or "Made in Bangladesh," labels on T-shirts made by American Apparel now read, in addition to "Made in U.S.A.," "This garment was manufactured by American Apparel in a sweatshop free environment at our downtown Los Angeles factory." The phrase "Sweatshop Free T-shirts™" is now a trademark owned by American Apparel.

The term "sweated labor" has been found in the language of 1800s to refer to the work done in miserable, sweltering environments and the phrase "sweating system" applied to this form of production. Today, sweatshops are imagined as workshops, generally in poorer countries, where rows and rows of workers (men, women and children) labor in squalid, cramped spaces, under bullying supervisors, for poor pay to create products for brand name multinationals. There is some disagreement on what qualifies as a sweatshop and what does not. Labor activists have taken the position that any single form of exploitation (low wage, poor working conditions, child labor, etc.) within a factory marks it a sweatshop. The U.S. General Accounting Office uses the term for factories that violate any labor law. Government officials, some economists and other proponents of free trade and globalization who believe that low paying jobs in poorer nations created by multinationals are beneficial to both parties and a necessary step in economic development, oppose the use of the term. They argue that it is extremely imprecise, highly politicized, used indiscriminately and therefore problematic to include in serious economic discourse.

Though subhuman working conditions have existed for centuries in several manu-facturing sectors, the term sweatshop is most often attached to the apparel industry. Rapid changes in fashion, the unpredictability of consumer desire, need for batch production, fear of unsaleable inventories and low profit margins are some of the reasons why this industry seems particularly drawn to sweatshop labor. "The industry has historically dealt with this unpredictability by pushing risk down through the production chain: from retailer to manufacturer to contractor to subcontractor and ultimately into the worker's home" (Howard 2007: 31). The economic risk faced by the retailer at the top transfers down through the chain and becomes economic, physiological, psychological and social risk for the worker. Labor scholars say that this system has not changed in over a century and the few stories of the disenfranchised from the 1800s resonate with those heard from sweatshop workers today. "Enormous changes were taking place in the industry—the use of electric power, the emergence of a mass market for ready-made clothing, economies of scale that concentrated large numbers of workers, even an insurgent labor movement—and yet the sweatshop remained intact and grew even more pernicious" (Stein in Howard 2007: xv). This is anonymous production. Consumers wearing clothing manufactured in Bangladesh have absolutely no idea which individual, subcontractor or contractor was involved in making the T-shirts they wear. Similarly, soccer players do not know the anonymous hands of Pakistani women, men and children who stitched the ball they kick around. These things are opaque; their form reveals nothing of their origins. The label only tells you where it was made, not how.

In the 1900s, garment manufacturing had not yet been outsourced to other nations and sweatshops were found in states like New York, New Jersey and Pennsylvania. Since then, several events have led to improved conditions for workers in sweatshops. The birth of the International Ladies' Garment Workers' Union (I.L.G.W.U.) and the Amalgamated Clothing Workers of America (A.C.W.A.), strikes in sweatshops, louder outcry about fires that killed scores of workers, growing public recognition and government oversight are some factors that have played a big role in minimizing the problems.

EXPORTING SWEATSHOPS, IMPORTING COMMODITIES

The sweatshop problem did not really disappear; it merely vanished from sight in the U.S. because it migrated to poorer nations in the world, where labor scrutiny was less rigorous, wages low and large populations willing to work. "In 1961, 4 percent of the clothes sold in the U.S. market were imports. Fifteen years later imports accounted for 31 percent. Today [2007] it's approaching 90 percent and still climbing—about $100 billion a year worth of clothing" (Howard 2007: 38). Apparel is now manufactured in several countries in Asia, Central America, South America, Africa, and to a lesser extent, in Eastern Europe as well. In some cases, the labor costs in these nations can be fifteen times lower than those incurred by hiring a unionized U.S. worker. Over the last couple of decades, scores of well-known brands such as Nike, Guess, Gap and others have been implicated in sweatshop scandals. As one of the leading manufacturers of athletic wear and sports shoes, Nike sits right in the middle of all the sweatshop controversies that have involved several multinationals. In Asia, Nike contracts work to factories in Indonesia, China, Vietnam, Thailand, the Philippines, South Korea and Taiwan. Indonesia is one of the larger producers of shoes for Nike (and several other corporations). With most contractors, the key issues of exploitation generally revolve around compensation, workplace conditions, collective bargaining and child labor, with compensation being possibly the most contentious.

Disagreements over compensation led 10,000 Indonesian workers to walk out of a Nike contract factory in April 1997. The case over wages generally revolves around the question of whether successful multinationals that charge premium prices for their products and spend exorbitant amounts of money on advertising should pay living wage or mandated minimum wage. Living wage is wage that is high enough to maintain a normal standard of living, while minimum wage is the lowest wage permissible by law or an agreement with a union. For example, in 1998, Nike contractors in Jakarta, Indonesia paid $2.60 a day, which met the legal requirements, but the A.F.L.-C.I.O.'s Asian-American Free Labor Institute (A.A.F.L.I.) contended that to cover basic needs of food, clothing and shelter in

Jakarta a worker would need $4 per day (Varley 1998). Officials at Nike said that their wage was better than what most Indonesians made, such as subsistence farmers who earned less than $1 per day. Critics responded to this argument by saying that Nike could pay more considering their profit margins (especially on shoes), and that wages should not be compared to farmers because cost of living in cities was significantly higher. Nike added that the factories also provided other benefits such as free food, transportation, uniforms, subsidized food markets, leave, health benefits, bonuses and overtime pay. Arguments and counter-arguments fly back and forth with little resolution.

Workplace conditions tend to be another major issue in contract labor. This includes abuse by factory managers, which can sometimes be physical, and often directed towards women. In response to such behaviors, Nike has said it disciplines and in some cases fires the responsible supervisors. In some cases, workers do not have direct access to managers at multinationals to file grievances. In Indonesia, Nike works through a labor union called the Federation of All-Indonesia Trade Unions (F.P.F.S.I.) for talks and negotiations. It also hires third party inspectors, who not only check quality and safety but also serve the workers by listening to their complaints.

Though child labor was a significant problem in several sweatshop allegations, in some cases it can be easily dealt with by following government regulations. The Indonesian government requires operators who handle machinery to be at least 18 years of age, and Nike's contractors do not hire anyone younger. However, there have been cases in Pakistan of 10 and 11 year old boys stitching soccer balls for Nike and other companies. According to Nike, ball stitching is handled by cottage industries in villages, and therefore the work is performed under little supervision in unknown environments. In some cases, centralized factories are set up for soccer ball stitching in order to regulate employee age. All major companies involved in contract labor now publish guidelines and codes of conduct to minimize the exploitation of workers and bad press for themselves.

Just as activists have protested corporations who contract work with sweatshops, supporters of free trade and globalization have made economic arguments in their favor. "By and large, economists defend such low-cost factories as the best employment alternative available for most third world laborers and an important step in the economic development and future prosperity of these newly developing countries" (Varley 1998: 46).

The key arguments in favor of sweatshops are the following:

- They are a necessary step in moving towards global economic prosperity.
- These job opportunities are much better than others available for the workers in those countries.
- They are good for the economic growth of the nations involved.

Several economists hold the view that sweated labor is a phase that every developmental process necessitates in order to get to a more prosperous situation. To support this argument, they cite examples of Manchester (England), Osaka (Japan) and Lowell (U.S.A.) where sweatshops existed during the late 1800s and early 1900s but have now all but disappeared (or at least reduced significantly in number):

> The prevailing view of mainstream economists [is] that left to their own devices, market pressures will gradually increase productivity, ease sweatshop conditions, and push up adult wages, which will in turn allow families to support their children and eradicate child labor. By contrast, the imposition of labor standards above local norms would render these third world factories uncompetitive, leading to reductions of foreign trade and investment and a corresponding economic stagnation. (Varley 1998: 48–9)

However, not everyone agrees. Labor activists point out that workers in poorer nations are often left with no choice but to take these jobs in desperation. Therefore, though it may be argued that they choose to apply for these jobs, choose to work there and choose not to quit, these choices do not represent a freedom to pick from alternatives. Multinationals, unlike the workers, are in positions of power and can therefore provide living wages so that workers may achieve a decent and sustainable standard of living. The I.L.O. has pointed out that in most situations where child labor is instituted, high rates of unemployment exist for adults as well. If adults were provided living wages, they may be able to keep their entire families out of destitution and situations of indenture. Therefore, the suggestion that sweatshops are a necessary evil for development is not a valid argument.

Outsourcing may be perceived as a natural extension of the processes of specialization and division of labor. When the production of a commodity is segmented into phases, manufacturing steps and individual labor actions, it is easy to determine the best economic strategies to accomplish those tasks for the lowest cost. Companies routinely perform "make vs. buy" analyses and parcel out manufacturing to the most suitable contractor. Over the past few decades, as more of the contractors and subcontractors are companies located in nations with large labor capabilities and lower wages, a specific form of outsourcing called offshoring has become more prevalent. Multinationals doing business in these nations and local government officials view these activities as catalysts of economic growth. It is important to note that offshoring does not mean sweatshop labor. In several high-tech and service industries, working conditions are good and wages are high. The IT industry in India that has witnessed a significant boom from offshoring is an example of this. Suri (2007), a member of the Indian Foreign Service, lists the following as benefits:

- employment generation;
- income growth and subsequent enhancement in standard of living for the poor and lower middle class;
- higher disposable income for the affluent and increased consumption;
- empowering impact on women through employment;
- state of the art training for local workers, leading to spillovers and improvements in domestic firms;
- introduction of competition and therefore lower costs for consumers;

- boost in air travel;
- promotion in decentralized growth across India, starting with larger cities and spreading to others;
- healthy foreign exchange earnings, leading to better trade balance;
- movement up the value chain for India as a provider of high-end services;
- emergence of Indian multinationals that can compete with more established north american and european firms;
- sustained leadership for india in the global marketplace as key advocate of liberalized trade;
- growth of education and training institutions in India;
- higher quality awareness and changing perception of "brand India" from low cost/good value to high quality/high value;
- higher computer security overall due to pressures from international firms.

Though many of these benefits have indeed occurred in India, they cannot be seen as representatives of a larger phenomenon. The significant success of IT offshoring in India has benefited predominantly urban segments of the Indian population. In fact, by some accounts (Datt and Ravallion 2002), the rural-to-urban poverty in India increased in the 1990s. It is also important to note that service outsourcing or business process outsourcing (B.P.O.) occurs under significantly different conditions than manufacturing outsourcing. Outsourcing to India includes such services as call centers, data management, engineering, healthcare, software development, research and analysis, creative services, etc. "With the increasing education levels around the world, B.P.O. is no longer confined to routine manufacturing jobs or boiler-room telemarketing centers. Today's outsourcing involves complex work that requires extensive preparation and training" (Duening and Click 2005: 5). This type of work does not involve exploitative, sweatshop activity.

Some economists who see value in sweatshops consider human rights issues to exist beyond the scope of economics and therefore believe that that the development of labor standards should be left to the nations themselves. They often discuss wages but will not address health and safety considerations. The issues such as child labor, mandatory overtime, intense pressure to work faster and the use of old unsafe equipment are contentious ones in these discussions. Several economists do not support the inclusion of social clauses in international trade agreements and see them as expressions of protectionism and intrusionism (Bhagwati 1999). It is generally believed that such issues should be fought for through organizations like the I.L.O. Some supporters of free trade perceive voluntary corporate standards as an acceptable solution while some do not. Labor activists insist that allowing corporations to abide by their own voluntary standards is another way of letting them do what they want without the oversight of any external accountability. Most companies involved in offshoring have developed fairly detailed codes of conduct. The Investor Responsibility Research Center (I.R.R.C.) established in 1972 is a non-profit, independent institution that has cataloged several of these codes of conduct at their website (irrc.org) for such companies as Ford Motor Company, Gap, Levi Strauss & Co., Reebok International, Starbucks and Wal-Mart Stores.

Maquilas or *maquiladoras*, also referred to as twin plants or in-bond industries, are foreign-owned factories that import materials and equipment on a duty-free and tariff-free basis for processing (generally some form of manufacturing and very often assembly) and export the finished product back to the originating country or elsewhere in the world. The U.S.-Mexico border is a region that has witnessed a steady rise in the *maquiladora* industry since its inception in the 1960s. The industry experienced rapid expansion until the end of the twentieth century with one new factory added every day between 1995 and 2000 (Shorris 2004: 531). Since then, with offshore outsourcing reaching countries in Asia, Mexican *maquilas* have experienced a steady decline, but thousands of them are still operating close to the U.S.-Mexico border. As foreign companies own these factories, profits do not generate development within the Mexican economy. The primary impact is on labor, as *maquilas* provide employment to roughly 17 percent of the Mexican labor force (Hausman 2003). However, human rights watchers and labor activists have raised concerns about the type of work, the conditions within which the labor is performed, and wages made by workers at *maquilas*. In several cases, it has been documented that *maquilas* are not unlike sweatshops, and stories of long hours, low wages and discrimination against women are not unusual.

GENDER ISSUES IN LABOR

According to the U.S. Department of Labor's Bureau of Labor Statistics, a

> major development in the American workforce has been the increased labor force participation of women. In 1970, only about 43 percent of women age 16 and older were in the labor force; by 1999, that figure had risen to 60 percent. From 1999 to 2004, women's labor force participation rate receded slightly to 59.2 percent, still well above the rates that prevailed throughout the 1970s, 1980s, and much of the 1990s. Along with rising labor force participation, women also made substantial inroads into higher paying occupations. In 2004, half of all management, professional, and related occupations were held by women. (Chao and Utgoff 2005: 30)

The history of industrial capitalism reveals that while more men have held positions of power in the world of production, women have been employed in practically every industry, with higher percentages in apparel manufacturing, food production and now the assembly of electronic goods. A closer look at the production/manufacturing industry reveals gender-based division of labor. The higher percentage of women in occupations of assembly, administrative assistance and apparel production is in stark contrast to their lower percentages in occupations dominated by traditionally male skills like machining or engineering.

The Industrial Revolution had a significant impact on women's work—it destroyed their cottage industries (as it did for men), exposed women to severe exploitation and transferred skills that were traditionally within their domain (domestic production of clothing and food) to men who operated machinery and special tools. Cockburn (1985) points out a few positive outcomes for women as they entered the industrial workforce. As production moved out of the domestic environment and entered factories it created a division between work and home, an accepted fact of life today but novel in the early days of the Victorian era. As they became wage earners, women gained a certain amount of independence from their husbands and fathers. The income assisted in their movement from environments of poverty to improved living conditions. They had rights (though limited) in the workplace and therefore a collective voice. As industrialization expanded and more women entered factories, they were no longer wedded to specific kinds of work; they diversified from textiles and food into the heavy industries, coal mining and all forms of manufacture. Though working conditions in many of these factories were highly undesirable, they were able to exercise a certain amount of choice in selection of occupation, and they were no longer ghettoized to certain industry sectors. In accounting for women's labor, it is important to recognize the dual responsibilities shouldered by many women through employment in the

OCCUPATION	TOTAL NUMBER OF WORKERS (in thousands)	PERCENTAGE OF WOMEN
Production Occupations (Overall)	9,462	30.1
Secretaries and Administrative Assistants	3,522	96.9
Sewing Machine Operators	281	77.7
Electrical, Electronics, and Electromechanical Assemblers	226	54.9
Mechanical Engineers	311	5.8
Machinists	445	4.4

Figure 3.5.   Percentages of Women Workers in the U.S., 2005. U.S. Department of Labor's Bureau of Labor Statistics, illustration by Amethyst Saludo.

formal labor market and unpaid domestic work at home. Household duties that include cooking, cleaning and caring are seldom factored in as contributions to the overall labor input. Traditionally domestic and caring labor has been perceived as women's work, and this imbalance thwarts their full participation in paid employment.

According to the 2007 Human Rights World Report, gender-based discrimination takes several forms in *maquiladoras*:

> Women and girls working in the *maquiladora* sector, though formally protected under the law, encounter persistent sex discrimination in employment based on their reproductive status, with little hope for government remedy. Guatemalan *maquiladoras*, many of which are suppliers for well-known South Korean and U.S.-based corporations, discriminate against women workers in a number of ways—including requiring women to undergo pregnancy tests as a condition of employment; denying, limiting, or conditioning maternity benefits; denying reproductive health care to pregnant workers; and, to a lesser extent, firing pregnant workers from their jobs. (Hwr.org 2008)

TECHNOLOGY AND LABOR

New technological innovations are continually introduced in factories to speed up production, improve precision, reduce cost, create flexibility, and so on. Today, most manufacturing facilities incorporate such technologies as computer aided design, C.N.C. milling for tools and dies, C.N.C. routers, laser cutting, rapid prototyping, etc. These new devices have a direct impact on the labor force. Braverman (1974) has suggested that in capitalist modes of production, technology always serves to marginalize labor by deskilling work. This is only the partial truth. Deskilling certainly occurs but the introduction of new machines leads to upskilling of some tasks as well. For example, design consultancies as well as design units within corporations regularly employed modelmakers to create prototypes and appearance models of new designs. The profession of modelmaking has changed with the introduction of such innovations as selective laser sintering (S.L.S.), stereolithography (S.L.A.) or fused deposition modeling (F.D.M.). These new technologies are used in rapid prototyping machines that can directly output physical forms from 3D digital files. These machines (some referred to as 3D printers) have led to fewer jobs for modelmakers. Most designers these days are familiar with software such as Rhino, Solidworks, 3DStudio Max, and others with which they can create virtual computer models of their designs. Once the designer has created a virtual model, the digital files can be sent to the rapid prototyping machines, which "print" the digital data into a physical model reducing the need for hand crafted models and the skilled labor that accompanies it. However, as jobs for traditional modelmakers are reduced, new opportunities are created for operators of rapid prototyping machines. The downskilling is therefore accompanied with an upskilling in another area. In most cases though (like modelmaking), the new work shifts categories from unskilled to semi-skilled, or semi-skilled to skilled, or requires the learning of a completely new set of skills and substantial training and education. While mechanical tools require mechanical skills, C.N.C. tools require computer and at times programming skills. A highly skilled worker who can operate a manual Bridgeport milling machine with ease will require training to successfully operate a 5-axis C.N.C. mill. If this training is not available, the result can be a further separation between the designers/engineers and the workers.

In a brilliant and gut-wrenching examination of factory labor in Dongguan and Hong Kong, China and Ciudad Juárez, Mexico, Melissa Wright (2006) exposes the process by which global capitalism extracts value from the bodies of young assembly line women workers and disposes of them when they are no longer as productive. In a series of observations and conversations with male supervisors, she explains "the myth of the disposable third world woman" that exists transnationally and is responsible for the constant flow of consumer goods travelling across the globe into people's homes. In the factories Wright visited, women did most of the assembly work. Hired (for 11 cents an hour) because of their dexterity, docility, patience, attentiveness, and cheapness (Elson and Pearson 1989, Salzinger 2003), most women worked an average of 2 years or less, and were then "disposed." The twisted logic works like this. In the Dongguan factory, young women without any experience and full of all the qualities listed above, are trained to do mind numbing, repetitive work under immensely rigid conditions. After three months on the job, they achieve "full speed" in assembling electronic components for consumer products within the optimal cycle time to keep the production line running at the desired speed. The young women become a part of this cycle, and like the product components that pass through the factory, they too leave the premises as "disposable women," having provided the service of capital accumulation for the corporation. Here, the woman building products becomes yet another component, another machine in the process of manufacture. The structure of power and the force of the manufacturing system together swallow human agency in service of the object.

> Employing a worker beyond her prime opens up the company to the risk of maintaining a labor force whose fingers have stiffened, whose eyes have blurred, and whose minds wander... People in this line of work commonly experience injuries from repetitive stress, such as carpal tunnel syndrome, tendonitis, shoulder pains, back aches and eyestrain. Depression due to lack of future opportunities and advanced training is also considered a prevalent factor that leads to less productive labor forces. Moreover, those assembly line workers with more tenure and experience in the industry are more likely to organize grievance committees, subversive tactics, and work stoppages. Consequently, managers face the challenge of devising a strategy for keeping women electronic assembly workers just long enough to extract the value from their dexterity, attentiveness, and docility before processes of injury, illness, and anger overtake them (Wright 2006: 25–26).

Factory managers keep a tight control on the women's bodies. They are taught the precise movements required in the process of assembly to ensure optimal speed. How to reach for the parts bin, how to install components, how to push the pedal ... all these movements are carefully choreographed and adhered to. In addition, their menstrual cycles are monitored carefully (sometimes through forced examinations) to check for pregnancy and illness.

Pregnant, injured and women who may be sick slow down the line and are immediately replaced by younger, healthier women waiting for these jobs.

Similar stories emerge from the *maquiladora* in Ciudad Juárez, Mexico that Wright visited. This factory had incorporated principles of flexible manufacturing, and the women were assembling three different models of television sets, a total of 500 a day. Though there is some flexibility in the system and workers at times find themselves in situations that require limited use of their cognitive skills through problem detection, recommendation of solutions, etc., Wright observes that a majority of the work was of a dull, repetitive nature. The task list below for a television sub-assembly clearly demonstrates this.

> Ergonomic description of position 29 on the line [for a television assembly line in Ciudad Juárez, Mexico]
>
> 1. Transport time 3.0 seconds
> 2. Right hand inserts part A 1.8 seconds
> 3. Left hand inserts part B 1.9 seconds
> 4. Right hand inserts part C 1.8 seconds
> 5. Left hand inserts part D 1.9 seconds
> 6. Right hand inserts part E 1.8 seconds
> 7. Left hand inserts part F and check[s] the polarity 2.2 seconds
> 8. Right hand inserts part G 0.9 seconds
> 9. Release the pedal (to move circuit board down the line) 2.0 seconds
>
> Note: Do not grab more than 5 components at the same time.
> Rest time: 4.0 seconds
> Efficiency rate: 97 percent. (Wright 2006: 55)

These instructions were to be followed for one of the sub-assemblies for Model A. Model B needed 11 instead of the 7 parts listed above, and Model C required 7 parts, but two were different than those used in Model A. This was the nature of flexibility on the line. In some cases, women were labeled as untrainable, unwilling to learn, uninterested in moving up the ranks, and therefore limited to assembly line work. Men were perceived to be more interested in technical issues, better technicians and therefore more suitable to perform the tasks that were more flexible. Deep-rooted gender biases therefore create, within these flexible manufacturing systems, a division between mass production type labor for the women, and mass customization type of work for men. Therefore, women are often assigned tasks that require less skill as they are believed to be better than men at repetitive, monotonous tasks, and are often paid less.

"All things of value under capital originate with those energies we call 'human labor…' A story of a worker's devaluation is simultaneously a story of capital's valuation because even as this worker is said to lose value, she continues to generate value as she works" (Wright 2006: 12). The hopes and promises presented by flexible manufacturing systems to improve labor conditions by minimizing repetitive work, increasing worker engagement and upskilling workers do not always work. Examples such as the Volvo plant discussed in Chapter 4 seem to be the exception, while *maquiladoras* are the rule.

THE SWEATED COMMODITY

Things are the final manifestation of labor. The labor process ends when a thing appears into the world, but in this emergence, it erases the social story of its origin. Although it may be a repository of labor, conflict, negotiation, profit, coercion, etc., it hides its history and appears as an object with no memory. As it slips into the world of consumption, it leaves behind the world of production. Stories of alienation can exist in both of these realms of production and consumption. While workers stitching shoe uppers may experience the alienation of making something they do not possess (Marx 1968), consumers who might buy the shoe on credit face alienation through debt (Padgett 2007). Often these stories of alienation are replaced by other narratives. Some things enter the world of popular entertainment and enjoy celebrity status. For example, Nike's Air Force 1, a popular basketball shoe, is also the subject of a song by singer Nelly. The raw material that makes up the shoe is treated, ripped, molded and stitched by unknown workers in an unknown factory in a foreign land. It travels to the U.S. and makes its way into popular culture through Nelly's feet, through a hit song and a popular M.T.V. music video. If there were any conflicts and negotiations between workers and contractors, Western multinationals and Asian governments, profit maximization and cost reduction in its making, none of those are visible any more. In the object's journey from unrest (*Unruhe*) to being (*Sein*), all human labor has vanished. It becomes a possession, a signifier of identity, but of the consumer, not the laborer.

INVISIBLE LABOR

The story of labor is a story of human agency but simultaneously the story of the suppression of human agency. In the worst sweatshops of the world, labor breaks down the body, mind and spirit, and in the best conditions it uplifts the entire being. It is unfortunate that many things we use in our everyday lives do not emerge from the latter form of human toil. And it is a further shame that consumers are generally unaware of how things are made, who makes them, under what conditions they are made, and what price workers pay in this process. Labor, as Marx has said, is invisible:

> In a successful product, the role played by past labour in mediating its useful properties has been extinguished… On the contrary, it is by their imperfections that the means of production in any process bring to our attention their character of being products of past labour. A knife which fails to cut, a piece of thread which keeps on snapping, forcibly remind us of Mr A, the cutler, or Mr B, the spinner. (Marx 1990: 289)

In other words, it is only when things do not work do they remind us of the work that has gone in their manufacture, and the people involved in making them—an argument similar to Heidegger's, as we saw in Chapter 1. Any alienation the worker might have experienced in making the things we use is no longer visible to us. The only sign the object bears is a tag or an engraving that tells us the name of the country in which the labor was expended. And in most cases, that sign hides much more that it reveals.

The story of labor is the story of social injustice. It is the story of poverty, gender discrimination, child labor, lack of safety and disregard for human life. However, the story of labor is also the story of resistance, rebellion, victory and justice. Through fair trade, labor regulations, better corporate codes of conduct and worker empowerment, labor's dignity can be restored. It will be a better world when narratives of labor embedded in our soccer balls and T-shirts are those of equity and justice.

4 PRODUCING THINGS: A HISTORY OF SYSTEMS OF MANUFACTURE

> The auto industry has become the locus classicus of dissatisfying work, the assembly line its quintessential embodiment.
>
> John Goldthorpe, *The Senses Considered as Perceptual Systems*

> In handicrafts and manufacture, the workman makes use of a tool, in the factory, the machine makes use of him. There the movements of the instrument of labour proceed from him, here it is the movements of the machines that he must follow. In manufacture the workmen are parts of a living mechanism. In the factory we have a lifeless mechanism independent of the workman, who becomes a mere living appendage.
>
> Karl Marx, *Capital*

The preceding chapter focused on labor; this chapter examines systems of manufacture. The production of things has witnessed several changes over time, beginning with craft-based production as seen in cottage industries and leading to the flexible manufacturing systems adopted in some factories today. This chapter includes overviews of the historical developments, key characteristics and societal impacts of Fordism and Taylorism, both mass production systems of the past century that transformed labor practice in all industry sectors. The socioeconomics of these forms of production led to a world full of standardized things that started losing their appeal over time. This, along with several economic factors, resulted in the slow deterioration of Fordist principles. Several other systems of post-Fordism like flexible manufacturing, Toyota Production System and agile manufacturing started to emerge at this time. In order to create something unique for each consumer, companies today are struggling to adopt principles of mass customization. While a few industries have been successful in developing unique solutions that give consumers more design capabilities, this remains a difficult challenge. Things come to be what they are, in part due to the structures of production from which they rise; this chapter is an overview of some of those systems of manufacture.

EVOLUTION OF THE INDUSTRIAL SOCIETY

> Prior to the Industrial Revolution the human being was surrounded by tools, afterwards the machine was surrounded by human beings. Previously the tool was the variable and the human being the constant, subsequently the human being became the variable and the machine the constant. Previously the tool functioned as a function of the human being, subsequently the human being as a function of the machine. (Flusser 2000: 22–3)

In mapping the relationship between people, tools and their machines, Flusser points to the increasing marginalization of laborers by automation and the resulting subservience of humans to machines in the process of labor.[1] Economists and historians have listed four major phases of development in the industrialization of the Western world. The first, often referred to as the age of craft production, lasted a century from the mid-1700s through the mid-1800s. Craft production gradually started being replaced by a new mode of manufacturing developed by Frederick Taylor around principles of scientific management. Taylorism, as this form of production was called, was the second phase and it lasted until the First World War. The third phase, which spanned the early 1900s through the early 1970s is generally referred to as Fordism, and the last and current phase from the 1970s to the present has been termed by scholars as post-Fordism, neo-Fordism, flexible specialization and mass customization.

Though craft production can be traced back beyond the 1700s, it was between 1750 and 1850 that a large number of goods were made by skilled laborers working in cottage or proto-industries. This generally involved self-employed workers, low volume production, highly skilled work and decentralized ownership. Slowly, as industrialization expanded and the textile industry grew, factories operated by steam engines became the norm. Between 1850 and 1950 "gross transformations of the Industrial Revolution were completed in England— the creation of a national market, several manufacturing industries mature enough to export significant fractions of output, a considerable urban working class and so on" (Blackburn *et al.* 1985: 34). Manufacturing started transitioning from craftwork performed by individual workers to division of labor and simple co-operation between workers. Machine tools, capable of repetitive work, started displacing the simple tools of craft, leading to a new form of production that Marx called machinofacture. While steam engines provided power for the machines till the third quarter of the nineteenth century, electricity took over by the end of the 1800s. Gradually, machine tools gained in precision, new materials were introduced, and parts and components could be rapidly transported within the factory. However, it was not until Taylor introduced "scientific management" tools that work flow started shaping up towards an assembly line. In most industries, machines were clustered together by type (drilling machines, milling machines, lathes, etc.), with skilled workers shaping and grinding parts so that they assembled appropriately. Components traveled from machine to machine across the factory floor, but not always very efficiently. With Taylorism, assembly was no longer structured around skilled workers and their machines but by steps involved in the process, a technique that was eventually perfected by Ford. This time period is marked by the advent of new power sources, increased standardization and precision of components, high volume production and consumption of such consumer goods as automobiles, sewing machines, bicycles, etc. (Blackburn *et al.* 1985). The time frame between the world wars is referred to as Fordism, an era in which practices developed towards the end of the second phase of industrialization were perfected, amplified and expanded to several industries. Increased mechanization, especially in the transportation of materials, led to the deskilling of labor. Elements of craft quickly started disappearing as standardization took over. Clear work flows were established, tethering workers to a long steadily moving assembly line. By this time, high-volume mass production of homogenous commodities was perfected.

A need for heterogeneity in products and flexibility in manufacturing was recognized after the Second World War. The strengths of Fordist production mechanisms became hindrances to post-war consumption patterns. The need for batch production (which became a crisis for Fordism) was addressed and made possible through such inventions as numerically controlled machines, C.A.D./C.A.M., and robotic assembly. The need to counter deadening assembly line labor with more fulfilling and rewarding forms of work led to newer factory designs and models of production at such companies as Toyota, Mercedes-Benz and Volvo. Post-Fordist flexible manufacturing systems allowed companies to quickly change product lines to meet changing consumption patterns and led to better working conditions for workers. To suggest that such technological changes as standardization, interchangeability, robotics, computer-aided design, are the sole reasons for why commodities are manufactured the way they are today would tantamount to technological determinism. It is also important to consider the significance of social structures of corporations, globalization, workers' unrest, etc. as forces of change responsible for the practices of contemporary production. The social relations between workers, managers and shareholders, producers' roles as consumers, the global movement of capital, labor laws, unionization, government incentives, N.A.F.T.A., C.A.F.T.A., etc. cannot be neglected in an analysis of production labor. In Marxist analysis, workers are generally treated as powerless individuals who are ruthlessly manipulated by capitalists in the accumulation of profits. Neo-Marxist labor analysts point out that though manipulation is rampant and power rests heavily in the hands of the capitalist, workers always fashion subversive, overt, individual, collective, legal, political and creative means to buck the system. Reducing them to grease and cogs in the grinding capitalist wheel is an incomplete reading of their existence. Gartman (1986), in his brilliant analysis of automobile work, refers to the Marxist analysis of labor as functionalist, and the subsequent, more socially integrated version as the dialectical approach.

THE INFLUENCE OF CAPITALISM ON SYSTEMS OF MANUFACTURE

Capitalism is routinely defined in two ways—as an economic and political system built around trade and profit, and as a social structure connecting workers and institutions through employment. Economic definitions generally emphasize capitalism's fiscal function and its goal of maximizing profit for the private owners. Such characterizations describe it as a system in which investment of private capital drives the production and distribution of commodities. On the other hand, social definitions describe capitalism as a system in which social relations between individuals and institutions are structured around the exchange of commodities, private ownership of production and employment of wage labor. Capitalism is both; its economic function depends on the active participation of members of the social structure within which it exists, and its social network is supported by its economic engine. It is important to recognize capitalism as a *socioeconomic system*, and it is within this system that design exists and performs its own socioeconomic activity.

There is no consensus among Marxists or between Marxist and non-Marxist historians on the true origins of capitalism. Most accounts explain capitalism as an emergent form of mercantilism, a system of for-profit trade that existed between the sixteenth and eighteenth centuries. The capital that was accumulated by merchants led to industrial capitalism, marked by the invention of machines, development of factories, the hiring of wage labor— all the conditions that set the stage for the industrial revolution. By the mid-eighteenth century mercantilism was declining and industrial capitalism had firmly established itself as the dominant economic system. The time during the late nineteenth and twentieth centuries is marked by the emergence of monopolies and oligarchies, the accumulation of large amounts of capital in the hands of banks and financiers and the division of labor into workers, managers, owners and shareholders. This system is therefore called monopoly capitalism or finance capitalism. The time after the Second World War is labeled "state capitalism" because of the increasing expenditures by the governments of the industrialized capitalist nations in the general economy. The contemporary world is characterized by internationalization of trade, growing influence of multinationals and the globalization of capital.

PRINCIPLES OF THE AMERICAN SYSTEM AND MASS PRODUCTION

Prior to mass production as it is known today, companies in the U.S. followed a production model called the "American System of Manufactures" or simply the "American System." While the precise date of the origin of this phrase is not known with any certainty, some historians suggest that it was first used in England in the 1850s, perhaps to describe some of the American products seen at the Great Exhibition of 1851 at the Crystal Palace (Hounshell 1985). Hounshell himself suggests that it might have been inspired by a book published in 1916 by Joseph Wickham Roe called *English and American Tool Builders*. Described as "the sequential series of operations carried out on successive special-purpose machines that produce interchangeable parts" (Ferguson, in Hounshell 1985: 15) the American System was similar to mass production, but with a few missing components. Joseph B. Pine (1993) provides a succinct summary of the similarities and differences between the two.

Mass production, which eventually replaced the American System and was eventually called Fordism, maintained some of the principles of the American System, but most importantly introduced several that were ground breaking.

THE AUTOMOBILE ASSEMBLY LINE AND FORDISM

A job on the assembly line of an automotive company has served as an icon of mind-numbing and punishing factory work for decades. Black-and-white photographs of greasy men in overalls pushing heavy cast-iron engine blocks, bolting components on frames and

THE AMERICAN SYSTEM

- Interchangeable parts to minimize assembly time and make maintenance easy

- Specialized machines that could create the interchangeable parts with the required precision

- Focus on management of the entire process of production from beginning to end and seek improvement

- Division of labor to improve efficiency

- Reliance on suppliers for some of the specialized parts

- Utilize the skills of American workers instead of replacing them with machines

- Maintain flexibility in the work to incorporate past learning, and

- Emphasize continuous technological improvement in product and process

MASS PRODUCTION

- Interchangeable parts to minimize assembly time and make maintenance easy

- Specialized machines that could create the interchangeable parts with the required precision

- Focus on management of the entire process of production from beginning to end and seek improvement

- Division of labor to improve efficiency

New Principles Added:
- Maintain a flow of materials from worker to worker through an assembly line

- Focus on low cost and low prices and create a mass market that included lower income groups

- Reliance on economies of scale, i.e. high volumes lead to lower overall expenditures

- Product standardization so that costs could be kept low and assembly time could be reduced

- A high degree of specialization in machinery was required to create the volume of components needed with the speed necessary

- A focus on operational efficiency was necessary and plants had to be kept running at optimal capacity to prevent an increase in costs

- A hierarchical organization was necessary with professional managers (who used principles of Taylorism) to maintain the tight control required on the assembly lines

- These large organizations required vertical integration and had to manage the process from raw material through distribution

Figure 4.1. The American System of Manufactures and Mass Production. Compiled from Pine (1993). Illustration by Amethyst Saludo.

Figure 4.2.   A 1928 Model A Tudor on an Assembly Line at Ford's Rouge Plant. From the Collections of The Henry Ford

lifting sculptural sheet metal car body forms from larger than life stamping machines offer partial testimonies to this hard labor.

The precursor to the automobile industry that we know today was the horse-drawn wagon and carriage business, which depended on carpenters, cabinet-makers, machinists, upholsterers—workers with specific skill sets. Improvements in car designs, better weather protection, better engineering, lower prices and several other factors led to an increased demand in the second decade of the twentieth century. Car companies responded by introducing mass-production techniques to increase supply. In the early days of production, the assembly of a car involved individual adjustment of components that were far from standardized, and therefore it required talented and highly skilled workers who knew exactly what needed to be filed, ground and sanded so that the parts mated as necessary. At this time, cars were expensive, demand was low, and it could take two or three skilled crafts-people half a working week to finish a car. The manufacture of the parts required specific and unique domain knowledge of mold making, casting, machining, painting, etc., which made workers craftspeople. They were in high demand, they were paid well and they were able to resist the forces of capital that would soon transform the industry.

The first significant strategy that changed labor practices forever was the "scientific management" theory proposed by Frederick Taylor in 1911. Referred to as a managerial ideology and also as a form of work organization, Taylorism transformed Ford Motor Company's auto manufacturing plant completely:

> Taylorism involves systematic analysis of the labour process and the division of labour, followed by their decomposition in accordance with several principles. This systematic analysis of work (Taylor's First Principle) was in order to develop a "science of work". And this systematic job analysis forms the basis for the calculation of production costs, the establishment of standard times for every task, and the associated incentive payment system. (Littler 1978: 188)

As in case of the early English factories, here too, the primary goal was division of labor. Complex tasks were chopped up into smaller units leading to the following benefits:

- Production speeds increased dramatically.
- Workers could be trained much faster, as the jobs were easier, and the learning curve was not steep.
- It was easier to fire and hire workers.
- New workers did not need prior experience or any skill; therefore finding replacement workers was easy.
- It was easier to observe inefficiencies in the system.
- It was easier to identify poorly performing workers on an assembly line.

> By 1923, Ford reported that 43 percent of the jobs in its factories could be learned in one day, 36 percent could be learned within one week, 6 percent in 1 to 2 weeks, 14 percent in one month to one year, and 1 percent in up to six years. (Asher and Edsforth 1995: 6)

The jobs that could be learned in very short amounts of time offered the least amount of opportunity for skill development and were the most alienating.

FACTORY LAYOUT

Henry Ford, his engineers and his industrial architects like Albert Kahn introduced new innovations in factory layouts on a regular basis in order to streamline operations and minimize the time required for the assembly of each car. Since the introduction of the immensely popular Ford Model T, the company rapidly added new plants (1903 Mack Avenue plant; 1904 Piquette Avenue; 1910 Highland Park Old Shops; 1914 Highland Park New Shops; 1917 River Rouge) to expand capacity and introduce new systems of workflow management that led to what is now famously called Fordism. "Production rates were doubling almost every year: 1909—13,840 cars; 1910—20,727; 1911—53,488; 1913—

180,088. That is, a factory designed when the company produced roughly 70 cars per day, was turning out 630 cars per day four years later" (Biggs 1995: 47). In an examination of the changing layouts and their impact on workers as well as Ford, Biggs demonstrates how the "rational factory—special purpose machines, division of labor, the moving assembly line, and mechanized handling—was indeed a mechanical wonder that left the worker with few authorized freedoms" (1995: 63). In the early shops, such as the one on Mack Avenue, ca. 1903, manufacturing car components and getting them to fit together required a significant amount of skill and creativity, and workers were well paid. Parts were not standardized or interchangeable, production volumes were low, and job duties were anything but repetitive.

The first significant changes started appearing in the Highland Park plant, with the introduction of more finely tuned control of the manufacturing process (and therefore of workers' freedom) through division of labor and specialization of work. Assemblies for complex products with thousands of parts are generally broken down into sub-assemblies. Ford engineers, armed with time study research, created work areas for the sub-assembly groups, fully equipped with ready-at-hand bins for parts and tools. Car frames would be lined up in the factory, and the sub-assembly teams would move from one to the next, building each car from ground up. The parts bins were stocked by unskilled workers called pushers and shovers, whose job was to ensure that components were available at the assembly lines at all times. By the time the workers got to the end of the line, frames would be in place at the front of the line ready for assembly.

Inefficiencies still existed in this system, and Ford decided to add to the building by constructing the New Shops, where the speed of production picked up even more with a much larger moving assembly line fed by better material handling trains pulling into the factory. Ford engineers strove to minimize movement of people by using as many mechanical contraptions as possible, so that while the workers focused on getting the finished car out of the factory, trains, cranes, conveyor belts, chutes, elevators, rollaways and gravity slides brought parts in. The goal, which was successfully accomplished, was to save as much time as possible.

> When Ford's engineers introduced the assembly line to Model T production in October 1913, the amount of labour time spent making a single car dropped from 12 hours and 8 minutes to 2 hours and 35 minutes. Six months later, Model Ts could roll off the assembly line at the rate of 1000 a day, with the average labour time dropping to just over an hour and a half. (Pine 1993: 16)

The new assembly systems were ergonomically much better suited as they minimized such tasks as bending and heavy lifting, but they also cut down on the small rest periods between operations. This new progressive layout led to two forms of control of capital over labor—repressive and non-repressive (Gartman 1986). Non-repressive control is "a neutral instrument" that works towards increasing production and productivity within reason through coordination of labor activity. On the other hand, repressive control "establishes a level of control over the labor process beyond that necessitated by mere productivity" (Gartman 1986: 8). The redesigns of plant layouts, the hiring of pacesetters and foremen to track and enforce speed on the line, time studies and performance standards were all mechanisms of control.

The River Rouge plant was designed differently from the rest to increase speed, minimize dependence on unskilled human labor and allow for expansion. At this plant, through a complex network of transportation systems for materials and scientific management of labor, Fordism had reached its peak. The factory, which in the 1930s employed 100,000 workers who smelted iron ore, manufactured engines, built tires and assembled vehicles, has undergone significant changes over time. Production dwindled at this massive plant gradually over the years and in the 1980s it was all but shut down. In February 1999 a boiler explosion killed six workers and injured others, leading to questions about the plant's safety. In 2000, William Clay Ford Jr., Henry Ford's grandson, launched a $2 billion sustainability initiative to convert this industrial megalopolis into a green factory. The building now has a 10.4 acre green roof, which cuts down the light bill by allowing sunshine to filter through skylights and recycles rainwater. It is under this green roof that Ford manufactures its popular F-150 trucks.

In addition to the division of labor, the Highland Park (and later factories) also symbolized segregation of type of labor, as the blue-collar workers were in the industrial looking factory setup, while the white-collar workers were in an office-like environment. The plant building of steel, reinforced concrete and glass signified hard labor, while the administration building of marble flooring, curved staircases, and carved ceilings signified management (Biggs 1995). The fact that these two buildings were physically separate symbolized the separation between worker and manager.

IMPACT ON WORKERS

Testimonies of autoworkers prior to unionization echo some of the conditions that Marx has documented in *Capital*. Breakneck speeds of work, constant pressure from foremen, no time for bathroom breaks and the constant bending to lift heavy parts were just some of the realities of line work that were tantamount to physiological and psychological abuse of the workers. In doing the repetitive jobs, many of the autoworkers were no longer employing their skills in machining, carpentry, or upholstery that they had previously learnt. With the development of time studies in industrial engineering, assembly lines became highly structured. Each job on the line had performance standards that had to be met. Workers were to perform the specific tasks assigned to them and nothing else. The speed with which the assembly line moved was carefully calibrated to keep the workers in tight formation, rushing back and forth between the part bins and the line. Cars appeared from the chassis on up, hundreds of them a day, as teams of workers like industrious little ants toiled in hurried, coordinated gestures under the watchful eye of the foreman. Their movements on the factory floor were restricted to tight prison-like quarters during the shift. For the workers, the subordination to foremen and the utter lack of control on the nature of work often led to a sense of powerlessness. But because Ford paid well and jobs in other industries were sometimes worse and more dangerous, they were not in a position to leave. Those who could not perform were reminded of people lined up outside looking for work (which was indeed true), or were given worse assignments. Job security was low and dropped lower as workers got older. Younger, newly hired men were generally preferred as they worked faster and did not complain. Workers experienced alienation from the cars they were building, from the repetitive toil they performed, from the foremen and pacesetters and from the inescapable trap of work.

The unionization of labor limited some of these abuses. The United Automobile Workers (U.A.W.) union was formed in 1935, after the U.S. Congress passed the National Labor Relations Act allowing workers to organize and bargain collectively. The automobile manufacturers did not initially recognize the unions but after a series of sit-down strikes by workers between 1936 and 1937 at Goodyear, Bendix Products, Midland Steel, General Motors (125, 000 workers at 50 plants), Chrysler (17,000 workers) and other factories, things started changing. General Motors and Chrysler first agreed to recognize the United Auto Workers union and were willing to bargain with them. Henry Ford adamantly refused to allow unionization till 1941, but 10 days after 50,000 workers went on strike at Ford's River Rouge plant he too had to concede. From then onwards, all negotiations between workers and the management occurred though unions. Unionization has helped auto workers get better wages, better working conditions, healthcare coverage, retirement savings, and so on.

TAYLORISM

In 1911, in a book called *Principles of Scientific Management*, Frederick W. Taylor presented a system of work management that became instrumental in changing manufacturing practices all over the world. This system, which came to be called Taylorism, almost immediately became controversial and met with support as well as resistance. Supporters saw this system as one that could lower prices, improve efficiency, increase pay and maximize profits, while others viewed it as a form of industrial slavery. The controversies surrounding Taylor and his principles of management continue to date. Interestingly, evidence gathered since the late 1970s suggests it was an associate and colleague by the name of Morris L. Cooke who wrote generous portions of Taylor's book (Wrege and Stotka 1978). The authors have discovered reports suggesting that Taylor was wont to use other authors' writings for his own publications and speeches.[2]

As a young man, Taylor had worked in factories as a laborer, an apprentice, a machinist, a gang boss (supervisor of a group of workers), foreman, engineer and finally as chief engineer. It was when he reached these supervisory and managerial positions that he started to develop management tools to increase worker output. The systematic analysis of work, task control, time-study observations, separation of planning and making, salary incentives for increased labor output, etc. are the ideas that he defined as central to the "scientific management" of work. In a publication titled *Shop Management*, printed in 1911, Taylor defined the "art of management" as "knowing exactly what you want men to do, and then seeing that they do it in the best and cheapest way" (Taylor 1947: 21). It is evident in this definition that control and productivity were central to Taylor's notion of labor relations. He adds, "what workmen want from their employers beyond anything else is high wages, and what employers want from their workmen most of all is a low labor cost of manufacture" (Taylor 1947: 23). The singling out and amplifying of the monetary function of work crushes all other elements such as creativity, job satisfaction, pleasure, service etc. from the meaning of work. From this point of view, labor becomes a mere force in the accumulation and circulation of capital. Work is reduced to making and saving money. One of the primary critiques of Taylorism is that it treats workers not as human beings who can contribute intellectually and socially to the corporate enterprise but as mechanical power (not unlike machines) that has to be directed through the creation of precise, bit-size instructions.

Central to his system was the belief that the adoption of scientific management required a "mental revolution" on the part of workers and management. This revolution for Taylor meant an eagerness to embrace the creation of surplus-value (profit). "The great revolution that takes place in the mental attitude of the two parties under scientific management is that both sides take their eyes off of the division of surplus as the all-important matter, and together turn their attention toward increasing the size of the surplus until this surplus becomes so large that it is unnecessary to quarrel over how it shall be divided" (Taylor 1947: 29–30). However, in a hierarchical system where power is concentrated in the hands of a few and the labor force tightly controlled, a collaborative and frictionless pursuit of capital accumulation by employers and employees is a fantasy.

Taylor listed four key principles to scientific management:

- Development of a science to replace the old rule-of-thumb knowledge of the workmen. Taylor recommended time studies of worker activity to identify and document standard practices. Artisanal and informal forms of knowledge possessed by the workers were to be replaced by standardized processes.
- Scientific selection and progressive development of the workmen. A few select workers should be identified and trained to take on extra work for higher wage compensation.
- Bringing the science and the scientifically selected and trained workmen together. Managerial control and wage increase together can get workers to speed up their work.
- Division of work between management and workmen. All planning activities are performed by the management while the actual labor is performed, as per plan, by the workers.

"It is only through enforced standardization of methods, enforced adoption of the best implements and working conditions, and enforced cooperation that this faster work can be accomplished. And the duty of enforcing the adoption of standards and of enforcing this cooperation rests with the management alone" (Taylor 1947: 83). Though this form of coercion swept through industry and many of Taylor's principles were adopted in mass production facilities, it was also met with instances of worker resistance. Resistance from the labor force was visible in several forms: individual and collective, organized and informal, subtle and blatant. In some cases, workers assembled themselves into labor unions and fought for rights collectively; in some cases they staged sit-downs or strikes and refused to work at speeds dictated by management; and in some cases, they exercised their resistance by purposefully derailing production off schedule through such subversive tactics as incorrect, inaccurate or slow work.

Perhaps the best-known example of resistance to Taylorism was the worker strike at Watertown Arsenal in 1911 (Aitken 1960). Taylor was invited by the army in 1909 to help reduce inefficiency in its operations at government arsenals, and over the period of a few years one of his disciples by the name of Carl Barth was able to implement several of the ideas at the Watertown facility. It was when Barth wished to perform a time study and sought the participation of an experienced moldmaker, Joseph Cooney, that he ran into trouble. The worker refused, an altercation occurred, and the all the men on the line walked out in strike. This led to an investigation, a Congressional Hearing in which Taylor testified, and the eventual ban on Taylorist principles in government-owned arsenals. The event shows that worker resistance did have influence on management practices and at times it shook up the production power structure. Production is a social system where forces of scientific management are played out on the factory floor along with the ritualized resistance tactics of workers. And in spite of management's control over structures of power, it is not able to completely silence the labor voice. However, the extent to which labor can shift the direction of production and alter the politics of power is not clear. "In sum, workers were unable to resist the transformation of the labour process but they did modify its effects and shape its character, in ways which were real and historically significant" (Whitston 1997: 203).

In order to create the most efficient workflow, maximize production and minimize assembly time, Taylor employed time-and-motion studies. Workers on the assembly line were observed, their movements meticulously noted and carefully analyzed. This eventually led to the development of standards, and worker actions were redesigned to maximize performance. Although it has come a long way since, the profession of industrial engineering emerged from Taylor's scientific studies of workers and production systems.

BEYOND FORDISM

One of the defining characteristics of the Fordist era is mass production, which depends upon mass consumption and a distribution system capable of moving goods on a large scale. Ford seems to have been aware of his reliance on consumption and believed that it was this that separated him from Taylor. Baudrillard's analysis of consumer society amplifies this point by emphasizing that it is production that needs consumption, not the other way around. However, the surplus production, low prices, aggressive marketing and effective distribution were not enough to stimulate the levels of consumption necessary over time. The U.S. government stepped in, established a minimum wage, increased spending to stimulate demand and assisted in maintaining stability in the economy.

> The development of Fordism, with the aid of multinational corporations, technological advances in transportation systems, the growth of mass retailing systems, the development of the welfare state and Keynesian demand management policies [which suggest that the government should boost or deflate demand according to the state of the economy] stimulated a period of unprecedented economic growth in the U.S.A. (Wigfield 2001: 10)

The economic growth was not to last. Until the 1970s, principles of Fordism were successful for companies and they were able to accumulate capital, as this was a time of tremendous economic growth. The late 1960s saw worker empowerment and the growing strength of unions, which led to increased resistance to assembly-line work. At the same time, capital/output ratios increased and therefore it required substantially larger capital investments for companies to increase production output (the specialized machine tools required for mass production are generally highly capital intensive). These factors triggered a series of events that included a drop in productive growth and employment, increase in unemployment, reduction in demand, and therefore lower levels of mass consumption (Lipietz 1987, Wigfield 2001). At this time, multinationals started exploring international markets in hope of exporting to Brazil, South Korea, Mexico and other countries going through a wave of industrialization. These countries became not only target markets but also locations where cheap labor could be found. Fordism entered these countries and led to the rise of sweatshops. By some analyses, though, this opened up new avenues where American-style consumerism could be encouraged; it also led to a significant drop in wages of unskilled labor in the U.S., leading to a further drop in domestic consumption. One of the limitations of mass production is perfectly encapsulated in Ford's famous statement about the Model T— that one could have in any color as long as it was black. The inability to create variations without substantial expenditure, also referred to as production inflexibility, was a factor that led to consumer dissatisfaction and hence a drop in demand. Savvy and demanding consumers desired choice and well-designed products, something that large outfits were incapable of providing rapidly and at low cost.

The industrial engineers who were in charge of planning the manufacturing process, fragmented workers' tasks for maximum efficiency and speed. This meant that each worker was to perform simple repetitive tasks. The loss of worker skill caused by this division also created a labor force that was capable of one thing only. There were not trained to solve problems, think creatively or assist in any intellectual function, which further added to the system's inflexibility. Mass production was so good in doing one thing that it failed miserably in doing anything else. This was also the decade when the U.S. experienced the first effects of the upward spike in oil prices, which affected consumers and manufacturers alike. Some authors also contend that American consumers had reached a level of saturation with domestic appliances and demand dropped (Piore and Sabel 1984, Pine 1993). Manufacturers who had been previously successful in selling standardized goods to a homogenous market found themselves struggling. Other factors that played a role included a growing consumer rights movement, the ecological movement and accelerated technological change (Pine 1993).

Piore and Sabel suggest that "five critical episodes" in the 1970s led to the slow decline of Fordist mechanisms of industry.

> The first was the social unrest of the late 1960s and early 1970s. The second was the United States' abandonment of its commitment to exchange dollars for gold at a fixed rate, and the resulting shift, in 1971, of the international monetary system to a regime of floating exchange rates. The third and fourth episodes began with huge increases in oil prices: the first increase, accompanied by food shortages, dominated 1973 to 1979; the second increase, a result of the Iranian revolution, shaped events from 1979 to 1983. The fifth episode, beginning in 1980, was marked by the deep worldwide economic downturn produced by prolonged high U.S. interest rates.[3]

Economists have pointed out that the success of Fordism's rigid high-volume low-cost strategy started eroding in the 1970s, and new production models that allowed for much higher flexibility in product design such as flexible specialization (Piore and Sabel 1984, Amin 1989), post-Fordism (Leborgne and Lipietz 1988) and mass customization (Davis 1987, Pine 1993) started appearing.

As consumers started expecting choice, as the global economy turned and demand started dropping for mass produced goods, the network within which these mass-produced cars existed along with the other actors (workers, consumers, industrial engineers, factories, etc.) started taking a new form. Fordism was too rigid and inflexible to respond to these changes, leading to an emergence of a range of new production paradigms.

FLEXIBLE SPECIALIZATION/POST-FORDISM

Flexibility and customization in manufacturing rely on soft rather than hard solutions to the question of production, i.e. the operations of the cutting tools on machines are controlled through software and programming rather than being built in through physical capabilities and constraints. Therefore the machines can be reprogrammed to perform a diverse set of functions in the manufacture of a diverse range of products. Flexible production involves manufacturing in batches rather than mass quantities, a practice aided largely by computer and digital technologies such as computer-assisted design (C.A.D.), rapid prototyping, and computer-aided manufacturing (C.A.M.). This allows for continuous incremental innovation and shorter response times to consumer demands. Flexible labor refers to a workforce that has a diverse set of skills, capable of performing non-repetitive tasks that require problem solving. This workforce therefore enjoys a higher degree of freedom but also shoulders more responsibility. Scholars have traced the growth of flexible specialization in two arenas—industrial districts and multinational corporations. Industrial districts involve a network of small to medium size firms that rely on each other's products and serve as each other's vendors in the production of a set of commodities. As a group, therefore, they function as a large corporation, with the advantages of flexibility, rapid response, innovation and diversity. From a labor perspective, though the workers may have the opportunities to be involved in the manufacture of a variety of goods, the repetitive nature of production may still haunt them. Moreover, not all workers may gain new skills and if there is a drop in contracts for the firms they may quickly lose their jobs. Multinationals have had to reorganize their production models and labor strategies to achieve the goals of flexible specialization. One of the fundamental changes is that of teamwork, as demonstrated in the well-known case studies of the Volvo plant in Uddevalla, Sweden and Toyota's total quality management practice (T.Q.M.).

In 1989, after four years of design and planning that involved management, engineers, unions, researchers and the guidance of the general manager Pehr G. Gyllenhammar, Volvo opened up a new plant in the city of Uddevalla in Sweden to explore a new model of human-centered production (Sandberg 2007). The goal was to break through the paradigm of assembly line alienation caused by practices of Fordism and Taylorism through such mechanisms as worker involvement in work planning and decision making, worker learning, longer cycle times (instead of short repetitive cycles like tightening one bolt over and over all day), decentralization, etc. The 700 workers at Uddevalla were not stationed as individual cogs in the large assembly machine; instead, they worked in small teams of 8 to 10 to assemble the entire car. Each team member was trained to perform two specific functions, and the position of the team representative was rotated. The teams enjoyed a significant amount of freedom—they did their own hires and determined their own overtime. The teams were also paid for their knowledge, i.e. individuals were paid higher for picking up new skills on the job.

Comparative reports evaluating the Uddevalla plant with others in Volvo and elsewhere seem to suggest that productivity, quality, speed, etc. seemed to be equal to or better than other more traditional Volvo plants. This production system allowed significantly higher changes in the individual models being assembled, and also allowed customers to make changes to the specifications until three days before assembly started. Changes in models of cars required much less adjustment time on the assembly line; work was performed in smaller amounts of space and Volvo required lesser amounts of investment in tooling. Management at Volvo expected worker satisfaction to be very high in the Uddevalla plant; however, a survey revealed that it was no different than other plants (Adler and Cole 2007).

FLEXIBILITY AND LABOR

There are no easy answers to the question of whether mass customization and flexible manufacturing will benefit the labor force, not influence it at all, or work against it. With programmable machines, workers have a higher supervisory role and oversight of a series of machines rather than actual operation of a specific part, tool or machine. The nature of work therefore has the potential of being less repetitive and monotonous, workers have more responsibility and therefore more power and control. With increased pressures on model changes and reduced time to market, production cycles are speeded up—a fact that can lead to higher stress on the shop floor in meeting these demands. "Capital is mobile but labor is not" (Sherman 1987: 30). With global competition, several companies in the industrialized nations have moved manufacturing operations to highly populated nations where labor costs are low. The division of labor has therefore taken on an international dimension, leading to the proliferation of sweatshops.

When introduced, flexible manufacturing was expected to counter the deskilling caused by division of labor, where on-the-job worker training would increase skill levels for the entire manufacturing team. It was expected to lead to a new age of craft, where a certain skill set (operating and managing C.A.D./C.A.M., for example) would be the precondition in the manufacture of goods. Unfortunately, the need for programming and other computer/engineering knowledge increases demand for workers with a wider technical range of skills and jeopardizes the jobs of the least skilled workers (Schoenberger 1988). In addition, the increased responsibilities and pressures of productivity in conditions of high flexibility and rapid change can lead to long-term stress for all workers. Flexibility in manufacturing has also led to flexibility in the wage-contract, "allowing managers to hire and fire at will" (Leborgne and Lipietz 1988).

THE TOYOTA PRODUCTION SYSTEM

There have been several other experiments at improving factory conditions in the automobile industry. Perhaps the best known example is Toyota's fine tuning of the assembly process using mechanisms of what is now called "lean production." Toyota defines the Toyota Production System (T.P.S.) as "a production system that is steeped in the philosophy of the complete elimination of all waste and that imbues all aspects of production with this philosophy in pursuit of the most efficient production method" (Toyota.co.jp 2009). The fundamental goal of T.P.S. is the minimization or elimination of every form of waste to ensure that all activities performed on the product add to it some form of value. Another defining characteristic of T.P.S. is the notion of *kaizen* or continuous improvement. Though standards of production are established, they are constantly examined and improved. T.P.S. is based on two concepts:

> The first is called *jidoka* (loosely translated as "automation with a human touch"), which means that when a problem occurs, the equipment stops immediately, preventing defective products from being produced. The second is the concept of "Just-in-Time" (J.I.T.), in which each process produces only what is needed by the next process in a continuous flow. (Toyota.co.jp 2009)

The T.P.S. does rely heavily on standardization of procedures and therefore elements of Taylorism are central to its operation. Charts that identify the sequence of operations and cycle times are posted above each workstation. According to principles of *kaizen*, standards are only fixed until they can be improved. The performance of the workers and teams is connected to their engagement in the continuous improvement process, and hence to their wages. "The contributions made in the continuous improvement process and activities, the cooperation within the team, the social competence and the ability to lead and to motivate team members and subordinates are further criteria in the performance appraisal" (Constanze 2005: 107). This system therefore encourages workers to engage actively in problem solving and suggests that they are not employed purely for their physical capabilities, but also for their intellectual capabilities. Opinion is divided on whether this only adds to worker stress and expects too much from them (Berggren 1992), or whether it assists development through the creation of an active learning environment (Adler and Cole 1993: 5).

The development of teams is accompanied by decentralization of operating units. Each team handles a batch, a relatively small quantity of products, and is able to respond quickly to design changes. The J.I.T. methodology minimizes inventory by supplying raw materials and parts for processing just in time for each stage of the development cycle. It utilizes programmable machinery that can be easily reconfigured to accommodate changes in product design for low volume production. Critics have said that these technological mechanisms do not necessarily assist in the development of new skills for the workers; instead, they merely add a larger variety to the repertoire of jobs (Clegg 1990). It has also been noted that the hierarchy central to Japanese companies continues to exercise its presence in this situation as well, and does not provide more autonomy to the workers (Mehri 2005).

Some scholars (Aglietta 1979, Lipietz 1987) suggest that post-Fordism cannot be typified or explained with one new model of production; instead they outline several possibilities including Kalmarism, Toyotism and neo-Taylorism. Neo-Taylorism refers to a practice adopted by companies involved in batch production of employing and releasing workers as and when jobs arrive and disappear. This system does not provide any security to the workers. Kalmarism, developed after Volvo's experiments at the Kalmar plant, creates workgroups where each worker is able to improve skills, participate actively in decision-making and problem solving and enjoys a certain amount of autonomy. These workers are hired on a permanent basis and are not laid off abruptly with job changes. And Toyotism, a Japanese method developed around Toyota, is similar to Kalmarism, except for the fact that workers are not hired on a permanent basis. These production models together account for what is referred to as post-Fordism.

MASS CUSTOMIZATION

In the introduction to *Mass Customization*, Pine acknowledges Stan Davis, author of *Future Perfect* (1987), as the architect of the term and describes it as "a new way of viewing business competition, one that makes the identification and fulfillment of the wants and needs of individual customers paramount without sacrificing efficiency, effectiveness, and low costs" (Pine 1993: xiii). The goal of all the production models described in the previous section that have followed Fordism is to provide the consumer a range of choices in their purchases, while still ensuring profit for the corporation. "Today, a new paradigm of management is emerging, one in which variety and customization supplant standardized products, heterogeneous and fragmented markets spring from once homogeneous markets, and product life cycles and development cycles spiral downward" (Pine 1993: 34). Examples of mass customization can be found in almost every industry sector including such consumer products as automobiles, fast-food, shoes, coffee, as well as service sectors like insurance and banking.

It is important to make a distinction between an extreme variety of fixed goods and consumer-designed goods. Pine includes in his examples breakfast cereals that are now available in a dizzying array of varieties. Cheerios, for example, is not longer just Cheerios; one has the option of choosing between Honey Nut Cheerios, Apple Cinnamon Cheerios, Multi Grain Cheerios, and so on. In this case, the customization is conceived, managed and implemented by the corporation. Customers may be involved in the design stages in focus groups and marketing studies, but the process of design is under the control of the corporation. Mass customization essentially refers to the availability of a large number of fixed alternatives. The consumer has not really customized any of the options; the corporation has. Mass customerization, however, refers to those products that allow users to actively change some of the components or design elements that result in a unique product that no one else may own.

Customized goods, therefore, can be mapped out on a continuum, that includes, at one end, products designed and manufactured by corporations to, at the other end, products designed and (to a certain extent) manufactured by consumers. For example, the Nike iD site and the Puma Mongolian Shoe BBQ site allow consumers to log on, select a shoe body and design their own graphics and colors. Similarly Toyota allows Scion users to select a variety of options online and create a car of their choice. Figure 4.3 shows a series of alternatives mapped on an X-axis that represents the process of design and a Y-axis that represents the process of manufacture. By locating consumers and corporations at the ends of these axes, one can map a variety of products in the four quadrants.

The bottom left corner of the diagram provides the highly individualized and personalized object designed and made by the consumer, while the top right corner represents the highly generic commodity designed and manufactured by the corporation. The top left quadrant represents the mass customerized product that incorporates elements designed by the user, and the bottom right includes product designs sold by corporations as plans/drawings that consumers can produce themselves.

The continuum above represents a range of products from those designed entirely by consumers (customerized) to those designed by corporations (standardized). To be successful at the left end of the continuum, a corporation needs to operate as a highly flexible organization

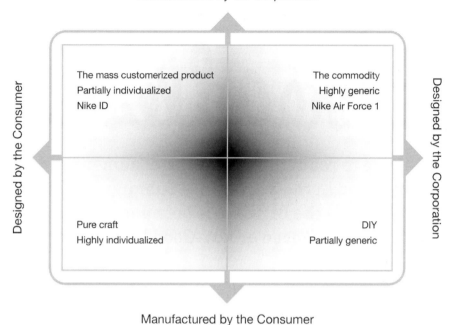

Figure 4.3.   Mass Production—Mass Customerization Map. Illustration by Amethyst Saludo.

that is able to meet the specific needs of an infinite number of consumers. In the middle is a newly emerging model in which customers submit designs that are selected through a system of voting, and those are the ones manufactured. Threadless, a T-shirt design and manufacturing company is an example of such an enterprise. The process is partially democratic because the selection of designs starts with people voting for their favorites,

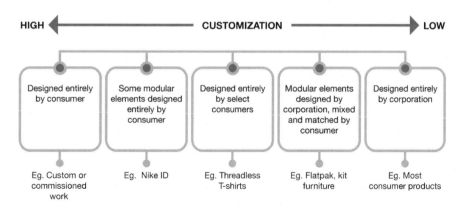

Figure 4.4.   Mass Customization Continuum. Illustration by Amethyst Saludo.

Be sure to read through all the documentation
provided in the Threadless Submission Kit.
It could mean the difference between having your
submission approved or not. *Good luck & have fun!*

Figure 4.5.   Threadless Logo and Directions. Image courtesy of Threadless.

but the final decision of manufacturing lies with Threadless. Similarly, Muji products from Japan follow a process of consumer selection prior to manufacturing. Threadless provides designers with templates they can use to create their designs.

FlatPak House by Charlie Lazor is an example of these concepts extended into the architectural world. In case of FlatPak, homeowners-to-be and designers engage in a process of co-creation. Through a palette of modular elements that can be selected from a "menu of components for living," a wide range of solutions can be generated (Flatpak.com 2009).

While mass production relies on economies of scale, mass customization focuses on economies of scope (Pine and Davis 1997). To keep costs low, mass production relies on a standardized product manufactured with processes so fine-tuned that every potential cost saving is exploited and realized. For mass customization, goods can be inexpensive if the process is designed to allow production of a variety of products quickly and efficiently. Effective use of digital technology can lead to economies of integration, so that design and manufacturing flow seamlessly from one to the other, allowing rapid design changeovers.

FLEXIBLE/AGILE MANUFACTURING

Agility is defined as "the ability to respond with ease to unexpected but anticipated events" (Oleson 1998: xvi), and is required of all divisions of a corporation including production, R&D, training and education, supply-chain management, etc. The agility in production depends on advanced manufacturing technologies (A.M.T.), which are used directly in the manufacturing process but also in the other support functions listed above. Automation

Figure 4.6. Threadless T-Shirt Template. Image courtesy of Threadless.

in flexible systems relies on computer-aided manufacturing (C.A.M.), a catch phrase that refers to machines controlled by numerical commands and software (numerical control machines and computer numerical control machines) as well as industrial robots. Automation can be classified into two major categories—hard automation, which refers to the automation of routine jobs of mass production, and soft automation, which refers to the use of programmable software to generate flexibility (Noori 1990). Manufacturing support functions are handled by such software as computer process monitoring (C.P.M.), computer process control (C.P.C.), computer-aided design (C.A.D.), computer-aided engineering (C.A.E.), computer-aided process planning (C.A.P.P.), machine vision (M.V.),

Figure 4.7. FlatPak House by Charlie Lazor. Image courtesy of Charlie Lazor.

automated guided vehicle systems (A.G.V.s), automated materials handling (A.M.H.) and manufacturing resource planning (M.R.P.).

Levi Strauss, renowned maker of the iconic blue jeans, started custom fitting clothing to individual needs in 1994. A customized pair of jeans started with four key measurements—waist, inseam, hip and rise (Lidgus 2003). The fact that these measurements were taken in the store by a specialist in fitting introduced the notion of craftsmanship to the process of customization. When these dimensions were keyed into a computerized database the program recommended a pair of jeans that the customer could try on. Modifications could be made at this stage based upon physical fit, and the final dimensions confirmed. The personalized pair of jeans became a digital file sent off to a factory. Within 10–15 days, the final pair of jeans would be shipped back to the customer.

Industrialization and mass production separated not only the designer from the maker (which in case of craft production was the same person) but also distanced the maker from the seller and thereby severed any possibility of a personal connection between the designer and the consumer. In certain ways, mass customization attempts to reconnect these unchained links by allowing the consumer to be the designer and facilitating a conversation between the consumer and the maker. However, establishing personal connections between designers, manufacturers and consumers is nearly impossible to achieve even for these mass customized goods. Products are still manufactured in remote locations by unknown workers. The only difference in case of the Levi's is that the consumer's identity is tagged directly to one specific commodity, prior to its manufacture. Mass produced goods generally become carriers of personal identities after they are acquired and used, whereas in case of mass customized goods such as the Levi's, the bar code and the digital file serve as repositories of consumer identity.

The manufacture of things is a long and complex undertaking that starts with the extraction of raw materials and ends with the delivery of finished goods. Each of these steps needs the participation of white- and blue-collar human labor. Millions of minds and hands fashion and build the things that we use everyday. The processes of their manufacture have undergone significant changes from craft-based production, through various forms of mass production leading to mass customerization. It is likely, as technologies of desktop manufacturing evolve, that we might be able to design and make our own things in the future. If and when that happens, it will signal a collapse of the boundaries between the designer, the manufacturer and the consumer. In the foreseeable future, this is possible with the simplest of objects. Massively complex devices that require substantial expertise will maintain the boundaries between designing, manufacturing and consuming. The future of labor in commodity production lies either in continued reliance on the human capital in poorer nations or on extreme automation. It is possible to imagine all goods being manufactured by robotic systems with minimal human interception or interruption. In the automotive and electronic industries, robotic arms already perform a large number of functions, and an expansion of this system to a much wider network of products is not unconceivable. On the other hand, if we consider the total human labor capital to be · composed of men and women between the ages of 20 to 64, it adds up to approximately three and a half billion of us today (U.S. Census Bureau 2009), an indomitable and unparalleled force. A few from this very large body of people will earn wages for knowledge labor and the rest will manufacture, assemble, pack, sort and handle things for worldwide consumption. Unfortunately, this latter form of labor has not seen radical changes since the Industrial Revolution.

• used examples of car production to show evolution of manufacturing-tech, + people

• production

5 BEAUTIFUL THINGS: THE AESTHETICS OF SURFACES

> The aesthetic in its broadest sense—sensuous appearance and the sense of the use-value—here detaches itself from the thing. Domination and separate production of this aesthetic aspect turn into means for the end of money.
>
> Wolfgang Haug, *Critique of Commodity Aesthetics*

> Regardless of how important the measure of innovation and environmental impact are, beauty is the number one criteria for good design.
>
> Tucker Viemeister, "Beautility"

The dictum "form follows function," known well to designers and non-designers alike, was a call by Louis Sullivan for an architectural aesthetic defined not by individual taste but by a rational objectivity. Widely accepted as the crux of what Modern design represents, the philosophy underlining "form follows function" has been adored and maligned equally in design. In addition to encapsulating the *Zeitgeist* of the time, "form follows function" also offered aesthetic guidance, and it has been held responsible for the clean-lined, unadorned and understated appearance of Modern objects. Since then, this axiom has been remixed into several versions including Krippendorff and Butter's (1989) "form follows meaning" and Harmut Esslinger's (2006) "form follows emotion." These phrases are expressions of design's struggle in defining for itself a clear agenda for the role of aesthetics in the creation of everyday objects. Creating beautiful things that meet the stylistic taste of user groups and market niches is generally perceived to be at the core of the industrial designer's job. Products manufactured by Apple are frequently cited as paragons of the kind of beauty that industrial design can produce, and the company is recognized for its attention to aesthetic detail in the design of its products, software, packaging and advertising, a fact that is evident in such landmark products as the iPod, iTunes, iPhone, iMac, etc. This attention to design is often described as an obsession that can be traced all the way up to the company C.E.O., Steve Jobs. Apple has built a reputation as a company that has been successful (in spite of occasional hiccups) due to a fierce emphasis on providing its customers with a total aesthetic experience. The Museum of Modern Art, which houses several Apple products in its permanent collection, describes the iPod as a product that has transformed the industry and people's tastes:

> The first-generation iPod has substantially influenced the quality and elegance not only of portable music devices, but of electronic products in general. The iPod has raised the public's expectations for all consumer products, thus stimulating manufacturers to

recognize the importance of good design and to incorporate design considerations at the highest levels of their corporate structures. (MoMA.org 2008)

This chapter offers an overview of some of the concerns that design faces in the creation of things of beauty. An introductory passage will demonstrate that the three key topics outlining the philosophy of aesthetics are art, aesthetic property and aesthetic experience. Of these the one most relevant to the aesthetics of everyday things is aesthetic experience. While design considers aesthetics one of its core duties and values, some cultural studies debates refer to it is a form of deceit and seduction of consumers. This chapter will also offer an overview of the process followed by designers in developing new aesthetic directions for everyday objects. However, the creation of new styles is not purely the domain of designers. Consumers, too, are designers in their own right, and exercise their creativity through *bricolage*. Aesthetics is often connected to ideas of taste and discrimination, concepts that are socially constructed and often divisive. Finally, the chapter suggests a new way to look at the aesthetics of things by treating their surfaces as skins. As most interactions with things primarily involve their external shells (except in case of maintenance and repair), the metaphor of skins can be use to explore a new typology of aesthetic surfaces.

The term "design" is frequently considered to be synonymous with the term "style". For designers, however, imparting good form is only one in a chain of iterative events that signifies the process of design. There are several reasons for this incongruity between the audience perception of design and the view from within the profession. For instance, articles about design in the popular press often tend to emphasize the sex appeal that it can impart to products. In addition, the most visible aspect of all design work is appearance, not research. Over the last decade, however, there is a perceptible shift in how design is "read" and therefore written about by journalists, critics and business writers. Design has been steadily gaining recognition as a key activity in processes of innovation, that offers tangible

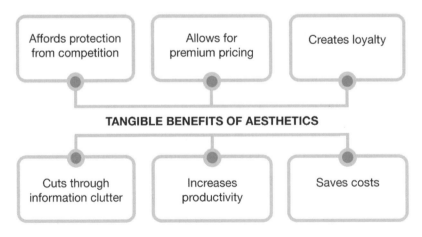

Figure 5.1.   Corporate Benefits of Aesthetics. Adapted from Schmitt and Simonson (1997) illustration by Amethyst Saludo.

and intangible benefits to all stakeholders including the users, manufacturers, society and the environment.

As evidenced in Figure 5.1, corporations clearly recognize the business advantages of aesthetics (Schmitt & Simonson 1997). The multiple benefits of well-designed products include financial advantages (people will pay more for beautiful things), strategic advantages (less competition) and human advantages (higher productivity).

PREVALENCE OF THE PRETTY: AESTHETICS IN POPULAR CONSCIOUSNESS

As some of the prime drivers of consumerism, beauty and desire are manifest all around us in various material and ephemeral forms. In the U.S., for example, the number of television makeover shows, the profusion of beauty magazines on newsstands, growing sizes of suburban malls and outlet stores, the ubiquity of gymnasiums, increased availability of "designer" goods, widespread obsession with low-carbohydrate body-conscious diets, societal embrace of Botox and cosmetic surgery, all are phenomena that signify a fixation on appearance in popular consciousness. According to Postrel, author of *The Substance of Style*, "recent cultural, business and technological changes are reinforcing the prominence of aesthetics and the value of personal expression" (2003: 39). Beauty is peddled incessantly and peddled hard to consumers. "When we declare that mere surface cannot possibly have legitimate value, we deny human experience and ignore human behavior" (Postrel 2003: xi). Postrel argues that aesthetics has become a significant and omnipresent component of everyday life in the U.S. and our increasing fondness of and dependence on beautiful surfaces is visible in things, environments, architecture, interiors and our own bodies. To Postrel, this is "the age of aesthetics." The desire to possess beautiful things is by no means a recent phenomenon, but over the last decade it has been commodified and its value as a driver for commercial success has been realized by a large number of American retail outlets such as Target, K-Mart, West Elm, Chiasso and many more. Clearly, there is a general increase in the variety of products available at these stores and many of them exhibit reasonably well-resolved formal characteristics. Increasing ranks of design professionals, growing media coverage and advice literature, and faster online shopping have increased access to these goods.

THE PHILOSOPHY OF AESTHETICS

Aesthetics, simply defined as the study of art and beauty, has its roots in philosophy. The history of the philosophy of aesthetics reveals that, in the treatises of Plato, Aristotle, Kant, Hegel, Schopenhauer and others, the discussion of aesthetics includes investigations into the nature of beauty, the judgment of taste, definition of art and craft, and subjectivity. Jerrold Levinson (2003) lists three main areas of focus for philosophical aesthetics, simply labeled as art, aesthetic property and aesthetic experience. "One focus involves a certain kind of *practice* or *activity* or *object*—the practice of art, or the activities of making and appreciating art, or those manifold objects that are works of art. A second focus involves a certain kind of *property*, *feature*, or *aspect* of things—namely, one that is aesthetic, such as beauty or grace or dynamism. And a third focus involves a certain kind of *attitude, perception*, or *experience*—one that, once again, could be labeled *aesthetic* (emphases in original)" (Levinson 2003: 3). The first—*art*—includes the following variations. Art is often concerned with form for the sake of form and is capable of being art simply because it possesses significant form.[1] It may also be perceived as a means by which an artist may express or communicate internal states of mind or emotional conditions. Art is also an imitation of life and of the world in which we live. Lastly, it is an activity that aims to create aesthetic experiences. The second—*aesthetic property*—refers to visible qualities that artworks might possess which allow them to be labeled as beautiful, ugly, unified, harmonious, calm, agitated, etc. These, in industrial design are often referred to as product personalities or characters. The third—*aesthetic experience*—as the name suggests, refers to a condition or state of mind, often defined in art as total engagement with form, contemplation of beauty and total disentanglement from wants. As the profession of industrial design broadens the boundaries of its concerns, and as the assignments undertaken by industrial design firms often include entire systems of interaction between people and the world, products are being considered in terms of experiences rather than as objects. In relation to such a notion of products, the third definition of aesthetics as *aesthetic experience* or a state of mind might be the most suitable to explore in relation to design.

The long history of the philosophy of aesthetics, evident in the several handbooks and compendia available on the topic (Levinson 2003, Kivy 2004, Gaut and McIver Lopes 2005), is too broad and too diverse to be covered here fairly or meaningfully. However, the following discussion will provide an overview of the ideas of a few philosophers whose work directly addresses the concept of "aesthetic experience." Eighteenth century German philosopher Kant's aesthetic theory is often considered "the first full attempt to deal in a systematic way with the major problems of aesthetics" (Crawford 1974: 11). Kant tackles such issues as the meaning of the aesthetic object, nature of beauty, taste, judgment and aesthetic experience:

> If we wish to discern whether anything is beautiful or not, we do not refer the representation of it to the object by means of understanding with a view to cognition, but by means of the imagination (acting perhaps in conjunction with understanding) we refer the representation to the subject and its feeling of pleasure or displeasure. The judgement of taste, therefore, is not a cognitive judgement, and not so logical, but is aesthetic-which means that it is one whose determining ground cannot be other than subjective. (Kant 1951: 31)

It is clear that for Kant, beauty is an illogical, subjective human response rather than a rational quality inherent to the object. According to Goldman, Kant also believed that "the experience of pleasure and subjective harmony in the presence of an object is central to proper aesthetic judgement" (2005: 259). American philosopher Dewey too explains the aesthetic in terms of experience:

The word "esthetic" refers … to experience as appreciative, perceiving, and enjoying. It denotes the consumer's rather than the producer's standpoint. It is gusto, taste; and as with cooking, overt skillful action is on the side of the cook who prepares, while taste is on the side of the consumer, as in gardening there is a distinction between the gardener who plants and tills and the householder who enjoys the finished product. (Dewey 2005: 49)

It is important to note that Dewey separates notions of skill and taste, identifying the former as an act of production and the latter as an act of consumption. In addition, notions of completeness, unity, fulfillment, and engagement of all faculties were critical in Dewey's description of the aesthetic experience. Monroe Beardsley (1958), recognized as one of the significant voices in the study of aesthetics in the second half of the twentieth century, described the aesthetic experience as complex, intense and unified, and related it directly to the complexity, intensity and unity of the aesthetic object. Beardsley constructed the concept of unity—which is often central to discussions of beauty in art and design education—around notions of coherence and completeness. In more recent work, Shusterman (1997) explains the features of aesthetic experience in four dimensions:

First, aesthetic experience is essentially valuable and enjoyable; call this its evaluative dimension. Second, it is something vividly felt and subjectively savored, affectively absorbing us and focusing our attention on its immediate presence and thus standing out from the ordinary flow of routine experience; call this its phenomenological dimension. Third, it is meaningful experience, not mere sensation; call this its semantic dimension… Fourth, it is a distinctive experience closely identified with the distinction of fine art and representing art's essential aim; call this the demarcational—definitional dimension. (Shusterman 1997: 30)

This explanation extends the concept of the aesthetic experience beyond formal judgment to include such higher order elements as meaning and intent, while clearly distinguishing it from routine events. Shusterman describes the aesthetic experience as a "heightened, meaningful and valuable phenomenological experience" that can restore our "ability and inclination for the sorts of vivid, moving, shared experience that one once sought in art" (1997: 39). In addition, he suggests that the goal of an aesthetic experience is to remind us of "what is worth seeking in art and elsewhere in life" (Shusterman 1997: 39).

These explanations of the aesthetic experience are not without their critiques. For example, recent critics of Beardsley point out that all aesthetic experiences do not always possess the characteristics of complexity, intensity and unity. In addition, it is rather implausible to imagine that these three qualities transfer directly from the object to the experience. Central to the characterizations by Kant and Dewey is the notion that an aesthetic experience is necessarily of a positive nature. However, this too has been challenged within philosophical aesthetics by such authors as Zemach (1997), who suggest that aesthetic experience may not always be positive and should include aspects that may be considered negative. The basis of Zemach's argument is that art engages the intellect, and in this process may not always lead to comforting or pleasing reactions and emotions. While negative encounters with designed things are by no means uncommon in everyday life, it would be very unusual for those to be classified by consumers as aesthetic experiences.

THE BEAUTY OF THINGS: AESTHETICS IN INDUSTRIAL DESIGN

Philosophical concepts of unity, completeness and intensity that are used in describing the aesthetic experience of art are often employed in design and design education in the evaluation of the beauty of everyday things. Objects are widely recognized as possessing enigmatic qualities that arouse desire, passion and lust in consumers. In a special issue of the journal *Innovation* on aesthetics titled "Beauty+Desire," the editorial outlines its primary task as helping to create a "better understanding of this mysterious phenomena" (sic) (Dziersk 2001: 37). The authors ask a series of questions aimed at understanding the role of aesthetics in processes of design and consumption. "Why should the expression of beauty cause us to become tongue-tied? Why is the beautiful, or its expression, a source of both desire and terror" (Dilnot 2001: 42)? "What is it about some products that gives us such a hankering" (Galway 2001: 50)? "These objects arouse the senses and create a longing for ownership. What evokes such strong human responses to inanimate objects?" (Kemnitzer and Grillo 2001: 45). The power of aesthetic appeal has several cited reasons, ranging from the grounded physical to the grand spiritual. Galway suggests that "newness, wit, Brand Me affirmation, exclusivity and you-can-have-it-all appeal are the sparks of product lust" (2001: 50). She attributes the desire for things to such product features as novelty, customizability, humor, etc. In true formalist tradition, Kemnitzer and Grillo (2001) believe that it is the mathematical precision of the Golden Section, Fibonacci Series and symmetry, which when followed in developing the forms of objects, imparts them the magical qualities of wide appeal. Dilnot (2001: 42) suggests that beauty holds the promise of happiness. In granting beauty this form of potential, Dilnot extends the reach of the aesthetic experience beyond physical sensation to the realm of psychology and spirituality. The question of why humans are attracted to beauty and repelled from ugliness has also been discussed from a biological perspective in the field of evolutionary aesthetics. Though limited largely to the discussion of natural beauty (faces, bodies, landscapes, trees, etc.), principles of evolutionary aesthetics have been applied to human-made things as well to show that our preferences for the beautiful over the ugly may be triggered by the logic of survival. Male peacocks enhance their chances of mating by the extravagance of their tail feathers. The lavish (and perhaps a little profligate) tail, in case of the peacock, is a signifier of a fit bird; it is a signal the female finds attractive because it signifies better genes and therefore healthy offspring. The female, it is assumed, knows that a fitter peacock is better equipped to get food, keep parasites at bay and flee from predators (although it is also argued that a long tail in fact hinders flight and could work against survival) (Mithen 2003).

Mithen posits a similar argument in the discussion of early handaxes created by hominids as far back as 1.4 million years ago. Archeologists have suggested that makers of these

Figure 5.2. A Peacock Displaying Feathers to a (Somewhat Indifferent) Peahen. Image courtesy of Tezzstock/IStockPhoto.

handaxes might have made aesthetic choices in their selection of the raw material and the shape of the final product. It is evident that in many cases they carefully "designed" the tools to ensure symmetry in front and side views, a feature that does not hold any specific utilitarian animal-hunting or carcass-carving advantage.

Rather like the peacock feathers, the "beautiful" handaxes "would have acted as reliable indicators for four specific dimensions of fitness: resource location abilities, planning ability, good health, and capacity to monitor other individuals within the group" (Mithen 2003). From an evolutionary point of view therefore, a sense of form signifies a better proclivity for physiological and social survival.

According to Veblen, who coined the term "conspicuous consumption," the acquisition and use of goods helps people gain, maintain and signal a sense of status. This form of consumption also leads to the "blending and confusion of the elements of expensiveness and of beauty" (Veblen 1973: 97). In other words, conspicuous consumers find beautiful that which is expensive. "The marks of expensiveness come to be accepted as beautiful features of the expensive articles" (Veblen 1973: 97). Veblen's evolutionary economics, partnered with Mithen's evolutionary aesthetics, provides a unique perspective on the meaning of the aesthetics of contemporary products. By this analysis, beautiful things indicate that

Figure 5.3. Ancient Handaxe Found in Italy (Date Unknown).
Image Courtesy Luca Maineri/IStockPhoto.

their owners—distinguishing, rich consumers—have access to resources and are therefore healthy. They are in positions of dominance and power, and therefore are likely to possess planning abilities. For instance, the owner of a large mansion, by principles of evolutionary aesthetics, should be resource-rich, in a position of power, in good health and in possession of good planning abilities. Though the first three characteristics are certainly connected to affluence, the fourth may not necessarily be true as expensive items can be acquired through unexpected windfalls like lottery winnings and inheritances. If the possession of a beautiful thing confers power on the owner, it is clear that beauty has its own politics. In this case politics refers to "arrangements of power and authority in human associations as well as the activities that take place within those arrangements" (Winner 1980: 123). Things of beauty actively participate in negotiating "arrangements of power" and in doing so demonstrate that they possess a unique agency capable of shaping human relations.

Designers are trained to create beautiful products with the goal of providing pleasurable experiences to users, which for the corporation leads to higher sales and enhanced profitability.

> The design professions are the only ones (perhaps besides plastic surgeons) whose job it is to create beauty. We are key players in the beauty business. It is important for us not to

shy away from style. We must not abdicate our role in making the world a better-looking place. (Viemeister 2001: 39)

Designers take the task of beautification as a natural right and an important responsibility. In situations where the designer's engagement is limited to the aesthetic manipulation of the surface of things, the practice is sometimes referred to as "styling." However, the industrial design profession often bristles at this word and is unhappy when its work is described as mere modification of product form for market differentiation and increased profits. Designers are often called upon to update the appearance of products through manipulation of form, color, material and textures but their practice involves much more. The increasing attention being given to ethnographic research, human-centered methods and sustainability testifies to the gradual shift in design's image—within and outside the profession—from a style-driven occupation to an empathic, problem-solving practice. This does not suggest that the larger humanitarian goals of design are all recently established. Ever since its inception, a segment of design's purpose and charter has been described as the improvement of the human condition.[2]

Form and its studied manipulation is central to design activity but scholarship in the area is limited.

> The concept of form is so basic to design and so denuded in meaning in the formalist tradition that designers and design historians have not realized the full implication or importance of the concept. Design as we are most familiar with is focused on giving import to the form of things. At worst, this focus degenerates into pure design estheticism; a valid, stock criticism of the most banal versions of design history is that this focus deals only with the most superficial issues of form and style. (Dilnot 1984: 18)

Dilnot makes it clear that issues of form, beauty and style, although central to design activity, have not received enough critical attention from historians. Histories of design have been written largely from stylistic perspectives, and those approaches provide only a partial understanding of the evolution of material culture. Therefore, a broader agenda for the study of the aesthetic in relation to design praxis, education, history and its theory calls for an evaluation of aesthetics, not merely from a formal perspective but from a socio-cultural perspective as well.

APPEARANCE, LANGUAGE, MEANING

Three key characteristics of things—form, surface and details—are often used in design praxis to illustrate the overall physical delineation and contours of objects. The term "form" is the primary criterion employed in the evaluation of aesthetic quality, and it refers to the overall shape and volume of the object; "surface" generally refers to type of material, color, texture and graphics visible on the skin of the object; and finally, "details" typically allude to buttons, grooves, grills, and other elements of the object's body. Descriptive critiques of objects based on these terms are similar to the traditional methods employed in art criticism derived from the formalism of early twentieth century. According to Raymond Williams, formalism's "predominant emphasis was on the specific, intrinsic characteristics of a literary work, which required analysis 'in its own terms' before any other kind of discussion, and especially social or ideological analysis, was relevant or even possible" (Williams 1976: 114). It is clear that this form of analysis is limited because in its appreciation of the artwork, it relies entirely on the object *per se*, rather than the object *in situ*.

In the pursuit of a unique and recognizable visual style, individual designers and corporations often develop their own signature design language, as is visible in the products designed by, for example, Philippe Starck or the design team at Apple. Of course, this is not unique to industrial design; all forms of cultural production, whether painting, architecture, film or literature, bear an imprint of the creative mind as well as the environment within which the artifacts are created. A unique design language can impart a specific character or personality to things. In other words, the unique forms, surface characteristics and details of things give them character. Physical attributes such as edgy forms, metallic finishes and sharp details can make objects (like Numark's NS7 Controller) look industrial, or the soft shapes, translucent materials and smooth details (like the Logitech headphones) can make things look playful.

Creative Director for Numark Industries Jonathan Hayes explained their process of generating ideas for form based upon linguistic devices. In the development of the NS7 Controller, Hayes (personal interview 2009) explained that their goal was "to be able to develop a design language that made the products look really pro." In other words, they were seeking the kinds of visual cues that would make the final product communicate to the user that this was a professional, not an amateur product:

> We talked to DJs to get their impressions on what "pro" really meant, and then started generating a list of adjectives that would get us there. For instance, words like "machined," "precise," "square," "non-organic," "fabricated rather than injection molded" started to emerge when we did this. And what you see as the final product embodies some of these ideas.

Designers often create these visual languages around the perceived lifestyle needs of target users. One of the goals of the growing field of design research is to find techniques by which to "read" people's lifestyles and aesthetic desires that can then drive the visual language for new product design. For example, in designing shoes for skateboarders, Nike recruited anthropologists to study skaters so as to incorporate their cultural, behavioral, athletic and stylistic needs into the design (Hampton 2006). In such cases, designers strive to create products that are aesthetic expressions of the social and cultural milieu within which the consumers live.

BEAUTY AS SEDUCTION AND VALORIZATION OF CAPITAL

In contrast to the usually positive value attached to product aesthetics in design, some accounts from cultural studies adopt a contrary view. Wolfgang Haug, in *Critique of*

Figure 5.4.   Numark NS7 Controller, by Numark Design Team. Image courtesy of Numark Industries.

Commodity Aesthetics: Appearance, Sexuality and Advertising in Capitalist Society, suggests that form, or the body of the commodity is deceitful as it is a mere appearance of use-value that "promises more, much more than it can ever deliver" (1986: 50). For Haug, commodity aesthetics represents a means by which capitalists seek to further the accumulation of wealth, without any regard for the genuine needs of people. In Haug's Marxist critique, people are afforded no agency to choose or resist this form of exploitation. However, this is a limiting and limited reading of people's agency and their power to exercise their will. People are not easily manipulated by corporations; they use processes of consumption as means of self-expression and development. In other words, consumption is not merely an act of being subjected to the powers of production. "Human beings, in engaging in acts of consumption and the relations surrounding consumption, achieve pleasures, exert powers, find meanings, construct diverse subjectivites, enact sociality in a creative and innovative manner" (Miller and Rose 1997: 1). It would be utterly inaccurate to suggest that aesthetics is merely an instrument that valorizes capital but it would also be equally incorrect to assume that it is entirely driven by user needs. No easy argument can reconcile these diametrically opposed production-centric and consumption-centric positions but it is critical for designers to be

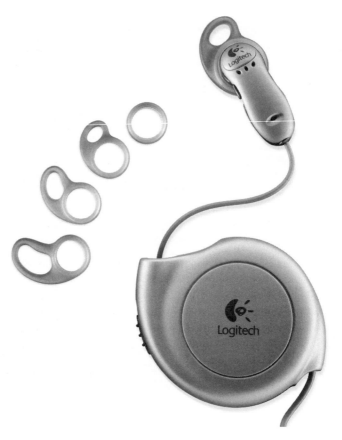

Figure 5.5.   Logitech Headphones, by Ziba Design. Image courtesy of Ziba Design.

aware of the role that design plays within the hierarchies of power that exist in today's socioeconomic systems. The argument that pitches good aesthetics against bad aesthetics is too simplistic and undermines the complexity of the role of aesthetics in design. The goal of critical discourse is to tackle these questions and offer a legitimate direction for design that, instead of adopting highly politicized positions, negotiates between them. There are countless situations in which the professions of design, marketing and engineering have been engaged in the development of things of questionable value—things that have poor utility, are unsafe, solve no known problem, are damaging to the environment and are discarded quickly. There are also countless examples in which these professions have played an important and critical role in saving lives, improving healthcare, providing education, promoting cultural expression and saving ecosystems. Design straddles the worlds of production and consumption, and is therefore well poised to develop critical knowledge that addresses the tension between these conflicting positions. With its interest in human-centered methods, design is an advocate for people and in its position as a value-adding entity to business it has agency to institute change from within.

One of advertising's harshest critiques portrays it as a profession that has adopted, as its primary goal, the employment of beauty towards the promotion of unfettered consumerism for the financial benefit of the corporation. Product design too, by giving sensual surfaces and seductive colors to gadgets is accused of the same crime:

> There are professions more harmful than industrial design, but only a very few of them. And possibly only one profession is phonier. Advertising design, in persuading people to buy things they don't need, with money they don't have, in order to impress others who don't care, is probably the phoniest field in existence today. Industrial design, by concocting the tawdry idiocies hawked by advertisers, comes a close second. (Papanek 1971: ix)

Papanek's critique of both industrial design and advertising is blunt, scathing and, although inappropriate in many cases, right on target for some of what these professions do. Haug views the aestheticized surface of the commodity as a second skin, much more beautiful than the first, and entirely detached from utility. "No one is safe any longer from its amorous glances, which the realization motive casts at the consumers with the detached yet technically perfect appearance of a highly promising use-value" (Haug 1986: 50). A discussion of the seductive nature of the object appears in the work of other cultural theorists such as Jean Baudrillard. "Consumer behavior, which appears to be focused and directed at the object and at pleasure, in fact responds to quite different objectives: the metaphoric or displaced expression of desire, and the production of a code of social values through the use of differentiating signs" (Poster 1988: 49). In other words, the objects appear to give us pleasure, while they are merely promoting a social structure through a system of signs. In a market saturated with homogenized products one of the means of creating distinction and stimulating desire is through aesthetics, a fact that is well known to design and marketing experts. "The vitality of aesthetics in customers' lives provides opportunities for organizations to appeal to customers through a variety of sensory experiences and thereby benefit both the customers and the organizations through customer satisfaction and loyalty" (Schmitt and Simonson 1997: 3).

What is contentious is not whether or not objects possess seductive qualities (it is clear that they do), but whether design is deeply implicated in this process and if ethical issues of power and abuse are being deliberately neglected. Through the artful manipulation of form, is design creating a false sense of needs in people's minds in the service of powerful corporations or is it facilitating people's processes of development and identity? Is it possible to create a responsible aesthetics that is more socially rather than formally informed? The answer lies at neither extreme. In its worst form, design's practice of creating beautiful things can be perceived as purely profit-serving and manipulative if it generates desire for things that people cannot afford to buy and rapidly discard into ever-growing landfills. On the other hand, design, by enhancing the beauty of everyday things allows people to inhabit pleasurable environments, encourages creative expression and fosters unique subcultures.

THE EMERGENCE OF FORM IN THE DESIGN PROCESS

Aesthetic development is not the only task of designers but it certainly is something that is expected of them. Designers often start the process of form generation by developing an aesthetic language appropriate to the product and its potential purchaser. Described using such terms as form, color, texture, character, etc. the aesthetic language is often derived from trend analyses, perceptions of user preferences and the creative inclinations of the designer. In new product development, the design language is represented in the form of image maps that include photographs of products, advertising, fashion, graphics, etc., which could serve as inspirations for the new product's appearance. In the design of Numark's turntable, the TTX, Roy Thompson formerly of design consultancy Continuum, discovered that extracting people's aesthetic preferences was not easy. "We wanted to create a design language that resonated with the DJs" (Thompson, personal interview 2007).

The TTX was created specifically for DJs who travel frequently with their turntables and their records, often performing at several venues within an evening. When record players were first introduced they were designed for use as stationary playback instruments. However, with creative techniques like scratching, DJs have transformed them into musical instruments and Numark's TTX was designed specifically for their unmet needs. In the design process, Thompson recollects that "when asked for their aesthetic preferences, DJs responded by saying that they really did not care about what products looked like; they merely cared for performance. But when asked about the types of clothing brands they preferred or cars they would prefer to drive, some of their stylistic preferences became more visible." Indeed, they did care about appearance, but did not want anything too flashy, too obvious, or with outrageous colors. Therefore the final design for the Numark TTX is subtle and incorporates some of these elements into its form. Thompson and other designers spent countless hours at clubs doing fieldwork, observing how DJs worked with turntables and incorporated innovative solutions to accommodate their practices. The scalloped curvature on the bottom edges has co-molded Santoprene (an elastomeric material) to make it easier to pick up the device easily. The Play/Pause button, duplicated on the top and bottom left edge allows the turntable to be used in two different situations—battle mode and club mode. The color palette—black, gray and silver—is a muted, understated choice that was the preferred aesthetic of the DJs.

Jeff Weber, designer of Herman Miller's latest chair called Embody, allows the aesthetic direction to emerge in the design process without predefining a set of potential options. He explained in a conversation, "we did not start the design process with pre-conceived notions of what the chair should or could look like. Our goal was to create something that was health-positive" (Weber, personal interview 2009). He describes design as the "connective tissue between people and the world." This metaphor allows him to think of things not as inanimate objects but as living bodies themselves. This perspective introduces a new sense of care in the process of making. The Embody Chair was launched in November

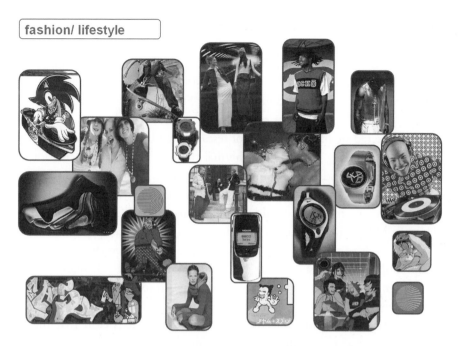

Figure 5.6. Fashion and Lifestyle Images for a New Design Language for Numark's TTX Turntable, by Roy Thompson Thorbin, Neu and Robin Warden (with Continuum & Numark). Image Courtesy Roy Thompson.

Figure 5.7. Numark TTX, designed by Continuum (Roy Thompson, Thorbin Neu and Robert Warden) and Numark. Image Courtesy Roy Thompson, Numark Industries and Continuum.

2008, and is aesthetically unlike any other office chair on the market. According to Herman Miller, "Embody's look communicates its performance. Its human-inspired form, which mimics the spine, is driven by its health-positive features. Its textile—more like a skin than a covering—is not intended to cover up, but to enhance" (Herman Miller 2008). While Jeff Weber of Studio Weber + Associates (formerly Stumpf + Weber Studio) served as the designer, a dedicated Herman Miller project team worked with him on all the phases of the process, conducted significant amount of research that included but was not limited to ergonomic studies of sitting, oxygen flow, thermal comfort, and spine articulation.

"The chair's narrow backrest and frameless silhouette ... removes the constraints found in a conventional, single-part backrest and allows healthful movement at the sitter's discretion for stretching the neck, shoulders, and lumbar spine" (Gscheidle, Stumpf, Weber 2008). Herman Miller's Research Lead Gretchen Gscheidle took on the task of testing the designers' initial health-positive hypotheses via expert opinion interviews. "I worked closely with Stumpf and Weber in establishing the health and comfort-enhancing criteria from which the design emerged. Once we started building prototypes and production chairs, I planned and managed laboratory and field studies to test and prove the physiological benefits to the user" (Gischeidle, personal interview 2009). It is clear that the aesthetic direction of this chair as well as the design thinking around it are inspired by the human body. Its surprisingly supple back, designed to flex and bend smoothly, looks like an organic fusion between the human spine and a branching tree.

Herman Miller's Executive Vice President for Research, Design and Development, Don Goeman referred to Embody's development process as "growing a chair." This interesting phytomorphic metaphor alludes to an organic design process. "This happens when you have a strong vision, a desire to set a new reference point with the design, but no idea of what the solution might grow into" (Goeman, personal interview 2009). The aesthetic direction of this chair seems to have emerged from the form and movement of the human body. While design often derives aesthetic direction from life-style, this chair seems to derive its inspiration from life-form.

The design of footwear, especially sneakers, is a unique blend between performance and fashion. A staggering number and variety of new sneakers are introduced into the market on a regular basis; this is an active, emotionally charged industry with a consumer base that is quick to fetishize. Gavin Ivester, former Senior Vice President and General Manager of International Footwear for Puma, cleaves the sneaker market into two very distinct groups—one driven by performance and the other by fashion. In a conversation, he explained the differences between these consumer groups. "The first group will spill blood and guts as sacrifice for high sports achievement. That is what Nike's personality is all about. It is made up of people who are completely dedicated to the sport" (Ivester, personal interview 2007). The industry caters to this group's desire by high-performance shoes and specialized designs for every imaginable sport. The second group is not driven to purchase by the functional characteristics of the sneaker; they seek out unique styles and new fashions. "This customer

Figure 5.8.   Embody Chair, by Jeff Weber, Bill Stumpf & Herman Miller, Inc. Image courtesy of Herman Miller, Inc.

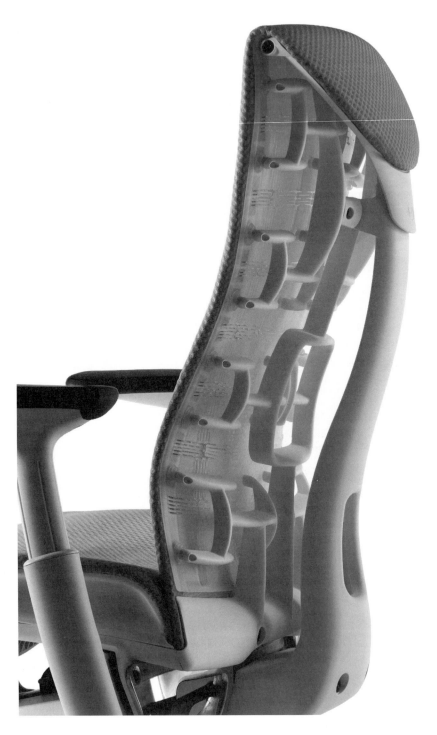

Figure 5.9.   Embody Chair, by Jeff Weber, Bill Stumpf & Herman Miller, Inc. Image courtesy of
Herman Miller, Inc.

follows all trends and is constantly on the lookout for the next cool thing" (Ivester, personal interview 2007). Ivester warns that this is a simplified typology for a much more complex and individualized consumer response. There are several consumers who do not fit the two categories listed above. For instance, he explains, "there are those who seek out vintage styles and are always on the look out for re-releases of classics. Another consumer, the 'hijacker,' is someone who will find a highly specialized product from the sports industry and wear it in the street and sometimes that will start a new trend". Aesthetic development in this industry is fast-paced. "When we see new trends in the fashion industry, we have little time to respond through design" says Ivester. But it is critical to do so to stay relevant in the business. Puma regularly targets specific sports for which to develop gear and in 2008, the focus was on sailing. "When sailing started entering the fashion industry, Puma started a sailing team. Our goal is to design extreme performance gear for the sport as well as fashionable lifestyle oriented gear" (Ivester, personal interview 2007).

The Puma Clyde was first introduced in 1973, named after Walt "Clyde" Frazier, fashion-conscious basketball player who was known to wear tailored suits and travel in a Rolls-Royce. The Clydes were the first shoes to be named after a basketball player. These shoes have developed a significant following and Puma has re-released them several times, often in limited editions of 250–300 shoes. The small production runs immediately transform the shoes from commodities into collectibles. The knowledge of their rarity catapults them instantly into fetish status.

STYLE BY CONSUMPTION

While designers and engineers drive the process that gives form to things, the creation of style cannot be attributed to designers alone. Style is as much a creative act of consumers as it is a result of the process of design. People consciously manipulate and use the aesthetic properties of objects in creating their own unique stylistic expressions. While clothing lends itself easily to expression of individual style and identity, other goods such as consumer electronics and automobiles play a significant role as well. Unique subcultures often emerge in the creative practices of product customizers (modders, lowriders, etc.), music fans (deadheads, punks, etc.) or people who adopt specific products into their lifestyles (bikers, skaters, etc.). These men and women often create and embrace unique styles (either for themselves or their possessions) by which they identify themselves and their social groups. In his landmark anthropological study of punks, teddy boys and other subcultures in England, Hebdige has shown that style performs several critical social functions that are central to the survival of the group (1991). People often re-appropriate objects by modifying their appearances and functions to express social identity and belonging, resistance to dominant cultures as well as defiant individualism:

> Objects borrowed from the most sordid of contexts found a place in the punks' ensembles: lavatory chains were draped in graceful arcs across chests encased in plastic

Figure 5.10. Puma Clydes. Image courtesy of Gavin Ivester and Benoit Duverger, Puma.

bin-liners. Safety pins were taken out of their domestic "utility" context and worn as gruesome ornaments through the cheek, ear or lip. "Cheap" trashy fabrics (PVC, plastic, lurex, etc.) in vulgar designs (e.g. mock leopard skin) and "nasty" colours, long discarded by the quality end of the fashion industry as obsolete kitsch, were salvaged by the punks and turned into garments (flyboy drainpipes, "common" mini-skirts) which offered self-conscious comments on the notions of modernity and taste. (Hebdige 1991: 107)

The things adopted by the punks transformed in meaning, becoming signifiers of a unique aesthetic style and mechanisms for communication within the group. And, as sub-cultures form in acts of defiance to dominant cultures, these items also become emblems of resistance. The punk ensemble with its black leather clothing, metal piercings and colored hair was spectacularly different from mainstream style, and while it was reviled by many it also attracted tremendous media attention. Gradually it started being admired, commercialized and reproduced outside the subcultural group. Eventually punk clothing and accessories were available for purchase in stores, co-opted by corporations who saw a commercial opportunity.

Early subcultural expression is always formulated around the creative *bricolage* of the members and initiated within the group but if the style is adopted and mass produced it becomes a form of design. *Bricolage*, an anthropological term, can be defined as the practice of using existing material forms from one's environment (such as safety pins in case of the punks) in unique ways that transform their meaning to create a new set of signs and discourses (as fashion items). The punk reappropriation of chains and bin liners as fashion elements is a form of *bricolage*. Subcultural *bricolage* and "professional" design are both creative forms of styling, the former initiated and managed by a social group as resistance to a dominant culture, the latter developed and promoted by a commercial entity for profit (mostly) within the dominant culture. However these broad classifications do not include *bricoleur*-entrepreneurs, who transform their own subcultural expressions into business enterprises. In such cases, small entrepreneurs continue their resistance to the dominant power structure but on economic and stylistic grounds.

CLASS AND TASTE

"The idea of taste cannot now be separated from the idea of the consumer," suggests Raymond Williams (1976: 266). This observation brings into doubt the traditional and elitist definition of taste (synonymous with good taste) as one's ability to gauge the aesthetic worth of something. The act of consumption is also an act of exercising taste but the nearly infinite variety of niche markets and target users makes it impossible to have a singular standard for taste. A fluid and problematic concept, taste possesses multiple, contested meanings, all of which are dependent on context and situation. In a comprehensive study, Lloyd Jones describes taste as "the acts and arts of appreciation, discrimination, critical judgment and the pleasurable savouring of man-made artefacts" (1991: ix). A departure from accepted understandings of what taste has meant in the past, this specific articulation does not explicitly differentiate between high or low forms of art and design, nor does it refer to a connoisseurship—gained either through education or class—of the individual. However, it does include the term "discrimination" which is fraught with the same contentious issues as is the word "taste." Generally defined as the capability to discern the good from the bad, it raises the age-old problem of "who decides what is good and why should the rest agree?"

In an essay titled "Discrimination", Jay Doblin examines the correlation between "price factor" and "discrimination factor" and offers "a new model that tries to explain why designers have better taste than normal people and why nobody else cares" (1988: 22). Admitting that this would "amuse a few ... [and] offend many more", Doblin proposed a nine-cell matrix as a means of describing the "inherent value" of products. "Value is a combination of price and quality, so the vertical scale of this model should not be controversial—it is quantitative... The horizontal scale, discrimination, requires making a judgment about whether items are good or bad. Discrimination is the ability to distinguish one thing from another and is specifically intended here to mean the ability to distinguish badly-designed products from well-designed ones" (Doblin 1988: 22). Doblin situates the following objects in these categories:

- *Flash.* Favored by people with too much money and too little taste; "Sheiks who own Bel Air mansions, and tastes of rockstars and Texas oil millionaires
- *Badmass.* Ugly, crude; Lazy-Boy rockers with Mediterranean styling, Buicks with hot-stamped, fake, burled walnut dashboard
- *Trash.* Junk sold in novelty or souvenir shops, inner city furniture emporiums and the mail order section of cheap magazines
- *Richtrad.* Products distinguished by strong brand identification; Mercedes-Benz cars, Cadillac stretch limos, Rolex watches
- *Goodmass.* Well-designed products; Honda, Sony, Apple, Black & Decker products
- *Disposable.* All consumable products; Toilet paper, Gillette razors, folding metal chairs, plastic cups, Swatch watches
- *Pro.* Highly technical, high performance products; Ferrari cars, Mies' Barcelona chairs, Cray supercomputers
- *Clean.* Well-designed products appreciated by enlightened consumers; Eames chairs, Braun appliances
- *Vernacular.* Simple and unstyled products; Pyrex beakers, futon bedding, metal industrial shelving, Eddie Bauer

Doblin's categorization is based on a worldview that is clearly informed by a European Modernist tradition, an education in art/design, and a preference for a specific typology of goods. Most classifications of taste and discrimination tend to categorize them into a tripartite scheme: highbrow, middlebrow and lowbrow (Lynes 1954), superior culture, mediocre culture and brutal culture (Shils 1978) and legitimate taste, middle taste and popular taste (Bourdieu 1984). Bourdieu's goal, however, is to expose and condemn the social divisiveness inherent in such classifications. "Bourdieu sees it as a pernicious by-product of illicit categorizations, generalizations and conflations, all of which are, in reality, merely theoretical abstractions deriving from the mindlessly ecumenical attitudes of curator-professionals, especially those in museums" (Lloyd Jones 1991: 160). In the 1960s, Bourdieu studied preferences and patterns of taste through a series of surveys conducted with people from all segments of French society. He discovered that social distinction, exhibited through the objects one possesses and the aesthetic one ascribes to, is a significant element that defines people's social lives. Bourdieu's critique focuses on this very difference between social groups that the notion of taste exaggerates:

> The denial of lower, coarse, vulgar, venal, servile—in a word, natural—enjoyment, which constitutes the sacred sphere of culture, implies an affirmation of the superiority of those who can be satisfied with the sublimated, refined, disinterested, gratuitous,

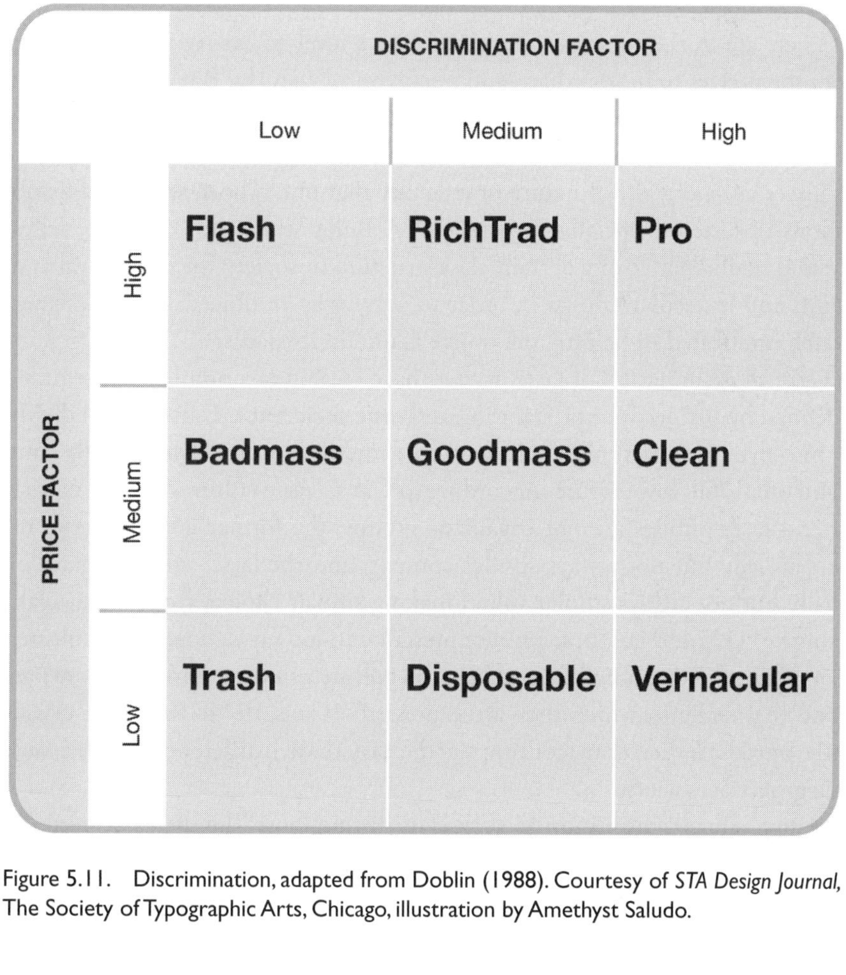

	DISCRIMINATION FACTOR		
	Low	Medium	High
PRICE FACTOR High	**Flash**	**RichTrad**	**Pro**
Medium	**Badmass**	**Goodmass**	**Clean**
Low	**Trash**	**Disposable**	**Vernacular**

Figure 5.11. Discrimination, adapted from Doblin (1988). Courtesy of *STA Design Journal*, The Society of Typographic Arts, Chicago, illustration by Amethyst Saludo.

distinguished pleasured forever closed to the profane. That is why art and cultural consumption are predisposed, consciously and deliberately or not, to fulfill a social function of legitimizing social differences. (Bourdieu 1984: 7)

Design has often considered the improvement of general taste as one of its tasks and, in the past, museums have aided it in this process. During the years when Modernism reigned supreme, good design was equated with a unique visual language that rejected ornamentation, and museums such as the Museum of Modern Art in New York took upon themselves the mission of educating people by showcasing specific designs. Whether or not people desired this aesthetic was not really questioned, and "common" taste was "otherized" as kitsch and unworthy. In such situations, design clearly becomes the vehicle by which class difference is exhibited and exalted, and objects become symbols of that differentiation:

Taste classifies, and it classifies the classifier. Social subjects, classified by their class-ifications, distinguish themselves by the distinctions they make, between the beautiful and the ugly, the distinguished and the vulgar, in which their position in the objective classification is expressed or betrayed. (Bourdieu 1984: 6)

If designers are in the business of maintaining a level of beauty in everyday life and if they deem themselves to be guardians and purveyors of taste, by Bourdieu's reckoning, they classify themselves in the process. Bourdieu's research showed that the distinctions between our preferences for certain forms of art depend upon level of education and economic status. He denounces taste as a gift of nature or a faculty that one is born with, and demonstrates how notions of taste are socially constructed. A Rolex watch, for example, relies on the existence and maintenance of a certain class structure in society for its survival at a certain price point, and it needs to do so in order to survive as an object. Is the designer of that Rolex watch implicated in helping the object maintain its status?

In the critical examination of taste, writers have created taxonomies that sequester social groups defined by socioeconomic standing and taste preference. Gans (1974) divided "taste publics" into five categories: high culture, upper middle culture, lower middle culture, low culture and quasi-folk low culture. According to Gans, "taste cultures are not cohesive value systems, and taste publics are not organized groups; the former are aggregates of similar values and usually but not always similar content, and the latter are aggregates of people with usually but not always similar values making similar choices from the available offer-ings of culture" (1974: 94). These publics prescribe to loosely defined taste cultures, which consist of "values and aesthetic standards for culture, cultural forms that express those values, and the media in which they are expressed" (Gans 1974: 10). Such classifications serve little purpose other than continuing the class-based differentiation between socio-economic groups in society.

Does design enhance or minimize such class distinctions? The increased visibility of in-dustrial design in museums and stores such as Target in the U.S. has definitely hastened its entry into the everyday life of every home, but does it also, through exclusive products, drive a deeper wedge between socioeconomic groups broadly characterized as the haves and the have-nots? Target Corporation's slogan "Design for All'" refers to an attempt to make designed goods more accessible and affordable. "Great design isn't limited to museums, and style doesn't have to be expensive. Since day one, our company founders recognized that the appeal of smart, stylish, well-designed products and stores would set Target apart" (Target.com 2008). The relationship between design and class structure is complex and not free of contradictions. Design activity is just as diverse as is the world of things, and while well-designed, high-end luxury goods continue to serve small, affluent segments of society, well-designed, inexpensive goods make life better, more convenient and pleasurable for large swaths of society as well. Economic divisions in society are a function of political mechanisms, historical traditions and social structures; design can only play a partial role in deepening or minimizing these divisions. However, design does possess agency, and its charter should clearly identify the pursuit of social equity as one of its goals.

SURFACES AND SKINS

"The aesthetics of products concerns the practical dealings with them and involves their bodily presence, rather than just what they look like or signify, or how they are to be interpreted or read" (Verbeek 2005: 211). Our relationship to the "bodily presence" of things, especially those that afford pleasurable aesthetic experiences, can be intensely physical. Though aesthetic experiences involve our entire bodies, the visual, auditory and the tactile dimensions play significantly larger roles in our interactions with products, during the process of production as well as consumption. Vintage cars, designer shoes, rare books and leather jackets are but a few examples of products that signify such relationships. As consumers, we eye their forms yearningly, we listen to their squeaks and beeps attentively and we caress their surfaces and contours with loving fingers. Most of this interaction with things is limited to a physical engagement with surface or the outer skin of the objects. Only in situations of maintenance, upgrade and repair are consumers required to dig deeper and meddle with parts and inner components. Designers tinker with the surface characteristics of form, contour, material, color and texture to create the aesthetic experiences that users seek and desire. These physical features of things are by no means the sole preoccupations of designers who strive to create aesthetic experiences and consumers who seek them. Price, performance, packaging, advertising, warranties and other factors play a role as well. Many of these attributes of the products are "written" on their surfaces. And just as the human skin operates as a protective, communicative, aesthetic layer of the human body so does the object skin.

Object skins are the boundaries between the insides of things and the outside world; they exist as visible surfaces that make technology invisible; they exist as designed interfaces for engineered utility. They may be conceived as borders that signify use-value and exchange-value, utility and fetishism, or art and machine. Rich in meaning, object skins can also be seen as signifiers of protection, desire, status, sensuality and deception. The epidermis of objects is polysemous; lacking fixity in meaning, it provides us with an "infinite range of meanings" (Hebdige 1979: 117). Object skins assume various forms in products—they maybe rigid, elastic, permeable, dense, translucent, clear, imitative, smart, green, ordinary, or fantastic.

COMPARING HUMAN AND OBJECT SKINS

Human skin forms the boundary between our viscera and the external environment and provides sensation and protection. It is also the most visible of all organs and one that records and exhibits all the markings of the aging process. Constantly in the process of change, the human skin regenerates itself on a regular basis, shedding its old self for newer, improved versions. It is the location of beauty and lust, but also of disappointment and despair. In humanities and cultural studies, the skin has been discussed mainly in relation to issues of race and profiling (white/black) or within psychoanalytic theory, in relation to the self and ego. According to Didier Anzieu (1989), who developed the notion of the "skin ego," the epidermis performs a series of functions for the body and the ego—supporting, containing, shielding, individuating, connecting, sexualizing, recharging, signifying and assaulting/destroying. These functions offer a framework by which to develop a typology of skins for objects that can help classify and organize the various meanings of the aesthetic surfaces that emerge in processes of production and consumption of objects. This typology consists of five major categories that signify the primary functions of the object skins: protective skins, informational skins, technological/intelligent skins and mythical/fetishistic skins. It is significant to note that the boundaries of these categories define the principal functions: they are permeable and therefore an object skin may be simultaneously sensorial (visual or tactile) and mythical/fetishistic, or intelligent and protective. These skins are aesthetic and utilitarian; this is where form and function merge.

PROTECTIVE SKINS

Skins that serve the specific task of safeguarding serve to protect and are further divided into shielding skins, green skins and faux skins. The protection a skin provides signifies the safeguarding of technology, the environment, or material identity.

SHIELDING SKINS

For a large number of products, the skin serves the primary function of providing an enclosure for technology, or to borrow Anzieu's terms, it supports, contains and shields the components. This is demonstrated in an early example of industrial design practice, the Gestetner duplicator redesigned by Raymond Loewy in 1929. "I decided to limit my efforts to amputation (the four legs) and plastic surgery on the body. By this I meant a face-lift job. I would simply encase all the gadgety organs of the machine within a neat, well-shaped, and easily removable shell" (Loewy 2002: 83). Loewy's use of corporeal metaphors in describing the object as well as the process of design testifies to his thinking of the product in animate terms. For Loewy, the visual quality of the skin was also important, but in this case, it was the primary function of shielding that gave it the desired aesthetic.

GREEN SKINS

The growing realization amongst designers and manufacturers about the need to embrace environmental responsibility and sustainability has led to significant research into recycled plastics, organic materials such as biopolymers and durable object skins. For instance, the skins of lampshades made from rock salt crystals are entirely organic, they dehumidify the air, they reduce air pollution, they can be composted, and their textured surfaces signify and exhibit their "greenness." Similarly, products made from such biopolymers as PLA represent green skin. University of Warwick engineer Kerry Kirwan has been working with the plastics industry to develop cellphone casings made from biodegradable materials that disintegrate when buried. The casings have sunflower seeds embedded in them that start to germinate in the soil; a plant is born when the cellphone ends its life.

FAUX SKINS

Semi-synthetic plastics were initially employed in the imitation of more expensive naturally existing materials. For example, in 1862, Alexander Parkes cooked up a doughy substance called Parkesine (cellulose nitrate produced by mixing cellulose with nitric acid and sulfuric acid), which could be pressed into molds to manufacture small objects. Parkesine could be colored or white, transparent or opaque, and was used to imitate materials such as ivory and tortoise shell. Further development of synthetic polymers led to materials such as acrylic that imitated glass and rhinestones, urea formaldehyde that reproduced the characteristics of marble or alabaster, and polyvinyl chloride that could look like leather or suede. The skins of objects made from these materials function as protectors of the true identities of these polymers, extending the length of their secret lives.

New polymers with better structural as well as visual and tactile properties are invented in laboratories everyday, often to precise requirements of designers and engineers. As these materials become more and more versatile, they become more and more difficult to distinguish from each other. This ability of imitation has led to a loss of recognition (Manzini 1989: 32) and increased anonymity of the plastic skins. It is no longer possible to recognize polymers by sight or touch; their stunning variety has made them as mysterious as ubiquitous.

INFORMATIONAL SKINS

The skins of products also serve an informational purpose, either through the material with which they are made or the through the graphics with which they are adorned.

Figure 5.12. Sunflower Phone, by Kerry Kirwan, University of Warwick. Image courtesy of
Kerry Kirwan, Peter Dunn, University of Warwick.

REVEALING TRANSPARENT SKINS

Informational skins act as message boards where designers and consumers of objects can pre-
configure meanings. Transparent skins first started to appear on small consumer appliances
such as radios and telephones in the 1970s, revealing all the operational details of the
gadgets. Looking into one of these, one could clearly see brilliantly hued wires snaking over
dull green printed circuit boards and tiny multi-colored electronic components. These skins
dissolve into their own transparence, becoming nearly invisible. Their clarity makes them
immaterial, bringing the design of the inside rather than the outside into sharp, stark focus.
Raymond Loewy's desire to shroud the machine is turned upside down into a voyeurism of
function.

SEDUCTIVE TRANSLUCENT SKINS

The iMacs from Apple introduced in 1998 led to an orgy of translucent objects, not only
in computer peripherals but in other product categories as well, including office products
and furniture. These translucent skins invite users to look inside, but offer only frosted-
glass glimpses of the inner secrets of the object; they seduce without revealing too much.

Referring to their translucent radios and CD players, Sony's Richard Gioscia says that "part of the idea is to show that the inside is as well designed as the outside" (Patton 1999). Unlike transparent skin, the translucent skin maintains its own presence against the backdrop of the dimly visible technology within.

TECHNOLOGICAL/INTELLIGENT SKINS

This group of skins contains two types: responsive skins, which employ smart or intelligent materials, and technological skins or the ones that use advanced materials such as polyamide composites.

TECHNOLOGICAL SKINS

New advancements in materials science filter their way into consumer applications pushing boundaries of aesthetic as well as functional capabilities of object skins. Jackets manufactured from Aramid fibers can be bullet proof or heat resistant, providing a second skin that is functionally far more resistant to the elements than human skin. Carbon fiber and epoxy composite helmets can withstand substantial shock in case of high impact crashes. Technological skins may also provide aesthetic value in certain cases. Titanium is a superior structural material with an excellent strength to weight ratio, but its application in the Apple G4 portable computer, in eyeglasses and wristbands also affords visual appeal.

RESPONSIVE SKINS

Certain object skins may be manufactured out of smart or intelligent materials that respond in ways previously unimagined, and have properties that can be dramatically altered with the appropriate stimuli. For example, photochromic and thermochromic materials change color when exposed to light and heat, electroluminescent and phosphorescent materials can absorb and emit light, and piezoelectric materials can generate small amounts of electricity when stressed. The insertion of microprocessor chips within objects also creates responsive skins that can adjust themselves to individual needs and desires. In 2002 Kyocera formed a partnership with Wildseed to create a new phone called the SmartSkins 7135 Smartphone. Designed specifically for the youth market, the casing of the product was embedded with a personalization chip that not only permitted changes in the appearance of the product but also in the software that triggered its features such as the organizer, mp3 player, camera, Internet connection, etc. Such skins are capable of "reading" the users' needs to provide the precise type of virtual environments they prefer. These skins could be removed and replaced with newer ones.

The SmartSkins website presented another phone with similar capabilities called Identity, as "the first phone that is designed to communicate who you are, and when you change your SmartSkin, you change your identity" (Smartskins.com 2006).[3] This skin was at once physical and virtual, able to change the phone from inside out; it was at once empowering and powerful, capable of changing its own identity to suit the consumer, and touted as powerful enough to change the consumer's identity.

MYTHICAL/FETISHISTIC SKINS

Semiotician Roland Barthes (1972) defined myths as modes of signification, or second order meanings of cultural forms. Through a semiotic analysis of ordinary products (such as margarine) and everyday phenomena (such as wrestling) he showed how society uses these cultural forms to assert it values. Barthes makes it clear that everything can be a myth, and object skins certainly can. Acting primarily as protective, visual, or technological surfaces, skins, at another level, can be seen as repositories of larger economic and political systems as well as individual desires and fetishes.

MYTH BY MATERIAL

Widely known for its fetishistic properties, latex is a "material whose clinical functionality cloaks the eroticism of contemporary design" (Lupton 2002: 36). A material of several seemingly contradictory applications and available in both natural or synthetic forms, latex can be used to increase bounce in a ball and reduce vibration in a machine base; to separate entities if used as an insulator and to join objects if used as a rubber band; as a means to constrain bodies in clothing and as a material that can extend through stretching. A latex skin used in surgical gloves signifies protection from contamination but used in skin-tight clothing for bondage can signify sexual arousal and fetish character.

MYTH BY CONCEALMENT

An object that is entirely closed off with an impenetrable skin conceals its mechanism and creates a sense of mystery. For instance, the iPod is a hermetically sealed object. It has no visible screws, it offers no access to its interior, it will mysteriously play endless music, and it suggests that it will never need to be opened because it will never break down. The skin of the iPod is flawless; it is uninterrupted by constraints of manufacturing, and is ripe for fetishization. "This tendency of design towards the perfection of surfaces and the disappearance of mechanical components radically transform(s) the relation of users to the products" (Kurtgözü 2002). This often leads to the subordination of use-value by brand-value and fetish-value. Media representations may add to its myth and fetish value as well. The description of the iPod as "an everlasting cigarette packet for those addicted to music instead of tobacco" (Arthur 2003), testifies to its fetish character.

The process of styling, or creating new skins on products that change appearance without added utility has drawn vocal criticism from design and cultural studies. Production-centric critiques, such as those of Haug, describe design as manipulative practice. By such accounts, creative operations are performed on the skin of the object to stimulate desire and to valorize capital, but are justified as attempts to satisfy a wider range of user needs. Based upon Marx's analysis of the commodity as composed of use-value and exchange-value, the

Figure 5.13. Fetishistic Latex Skins. Image courtesy of Martin-Carlsson/IStock Photo.

process of styling makes the skin a receptacle for its exchange-value rather than its use-value. Equating the buyer's gaze to voyeurism and the exchange-value to sexuality, Haug relegates the role of commodity aesthetics to the "sexing-up" of the object, a term that also appeared in Papanek's (1971: 151) writing. Papanek attacked design in its effort to create object lust merely by changing its skin, a process that has since been accelerated with the rapid replacement of electromechanical components with digital ones. In contrast to the production-based studies, consumption-based approaches and post-structuralist studies do not perceive humans as naïve and controlled by large, capital hungry corporations, but as discerning buyers who negotiate meanings with cultural commodities in contexts of use. The positions adopted by designers and cultural studies scholars regarding the relation-ship between people and things regarding aesthetics are often antagonistic. From a cultural studies point of view, some of the activities central to design praxis may be viewed as manipulative and driven by economic rather than humanistic concerns. Within design studies, aesthetics continues to be one of the least examined areas that deserves serious attention, and the research methods and interpretive techniques used by cultural studies can serve as appropriate models. Formalist evaluations of aesthetics and meaning, though valuable, are incomplete unless supplemented by other interpretive strategies that include social and cultural concerns.

AESTHETICIZATION OF THINGS IN EVERYDAY LIFE

The practice of design involves the creation of everyday things with the intent that they provide aesthetic experiences to people while simultaneously boosting sales for the manufacturer. The deliberate selection and specification of such physical attributes as form, color, texture, materials and graphics are the tools that a designer uses to achieve this goal. The beauty of things resides neither in the solid materiality of the object nor in the ephemeral mind of the consumer. It is neither entirely the result of the mate-finding instinct of our evolutionary history, nor is it a matter of pure social construction. Style is not fashioned by the designer in the processes of production, and neither is it organically created by the owner in processes of consumption. It is a fluid concept that holds different meanings to people across cultural and subcultural groups defined by ethnicity, geography, age, education, wealth, musical interest and so on. As most interactions with objects involve some contact with their external surfaces, object skins function as locations where the aesthetic experience originates. "The beautiful opens us into limitless possibility" (Dilnot 2001: 43). Design's goal should be to pre-configure skins of objects so as so offer users the possibility of generating their own aesthetic experiences through practices of *bricolage*.

6 THE GREED IMPERATIVE: USER NEEDS IN PRODUCT DESIGN

That man possesses certain needs is a biological fact; how he satisfies them is a social or cultural fact.

J. A. C. Brown, *The Social Psychology of Industry*

It must be borne in mind that the object being worked on is going to be ridden in, sat upon, looked at, talked into, activated, operated, or in some way used by people individually or en masse.

Dreyfuss, *Designing for People*

Commodities are not pitched to needs, which are limited, but rather to desires, which know no bounds.

Greg Kennedy, *An Ontology of Trash*

It is commonly assumed that we buy things because we have a certain need for them. People buy houses because they need a place to reside, cars because they need to commute to work, chairs so that they may satisfy the need to rest, and so on. However, a closer examination of why and what we buy reveals that the process of consumption and our motivation to consume cannot be easily explained away as response to need. Our need for houses, cars and chairs cannot be the sole explanation for the staggering variety of these products available to us. Clearly the need for transportation cannot explain the existence in the automobile market of the Hyundai Accent (approximately priced at $10,000) as well as the Bugatti Veyron (approximately priced at $1.4 million). Should the need for automobility be parceled into a finely distributed classification to accommodate the need for fast and powerful transportation, sustainable transportation, status-signifying transportation, affordable transportation, etc.? How much of consumer choice is driven by need? These questions bring into focus the difference between needs and wants, and the role of desire in the acquisition of things. Does the basic, universal human need for food, water and shelter extend to such things as Beluga caviar, San Pellegrino and a Manhattan penthouse when those needs can clearly be met more modestly? The abundance and variety of material goods suggest that the need for choice is just as critical as the need for things themselves. The concept of need is intricately and inextricably tied to the process of new product design and development. The identification and listing of the needs of potential users is typically one of the first steps in contemporary design practice. However, do designers create new products in response to people's needs or do they, inadvertently or by design, create new needs? Are new products designed for needs or are new needs designed for products?

Needs should be imagined, not merely as internal, individual compulsions that can be packaged into neat hierarchies (such as Maslow's), but as *forces in a network,* which are caused by, and which in turn impact, a large number of actors. The appearance of a need in a network may be likened to a ripple or a pulse. It may start at a specific location in the network but it quickly spreads outwards in space and time, impacting several other actors. All individual, group and institutional needs exist within a complex social network, and they are shaped by constantly changing cultural, economic, environmental and political dynamics. As the following survey of needs literature in several disciplines will demonstrate, there are several similarities in classification systems. Most attempts tend to broadly classify needs into two dominant segments—basic necessities (or survival needs) and unnecessary luxuries (or status needs). Two key ideological positions divide thinking on this topic— by Marxist analysis, needs are created by the system of production and corporations to maximize profit and keep them in business. The other position holds that things are designed, engineered and sold specifically in reaction to people's needs. Neither position can be wholeheartedly embraced or rejected and there is no reconciliation between them. Instead of pitching production against consumption, it is more beneficial to imagine that both have agency, and design's goal should be to channel these for the greater good.

While there have been countless efforts at organizing and categorizing needs, the contextual and networked nature of needs defies all taxonomies. Max-Neef, Elizalde and Hopenhayn (1989) offer a new model that refines this dichotomous structure and rids it of hierarchy. "Human needs must be understood as a system: that is, all human needs are inter-related and interactive. With the sole exception of the need of subsistence, that is, to remain alive, no hierarchies exist within the system. On the contrary, simultaneities, complementarities and trade-offs are characteristics of the process of needs satisfaction" (Max-Neef *et al.* 1989: 19). In addition, the authors introduce a differentiation between needs and satisfiers, "[f]or instance, food and shelter must not be seen as needs, but as satisfiers of the fundamental need for subsistence" (Max-Neef *et al.* 1989: 20). They suggest that needs are universal but what is different is how people choose their satisfiers in meeting those needs. On the one hand, "[f]undamental human needs are not only universal but are also entwined with the evolution of the species." On the other hand, "satisfiers behave in two ways: they are modified according to the rhythm of history and vary according to culture and circumstance" (Max-Neef *et al.* 1989: 29). A non-hierarchical network more accurately represents the nature of needs formation in society. "There is a complex network of what we might call positive and negative feelings, constantly forming, dissolving and re-forming, that constitutes the dynamic bond between the individual's perceptions of his needs and his judgments about what can satisfy those needs" (Leiss 1978: 49). Leiss refers to needs as "symbolically mediated impulses," a smart characterization that recognizes individual urges as well as the sociocultural process of their transformation. Human needing, according to Leiss (1978: 65), has two inseparable components—a "material correlate" and a "symbolic correlate"—and needs should be considered holistically without being split into hierarchies and classifications.

THE PHILOSOPHY OF NEED

The scholarly examination of human needs has a long history that can be traced to the ancient Greek philosophers Aristotle, Socrates and Plato. However, "the concept of need plays a significant but still relatively unexplored role in philosophy" (Reader 2005: 1). The conversation around need automatically leads to a discussion of wants, desires and necessities as these terms are semantically linked. Aristotle explains the core concept of necessity ✳ as that which cannot be otherwise, and lists four primary reasons or senses (Barnes 1984). "The first sense is for being required for life or existence. The second is of being required to achieve a good or avoid an evil. The third is of being coerced against will or nature. And the fourth is of being logically compelled…" (Reader 2005: 114).[1] Basic needs such as food, shelter and clothing may be classified under the first sense as necessary for survival. The second category of necessity includes the need one may experience to save someone from harm, help alleviate poverty and disease, or protect the environment. In the third case of need by coercion, one may imagine pressure exerted by one's peers or the force of advertising inducing a need to buy things. Finally, the fourth sense of Aristotelian necessity refers to need by logic and can be translated to situations where the acquisition of one thing creates, by logic, the need for other things. The purchase of a laptop computer creates the need for a mouse, and therefore a mouse pad, and an ergonomic rest and a wrist brace and so on.

Socrates does not directly address the notion of needs, but discusses it as desire, adding that all desire is good because no one intentionally desires bad things or does wrong willingly. He believed that wisdom is good in itself and "if all human desire is for the good, all human desire is for wisdom" (Rowe 2005: 107). Following Socrates, the stoics claimed that "wisdom alone is the one secure possession because it will reliably tell you how to extract the maximum good from every situation" (Rowe 2005: 108). This line of reasoning, of wisdom as possession, leads to a rather non-material conceptualization of desire that forces a reconsideration of the idea of material need. With wisdom established as the only reliable thing, the stoics believed that all the other materials things one needed were not good in themselves, but dependant upon circumstance. No clear concept of need therefore (for anything other than wisdom) emerges in Socratic thought.Philosopher Garrett Thomson defines need as a "disposition … [that] does not imply a lack" (2005: 175). The idea of need as a *disposition* that is not necessarily triggered by a lack of any kind is a departure from its generally accepted meaning. Thomson classifies needs into three categories: minimal, fundamental and instrumental. Such things as food and water, which are imperative for survival, are minimal needs. Fundamental needs refer to inescapable and necessary conditions that we rely on to protect ourselves from harm. He defines harm not necessarily in physical terms but as deprivation from experiences that are deeply and meaningfully interesting. To Thomson, interests are different from desires and should not be interpreted purely as material wants. Instrumental needs are those that signify necessary conditions for attaining a specific objective (necessary or unnecessary, good or bad) or satisfying a desire. Fundamental needs refer to natural necessities; instrumental needs refer to desire

NEED	EXPLANATION
1 Minimal Needs	• Basic • Necessary for survival
2 Fundamental Needs	• Non-derivative • Necessary to avoid harm • Inescapable
3 Instrumental Needs	• Necessary conditions • For obtaining a goal • Satisfaction of a desire

Figure 6.1.   Minimal, Fundamental and Instrumental Needs. Illustration by Amethyst Saludo.

satisfaction. Thomson's classification of needs and emphasis on *interest* over desire can be used to construct a concept of critical consumption as a form of sustainable development.

THEORIZING NEEDS

The discussion of human needs in economics, consumption studies, philosophy and marketing revolves around several fundamental issues about their origin, classification, subjectivity and role in the process of design. It involves an examination of whether needs are universal or culturally determined, and whether they are objective or subjective. Do we, as consumers and producers of material culture, determine what we need by choice or are we coerced into needing things through systems of production? While it seems logical to assume that things are made available to us because we need them, it is critical to ask if we need these things because they are available. Do designers create products to satisfy people's needs, or do they actually design new needs that can only be satisfied by the acquisition of new products? The need for things does not stop at the individual level; things also exist to meet the need for corporations to make a profit and for nations to meet goals of gross domestic production. In *The Green Imperative*, Victor Papanek (1995) urges designers to act ethically by incorporating ecological and humanistic principles in their work. He asks if their designs assist the needy, minimize resource use and foster well-being. Are designers and corporations heeding this urgent call or are they instead driven by a greed imperative to maximize profits? These questions represent polarizing positions on what human needs mean, and the answers to most of them lie at neither extreme.

In mainstream economic theory, those human wants that can be met through consumer spending serve an important function in the determination of the economic health of a nation. Accounting for up to 70 percent of the economy in the U.S., consumer spending is perceived to be a critical barometer of the nation's fiscal health. Therefore, consumption is perceived as a driver of production, and when a slow economy needs a push to prevent it from slipping into a recession, consumers are generally urged to go shopping. This point of view, widely embraced by free market theorists, generally regards production as the mechanism designed to meet people's needs and improve their standards of living. However, economists such as Kenneth Galbraith view things a little differently. He suggests that needs are in fact the *results* of production (Galbraith 1998). In other words, what we refer to as human need may be created by manufacturers who *need* to sell goods. In confirming and extending Galbraith's position, Baudrillard says: "by producing particular goods and services, companies at the same time produce all the means of suggestion tailored to gaining acceptance for them and therefore, ultimately 'produce' the needs which correspond to them" (1998: 74). There are two ideologically contrasting positions on need: one views production as a positive force that creates things to meet people's needs, and the other frames production as a force that creates needs. Neither position alone accurately describes consumption in contemporary society. While some predatory corporations continue to manufacture needs and commodities to satisfy them, many design and produce goods to address genuine needs of people.

NEEDS, WANTS, DESIRES, DEMANDS AND EXPECTATIONS

Though needs, wants, desires and expectations are terms that often share common meanings, there are subtle differences among them in marketing and economic literature. In 1960, Robert Keith, Executive Vice President and Director of the Pillsbury Company wrote of a "marketing revolution" that was occurring in industry. "Soon it will be true that every activity of the corporation—from finance to sales to production—is aimed at satisfying the needs and desires of the consumer. When that stage of development is reached, the marketing revolution will be complete" (Keith 1960: 38). Indeed, the interest in consumer desire has sustained and become one of the fundamental concepts of marketing. Corporations strive to create marketing campaigns that speak to consumers' needs, desires and expectations through advertising, packaging and other sales communications:

> Expectations are beliefs about the likelihood that a product is associated with certain attributes, benefits, or outcomes, whereas desires are evaluations of the extent to which those attributes, benefits, or outcomes lead to the attainment of a person's values. Expectations are future-oriented and relatively malleable, whereas desires are present-oriented and relatively stable. (Spreng *et al.* 1996: 17)

For Ramsay, fundamental needs are essentially all biological and psychological needs, which are objective and unchanging. On the other hand, felt needs are subjective, they change all the time and they have socio-historic form (Ramsay 1992). She describes wants as "demonstrable dispositions to desire or prefer something" (Ramsay 1992: 10). Wants are instrumental because they generally signify the want for something—either an object or a goal that can be achieved with that object. She refers to these goals as "desirability characteristics." It may be argued that, through careful manipulation of such features as form, color, texture and materials, or devices used in advertising, designers play a significant role in fashioning these desirability characteristics into things:

> A demand is a want for which the consumer is prepared to pay a price; a want is any thing or service the consumer desires or seeks; and a need is any thing or service the consumer ought to have to keep alive and healthy or to keep efficient or simply because somebody (not necessarily himself) thinks he ought to have it. Thus while demand is an economic conception, want is psychological, and need, partly at least, ethical. (Boddewyn 1961: 18)

In the descriptions above, needs, wants, desires, expectations and demands are associated almost entirely with consumers. The creation of needs is a complex process that includes the influence of multiple individuals and institutions such as friends, peer groups, family members, corporations, advertising agencies, media outlets, governmental bodies and so on. These agencies function within an intricate network, and when someone buys something, it is not simply an independent individual decision but a response to a change in the network.

THE NEED FOR THINGS

Perhaps the best known and most frequently quoted common and popular discussion of need is a hierarchy that psychologist Abraham Maslow proposed in 1943 in a paper called *A Theory of Human Motivation*.

Maslow stratified human needs into five categories, a classification often represented as a pyramid with five levels. Maslow referred to the first four—physiological, safety, love/belonging and esteem needs—as deficiency needs that had to be satisfied before the final self-actualization needs could be met. "Human needs arrange themselves in hierarchies of pre-potency. That is to say, the appearance of one need usually rests on the prior satisfaction of another, more pre-potent need" (Maslow 1943). However, hierarchical structures of needs do not accurately represent patterns of consumption or the somewhat irrational nature of human behavior. It is common for people to experience the need to acquire status-bestowing, expensive objects while physiological needs are still unmet or only partially met. Explanations of human need based upon hierarchical structures that move from physiological to cognitive/spiritual or material to non-material tend to oversimplify complex human response. Though we experience physiological needs, several needs are socially and culturally constructed. According to Postrel (2004), the hierarchical model can lead people to conclude falsely that we are attracted to beauty (which may be classified as a higher-level growth need) if and only if all our basic needs are met. She suggests that "human beings do not wait until they have full stomachs and a roof that doesn't leak before they satisfy their aesthetic needs. Given a modicum of stability and sustenance, people have

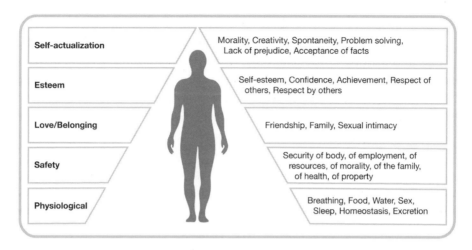

Figure 6.2. The Common Pyramidal Representation of Maslow's Hierarchy of Human Needs. Illustration by Amethyst Saludo.

always enriched the look and feel of their lives through personal adornment and decorated objects" (Postrel 2004: 35).

THE CONCEPT OF NEED IN MARX

"The commodity is, first of all, an external object, a thing which through its qualities satisfies human needs of whatever kind. The nature of these needs, whether they arise, for example, from the stomach, or the imagination, makes no difference. Nor does it matter here how the thing satisfies man's need, whether directly as a means of subsistence, i.e. an object of consumption, or indirectly as a means of production" (Marx 1990). It is clear in this quote that Marx considered the need-satisfying function of commodities as an essential component of their existence. Though Marx does not provide definitions or detailed explanations of the term "need," he does approach the concept of need through the lens of value. The use-value of a commodity, according to Marx, is that property which connects · it to a certain need experienced by the owner. It is the utility of an object that binds it to human need. Exchange-value can also be tied to the notion of need, but in this case, to that of the capitalist. The reason the capitalist is able to sell commodities is because the worker ⌄ is able to produce surplus-value. The capitalist needs this surplus to increase capital. Marx associates need to use-value as well as exchange-value, in the former case to the worker and in the latter case to the capitalist. In either case, "satisfaction of a need is the *sine qua non* [an essential condition] of any commodity" (Heller 1976: 23).

In addition to this economic analysis of need (in relation to value), Marx also explained needs from historical, philosophical and anthropological perspectives. The terms that appear in his writings include natural needs, necessary needs and socially produced needs. Natural needs (need for food, shelter, clothing) can be distinguished from socially constructed needs only if we accept that certain needs are universal while some are culturally and contextually determined, and that is the distinction that Marx makes clear in *Capital* and *Grundrisse*. "Necessary needs" are those that are satisfied through the mediation of labor power and money. We are all born with natural needs, which are generally satisfied through the wages earned. Individuals go to work to sell their labor power, and it is the value of the earned wages (and therefore the value of the labor power) that determine their necessary needs. As labor power increases, the necessary needs rise as well (Fraser 1998). "Luxury needs," a third category of needs posited by Marx, are not deemed as necessary to be exchanged for wages and labor power. Therefore they generally reside beyond the reach of the working class and within the consumption world of the capitalist. However, as worker wages increase and they gain more spending power, these luxury needs too can transform into necessary needs for them. Marx's notion of "social needs" is more than another category of needs; it is a concept that has "rational meaning in every society" (Heller 1976: 67). There are several interpretations of "social needs" in Marx's *Capital*, but "the most important meaning (and the most frequently used) is that of "socially produced" need (Heller 1976: 69). A social need is a type of demand, which "always has the money to back it up" (Marx 1981: 282) and is therefore recognized by the market. A variation on this concept, which Marx called "real social need," refers to an invisible and aspirational level of need that individuals would seek to satisfy in a different set of economic circumstances (if for example, they were richer). In other words, a new set of circumstances automatically means a new set of needs.

These forms of need (natural, necessary, luxury, social and real social) represent a structure of need creation in capitalist society. "Hunger is hunger, but the hunger gratified by cooked meat eaten with a knife and fork is a different hunger from that which bolts down raw meat

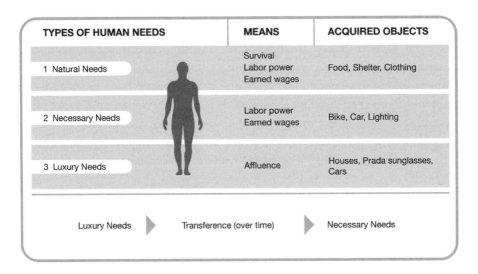

Figure 6.3. The Concept of Needs in Marx. Illustration by Amethyst Saludo.

with the aid of hand, tooth and nail" (Marx in Fraser 1998: 128). The natural need for food can be met, for the most part, without the need for any kind of a utensil; one can eat with ones fingers. When forks and knives were first introduced in the Western world, they were a luxury need, available only to wealthy aristocrats. Over time, though, their use spread and was normalized in several European and North American societies. Gradually eating with forks and knives transformed into a necessary need and now their use is ubiquitous in many Western and non-Western societies. Once signifiers of aristocracy and wealth, they are now objects of common use. As a large number of socioeconomic groups now use these utensils, distinction between classes can no longer be maintained through their possession and use. Instead it is their design, i.e. material choice (silver or stainless steel or plastic), number of different kinds used in a meal (determined by number of courses and therefore the economic and social worth of the meal), style (bought in a museum store of high design or at an unexceptional retail outlet), etc., that help maintain the class distinction.

THE ROLE OF NEEDS IN THE DESIGN PROCESS

Human-centered design (also referred to as user-centered design) is a response to new product development driven purely by styling or by engineering. Those products designed

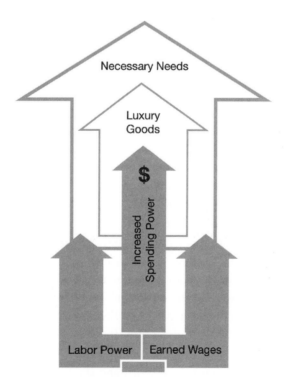

Figure 6.4.   Needs Drivers: Luxury to Necessary Needs.
Illustration by Amethyst Saludo.

with the primary motive of creating a better aesthetic variation on an existing device are not perceived as solving pressing problems faced by consumers. Similarly, products driven by technology rather than people's needs and desires may end up having features and functions that nobody wants or cares about. Human-centered design rejects aesthetics or technology as the sole drivers for product development; instead, it emphasizes the need to understand the context within which people interact with things, and using that knowledge to generate new design. The rapidly growing field of design research addresses this very need, largely through such qualitative methods as interviews, observations, shadowing, and journaling. The goal of these methods is to be able to identify people's articulated as well as unarticulated needs. Corporations involved in human-centered new product development operate on the principle that knowing people's needs will lead to designs that are more readily assimilated into their everyday lives. Though the tradition of user research has existed in the design discipline for several decades (especially in the work of such visionaries as Robert Propst and Henry Dreyfuss), the explicit and widespread use of rapid ethnography is relatively new. In design research, it has been defined as "a research approach that produces a detailed, in depth observation of people's behavior, beliefs and preferences by observing and interacting with them in a natural environment" (Ireland 2003: 26). This embrace of user needs is not limited to design. Market researchers use business tools to identify the needs of large segments of target populations. Engineers involved in new product development too have altered the traditional process of designing products from a purely technical focus to one that includes the "voice of the customer." Widely accepted practices such as total quality management (T.Q.M.), Zero Defects and Six Sigma take into account customer needs in the process of design.[2]

Countless examples of well-designed products make it clear that identification and listing of user needs help in creating products that solve specific problems for users. Design research can be highly successful in identifying needs, recognizing opportunities and recommending appropriate solutions, but there are certain issues that it often may not deal with. For example, the critical question of whether there really is a need for a new product in a given situation or context is often not posed. Can users sufficiently make do with an existing product? And should they be encouraged to? The central premise of industrial design practice is the creation of new products, and therefore designers question what the object might be like, how it may satisfy a need, or how it may perform better than an existing device, but not whether it needs to exist at all. The critical vocabulary of design for need should include the question of the very existence of a new object a part of its lexicon. Through the design of new consumer products, designers introduce incremental changes to prevailing ways of executing everyday tasks. The iPhone makes it easier to selectively retrieve voicemail messages, the Gillette Fusion razor with five pulsing blades and a built-in spotlight promises a chin with no missed spots, and the Rabbit corkscrew, which by web accounts "pulls a cork in 3 seconds flat," speeds up the process of opening a wine bottle. Are these design interventions vital to the improvement of people's everyday lives; do they solve existing problems in significantly improved ways; do the benefits of acquiring the new product outweigh the drawbacks of its consumption? The general argument in favor of continuous innovation is that these designs offer better user experiences, their manufacture implies jobs for workers, they signal economic growth, they are a necessary form of technological progress and that people want them. The counter argument posits that the steady and rapid introduction of newer devices in the marketplace creates an unsustainable consumer culture, fetishizes our relationships to things, generates environmentally damaging waste and increases social distinction.

The introduction of a new device may satisfy specific needs but it often leads to the creation of new needs. The acquisition of a new product, at times, necessitates the purchase of additional ones. All things exist within a network that includes other things. The desktop computer lives within an environment that contains other essential objects—a keyboard, a mouse, a wrist support, a mouse pad, an external hard drive—that constitute the network of computer accessories. This network intersects another. The desk, the ergonomic chair, the footrest, the partition and the task lamp constitute the overlapping furniture network. The task light belongs to yet another network—lighting—which also includes overhead lights and indicator LEDs. It is evident that the need for individual things is in fact a need for a network of things. The existence of this object network can be attributed to several reasons, some of which relate directly to processes of new product design and development. At times, the introduction of new products renders existing infrastructures insufficient or incapable. Computers brought along with them an untidy web of Ethernet cables and power cords that necessitated the design of desks and other furniture systems with wire management capabilities. In other cases, designers are required to redress the poor designs of particular products through additional products. Ergonomic pads and wrist braces are perfect examples of corrective devices designed to compensate for the shortcomings of the computer keyboard. Yet another reason for the proliferation of products and the exponential cluttering of the object network is the design of specialized tools and equipment.

Stores such as Williams-Sonoma, a high-end repository for kitchen devices like garlic presses, apple wedgers, corn zippers and mango pitters, is a "place for cooks" that offers a specific tool for every culinary task imaginable. While all of these gadgets are clever, and some perform critical functions, others raise questions. Indeed, some tools such as the Pineapple Easy Slicer, which cleverly cores and slices the thorny fruit, perform functions that would be substantially more taxing with a simple kitchen knife, and some such as the Flexible Finger Guard, which shields fingertips during chopping, make potentially dangerous tasks significantly safer. However, it is difficult not to question the need for such items as avocado mashers tailor-made to perform specialized duties. Surely, a universal masher can pulverize cooked potatoes and avocados with equal ease without the need for two distinct designs. The process of identification of every possible consumer micro-need can easily lead to the design of a series of discrete products that only marginally improve upon a universal device. And if such an assortment of objects rates high on desirability but low on added utility, what type of a need do they fulfill? This by no means suggests that the solution is a single universal device for all tasks possible. Clearly, the strategy of one-size-fits-all creates a condition of one-size-fits-one leaving many straddled with the problem of too big, too small, too loose, too tight, too heavy, too light and so forth. The other extreme, of a different product for every possible need leads to the rabid proliferation of variety, creating conditions of fetishism and waste.

The hammer is a universal tool for nailing things. However, situations of occasional use and intense use can present a different set of needs to the designer. A framer, who constructs the structural wood frame for a house, is an intense user who works rapidly and might have to hammer hundreds of nails in a day. According to designer Yani Deros of ATOMdesign:

> we discovered during the research that framers need a hammer that absorbs shock well because they are prone to getting repetitive stress injury. In addition, because they work really fast, they tend to overstrike and in process destroy the handles of the hammers. There were many other problems like making it easy to align and start the nail so that both their hands are not tied up ... creating a balanced hammer and so on. (Deros, personal interview 2008)

The S-2 hammer designed by Deros specifically addresses these needs. The head is split in two parts with a shock gasket in between so that it dissipates impact energy to minimize recoil and repetitive stress injury. It has overstrike plates that protect the wooden handle from getting split. The wooden handle is made of hickory that is farmed sustainably by the company (they plant more trees than they cut down).

"This product had very important tactile constraints ... it had to feel right. So we took prototypes to the field and asked framers to use them because we wanted to make sure that the needs we were designing for were being met" (Deros, person interview 2008). In this case, the design process started with an identification of the user needs and those became the driver for the project.

Marx observed this variety in the tools that were used in England's nineteenth-century factories:

> Manufacture is characterized by the differentiation of the instruments of labour—a differentiation whereby tools of a different sort acquire fixed shapes, adapted to each particular application—and by the specialization of these instruments, which allows full play to each special tool only in the hands of a specific kind of worker. In Birmingham alone 500 varieties of hammer are produced, and not only is each one adapted to a particular process, but several varieties often serve exclusively for the different operations in the same process. The manufacturing period simplifies, improves and multiplies the implements of labour by adapting them to the exclusive and special functions of each kind of worker. It is thus creates at the same time one of the material conditions for the existence of machinery, which consists of a combination of simple instruments. (Marx 1990: 460–1)

Figure 6.5. Framing Hammer, by Yani Deros of ATOMdesign for Vaughan & Bushell. Image courtesy of Yani Deros, ATOMdesign.

Marx suggests that designing this type of variety into tools creates a need for those machines in factories, thereby enslaving the worker. Instead of controlling the machines, the worker is controlled by them.

In the design process, identification of user needs generally occurs during the phase referred to as the "fuzzy front end" in new product-development literature. Over the last decade, ethnographic research methods such as user observation and cultural immersion have become common practice in design as a means of identifying people's needs. While it is truly beneficial to identify, list and categorize all possible needs observed during research, which ones and how many of them design should address is debatable. As is evidenced in the quotation below, in some cases researchers identify needs that consumers did not know they had.

> "The user" is a central trope for designer, the focus of their professional attention: identifying and meeting "the user's" needs and wants is the central mission of designers. Of course, this is never a straightforward process. Consumers have complex, multiple needs,

which they are not always able to articulate. Also, designers may create new product ideas that satisfy needs consumers did not know they had. The popularity of Post-it notes is an example. (Wasson 2000: 377)

Engineering and marketing literature also recommends that customer needs be identified early in the design process and certainly before settling on technical specifications. The process involves discovering the "voice of the customer," defined as a "hierarchical set of 'customer needs' where each need (or set of needs) has assigned to it a priority which indicates its importance to the customer" (Griffin and Hauser 1993: 2). This list can vary in length depending upon the complexity of the product but an inventory of over 200 individual needs is common. The voice of the customer is a component of a total quality assurance and management system called quality function deployment (Q.F.D.). Yoji Akao, who introduced Q.F.D. in Japan in 1966, defines it as a method aimed at "translating the consumer's demands into design targets and major quality points to be used throughout the production stage" (Akao 2004: 3). These needs guide the determination of features and functions for the product and are eventually transformed into technical specifications. The hierarchical ranking of the needs allows designers and engineers to focus on those needs that are perceived to be the most significant for consumers and the most achievable for the corporation. Needs are generally grouped into categories such as primary, secondary and tertiary, and though N.P.D. professionals (designers, engineers, market researchers, etc.) may identify hundreds, not all can be met through the design of the product. Several choices and tradeoffs—technological, deadline-based or financial—are made during the process of development in order to get the product to market. During the research phase as these needs are being identified, potential users are also asked to prioritize them, so that designers may make the most appropriate tradeoffs. However, the final decision about which needs are translated into product features lies with the N.P.D. professionals, and it is likely that some needs deemed important by users are not met through the design of the new product.

NEEDS IN MARKETING AND ENGINEERING

In marketing and engineering, the classification of needs is often based upon their nature or level of importance:

- primary, secondary and tertiary needs (Akao 2004);
- basic, articulated and exciting needs (Griffin and Hauser 1993);
- psychological, physiological, sociological needs (Gutman 1982);
- individual, societal, environmental, corporate, government (stakeholder analysis).

One of the simplest forms of classification used in Q.F.D. methodology groups needs into primary, secondary and tertiary based upon their importance value to consumers. The prioritization of needs allows engineers to rate the importance values of specific features in the product design. Primary needs are also referred to as strategic needs and they are the ones that generally determine the major design direction the product takes. Secondary

CLASSIFICATION OF NEEDS

Primary	Basic	Psychological	Individual
Secondary	Articulated	Physiological	Societal
Tertiary	Exciting	Sociological	Corporate
			Government
			Environmental

Figure 6.6.   Classification of Needs. Illustration by Amethyst Saludo.

needs, also referred to as tactical needs, allow the product engineers to better understand the means and tactics by which the strategic needs can be met. And lastly, the tertiary needs, also called operational needs, provide the maximum amount of detail so that specific functional solutions may be generated through appropriate engineering and component design. This grouping is often used in the construction of the House of Quality that helps convert customer needs into functional operations through a one-to-one correspondence (Kamrani and Salhieh 2002).

Using the example of a computer monitor, authors Griffin and Hauser classify needs into three broad categories. "These customer needs include basic needs (what a customer assumes a monitor will do), articulated needs (what a customer will tell you that he, she, or they want a monitor to do), and exciting needs (those needs which, if they are fulfilled, would delight and surprise the customer)" (1993: 4). Exciting needs are often the most challenging to identify but they are also the ones that give corporations a higher sales volume and therefore a significant competitive advantage.

Jonathan Gutman (1982) introduces the concept of "consequences" in relation to the notion of need, and classifies them into three main categories—physiological, psychological, and sociological. He defines consequences as "any result (physiological or psychological) accruing directly or indirectly to the consumer (sooner or later) from his/her behavior" (Gutman 1982: 61). Physiological consequences include satisfying hunger, thirst and other bodily needs, psychological consequences include such conditions as self-esteem and sociological consequences refer to enhanced status, group membership, etc. Gutman suggests that "consumers choose actions that produce desired consequences and minimize undesired consequences" (1981: 62). The use of the term "consequence" locates responsibility into the hands of consumers and makes them active agents not only in the outcomes of their buying decisions but also in their experience with the goods bought. Indeed, consumers exercise a certain amount of choice in the selection of goods, but they are not solely responsible for how these products function. Decisions about which consumer needs should be translated into product features lie largely in the hands of designers, engineers and corporate executives, and therefore so does their operation.

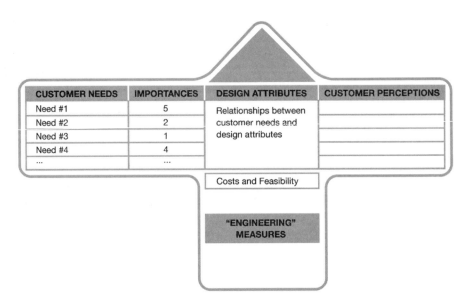

Figure 6.7. House of Quality Customer Needs and Design Attributes. Adapted from Griffin and Hauser (1993: 4).

Needs of the immediate user generally receive most attention and consideration during product development, especially from engineering and design. However, needs are also often identified by stakeholders—entities directly or indirectly affected by the entire lifecycle of a product system. Typical stakeholders for products include individuals (users, purchasers and influencers), society (cultural, social and political groups/institutions), the environment, corporations (for and non-profit), financial institutions (banks and venture capitalists), the media (print and online) and the government (states, nations and the international community). It is evident that even the most mundane and small products may involve and impact large numbers of individuals and institutions. Though several strategies exist to prioritize customer needs, few mechanisms exist to rank stakeholder interests. Stakeholders typically constitute a large, complex and amorphous network of individuals and institutions and they never have one spokesperson or advocate. Of the several needs taxonomies discussed, it is the stakeholder needs approach that casts the widest net in meeting needs of a diverse group of people involved in the production, distribution and consumption of goods. The needs of the various stakeholders may often compete with and oppose each other. A consumer's need for convenient, disposable goods directly violates the needs of environmental groups that might demand durable products; the needs of a large corporation to dominate markets may intrude upon the needs of a smaller entrepreneurial business as well as the guidelines of governmental regulatory bodies. The resolution, in such situations, depends entirely on the politics of power and the nature of the relations between the groups involved.

DESIGNING NEEDS OR DESIGNING FOR NEEDS

Nigel Whiteley (1993) distinguishes between several forms of design practice around the notions of those that benefit society and those that do not. He explains consumer-led design, for example, as the widely adopted practice of designing products that, instead of improving human, social or environmental conditions, worsen them. In such cases, design appears to be driven more by corporate profit margins rather than pressing human needs. Whiteley quotes Terence Conran, founder of Habitat, who explains a shift in design practice as well as consumption patterns. "There was a strange moment around the mid-60s when people stopped needing and need changed to want… Designers became more important in producing 'want' products rather than 'need' products, because you have to create desire" (Whiteley 1993: 18). This situation never reverted back, and the world has witnessed the steady population growth of things that often do little to satisfy people's urgent needs:

> There is a worldwide concern that despite the material benefits arising from advanced technology and industry, there is a deterioration in the quality of life and failure in the provision of many essential needs. This is accompanied by an increasing awareness of a waste of resources and a despoliation of the environment.[3]

These words, published at the "Design for Need" conference organized by the Royal College of Art in London in 1976 are just as relevant today. In fact, it is easy to argue that conditions are substantially worse than they were in 1976. Does this signify that conversation about responsible design continues without any significant or measurable success? Has the design community ignored humanity's long present, pressing needs for shorter gain? Or, are a good number of designers seriously following principles of sustainable development and in process creating responsible products? The world of design cannot be cleaved cleanly into responsible and irresponsible or good and bad. Instead, design straddles a spectrum of possibilities, with wasteful and damaging objects at one end and socially uplifting experiences at the other end. Whiteley suggests green design, responsible design and feminist design as alternative approaches that hold the potential of addressing the broader social problems that "consumerist design" does not.[4]

SOCIAL CONSTRUCTION OF NEED SYSTEMS

Baudrillard, on whom one can always rely for extraordinary and occasionally bewildering ideas, upends the notion of a taxonomy of needs, suggesting that primary or fundamental needs are a myth and that this form of differentiation between primary or secondary needs or survival and luxury needs is an ideology determined by the economic system. Baudrillard summarizes his concept of need succinctly by explaining that "the system of needs is the product of the system of production" (1998: 74). According to Baudrillard, needs do not exist in atomized form within individuals, and there is no such thing as a one-to-one relationship between our needs for objects and those objects. In general, practices of consumption cannot be directly traced to the notion of human need for things. Instead,

Baudrillard suggests that within a capitalist framework production creates a waged labor force, and hence creates a system of needs; in fact, he views needs as well as consumption as "an organised extension of the productive forces" (1998: 76). In other words, we do not need things due to our physiological or psychological conditions; we need things because of the system of production within which we live. Needs, for Baudrillard, are not innate or instinctive but "better defined as a *function* induced (in the individual) by the internal logic of the system: more precisely, *not as a consummative force liberated* by the affluent society, but *as a productive force* required by the functioning of the system itself, by its process of reproduction and survival. In other words, there are only needs because the system needs them" (Baudrillard 1981: 82). As with other production-centric approaches, Baudrillard's position affords too much agency to the system of production at the expense of the agency of consumers.

While the production engine can exert significant force, individual human agency cannot be simply written off as impotent or inconsequential. Economist Galbraith critiques the economic system for focusing on more frivolous needs while ignoring critical ones:

> Economic theory has managed to transfer the sense of urgency in meeting consumer need that once was felt in a world where more production meant more food for the hungry, more clothing for the cold and more houses for the homeless to a world where increased output satisfies the craving for more elegant automobiles, more exotic food, more erotic clothing, more elaborate entertainment—indeed, for the entire modern range of sensuous, edifying and lethal desires. (Galbraith 1998: 115)

Often, it is the practice of design that imparts this elegant, exotic, erotic and elaborate character to things, and by Galbraith's account, therefore, assists in the creation of extravagant and misguided craving. Entire economic systems of nations are tied to the bulk of production (gross domestic product) and volume of consumption (consumer spending index). Economic growth naturally leads to the simultaneous creation of products and needs. However, Baudrillard observes that this creation occurs at different rates, leading to a continuous condition of a surplus of needs over the supply of goods. While the rate of goods production depends upon industrial and economic activities, the rate of needs growth depends upon class distinction. The purchase of more goods and the acquisition of more needs go hand in hand with affluence. Needs exhibit a trickle-down effect, as those of the affluent and the elite lead those of the poor.

Baudrillard rejects the notion suggested by conventional economic theory that human needs can be satisfied and that the process leads to a state of equilibrium. He disagrees with Galbraith's suggestion that "production only fills a void that it has itself created" (1998: 125). If needs exist as a systemic, organized extension of the productive force, it is erroneous to imagine a condition of satisfaction; they should not be conceived as a void that can be filled by consumption. The system of needs is maintained in a state of perpetual motion by the system of production; a state of human satisfaction that ends needs does not exist. While it is generally assumed that the market offers a plethora of things from which one can choose to satisfy one's needs, Baudrillard suggests that choice is illusory because the system of production *forces* choice on consumers. "How am I free *not* to choose?" (Baudrillard 1981: 81). He suggests that discretionary income—generally defined as a sum of money that one has available to spend as one chooses—itself is absurd, because one is no more free while shopping for a second automobile than when one is buying food. "Is the loss of status—or social non-existence—less upsetting than food?" (Baudrillard 1981: 81). The system of needs therefore is not organized in a hierarchy that makes the need for food any different than the need for a car. Instead, he suggests that the system of production prescribes a level of "imposed consumption," and anyone who does buy into this "standard package" is an "outcast" (Baudrillard 1981: 81). Through these arguments, Baudrillard recasts the notion of need as a system of control devised by the system of production.

THE MULTIPLE DIMENSIONS OF NEED

In spite of the multiple taxonomies and classifications of needs, it is clear that there is no universality in what makes a need fundamental, basic, minimal or essential for survival, and what constitutes as secondary, tertiary, instrumental or luxury need. What is clear that they certainly exist as a force in our lives, as drivers of the design process, and as elements of philosophical, economic and social discourse. In design, engineering and marketing, needs are defined in functional terms—as opportunities that have to be met with goods and services. However, critical analyses by economists and sociologists suggest that the needs being satisfied, in many cases, may be not simply be those of individuals but of the entire system of production. From this point of view, they appear as instruments set into momentum by corporations to maintain the system in place. Needs are dynamic in nature and they change over time as patterns of consumption change. The notion of a satisfied need can often be a myth; needs are not satisfied, they are replaced with other needs. The proliferation and escalation of needs impacts individuals, corporations, societies, the government and the environment:

> Consumer-led design in a market economy goes far beyond the idea of meeting human needs: it seeks to create and constantly to stimulate human *desires*. The modern consumer's condition is characterized by dissatisfaction and a consequent state of longing. A continual stream of 'new' goods is produced to satisfy temporarily the desires which the market has, if not created, then certainly kindled. (Whiteley 1993: 3)

Containing this form of needs escalation will require nothing short of structural changes to the way we consume, the way in which corporations function and the way governments regulate processes of production. Practices of sustainable design and manufacturing have to be accompanied with practices of sustainable consumption. The United Nations Development Programme estimates that "some 1.2 billion people around the world live on less than a dollar a day, while almost 850 million go hungry every night." In addition, some

1.6 billion people lived without access to electricity in 2004.[5] Are we, in the words of Guy Debord "replacing the satisfaction of primary human needs (scarcely met) with an incessant fabrication of pseudoneeds" through our economic, political and manufacturing empires? (2006: 24) The escalation of needs translates into an ever-enlarging variety and abundance of things. Needs beget things, which in turn beget needs for other things and so on, in an infinite chain that creates an inescapable stranglehold on the consumer's life:

> Much recent design has satisfied only evanescent wants and desires, while the genuine needs of man have often been neglected. The economic, psychological, spiritual, social, technological, and intellectual needs of a human being are usually more difficult and less profitable to satisfy than the carefully engineered and manipulated "wants" inculcated by fad and fashion. (Papanek 1971: 15)

Though Papanek's accusation is certainly justifiable in many ways, what qualifies as a "genuine need" is by no means simple to determine. The need for status, convenience and style is no less genuine than the "fundamental" need for food and shelter.

In the world of social policy, Doyal and Gough suggest that human needs "are neither subjective preferences best understood by each individual, nor static essences best understood by planners or party officials. They are universal and knowable, but our knowledge of them, and of the satisfiers necessary to meet them, is dynamic and open-ended" (1991: 4). The authors argue for a theory of needs that recognizes the individual as well as the collective, that draws upon "both liberal and socialist thought," that represents a "third way forward which rejects both market individualism and state collectivism" (Doyal and Gough 1991: 3). Such a strategy would require the active participation of all stakeholders: corporations and consumers, governments and citizens, institutions and individuals. Responsible design and ethical consumption are both practices that can together serve as the mechanisms by which to create a "third way forward" of needs-satisfaction, the goal of which should be global human welfare.

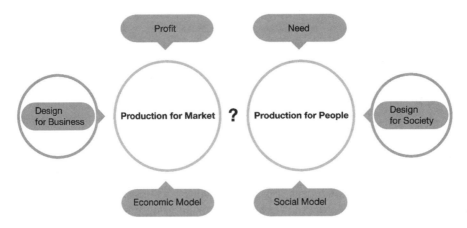

Figure 6.8.   Design for Need. Illustration by Amethyst Saludo.

7 PLANNED OBSOLESCENCE: UNSUSTAINABLE CONSUMPTION

We cannot conceive how to serve the consumer unless we make for him something that as far as we can provide will last forever. We want to construct some kind of a machine that will last forever. It does not please us to have a buyer's car wear out or become obsolete. We want the man who buys one of our products never to have to buy another. We never make an improvement that renders any previous model obsolete.

Henry Ford, *My Life and Work*

Goods fall into two classes, those we use, such as motorcars or safety razors, and those we use *up*, such as toothpaste and soda biscuit. Consumer engineering must see to it that we use up the kind of goods we now merely use. Would any change in the goods or habits of people speed up their consumption? Can they be displaced by newer models? Can artificial obsolescence be created? Consumer engineering does not end till we can consume all we can make.

Ernest Elmo Calkins, "Introduction: What Consumer Engineering Really Is"

To a designer, anything that is, is obsolete.

George Nelson, "Obsolescence"

You know, you keep on innovating, you keep on making better stuff. And if you always want the latest and greatest, then you have to buy a new iPod at least once a year.

Steve Jobs, *Brian Williams, Nightly Report*[1]

When Apple first started offering the option of custom laser engraved lettering so people could personalize their iPods, an acquaintance wanted to get the words "obsolete" etched into his brand new machine. This would be, he reasoned, a means of asserting his awareness of the extremely short lives of hi-tech electronic devices while succumbing to their allure. He said he knew he would probably be buying another iPod before too long as he had done with computers. Regardless of whether he went ahead with his plan (and whether Apple agreed to do it), the anecdote reveals the irony that consumers sometimes perceive in their consumption habits.

Generally speaking, electronic products tend to have limited lives. Jobs' quote above suggests that consumers exercise choice in purchasing the "latest and the greatest" devices but, in many cases, the further older products recede from the cutting edge of innovation, the less likely they are to work harmoniously with the ever-changing infrastructure of software, file formats and compatibility. Since 2001, Apple has introduced several variations/models of the iPod either with newer features such as image and video capabilities, smaller sizes, additional storage, newer colors and sleeker forms. For consumers, the responsibility to preserve the old and worn thing is continually challenged by the desire for the seductive and fashionable new thing. For corporations, the need to support old designs faces the constant pressure of keeping up with cutting-edge technologies. This duality and ambivalence between the antiquated and the nascent, durability and disposability and conserving and discarding, makes obsolescence a difficult problem to tackle.

This chapter examines the social, economic and environmental impacts of the life spans of things. Obsolescence and durability are two of many critical topics that constitute the discourse of sustainability. Planned obsolescence, the practice of deliberately shortening the life of products to stimulate sales, can be traced back to the early 1900s. It has had a long history in a variety of industry sectors and while it has enjoyed significant support from economists, marketing experts and designers, it has also been subjected to scathing critiques by writers, some industry officials and some designers. This chapter presents overviews and critiques of some of their thinking. A discussion of the various types of obsolescence will demonstrate the wide reach and impact this practice has had over the years. We live in a world of durable things and disposable things; while disposing things rapidly has taken a significant toll on our social practices and environmental quality, designing durable things might serve as a strategy by which to minimize some of these problems. This chapter will also discuss some of the challenges designers face in designing for durability.

In 1987, the Brundtland Commission published its oft-quoted definition of sustainable development as "development that meets the needs of the present without compromising the ability of future generations to meet their own needs" (WorldinBalance.net 2009). In 1994, John Elkington urged corporations to think not only of the economic bottom line but also to consider social and environmental factors in their business strategies. Widely referred to as the triple bottom line, this idea was elaborated in Elkington's *Cannibals with Forks* (1998) as development that strives for economic prosperity, social equity and environmental quality. In other words, it is development that manages its resources of people (human capital), profit (financial capital) and the planet (natural capital) in a responsible fashion. Sustainable design refers to the development of artifacts in compliance with the principles of sustainability as explained above. Green design, ecodesign, design for the environment (D.F.E.), design for the majority, etc. focus on specific areas (environmental or social) within the realm of sustainable design. These forms of design recommend a series of strategies by which to mitigate the damaging effects of unsustainable production and consumption. For instance, minimizing the weight of products, reducing waste, limiting transportation, avoiding toxic materials, and reducing energy use are but a few of the strategies of sustainable design. By increasing waste, increasing pollution and squandering energy resources, the practice of planned obsolescence directly contributes to negative environmental impacts. On the other hand, durability, by extending product life and minimizing waste serves as one of the strategies by which to combat unsustainability. Literature in sustainable design lists several approaches and strategies of lifecycle impact assessment—some, such as multi-score life cycle assessments (with original inventory data) are very comprehensive as well as objective and others such as Total Beauty are much more subjective and do not consider several categories of environmental impact (White, St. Pierre and Belletire 2007).

Other well known methodologies and approaches, many of which are based on life-cycle assessment (L.C.A.) include the Okala Impact factor Assessment (White *et al.* 2007), MDBC Cradle-to-Cradle (McDonough and Braungart 2002), Bhamra and Lofthouse (2007), Walker (2006), Fry (2009) and Eternally Yours (van Hinte 2004).

The scope of this book does not permit a lengthy discussion of sustainable design, but planned obsolescence (in all its forms) sits squarely in the middle of the issues it faces. In all life cycle assessments, product lifetime is a critical piece of quantitative data that has significant impact. It is often calculated in the number of hours a product will be used in its lifetime. While performing L.C.A.s of products, many manufacturers are reluctant to share this data (White *et al.* 2007: 45). Lengthening the life of goods is one of the key strategies to reduce some of the environmental impact of products. In addition, it also holds the potential of slowing down individual consumption and reducing quantity of waste.

EARLY ATTEMPTS AT PLANNED OBSOLESCENCE

Though the original author of the term "planned obsolescence" is not known with any certainty, Slade (2006) traces one of its earliest known uses to 1932, to Bernard London, a real-estate broker in Manhattan. In a publication titled *Ending the Depression through Planned Obsolescence*, London outlined his plan for stimulating the economy in tough times. He suggested that all goods be assigned a specific lifespan when sold. At the end of this time frame, people would return these "dead" things to the government in exchange for a receipt that indicated their value. This would generate the need for new "live" things that factories would produce continuously. This was a time when there was widespread and tacit understanding in the business community that obsolescence was one of the surest mechanisms of economic gain. However, ambivalence about the concept was common. Such authors as Sheldon and Arens (1932), in explaining obsolescence, referred to it as a positive force and saw no problems in its operational model. Over the years, of the designers who have spoken in favor of obsolescence, Brooks Stevens, Gordon Lippincott, George Nelson and Harley Earl were perhaps the most vocal. At the other end of the ideological spectrum, scholars who have critiqued the practice as wasteful and manipulative have included writer Vance Packard, economist John Kenneth Galbraith and several designers including Walter Dorwin Teague and Victor Papanek.

THE ECONOMICS OF OBSOLESCENCE

"Planned obsolescence may be a necessary condition for the achievement of technological progress and that a pattern of rapidly deteriorating products and fast innovation may be preferred to long-lasting products and slow innovation" (Fishman, Gandall and Shy 1993: 361). The proponents of planned obsolescence—economists, manufacturers, designers and marketers—argued that it was a means of promoting innovation and progress, it allowed manufacturers to give people what they wanted, and it made economic sense. The practice seems to have taken root during the 1920s and 1930s and flourished during the 1950s and 1960s. Prior to London's use of the term "planned obsolescence," other phrases such as "creative waste" (by Sheldon and Arens) and "progressive obsolescence" (Frederick 1928) were circulated in business literature. George Frederick suggested that corporations should encourage consumers to buy products more frequently to promote a "sense of modernness" (Frederick 1928). In her book, *Selling Mrs. Consumer*, Christine Frederick advocated progressive obsolescence as a means of achieving "human satisfaction" (1929: 245). Presenting women as avid practitioners of obsolescence, she guided businesses in creating marketing strategies to appeal specifically to women. She explains progressive obsolescence as a personal ambition for every American and a mechanism for the great American triumph. In 1932, Sheldon and Arens published *Consumer Engineering*, in which they outlined a "new technique for prosperity." In the introductory chapter, Ernest Elmo Calkins explained consumer engineering as "shaping a product to fit more exactly consumers' needs" (Sheldon and Arens 1932: 1). Though this definition is not unlike the notion of human-centered design, for Calkins it meant "any plan which stimulates the consumption of goods" (Sheldon and Arens 1932: 2). By means of this explanation, Calkins included consumption itself as a human need. "We can no longer take it for granted that because people buy a thing they are satisfied with it. A larger market may be obtained by some change in the product" (Sheldon and Arens 1932: 6). Engineering for need became a mechanism by which to increase consumption and profits. In this equation of production and consumption, waste was not considered seriously. "People are persuaded to abandon the old and buy the new to be up-to-date, to have the right and correct thing. Does there seem to be a sad waste in the process? Not at all. Wearing things out does not produce prosperity but buying things does" (Sheldon and Arens 1932: 7). Calkins describes "obsoletism ... [as] another device for stimulating consumption" and adds "any plan which increases the consumption of goods is justifiable if we believe that prosperity is a desirable thing" (Sheldon and Arens 1932: 7). It is arguable that, in 1932, when Calkins wrote this essay, the ills of reckless consumption were yet unknown but the fervent promotion of consumption by "any plan" has resulted in serious environmental, social and financial problems.

Sheldon and Arens recast the meaning of usefulness by separating it from functional utility. "Just because a motor will run five years more and propel an uncomfortable and unsightly touring-car over our roads for an additional 50,000 miles it is no proof that that car has not finished its usefulness" (Sheldon and Arens 1932: 62). They supported the replacement of that which was *passé* with that which was *en vogue* because "the things we use sometimes break down from wear and tear, but much more frequently their style wears out before their gears" (Sheldon and Arens 1932: 63). While admitting that the constant exploitation of natural resources for increased production is imprudent and short-lived, they continued to serve as its advocates, proclaiming it as the American way. "We still have tree-covered slopes to deforest and subterranean lakes of oil to tap with our gushers" (Sheldon and Arens 1932: 65).

DESIGNERS FOR OBSOLESCENCE

Although he may not have been the originator of the term, American designer Brooks Stevens, certainly played a role in popularizing planned obsolescence in the 1950s. He referred to it as "instilling in the buyer the desire to own something a little newer, a little better, a little sooner than is necessary" (Heskett 2003: 4). The following excerpt from a presentation he made to Midland Corporation in Minneapolis in 1954 is worth quoting at length.

> In America, today, the economic situation is such that we definitely lean heavily on what we call planned obsolescence. This may at first sound like a startling statement, but unlike the European approach of the past historical days, where they tried to make the very best product and make it last for ever, meaning that if you bought a Rolls-Royce that you owned it throughout your lifetime and never had to trade it in, or you bought such a fine suit of clothes, that you were married in it and then buried in it and never a chance to renew it. The approach in America is one of making the American consumer unhappy with the product that he has enjoyed the use of for a period, have him pass it on to the second hand or second used market, and obtain the newest product with the newest possible look. This philosophy is not wasteful, it means that that product which you have had for a while … let's say it's a Buick sedan or a Ford station wagon, with twenty-three thousand miles on it, suddenly is not completely up to snuff from a standpoint of appearance, design and styling, and you aspire to having the 54 model. You turn in your perfectly good automobile which has another fifty thousand miles good in it, and it goes to the used market where another person with slightly less means can obtain a finer product than he can ever hope to have new. This can go through the refrigerator, the washing machine, the clothes dryer, the television set, and right on down the line. I want you to realize then that the planned obsolescence theory is what makes our productive plants continue at a high peak. Because of this definite trend in merchandising in America, I see no reason for any alarm or concern about depression or even recession. I think the words should be left out of everyday conversation. That means that the appearance design of any approach to the consumer should be the newest, freshest, and most remembered impression we can possibly make.[2]

Stevens' justification for planned obsolescence relied on a smooth transition of discarded products into the used goods market. The argument that goods discarded by one group could neatly serve the needs of another is not as tidy a situation as is portrayed. First, although automobiles in the U.S. exist in a thriving pre-owned market, other products do not enjoy elaborate dealer networks and financial structures to support their resale after their first use. Second-hand goods are sold in garage sales, thrift stores and such online environments as Craigslist but they often end up in junkyards to decay for years. Second, a consumption model in which the affluent have monetary access to new products while the middle, lower-income and indigent classes are expected to buy used products can only promote economic and social stratification. The conscious separation of buying habits by economic class can further distance the consuming identities of the various groups of people. Third, a population habituated to a rapid turnover in their material possessions exhibits neomaina and is likely to value the act of possessing over that which they possess. Such material lust can quickly turn into an addiction that cannot be beneficial for the individual, society, or the environment.

In addition to Brooks Stevens, George Nelson too spoke up in favor of obsolescence. In an essay published in 1956, he laid out an argument about the economic virtues of obsolescence. "If rapid change comes from a continuing demand for the best possible product, then why do we look on accelerating obsolescence as if it were fostered by a conspiracy of stupid consumers and irresponsible manufacturers?" (Nelson 1967: 174). Nelson attributed obsolescence to pressures of competition, need for change and fashion. In addition, he suggested that designers are temperamentally inclined to favor obsolescence. "The designer has a good bit more to do with obsolescence than one might think, because he is temperamentally unable to leave things alone" (Nelson 1967: 175). If this is the case, it is not only design's institutional relationship to economics, but individual designerly disposition that is to blame. Obsolescence, planned or unplanned, was perceived as an inevitable force to be embraced and supported as a mechanism for technological change, economic success, social prosperity and human satisfaction.

AGAINST OBSOLESCENCE

The positive rhetoric of obsolescence has also had its enemies in writers, designers, engineers and economists who found the practice distasteful on social, economic, environmental and moral grounds. In a series of highly influential and widely read books, Vance Packard launched one of the most fervent and vitriolic attacks on planned obsolescence. It was *The Wastemakers* published in 1960. In it he thoroughly examined several corporate and consumer practices surrounding obsolescence with examples of scores of disposable, malfunctioning, short-lived and wasteful products that included food packaging, kitchen appliances, cars and homes.

Packard identified three major types of obsolescence. Obsolescence of function, the first type, refers to a situation in which an existing product becomes outmoded when the new, better functioning product is introduced into the market. Obsolescence of quality refers to a situation in which a product is designed to break down or wear out at a given time, usually in a future not too distant. This generally results in short-lived, low-performing goods. Obsolescence of desirability, the third kind, refers to the situation in which a product that is still sound in terms of quality or performance becomes worn out in our minds because of fashion or other change that makes it seem less desirable. Packard applauds and welcomes functional obsolescence, the first kind but rejects the other two as manipulative and dishonest. Offering a dizzying range of examples including light bulbs engineered to last a fewer number of hours than technologically possible, portable radios with shortened life spans, low quality toasters that broke down frequently during testing and rugs that faded quickly when prototypes, Packard demonstrated that this practice was then common in every imaginable industry sector.

Packard warned against increasing consumption by spotlighting the rate of resource depletion, lifestyle degradation and the changing character of Americans. The constant thirst for raw materials and fuel to support production, the careless, wasteful and unregulated habits of corporations and the despoliation of virgin lands were identified as key environmental problems. He referred to a second set of problems as commercialization of American life evident in the constant bombardment of advertising images through all possible forms of media in addition to radio television and print. Advertising techniques like sky billboards dragged by low-flying aircraft, posters on park benches and projections on clouds appalled Packard but would scarcely raise an eyebrow today. Such "thingmindedness," Packard suggested, made Americans hedonistic, materialistic, soft and passive, causing them "to find their main life satisfactions in their consumption role rather than their productive role" (1960: 233). Citing several studies, Packard suggested that this form of continuous consumption had led to deterioration of family structures, juvenile selfishness, general apathy and criminal behavior. As solutions, Packard suggested consumer education, activism and prudence; he urged corporations to exercise rigorous quality control and put emphasis on utility rather than fashion; he recommended product testing and labeling for such non-profit consumer watchdog groups as the Consumers' Union; and he favored more governmental oversight.

In 1971, Victor Papanek published the classic *Design for the Real World* in which he admonished designers for the frivolity of much of their work. "By designing criminally unsafe automobiles that kill or maim, by creating whole new species of garbage to clutter up the landscape, and by choosing materials and processes that will pollute the air we breathe, designers have become a dangerous breed" (Papanek 1971: ix). He too, like Packard, identified three kinds of obsolescence "technological (a better or more elegant way of doing things is discovered), material (the product wears out), and artificial (the death-making of a product; either the materials are substandard and will never wear out in a predictable time span, or else significant parts are not replaceable or repairable)" (Papanek 1971: 34).

Papanek suggested leasing rather than buying, successful in several industries including automobiles, office equipment, movies and heavy tools, as one of the strategies that could be applied to products, especially those that undergo rapid upgrades. Leasing has been successful with several product categories and has potential for success. A cultural shift in the way we imagine and conceptualize our possessions would also be necessary to make this strategy a success. Will people exhibit sufficient care for things they do not own? Will we instead create attitudes and cultures of everyday life where nothing is cared for because it is only temporary, where things are not cherished because they will move into other hands?

If adopted on a large scale, this could signal a different form of material culture, where identities are generated collectively rather than individually.

THE ANNUAL MODEL CHANGE

The practice of planned obsolescence, in case of automobiles, generally refers to stylistic modifications unaccompanied by improvements in functional characteristics. This was certainly true in case of GM, which first introduced the annual model change in 1923 and quickly "increased its share of total industry sales dramatically from 13 percent to 43 percent in the five years between 1922 and 1927" (*Yale Law Journal* 1971: 579). Henry Ford, who had adamantly refused any form of restyling of the Model T, finally halted its production on 27 May 1927 to make way for the new Model A. "While Ford's market share had dropped from 51 percent to 9 percent between 1922 and 1927, the new model A picked the figures back up to 30 percent by 1929" (*Yale Law Journal* 1971: 567). Chrysler too, though at a smaller scale, reaped financial benefits of the practice of stylistic obsolescence.

A direct result of this policy was consolidation of market into the clutches of the three largest automakers: Ford, GM and Chrysler who, between 1923 and 1935, increased their combined market share from 65 percent to 90 percent. The impact on the industry was sizeable, and created tremendous hardships for smaller producers who were unable to scale up their operations. The *Yale Law Journal* (1971) identified "components integration, heavy advertising, franchised distribution [and] enormous capital requirements" as the four prime factors that gave the big three auto manufacturers their market advantage. In order to create new models on a yearly basis, manufacturers had to integrate components of the body and the engine and produce them internally. This replaced the standard procedure of buying components from suppliers and assembling them internally. Such integration was not possible for smaller manufacturers on a similar time scale. The new models had to be advertised widely and heavily to generate consumer interest, causing a substantial expense that only corporations with vast financial resources could afford. The rapid entry of new models complicated the maintenance of these cars and the big three were again able to establish and support dealer networks capable of being able to service the myriad variations. The *Yale Law Journal* declared, "annual styling change should be declared an unfair method of competition" in the automobile industry. General Motors, Ford and Chrysler have held a substantial grip on the American automobile market for decades but that has been shaken up by the financial crisis that commenced in the last few months of 2008 as C.E.O.s of the big three sought several billion dollars of "bailout funds" from the U.S. government to rescue their companies.

VARIATIONS ON THE PRACTICE OF OBSOLESCENCE

Slade (2006) distinguishes between three distinct versions of deliberate obsolescence in the history of its practice —technological, psychological and planned—and traces their emergence back to the second, third and fourth decades of the 1900s. As the name suggests, technological obsolescence occurs when emerging technologies start appearing in the form of new products displacing existing goods and services. Slade tracks this back to 1913 when the electric automobile starter replaced the hand crank, making older cars immediately undesirable. Today, this phenomenon is visible in the computer industry, where both hardware components and software rapidly become unusable as newer versions are released. In the 1920s, in order to increase sales and gain an edge over the competition, designers and manufacturers in the auto industry started introducing rapid changes in the appearance of things without improving technical performance, making older cars unfashionable and dropping them out of favor. General Motors, famously recognized as the pioneer of this sales mechanism in the automobile industry, called it dynamic obsolescence. Slade refers to it as progressive or psychological obsolescence. Finally, Slade explains planned obsolescence as "the assortment of techniques used to artificially limit the durability of a manufactured good in order to stimulate repetitive consumption" (2006: 5). In this case, he refers to the intentional use of weaker materials, the practice of adulteration and the purposeful reduction of component life spans.

The evolution of personal, portable stereos offers a classic case for the examination of technological obsolescence. Introduced in 1979, the Sony Walkman was the first such device that allowed people to listen to recorded music while on the move. It was quickly adopted, largely by young people, and became a substantial market success. Several variations later, it was pushed aside by the compact disc player, the Sony Discman, which signaled a shift away from analog to digital music. This device was followed by a brief interlude of the relatively unsuccessful mini disc player, the Sony M.D. Walkman. By this time, a large number of major electronics manufacturers had entered the market and Sony no longer had its competitive edge. Finally, the version we know today, the mp3 player, appeared in 1998 and is now manufactured by over 75 different companies, in hundreds of different designs. All these devices operate on a variety of different technological platforms and have spawned several software and hardware solutions to allow interoperability among them. As emerging technologies appear through new products and are popularly adopted, they displace older technologies and products. However, it is important to recognize that these earlier technologies do not entirely die off; they continue to have an afterlife in some form within specific groups of people. As new products are introduced, the material landscape undergoes gradual mutation. The new and the old often co-exist during the transition phases, and with greater and greater disconnect as the newer technologies diffuse and become central to everyday life. As the devices used in the consumption of music slip away from popular use, so do the media associated with them. The first long-playing records (LPs) were pressed in 1948, cassettes were introduced in 1964, compact discs in 1982, and the mp3 format for digital audio in 1987. Though the ubiquity of mp3 players may suggest otherwise, all formats are still being actively produced and consumed. It is not entirely unusual to find music lovers who own and maintain certain sections of their collection in vinyl, CD, and mp3 formats simultaneously although they may routinely only use one media type. In many cases, certain media forms have lost some of their use-value but in process have acquired much more symbolic and nostalgic value: "Vinyl records are just a small scratch on the surface when it comes to total album sales—only about 0.2%, compared to 10% for digital downloads and 89.7% for CDs, according to Nielsen SoundScan--but these numbers may underrepresent the vinyl trend since they don't always include sales at smaller indie shops where vinyl does best" (Dell 2008). Can vinyl be declared obsolete when it continues to be used, albeit in significantly lesser quantities and in niche markets? According to the Recording Industry Association of America (R.I.A.A.) statistics, vinyl LPs constituted 9.2 percent of the total U.S. music sales in 1989, and 0.6 percent in 2006. Similarly, full-length cassettes for the same time period made up 54.8 percent in 1989 and 0.8 percent in 2006.[3] When, therefore, can things be declared obsolete? Probably never. Large quantities of products are discarded as they fall out of use but it is common to find a few samples handed down to others, stored in garages for nostalgic value, re-purposed for other applications, or displayed in museums. Their quantities, however, are too insignificant to have substantial impact on the durable goods economy. Though many of these products may be declared technologically obsolete, they are by no means culturally obsolete.

One of the first personal digital assistants (P.D.A.s) in the market was the Newton, introduced by Apple in 1993. Too large to be truly mobile, too expensive to be popularly affordable and too early to be adopted widely, Newton was officially, and amidst sincere protest, discontinued in 1998. However, the product never really died:

> Fans still take their Newtons to Jobs' keynote speeches at Macworld and wave them in the air in silent protest. It doesn't seem to matter. Without any help from Apple, Newton users have kept the platform current with technological changes through a series of software hacks and hardware fixes, most of which are freely available. (Kahney 2004: 220)

Through their devotion to the product, a few enthusiasts have steadfastly held the Newton at the brink of total obsolescence. Though a large number of electronic products are pushed into obsolescence due to technological upgrades, the Newton was not intentionally killed off to introduce a new and updated version of the product; it was discontinued due to poor market performance. Apple stopped production of the Newton within five years of its launch but it inspired a community of followers who, through their obsession with the product, have protracted its life, defying its "official" death.

Not deterred by the lack of support from Apple, and often ignoring the incredulous looks they get from technophiles and early adopters, the "abandoned Apple Newton brand community" (Muniz and Schau 2005) continues using the "discontinued" product. In their analysis, Muniz and Schau find parallels between the communal activities of Newton fans and those of religious groups, as "supernatural, religious, and magical motifs are common in the narratives of the Newton community" (2005: 739). The authors list five shared narratives that hold the Newton community together—persecution, faith, survival, miraculous recovery and resurrection. Newton users feel Apple persecuted them by abandoning them and not providing any support in spite of their loyalty. The second narrative theme of faith refers to the belief they have in the community in being able to keep Newton alive in spite of all odds. The faith is sustained by technological success stories that are shared by community members. Tales of survival refer to the ordeals through which individual Newtons are able to prevail in their constant struggle to stay alive. Stories of miraculous recovery included in the fourth narrative, not entirely unusual in the use of computing devices, essentially refer to accounts by users of failed components inexplicably starting to work again, rather like magic. The final narrative refers to the hope of Newton's resurrection by Apple, a sentiment that played a significant role in generating excitement amongst members. These were rumors that never did transform into reality. However, the metaphor of religiosity is only partially successful in explaining the rituals adopted by the Newton community. Narratives of faith and resurrection are structurally pliable enough to be meaningful in the context of commodity fetishism but concepts of persecution, survival and recovery function better as anecdotal instances rather than community strategies. Religion also does not help explain the creativity Newton owners exercise in keeping their products alive. Here Stuart Hall's study of post-war British youth offers a more apposite model.

> Negotiation, resistance, struggle: the relations between a subordinate and a dominant culture, wherever they fall within this spectrum, are always intensely active, always oppositional... The subordinate class brings to this "theatre of struggle" a repertoire of strategies and responses—ways of coping as well as resisting. (Hall *et al.* 1993: 44)

In their efforts to keep an obsolete product alive, Newton users operate as a subordinate culture, negotiating with, resisting the pressures of, and struggling against two dominant groups—an unheeding corporation (Apple) and a mocking public. In order to maintain the usability of their products, they have to hack software, fashion their own hardware and stave off rapidly advancing newer technologies. It is clear that this involves strategies of coping and resisting—coping with the lack of upgrades, difficulty of repair, and the constant fear of not being able to keep their machines working, while resisting the pressures of such devices as the Palm Pilot, the Blackberry, the iPhone, etc. According to Muniz and Schau, Newton users "are rejecting a system that caters to the lowest common denominator and perpetuates a short life cycle in the name of incremental innovation and planned obsolescence" (2005: 744).

It is important to note that ingenuity and creativity form key driving forces of inspiration for the Newton community. Users create software and hardware solutions for the Newton and share them with others at such sites as NewtonTalk.net. Almost 600 messages were posted at this site in the month of January 2008; a statistic that serves as testimony to popularity of the product and the need for the members to communicate and share. By publishing tips on enhancing the capabilities of the Newton and solutions for fixing problems, users are able to share their creativity with other members of the community.

The Newton connotes several meanings within and outside the product's community. It is at once an obsolete product and a resurrected object, a product of ridicule and one of pride, a location for creative production and sustainable consumption. It is a signifier of community and resistance, struggle and success. Arguably, the Newton may not be classified as a traditional example of technological obsolescence, because though deliberately killed off by Apple, the reasons had more to do with market failure rather than the need to stimulate desire by introducing a new version.

THE ECONOMICS OF DURABILITY

In marketing literature, obsolescence is defined as "the relative loss in value due to styling changes (style obsolescence) or quality improvements (functional obsolescence) in subsequent versions of the product" (Levinthal and Purohit 1989: 35). When obsolescence is anticipated or expected, consumer willingness to pay for existing products drops while increasing for the newer models, often leading to a decrease in sales. Consequently, this results in a loss of revenue, especially during times of joint production when both the old and the new products are manufactured. By financial analyses, buy-back and trade-in programs are truly successful when the new product offers substantial advantage. Considering these conditions, is there incentive for the corporation to manufacture products that are durable over a long period of time?

If not carefully monitored and managed, an economy of deliberate obsolescence, in which profits are tied to short life cycles of durable goods and rapid consumption of non-durables, can quickly lead to hyper-consumption, generation of excessive waste and environmental degradation. Therefore, extending the life of durable goods and minimizing quantities of non-durables are both recognized strategies of sustainable design. In part due to economics of the used goods industry and in part due to design, most consumer products start depreciating in value soon after their purchase. This degradation in value is primarily economic, but the passage of time often diminishes our attachment to goods and therefore also signals a decline in symbolic or emotional value, hastening their demise. There are, of course, some things that do not lose value as they age, and some that appreciate over time. Family photographs, wedding rings, the Eames lounge, antiques, leather jackets, jeans are but some examples.

DURABILITY IN JEANS

According to a market research study published in 2006 by the Mintel International Group (Mintel.com 2008), Americans buy roughly 450 million pairs of jeans each year.

> The history of Jeans begins in the mid-nineteenth century in California. A robust, indigo-coloured cotton from Nîmes, denim ("de Nîmes") was imported via Genoa (French "Gênes", hence English "jeans") for the manufacture of a work pant durable enough for the needs of the gold-miners. (Kramer 2006: 289)

In their journey from the mine as sturdy work pants to the metropolis as urban hipwear, jeans have acquired several social meanings. In the early 1900s, denim overalls served as uniforms for women involved in war production, becoming icons of American solidarity. Later, during the depression years of the 1930s, urbanites vacationing on dude ranches in the American heartland brought them back to wear in the city. In addition, artists and painters started wearing them as well. It was in the 1950s when they gained significant popularity through Hollywood and the star power of such men as James Dean and Elvis Presley. In the 1960s and 1970s, blue jeans became the pants of choice for left-leaning opponents of the Vietnam war and hippies as symbols of their resistance. In many cases, they signified the wearer's opposition to a middle-class, conservative, consuming America.

Today, jeans signify both utility as well as style, casual wear as well as fashion wear and ordinariness as well as exclusivity. Though these terms are conceptually opposite in meaning, users do not typically perceive them as conflicting and are able to negotiate between them with ease:

> Framing the garment's status dialectic was the contest of polarities, one pole continuing to emphasize and extend blue jeans" "base-line" symbolism of democracy, utility, and classlessness, the other seeking to reintroduce the traditional claims to taste, distinction, and hierarchical division. (Any individual wearer, and often the garment itself, might try to meld motifs from both sides in the hope of registering a balanced, yet appropriately ambivalent, statement). (Davis 1989: 73)

In view of such ambivalence, what individual, group or social identities do jeans express? Or, what are we trying to say (if anything) through our clothing? Theories of fashion have suggested that what drives fashion is "sexual allure, relief from boredom, generalized zeitgeist effusions, economic self-interest (i.e., a clothiers' conspiracy) and the symbolic representations of invidious class distinctions" (Davis 1989: 338). Clearly, blue jeans are available in styles abundant and diverse enough to accommodate all the characterizations listed above, including low and snug jeans designed to display human form, baggy jeans that completely hide the body, inexpensive casual jeans and $4,000 personalized designer pairs studded with diamonds. Davis also suggests that fashion in general is replete with polarities, the more prominent ones being "youth versus age, masculinity vs. femininity, androgyny vs. singularity, inclusiveness vs. exclusiveness, work versus play, domesticity vs. worldliness, display vs. modesty" (1985: 18). This polarity inherent in the social meanings of jeans is in part responsible for the wide transgenerational, crosscultural, multinational and all income group popularity they enjoy. "Blue jeans cover and express, turn us into members of a tribe and hug our body, are generic, simple, and yet expressive. They do not so much exhibit a use or our body as they evoke both while working as the most versatile parts of the complicated wardrobe of our lives" (Betsky 1997: 124). It is this versatility and polysemy that make jeans durable goods.

In the discussion of durability, jeans serve as a category of product that has engendered a new relationship between form and function. As their functionality erodes, as jeans get thinner and start to tear though use, they do not lose any of their stylistic value. In fact, form gains value. In other words, jeans, in a direct reversal of planned obsolescence, look better as they age. Worn, torn, well-washed and threadbare jeans are not only more comfortable— they are (often) hipper, cooler and more stylish. The tough denim fabric is able to withstand use and abuse, and over time becomes a repository for the wearer's experiences. Woven into the faded fabric and ripped seams are memories and stories. The market, quickly realizing the potential of the worn look, started offering pre-faded, pre-ripped jeans to appear old while still new. According to the popular *People* magazine that chronicles lives of Hollywood stars, singer Faith Hill does not quickly discard her jeans: "I wore one pair until the seat came off ... good jeans are like wine-they get better with age" (*People* 2007: 19). If products can be designed to become more desirable over time, if engineers can create materials that wear gracefully and in such ways to become more stylish, people might be less apt to discard things quickly. As Ezio Manzini notes, "it's time for a new generation of products that can age slowly and in a dignified way, become our partners in life, and support our memories" (Chapman 2005: 24). The strategy of increasing the emotional value of things and therefore their usable life is one mechanism of battling obsolescence.

However, it is important to ask what level of durability should be designed into things. Can things possess permanent durability or eternal life, and if yes, what would be their cultural import? How would you value something that was "eternally yours?" In 1995, Henk Muis and Arnoud Odding founded Eternally Yours, an organization committed to collecting and sharing knowledge about mechanisms by which to extend the cultural lives of products. Through publications and projects, this self-described "tiny group of enthusiasts" has gathered information for designers about product endurance. Like the classification of mechanisms of obsolescence, researchers at Eternally Yours categorize product life spans into three groups—technical, economical, and psychological. The inability to get something repaired signals an end to its technical lifespan; the introduction of a new version automatically refers to the end of an existing product's economic lifespan; and when a thing does not fit the lifestyle needs of the user, it has outlived its psychological lifespan.

Statistics from the Okala Ecodesign Guide show that functionality is often not the reason we discard products (White, St. Pierre and Belletire 2007). Figure 7.1, adapted from the research compiled by Eternally Yours, makes it instantly obvious that computers often get discarded while they are "still functioning." However, in case of electronic goods "still functioning" may not necessarily mean fully operational. As newer versions of hardware and software are released, older computers start losing their upgradeability, connectivity with newer machines and compatibility with peripheral devices, quickly making them useless while still functional.

How long should things be designed to last? If things did not break down, did not need to be replaced with more fashionable versions, or did not routinely become technologically

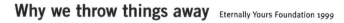

Why we throw things away <small>Eternally Yours Foundation 1999</small>

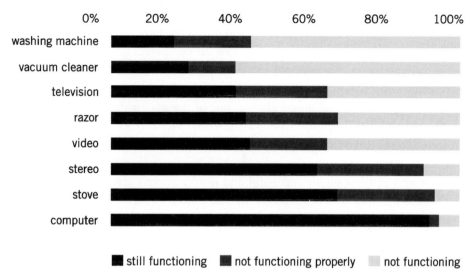

Figure 7.1. Why We Throw Things Away. From the Okala Ecodesign Guide (original from Eternally Yours, Van Hinte 2004).

unusable, we would undoubtedly generate less waste and minimize impacts on the environment. Current manufacturing practices and consumption patterns suggest that the desirability of durability is questionable. Companies are urged to innovate and improve upon what exists. In addition, people get tired of things; neomania sets in. Though durable goods could signify cost-saving, many consumers may not find them desirable over long periods of time unless the objects have the potential of accruing antique or symbolic value. Durability holds value for consumers who are sensitive to environmental issues and keen on changing their lifestyles to minimize their ecological footprint. The Natural Marketing Institute refers to this group as LOHAS (Lifestyles of Health and Sustainability) consumers. They are individuals who:

> are interested in products covering a range of market sectors and sub-sectors, including: green building supplies, socially responsible investing and "green stocks", alternative healthcare, organic clothing and food, personal development media, yoga and other fitness products, eco-tourism and more… Approximately 16% percent of the adults in the U.S., or 35 million people, are currently considered LOHAS Consumers.[4]

Durability may also be valued in lower income group markets, where financial hardship may make durable and repairable goods more desirable. The lifecycles of consumer goods in poorer nations is significantly higher than in more affluent countries, often due to necessity, access to inexpensive forms of repair, availability of parts and a culture of frugality and prudence.

DURABLE THINGS

The anti-obsolescence literature, produced by such scholars as Vance Packard (1960), John Kenneth Galbraith (1998, original in 1958) and others did have its effect, especially on the automotive industry in the 1960s. One of the first car companies to promote the culture of durability through its smartly minimal anti-obsolescence advertisements was Volkswagen. The advertising copy critiqued planned obsolescence and poked fun at American cars. In a direct mockery of the annual model change, one of the ads for the Beetle shows a single image of the car with the caption "The '51, '52, '53, '54, '55, '56, '57, '58, '59, '60, '61 Volkswagen." In the advertising copy, Volkswagen reassures readers by saying, "We don't make changes lightly. And never to make the Volkswagen look differently, only to make it better." Several of these highly successful and quirky adverts, designed by Doyle Dane Bernbach, used the notion of obsolescence for the contrary effect. Other companies, such as Volvo, ridiculed consumers who succumbed to the practice of the annual model change. In a 1967 advertisement, Volvo sarcastically suggests that a paper car is the next step in the evolution of the stylistic obsolescence of cars. The text reads:

> at a time when people trade in their cars every two or three years, it's reasonable to assume that the next step might be paper cars. After all, we're living in a "throw-away society." So why not jump in with both feet? Why not have a car you can trade every

Figure 7.2.   Volvo Ridicules the American Practice of Planned Obsolescence. Image courtesy of Dan Johnston, Volvo.

month? Why not have a dandy polka-dot one for weekends and a swinging striped one for going out on the town and, of course, a plain black one for when you want to be serious?

Further along, the ad promotes durability because Volvo knows that "to make a car that lasts, you begin with nice, thick steel."

Volvo owners are known to keep their cars for a long time, and some are proud members of the Volvo High Mileage Club, affiliation to which is available only to those how have clocked more than 150,000 miles (241,406 kilometers) on their cars. According to this club (and the Guinness Book of World Records), Irv Gordon of East Patchogue, NY holds the leading spot on the list with a stunning 2.7 million miles clocked on one vehicle. The car, miraculously surviving with the original engine, radio, axles and transmission is certainly one in a million, and has become an icon of durability. "I'll keep on driving," Gordon said, "but whether I drive three million miles is more up to me than it is the car. The car's parts may be able to take it, but I'm not so sure about my own."[5] This car is eternally his. In a phone conversation, Gordon said, "I bought it on June 30th, 1966 from the Volvo showroom for $4,150 ... when it had one-tenth of a mile on it." As of July 2009, the odometer read 2,715,000 miles.

Gordon recognizes the impact that this vehicle has had in his life. In a conversation, Gordon (2009) said: "You never know how these decisions could affect the rest of your life. If it wasn't for the car, everything that I do these days would be totally different. I've had

Figure 7.3.   Irv Gordon with his 2.7 Million-mile Volvo. Image courtesy of Irv Gordon and Volvo.

opportunities to go places and meet people that I wouldn't have had if I didn't own this the car." And, as he suggests, if he is outlived by his car, he will have achieved the status that Ford desired for all his consumers when he said, "we want the man who buys one of our products never to have to buy another" (Ford 1922: 149). In such scenarios the culture of durability is embraced and encouraged.

Ray and Charles Eames designed their classic lounge chair and ottoman for Herman Miller in 1956. Joe Schwartz, then Marketing Director for Herman Miller recalls, "I think it sold for about 900 U.S. dollars at that time. And not a lot of people liked its aesthetic then … it was an unfamiliar visual object. Eames made it to give it as a gift for his friend Billy Wilder. It was not originally designed as a Herman Miller product" (Schwartz, personal interview 2008). Over 50 years since their introduction, the lounge chair and ottoman are still being manufactured with minor modifications and they continue to sell. Durability, endurance and timelessness are not easy to capture in the design of products. Herman

Figure 7.4.   The Eames Lounge Chair. Image courtesy of Herman Miller, Inc.

Miller C.E.O. Brian Walker believes that planned obsolescence is by no means a necessary condition for either innovation or market success. "By increasing durability, extending 12 year warranties to customers and developing long lasting design solutions, we strive to create a sustainable world. In the contract furniture business, customers do not want short-lived goods; they want their furnishings to endure over time" (Walker, personal interview 2008).

According to Walker, "functional and aesthetic durability, a sense of timelessness has always been the ethical underpinning of Herman Miller design. This translated into the company's environmental stewardship. We have always believed that we would be doing the right thing ethically if we built products that lasted a person's lifetime." When asked how the company keeps up with trends and changes inspired by fashion, Walker introduced the notion of a timeless platform on which stylistic updates could be easily designed:

> When you have a product that is durable aesthetically and functionally, it is important to celebrate and nurture that timelessness, but you also have to plan design strategies that can keep the product contemporary and fashionable. For example, for the Eames Aluminum Group, a couple of years ago, we introduced a series of new textiles that could play on that very timeless platform. While products can have long lifecycles, we also have to attend to the fact that there is a fresh fashion element is brought forward on a regular basis. This extends the durability and sustainability of the platform even further making it relevant to the consumers coming back to it.

The ethic of durability at Herman Miller seems to emerge from a solid research foundation and the desire for a timeless aesthetic. Walker mentions that for systems furniture like

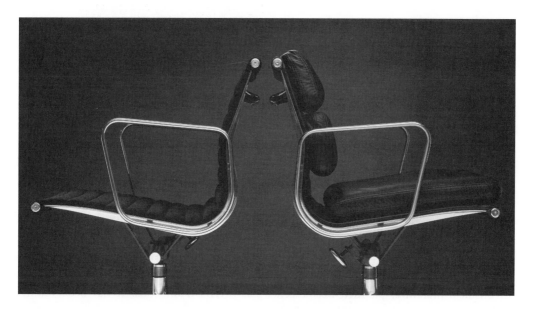

Figure 7.5.   Herman Miller Aluminum Group. Image courtesy of Herman Miller, Inc.

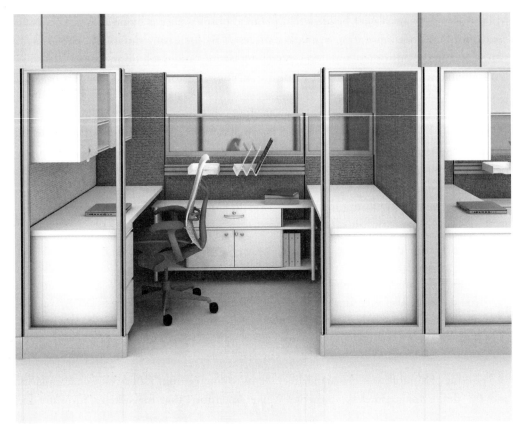

Figure 7.6.   Herman Miller Action Office. Image courtesy of Herman Miller, Inc.

Herman Miller's Action Office, durability made sense from two perspectives "When you combine the Propstian approach of non-obsolete, expandable systems, and the Eames ethic of 'good goods,' you get a situation where these ideas play symbiotically with one another to create not only a sustainable platform but also great individual products." Walker here refers to one of the pioneers of design research and systems thinking in furniture, Robert Propst. The phrase "good goods" is attributed to Charles Eames and it describes "purposeful and practical solutions that have integrity, clarity, and honesty" (Herman Miller Materials Program 2009). "For Charles Eames, these were simple things, like ... a ball of twine or a box of chalk ... honest and simply beautiful. That's why they were so enduring" (Schwartz, personal interview 2008).

THE ECONOMICS AND MARKETING OF OBSOLESCENCE

In business literature, planned obsolescence has several definitions. It has been bluntly defined as "a marketing practice that capitalizes on short-run material wearout, style changes, and functional product changes" (Evans 2004: 120). Another characterization of planned obsolescence is based upon features and attributes. "We define a situation of planned obsolescence as one in which a supplier deliberately withholds attributes that could be added costlessly to the good and provide positive utility" (Grout and Park 2005: 597). Yet another definition is derived from the notion that new goods deteriorate the value of existing ones, making them obsolete. "Obsolescence is defined as the relative loss in value due to styling changes (style obsolescence) or quality improvements (functional obsolescence) in subsequent versions of the product" (Levinthal and Purohit 1989: 35). In his seminal paper titled *An Economic Theory of Planned Obsolescence*, Jeremy Bulow defines the term as "the production of goods with uneconomically short useful lives so that customers will have to make repeat purchases" (1986: 729). In some economic literature, planned obsolescence is defined as "a strategy of shortening the lifetime of a product after it is released onto the market. Under this strategy, the manufacturer 'convinces' the consumer to replace an old product with a new one, thereby rendering the lifetime of the old product shorter than its actual useful lifetime" (Orbach 2004: 26). In this case, planned obsolescence is presented in contrast to *contrived durability*, which according to Orbach refers to "a strategy of shortening the product lifetime before it is released onto the market" (2004: 25). Such distinction is not found outside the economic literature, where these terms are used interchangeably. Orbach gives annual model changes of cars and revising editions of textbooks as examples of planned obsolescence. On the other hand, contrived durability refers to the choice a corporation may have to make between manufacturing a light bulb that can last one year or ten years. A manufacturer may possess the technological and financial means to produce both, and production cost for both may be identical, but Orbach's analysis demonstrates that the durable goods monopolist will prefer to produce the one-year bulb. If the manufacturer produces the ten-year bulb, it will be offered for a premium price ($10 for example) in comparison to the one-year bulb, which may be relatively inexpensive ($1 for example). At launch, the ten-year bulb is expected to attract only high-valuation customers, those who can afford to and do not mind the high cost, while the low-valuation customers continue using other technologies. Consumers generally expect that, over a period of time, when everyone who can afford the ten-year bulb has one, prices will start to drop. This expectation minimizes initial sales and forces manufacturers to lower price, thereby lowering profit margins. In contrast, the lower priced one-year bulb does not create such consumer expectations, sells in larger quantities, allows the manufacturer to maintain optimal pricing and therefore boosts profits. This argument makes it clear that, considered purely from an economic perspective, the manufacturer is more incentivized to promote products with lower durability.

Arguments for and against this practice are plentiful in the scholarship from economic as well as ethical points of view. On one hand, the practice of obsoleting products is critiqued as inefficient, welfare reducing, unfair to consumers and competitors, wasteful, unsustainable and monopolistic. On the other hand, it is perceived as an active means by which to stimulate the economy, enhance innovation, keep up with technology and satisfy consumer demand. The response to the disapproving judgment of obsolescence is well summarized in the following comment:

> Marketers respond to criticism thusly: Planned obsolescence is responsive to people's desires as to prices, styles, and features and is not coercive; without product turnover, people would be disenchanted by the lack of choices; consumers like disposable items and often discard them before they lose their effectiveness; firms use materials that reduce prices; competition requires firms to offer the best products possible and not hold back improvements; and, for such items as clothing, people desire continuous style changes. (Evans 2004: 121)

Through mathematical modeling—the discussion of which extends beyond the scope of this text—economists have demonstrated that obsoleting products is of economic advantage to firms operating in competitive as well as monopolistic markets (Waldman 1993, Grout and Park 2005, Levinthal and Purohit 1989). Interestingly, this practice is not considered unlawful by the U.S. antitrust laws. In fact, it is perceived as a strategy that will promote competition by inviting other companies to create more durable goods, a market condition favored by those very laws. Entirely absent from this equation is the discussion of the creation of waste, generation of desire, material inequities and ethics.

According to economic theory, the launch of a new version (Model B) fractures the life of the existing product (Model A) into two economic time intervals, generally labeled Period 1 and Period 2. Period 1 characterizes the duration when Model A is the latest version available from that firm, and Period 2 signifies the downgraded and therefore less desirable status of Model A on account of the appearance of Model B. Introduction of Model B dramatically drops the demand and therefore price of Model A. In such cases, corporations have three options—to immediately halt the production of Model A, to continue simultaneous production of Models A and B, or offer buy-back programs for Model A. Economic analyses recommend that companies should commit to a phasing out of Model A in Period 2, as it could potentially cut into the profits of Model B, a process referred to as cannibalization.[6] Additionally, buy-back programs are financially successful only if Model B has substantial feature improvements and user benefits over Model A. In the high-tech industry, where technological obsolescence is rampant and therefore expected by consumers, rumors and information leaks of the impending introduction of Model B often lead to reduction in the perceived value of Model A, a substantial drop in its demand, and a willingness on the part of consumers to delay purchase.

Bulow suggests that monopolistic corporations,[7] when they do not face the threat of competition from other corporations trying to enter the same market with a similar product, will create products that have inefficiently short useful lives, thereby promoting obsolescence. By his analysis, monopolies and oligopolies that do face entry by competitors can benefit financially by increasing product durability. When people own products that have long lives, they are less likely to switch them out for a competitor's offering. In such cases, durability deters entry. He also notes that oligopolies may gain by colluding to increase the rate of obsolescence. In other words, lowered durability can lead to higher industry profits, bringing windfall to all firms. "If an oligopoly such as the American automobile industry were colluding on durability, then, it would likely be in the direction of planned obsolescence. The entry of foreign competitors to make the industry more competitive would then move durability toward efficient levels" (Bulow 1986: 742). Therefore, by Bulow's analysis, as an industry moves from monopolistic or oligopolistic conditions to competitive market, there are lesser gains from higher obsolescence and higher gains from increased durability.[8]

Supporters present technological progress as a vital result of planned obsolescence. "If products are too durable, potential innovators may lack the incentives to invest in the development of a new technology and the economy may stagnate as a result" (Fishman, Gandall and Shy 1993: 361). This argument is founded upon the erroneous assumption that investment in innovation is only possible in situations where a corporation is able to garner profit on short-lived goods. The authors suggest that if consumers are in possession of a durable, well-functioning Model A, the firm has no incentive to innovate. By this account, durable products become signifiers of economic stagnation and technological sluggishness. This characterization stands in diametric opposition to the meanings of timelessness and enduring design. Technological progress, understood on these terms only leads to further obsolescence. "When progress is understood as the historical consequence of an increasing technological perfection that raises our expectations, then it can no longer simply satisfy appetites—it also provokes a competing new desire for more new experiences (and thus more objects)" (Scanlan 2005: 133). It might serve us better to measure technological progress through social indicators rather than in purely technological or economic metrics.

CULTURE OF DISPOSABILITY

What happens to goods that become obsolete? Where do they go? Many continue their existence in households within closets, attics, basements and garages; some may be donated to charities or handed down to family members; several others get tossed as rubbish to be picked up by utility services; a scant few are recycled; even fewer reappropriated and converted into other goods; and some destroyed. Where something ends up at the conclusion of its useful lifecycle is determined by a myriad of factors including the life of the product, its price, its value to the owner, the materials it is made of, city waste management regulations, and so on. Of all non-reusable items, product packaging often has the shortest lifespan as it is discarded almost immediately after purchase. Consumables such as disposable razors, diapers and batteries that have life spans of a few months follow suit. On the heels of these short-lived goods are such products as mobile phones, computers, keyboards, etc. with lives of one to three years. "[M]odern society remains largely ignorant, often willfully so, of the inevitable end that the once cherished and shiny new objects of consumer society will find" (Scanlan 2005: 131). All things are waste in the making. Once in pristine condition, and having lived their useful lives, our personal possessions make their way out of our homes into public locations of discard where they rot as anonymous heaps of rubbish.

Things are not static, inanimate objects. They are entities in constant animation, steadily marching from the time of their birth toward the landfill, the incinerator, or the recycling station either to be condemned to eons of slow decomposition, rapid reduction to ash, or pulverization and reappearance in modified form. It is only for a brief pause that they are in contact with humans. And, the less durable these things are, the faster their journey and transformation to waste. By reducing product life, mechanisms of contrived durability and planned obsolescence directly contribute to the speed with objects go in and out of our lives. Once discarded and outside the home, the object loses value becoming no more a possession of the individual or the family, but that of the city, the waste management system and society. Divested of our control, the object becomes invisible to us in physical terms, its materiality no longer a matter of our concern. Only in abstract terms may it reappear into our lives, either through images of landfills, through recycled content in products, or through some form of air, water or soil pollution.

Prior to the twentieth century, Americans did not generate the volume or type of waste produced today. Individualized packaging was not the norm as household supplies were sold in bulk; disposable paper products were neither available nor acceptable and some use was found for almost all domestic scrap. When products broke down, they were repaired rather than replaced. Handing down used goods to family members was the norm. Nothing was really classified as junk; everything was salvaged and turned around as raw material for some other process. In the early part of the twentieth century, the mechanized mass manufacturing of goods started changing the landscape of how goods were produced, promoted and purchased. Strasser (1999) catalogs a variety of events that led to the demise of these practices. New packaging materials such as aluminum foil and cellophane were introduced, and corporations such as Procter & Gamble and Heinz started offering goods in individualized, branded packaging. Scavenging and salvaging practices, so far carried out by individuals or groups, were taken over by city-wide waste management systems. Advertising grew rapidly and with it ushered consumer culture. The steady growth of affluence gave people the means to buy, discard and buy anew rather than save and reuse. Towards the late 1800s, the price of paper started to drop, leading to its use in a host of applications including clothing, utensils, toiletries and home décor. In spite of initial resistance, single-use shirt collars, cups, toilet paper, towels, buckets, curtains, carpets and several other disposable items eventually started gaining acceptability, primarily for two main reasons: convenience and hygiene. Personal cleanliness and hygiene, signifiers of class, were made available to a much larger population. "The selling points of modern products—styling, technological superiority, convenience, and cleanliness—all amounted to arguments for disposing of things rather than seeking ways to reuse them. Together they fostered a new kind of relationship to the material world, to production, and to disposal" (Strasser 1999: 173). Cleaning products of all kinds—paper towels, soaps, sinks and tubs—were flooding the market. These chemicals and devices were put to use to combat the newly formulated fear of and disgust for germs, popularized by germ theory, which attributes all infectious and contagious diseases to invisible microorganisms. Suddenly, cleanliness involved not only the removal of dust and dirt, but also the annihilation of these ubiquitous germs purportedly crawling on every surface. Items of common use became harbingers of disease, and disposable items the panacea. Dixie Cups, one of the largest manufacturers of disposable paper cups in the United States were previously called Health Kups. Manufactured by the Individual Drinking Cup Company, the foldable Health Kups were impossible to reuse; indeed, the company itself claimed that it would be "destroyed if you fold it for second use."[9] Despite initial resistance to the single-use cups, they quickly become the norm, accepted and used at all public venues. Paper straws, paper napkins and paper plates followed the cups in quick succession, and have survived to date. Manufacturers launched campaigns about the sanitary qualities of paper napkins over germ-infested handkerchiefs, and magazines such as *Good Housekeeping* promoted their use.

The single-use disposable product therefore gained currency as the healthy and safe alternative to the durable, reusable good. The combination of cheap paper, aggressive advertising and the wide acceptance of germ theory were effective in this transition. It is evident today that this practice has been tremendously wasteful and damaging to the environment. Disposable goods were promoted as being hygienic and convenient, especially to the woman of the household. Frederick (1929), through her articles and books, recommended them so that the woman could increase her household efficiency, save time and therefore gain some freedom from endless domestic toil. Paper towels started being used in public bathrooms in the early 1900s, and gradually migrated to the home where, it was suggested by Frederick, they could be used in the kitchen to soak up oil from frying, wiping counters, and wrapping leftovers. During the postwar boom in the 1950s, as new materials and technologies discovered during wartime research were spun off into domestic applications; more disposable goods appeared on store shelves. In addition to paper products and aluminum foil, disposable packaging in the form of TV dinners and other frozen foods also created significant volumes of waste.

The disposable item is simultaneously one and many. The paper cup, for instance, embodies the meaning of singularity through its one-time use, but also that of infinitude; although one is discarded immediately after use, there are identical millions waiting and ready at hand. Their value, positive or negative, lies not in their individuality, but their collectivity. The paper cup is joined today by its cousin, the expanded polystyrene (E.P.S.) cup, another ubiquitous commodity in fast-food restaurants, manufactured from petroleum-based chemicals. In his ontological analysis, Kennedy finds the E.P.S. cup "shrouded in a veil of obscurity" and attributes this mystery partly to the material and its mode of manufacture (2007: 137). Thicker than paper and yet lighter, it seems to be made out of something "immaterial, a substance imperceptible to the body" (Kennedy 2007: 137). People do not know how E.P.S. is made or what it contains. The length of time it spends

Figure 7.7.   Paper, E.P.S. Foam and Earthenware Cups.

in the hands of people is infinitesimally small compared to the millions of years required in the natural production of the crude oil from whence it comes, or the centuries it may spend in a landfill stubbornly unwilling to surrender to the natural order of decay. Disposable in life, it is durable in death. The cup is never what one pays for—it is free; what one pays for is the liquid it contains. Stripped of value, stripped of durability, the cup inspires no caring. It is never washed, dried and reused, never on proud display in hutches, never attached to personal memories. Its fleeting existence in our lives signifies convenience, efficiency and sanitariness.

The growing awareness of the climate crisis has foregrounded the environmental issues surrounding disposability. While the single-use paper and E.P.S. cups signified convenience and cleanliness a few decades ago, they now also signal the wasteful practice of affluent societies. It is generally assumed that reusable porcelain or earthenware cups that do not generate waste are environmentally better. However, such assumptions about the greenness of products can be refuted through scientific, peer-reviewed studies. Scientists have determined that life cycle assessment (L.C.A.), the process by which "to evaluate the environmental effects associated with any given activity from the initial gathering of raw material from the earth until the point at which all residuals are returned to the earth" is one of the best ways to gauge the environmental impacts of a product (Vigon *et al.* 1994: 1). Performing an L.C.A. of a product is an incredibly complex process that requires significant amounts of data. The impacts are generally calculated over five distinct phases of the product's life: "extraction and processing of raw materials; manufacturing; transportation, and distribution; use/reuse/maintenance; recycling and composting; and final disposition" (Vigon *et al.* 1994: 6). The objective of an L.C.A. is to quantify the embodied energy and resource use involved in manufacturing the product, and determine the harmful effects of the environmental releases to humans, air, water and land.[10] Scientists can then use this data to recommend strategies by which to minimize the harmful impacts of the products.

Several L.C.A.s of single- and multiple use cups have been performed and the results are far from conclusive. The Netherlands Organisation of Applied Scientific Research performed L.C.A.s on a reusable porcelain cup and saucer, a reusable earthenware cup, a disposable paper cup, a disposable paper cup with a reusable sleeve and a disposable polystyrene cup (Ligthart and Ansems 2007). All were benchmarked against 1000 servings of hot drinks (coffee, tea, etc.) from a vending machine or dispenser in a work environment and the results showed no clear winner. The largest impacts from reusable cups were due to water and energy usage in cleaning, while the largest impacts for the disposable cups were found to occur during the extraction of the raw materials and production of the cup (Ligthart and Ansems 2007). Another study in the journal *Science*, which unfortunately does not include an examination of multiuse cups, suggests that paper cups pose a bigger environmental threat than E.P.S. cups (Hocking 1991). Yet another study suggests that for a multi-use cup to be environmentally superior to a single use cup in "serving 1000 liters of draught beverages" (Garrido and Alvarez del Castillo 2007), it has to be used at least ten times. All analyses are based on life cycle assessment. According to Philip White, Chair of the Ecodesign Section for the Industrial Designers Society of America:

> the variation in conclusions depend upon process inventory data (the specific emissions, land use changes and resource depletion values that are measured by the data collectors for each process and material in the system), assumptions about the various parts of the system being assessed (how far it travels and by what mode, whether or not the wood in the paper is considered to be biogenic or anthropogenic, energy required per wash, how many times it can be reused prior to disposal, whether it will be recycled, landfilled or incinerated, whether the landfill captures methane or releases it into the atmosphere), and the impact characterization method (some 15 characterization methods are commonly used at this time). (White, personal correspondence, 22 November 2008)

The environmental meanings of things (green or not green, benign or toxic), which may seem easy to judge for such simple products as cups, are in fact shrouded in a decision-making process that involves complex data sets, system boundary conditions and characterization methodology. It is possible that the selection of soap, type of dishwasher and frequency of washing could tilt the greenness scale of an earthenware cup from the best to the worst environmental choice from a set of alternatives.

Another single-use everyday product central to the life of consumption is the disposable plastic grocery bag:

> In January [2008] almost 42 billion plastic bags were used worldwide, according to resuablebags.com; the figure increases by more than half a million bags every minute. A vast majority are not reused ending up as waste—in landfills or as litter. Because plastic bags are light and compressible, they constitute only 2 percent of landfill, but since most are not biodegradable, they will remain there. (Rosenthal 2008)

Such facts have spurred several cities and nations to ban or tax plastic single-use bags. In Ireland, the introduction of a 33 cents per bag tax has led to a 90 percent reduction in use and a drastic change in the meaning of the once free plastic bag. "Plastic bags were not outlawed, but carrying them became socially unacceptable—on a par with wearing a fur coat or not cleaning up after one's dog" (Rosenthal 2008). People quickly acquired reusable cloth bags, and the plastic versions have all but vanished from the streets in Dublin.[11] These products, once signifiers of convenience have become semantically loaded with connotations of shame and environmental irresponsibility.

THROWAWAY CULTURE OF THE SIXTIES

The adoption of disposable goods in the 1950s found some unusual and experimental applications in the 1960s. Many of these were inspired by the Pop movement, which may be traced back to the work of the Independent Group (IG) and particularly Richard Hamilton, who explained Pop as "popular; transient; expendable; low cost; mass produced; young; witty; sexy; gimmicky; glamorous; and Big Business" (Hamilton 1985: 25). As a cultural movement, the roots of Pop can be traced to the affluent youth of the U.S. and Britain of the mid-1950s. In its evolution through the 1960s, Pop went through several mutations. Referred to in its initial years as Early Pop, it transformed into High Pop in the 1960s and eventually into Late Pop, which lasted until the early 1970s.[12] The "transient; expendable; low cost" attributes led to such products as cardboard furniture and paper clothes, and such ideas as expendable rooms within an expendable architecture. According to Nigel Whiteley, expendability was "a central aspect of much of the culture of the 1960s: it was both a phys-

Figure 7.8. Vintage Paper Dress from the 1960s. Image courtesy of Jennifer Karpin-Hobbs, Morning Glorious Vintage.

ical fact of many products, and a symbol of belief in the modern age. Obsolescence was not only accepted by the fashion-conscious young, often it was positively celebrated" (1987: 3).

Pop found its voice in Britain's fashionable Carnaby Street in London, where much that was expendable was on exhibit. Though they never really caught on, paper dresses and skirts, available in eye-popping colors and graphics, were introduced in the late 1960s to be worn for a night out, and discarded in a day or two. Several designers who believed that "furniture should be cheap enough to be expendable" created highly affordable paper tables and chairs for mass consumption (Whiteley 1987: 19).

Archigram was an avant-garde group of architects who explored the ideas of plan-ned obsolescence in buildings through their conceptual projects such as "Plug-in City." Designed by Peter Cook in 1964, this city was built around several modules that could be plugged in and out of the system depending upon necessity. Kitchen plugs would last four years, bathroom plugs would last five years and so on. Everything was designed to become obsolete and replacement was at hand. Cook said, "Why is there an indefinable resistance to planned obsolescence for a kitchen, which in twelve years will be highly inefficient (by the standards of the day) and in twenty years will be intolerable, yet there are no qualms about four years obsolescence for cars?" (Cook 1972: 16). Plug-in City exemplified the extent to which the concept of obsolescence could be stretched.

By the late 1960s, Pop started waning, and with it so did the emphasis on disposability in fields of design and fashion. The student movements of 1968, increasing effects of drugs and peace movements, and the failing Vietnam war are recognized as events that changed the mood of the 1960s. Victor Papanek, who referred to the American propensity for disposable goods as the Kleenex culture in his distinctive, hyperbolic style warned against the dangers of

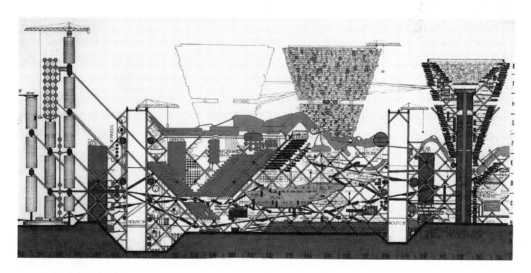

Figure 7.9. Plug-In City, by Sir Peter Cook. Image courtesy of Sir Peter Cook.

throwaway attitudes: "The risk is the expansion of this attitude: from changing automobiles every few years, we may move to considering everything a throwaway item, and considering *all* consumer goods, and indeed, most human values, to be disposable" (Papanek 1971: 87).

MANAGING PRODUCT LIFECYCLES

Planned obsolescence can lead to a series of social and environmental problems:

> The International Association of Electronics Recyclers (IAER), which has done the most detailed surveys of U.S. e-waste to date, expects that somewhere in the neighborhood of "3 billion units of consumer electronics will become potential scrap between 2003 and 2010." They expect 250 million computers to become obsolete between 2007 and 2008 alone and that at least 200 million televisions—about 25 million a year and—will be discarded between 2003 and 2010. (Grossman 2006:146)

The staggering numbers of products that are fated to join these ranks make it evident that this is a pressing problem.

The Eternally Yours Foundation, a collective of designers, philosophers and other thinkers was established in 1996 to study the problem of disposable goods, and strives to create design methodologies to extend product life where appropriate. They seek design methodologies by which "to help products age with dignity in cases where this is relevant for the environment" (EternallyYours.net 2009). They suggest that in order to increase product lives, it is important to create better attachments between people and things, and offer three strategies by which to lengthen the psychological lifetimes of things: Signs 'n Scripts, Shape 'n Surface and Sales 'n Services (Verbeek and Kockelkoren 2004). The strategy of Signs 'n Scripts seeks to create stories of products so that they become a part of people's personal narratives. Stories can impart character to things and, in the process, help build attachments to people. Shape 'n Surface refers to the use of forms and materials that age gracefully making them more desirable. This automatically urges people to take good care of their things. Finally, Sales 'n Services suggests that along with the sale of the product, the company also builds a relationship with the user, helping with repair and maintenance to extend product life. These promising strategies can help generate a new aesthetic that is tied closely to ethics (Verbeek 2005). Chapman (2005), too, suggests several design tools that can be employed in building "emotional durability" into things. The question of how long a product should be designed to last is not easy to answer. From an environmental perspective, durable things are generally preferable because they provide a better return on the resources used in their manufacture. However, if a durable object is highly polluting and requires significant natural resources to operate, its durability becomes an environmental liability. In such cases, if it can be removed from its useful life without generating unmanageable waste, and if it can be replaced with a better alternative, hastening its death might be preferable. The longer a harmful product survives, the longer it can continue inflicting harm. On the other hand, life cycle assessments demonstrate that single-use items or short-lived objects

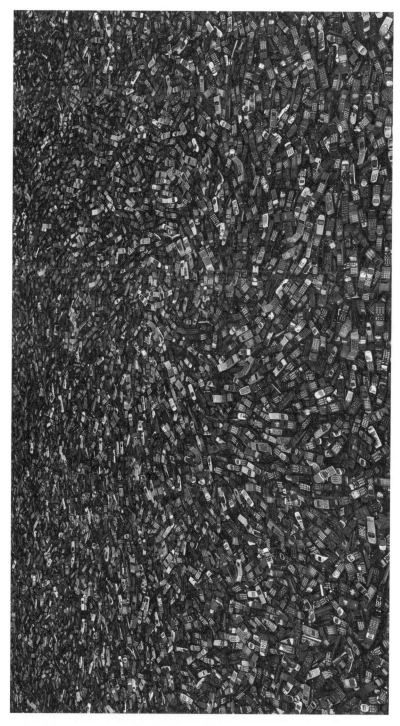

Figure 7.10. Discarded Cellphones, Photographed by Chris Jordan.
Chris Jordan Photography.

may not necessarily pose problems if they are environmentally benign. Decisions regarding the suitable life of an object should be based upon thorough life cycle assessments. The rapid acquisition and disposal of goods (whether caused by changes in technology, drop in quality or *démodé* appearance), is a unique form of consumption that leads to a new form of conspicuous waste:

> By *conspicuous waste*, Veblen meant using excessive amounts of goods or discarding something rather than reusing it or repairing it. Examples might be buying the latest model of a consumer item and throwing out the old, running a gas-guzzling power-boat at top speed, or routinely leaving food on your plate. Those who can afford to waste in these and countless other ways thus demonstrate their elevation above material concerns. (Bell and Carolan 2004: 37)

Designing and engineering goods that swiftly slide into obsolete status after acquisition accelerates the creation of conspicuous waste, and encourages the conspicuous display of unsustainable consumption. If our identity is wrapped up in what we consume and if our status is tied to what we waste, the cultural import of planned obsolescence is significant. Designers need to pay close attention to the life spans of things they design; their decisions affect individuals, societies and the environment.

8 OBJECT AS SIGN: WHAT DO THINGS MEAN?

> This universe is perfused with signs, if it is not composed exclusively of signs.
>
> Charles Sanders Peirce, *The Essential Peirce*

> Semiotics is in principle the discipline studying everything which can be used in order to lie.
>
> Umberto Eco, *A Theory of Semiotics*

The world of things is a world of signs.

The quest to uncover the meanings of things pervades several disciplines. What do things signify and how? Semiotics is one area of study that has undertaken the answering of this question as one of its central missions. Semioticians view the world as a collection of signs and have created analytical tools by which to decode meanings of material objects, texts, media forms and other cultural artifacts. Can words, images and objects be perceived as signs? And if so, how do these signs operate, how do they make sense to us and how do they relate to each other? These are questions explored by semiotics, often referred to as the *doctrine of signs*. The initial focus of semiotic inquiry—language and words—has since expanded to include a variety of other entities—images, objects, film, sports and several other forms of cultural praxis. The semiotician's trade involves the answering of three questions: "What does something mean? How does it mean what it means? Why does it mean what it means?" (Danesi 2007: 24). Semiotics has evolved into a discipline, and has since inspired several variations such as cultural semiotics, social semiotics and postmodern semiotics.

This chapter offers an introduction to the life of signs in society and though a comprehensive overview of semiotics is not possible, some of the key ideas that bear direct relevance to design and meanings of objects are discussed through theory and case studies. The first use of signs can be traced back to Hippocrates and the medical procedure of diagnosis, which uses the body's signs to look for illnesses. The discipline of semiotics took shape when early semioticians used the idea of signs to understand the fundamental workings of language, and realized that the basic structure they were uncovering could be extended beyond words. Since then, semiotics, which can be characterized as a discipline, a theory and a methodology, and has found applications in academia and industry in areas as diverse as advertising, marketing, cultural studies, material culture studies, anthropology, and of course, design. In the 1980s, design scholars developed some of the basic thinking of signs further into an area of study called product semantics, which inspired unique methodologies and forms of analysis. This chapter will map this story of the evolution of semiotics since the time of Hippocrates. The meanings of things, one of the primary concerns of semiotics, will be explained as a dynamic structure that exists in a network of people and things; and it is the reciprocity of agency between people and things that is responsible for how meanings emerge and change in the network. Finally, the chapter will list some of the limitations of semiotics and some of the new directions (such as socio-semiotics) they spawned.

THE MEANING OF WATER

BlingH$_2$O is not simply bottled water. It is "couture water" that is packaged in a limited edition, corked, frosted glass bottles with the letters Bling and H$_2$O spelled out in Swarovksi crystals. According to the company website, this unique packaging was designed specifically in response to an observation by Hollywood writer-producer and founder of BlingH$_2$O Kevin Boyd, that "you can tell a lot about a person by the bottled water they carried"

Figure 8.1. BlingH$_2$O Corked Glass Bottles with Swarovski Crystals. Image courtesy of Kevin G. Boyd, BlingH$_2$O.

(BlingH$_2$O.com 2007). Boyd compares BlingH$_2$O to the Rolls-Royce Phantom and Cristal champagne, other products that are signs of extreme exclusivity, status and affluence.

Consumers may have to pay anywhere between 20 to 480 U.S. dollars per bottle depending upon design, but this is a luxury experience "that's not for everyone, just those that Bling" (BlingH$_2$O.com 2007). While BlingH$_2$O might be one of the most expensive bottled waters, there are a few other brands in this market space. Evian's Palace, another luxury water brand, <u>accessorized with</u> its own no-drip pouring top and a stainless steel coaster, is sold at restaurants for 15 to 20 U.S. dollars a bottle. Tasmanian Rain, collected rainwater that "never touches the ground … contains only 17 parts per million of dissolved solids (impurities) and is more than nine times purer than the leading spring and artesian waters" (TasmanianRain.com 2007). Antipodes water, sold for 60 U.S. dollars for 12, 1000 ml bottles, "comes to the surface from a deep aquifer and is bottled at source in Whakatane, Bay of Plenty, New Zealand" (Antipodes.com 2007). Distinguished from commodity bottled waters by the label "fine waters," they signal a growing trend in the world, with

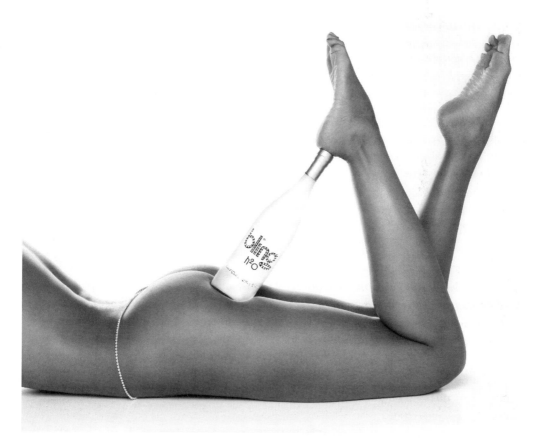

Figure 8.2.   BlingH$_2$O Advertising. Image courtesy of Kevin G. Boyd, BlingH$_2$O.

an estimated one new bottled water brand emerging everyday (Mascha 2007). With its premium packaging, sold to a specific target market, branded as a luxurious necessity, BlingH$_2$O signifies an entirely different set of meanings than the mundane bottled water like Arrowhead Water (owned by Nestlé Waters North America, Inc.), which retails for no more than a tenth of the price of BlingH$_2$O.

Boyd says "this is pop culture in a bottle," referring to the Hollywood celebrities like actors Jamie Foxx who drinks it during concerts and Ben Stiller who had cases flown to a movie set in Cabo San Lucas, Mexico (Mayer 2007). Some of BlingH$_2$O's advertising is highly sexualized. The company's website features an image of the BlingH$_2$O bottle held up suggestively by a woman between her derrière and her heel. The phallic symbolism is hard to miss.

Both BlingH$_2$O and Arrowhead share certain utilitarian meanings. They are containers of drinking water; the water they contain is sourced and treated differently from tap water, but that is where the similarities end. Bling H$_2$O is designed for a high-end market; this is water for the wealthy. The incorporation of the word "Bling" and the Swarovski crystals are both direct references to visual elements of hip-hop culture. The frosted glass, 750 ml bottle with its corked top makes aesthetic references to wine rather than water. This is water for the status conscious. None of these meanings apply to the Arrowhead Mountain Spring Water bottle. This is commodity water. The name Arrowhead, derived from the location in California from where the water is collected from a natural spring, is not connotative of any of these luxury meanings. It is a banal product, manufactured, distributed and consumed in large quantities, nondescript in design, arguably indistinguishable from several others within the same price range in the market, blow-molded from a commonly used polymer called PET (polyethylene terephthalate), and rather unremarkable and prosaic. BlingH$_2$O and Arrowhead exist at the opposite ends of the semiotic spectrum: one exorbitant, the other cheap; one highbrow, the other lowbrow; one glass, the other plastic; one exclusive, the other mundane.

Peter Thum founded Ethos, a bottled water brand—now owned by Starbucks Corporation—with the goal of "linking the product to a related humanitarian cause" (Walker 2006). Five cents from the sales of each bottle (which costs approximately 2 U.S. dollars) is set aside for water-based projects in poorer nations, and according to the company website, to date Ethos has committed grants of "6.2 million [U.S. dollars] that will benefit more than 420,000 people across Africa, Asia and Latin America" (Ethos.com 2008). The Ethos water bottle takes on a unique set of meanings in this case, and becomes a signifier of a worthy cause. This is water for those with a social conscience. However, this new meaning masks the fact that Ethos is still a single-use, disposable water bottle and begs the question that Walker raises: "isn't this all a bit like an S.U.V. whose profits finance third-world alternative-energy projects?" (Walker 2006).

Objects symbolize much larger social phenomena. A simple water bottle, harmless and innocuous as it may seem, stands for all the bottles in the world, for consumer attitudes, for environmental degradation, for waste and so on. It means a whole lot more than is immediately apparent, and regardless of the various meanings, it continues to be "a durable symbol for silly conspicuous consumption" (Walker 2006). Semiotics takes on the critical investigation of such mundane objects to uncover their meanings and significance in society.

WHAT IS SEMIOTICS?

Semiotics is the field of study that has undertaken the examination of signs and their meanings in society as its primary task. "Semiotics is the theoretical accounting for signs and what they do" (Deely 1990: 105). Construed broadly, "the goal of semiotics is to unravel the meanings that are built into all kinds of human products, from words, symbols, narratives, symphonies, paintings and comic books to scientific theories and mathematical theorems" (Danesi 2007: 3). It is, in this regard, a study of culture and all of its components, physical or virtual, ordinary or extraordinary, verbal or visual. Semiotics treats everything as a sign; it is "consumed with everything that can be (taken) as a sign" (Eco 1979: 7). And, in its analysis, it decodes the processes of sign production as well as the meanings of the resulting signs. Very simply, it can be defined as the science of signs, where a sign refers to anything that means something to someone.

Design is sign making. In fact, the root of the word design is the Latin *designare* which means "making something, distinguishing it by a sign, giving it significance, designating its relation to other things, owners, users, or goods" (Krippendorff 1989: 9). The word designate is derived from Latin *designatus* "designated" past participle of *designare*, based on *signum*, or mark. Designing, from this original meaning, can be referred to as creating signs (objects, graphics, building, etc.) and making marks (impact) on the world. Critiquing the practice of design therefore involves understanding and deciphering these signs.

Semiotic theory contains conceptual models of signs that offer themselves to wide application. Semioticians suggest that there is practically nothing that cannot be perceived as a sign and therefore there is nothing that cannot be examined semiotically. This proclaimed breadth of scope has resulted in suspicion of overreach and domination. "This project of semiotics, to study the whole of culture, and thus to view an immense range of objects and events as signs, may give the impression of an arrogant 'imperialism' on the part of semioticians" (Eco 1979: 6). And though the world of objects may rightfully and arguably be perceived as the world of signs, semiotic methods do have limitations.

A BRIEF HISTORY OF SEMIOTICS

Though French linguist Ferdinand de Saussure is often considered to be the pioneer of modern semiotics, it was Greek physician and father of Western medicine Hippocrates (ca. 460 B.C.E. - ca. 370 B.C.E.) who first coined the term *sêmeiotikos* (observant of signs) (Danesi 2007). One of the central mechanisms of medical practice of diagnosing conditions on the basis of symptoms is the earliest expression of semiotic theory. The body displays *semeions* ("marks" or "signs"), which the doctor "reads" as visible expressions of disease in order to prescribe treatment. In this context, elevated body temperatures, skin rash and swollen organs are all examples *semeions* or signs of an afflicted body. They provide physical, visual, tangible evidence for a sub-visual condition (disease) inside the body. This basic meaning of the sign has not changed since the time of Hippocrates. Several developments followed his work as philosophers like Plato, Aristotle and St. Augustine debated the nature of human made and natural *semeions*, thereby expanding the scope of the inquiry beyond the body. Natural signs are those caused by environmental and biological processes such as the falling of leaves, floods, etc. and lack human intentionality, while human-made signs, physical and abstract, are those created by people for specific purposes. Words and gestures are some examples of abstract human-made signs. St. Augustine referred to natural signs as *signa naturalia* and the human-made signs *signa data*.[1] Words were eventually included as *semeions* though they may express abstract ideas and mental states rather than physical entities. Plato believed that words were mental images of properties of things. Or, in semiotic terms, words *signify* properties of things. For example, we recognize all shapes, types and conditions of tomatoes as tomatoes because we recognize a certain property of "tomatoness" they embody. Aristotle, on the other hand, believed that words are practical mechanisms we use to name, recognize and categorize things. Aristotle would say we name singular tomatoes first, then recognize properties of other tomatoes that share a certain tomatoness and then classify them into categories. Neither Plato's approach, referred to as the mentalist theory, nor Aristotle's, referred to as the empirical theory, can be proved correct or incorrect. The recognition of words as *semeions* was a key development in the history of semiotics. The Stoics (Greek philosophers who lived between ca. 300 B.C.E and 100) also formulated a theory of signs, which bears some resemblance to those developed in the twentieth century. By their accounts, the sign connected three components together: the material *signifier*, the *signified* or meaning and the *external object* (Nöth 1990). The Stoics considered this relationship between the three elements as inferential, or that a meaning can be logically derived from the signifier: "From the observable signifier, we infer by mediation of the signified in a process of drawing a logical conclusion abut what the sign stands for" (Nöth 1990: 16). The signifier is visible, and by reason, it is possible to decipher the meaning it represents.

After centuries of relative inactivity in sign theory, English Franciscan William of Ockham (ca. 1285–ca. 1349) along with John Duns Scotus (c. 1266–1308) suggested that signs did not really refer to things or their properties. Instead, signs merely pointed to other signs. In 1632, John Poinsot produced *Treatise on Signs*, a highly regarded work in which he defined the sign as an "intermediary between thoughts and things" (Danesi 2007: 9). By this conception, signs may be perceived as our link to reality, entities that connect our inner worlds to external physicalities. The last philosopher who deserves mention before we address the work of twentieth-century thinkers like Saussure and Peirce is John Locke, who is credited with the term "semiotic" for the doctrine of signs. In his seminal work in 1690 titled *Essay Concerning Human Understanding* he suggested that semiotic would "afford us another sort of Logick and Critick, than what we have hitherto been acquainted with" (Deely 1990: 114). He believed that philosophy could benefit from the doctrine of signs, and that the "first task for semiotic [was] the bringing of 'ideas'—the inner side of knowing—along with "words" the outer manifestation of knowing—into the perspective of the sign" (Deely 1990: 51). These earlier works, from the ancient Greek thinkers to the seventeenth century European philosophers, the "proto-semioticians" (Cobley and Jansz 1999: 7) laid the groundwork for twentieth-century semiotics.

The roots of modern semiotics are, by most scholarly accounts, traced back to the work of two men, Swiss linguist Ferdinand de Saussure and American pragmatist Charles Peirce, who independently and contemporarily developed their own theories of signs. Saussure used the term semiology and described it as a "science which studies the role of signs as part of social life" (Chandler 2002: 5). He is best known for splitting the sign into two components and creating a dyadic relationship of the signifier and signified. The signifier refers to the acoustic image of the word as it is spoken, and the signified refers to what it means to a listener. In other words, the signifier is the sound uttered when someone says something and the signified is the sense the listener makes of it. Taken together, they constitute the sign. Saussure also points out to that the relationship between the signifier and the signified is arbitrary, and only held in place by convention. A bottle is called so simply because it is designated by a code, a convention called the English language. If it were called by any other name, it would work just as well, as long as we all agreed to it and accepted it. Saussure also believed that signs possess intentionality, that they were devices for communication between people.

Equally important as Saussure's is the work of Charles Peirce. Like Locke, Peirce referred to the study of signs as semiotics, rather than semiology, and that name has endured. According to Peirce, a sign is composed of three connected components: the representamen,

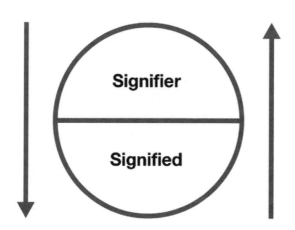

Figure 8.3. Saussure's Dyadic Model of the Sign.

the interpretant and the object. "A sign stands *for* something to the idea which it produces, or modifies. Or it is a *vehicle* conveying into the mind something from without. That for which it stands is called its object; that for which it conveys its meaning; and the idea to which it gives rise, its interpretant" (Gottdiener 1995: 9–10). Gottdiener explains that this triadic model does bear some resemblance to Saussure's dyadic version. "His [Peirce's] model of the sign . . . encompassed three entities, although strictly speaking . . . with regard to Peirce, the object world lies in the background and semiosis consists of the cognitive relationship between the representamen, which is very much like the signifier, and the interpretant, or Saussure's signified" (Gottdiener 1995: 11). The representamen is the physical sign itself which does the representing, the object is that which the representamen stands for, and the interpretant is the resultant image or psychological event or meaning that it gives rise to in the mind of the interpreter.

For example, an Aeron chair that exists as a material object in the world is the representamen. It is so named because it is that which does the representing, it is a vehicle. The concept that it encodes, in this case, possibility of sitting, is the object. It is referred to as such because it is something that is presented to the world for observation. The interpretant refers to all the meanings that the Aeron chair gives rise to in the mind of the interpreter. These meanings, of course, depend upon the cultural context within which the interpreter is submerged, and are therefore unique to each individual. The Aeron chair

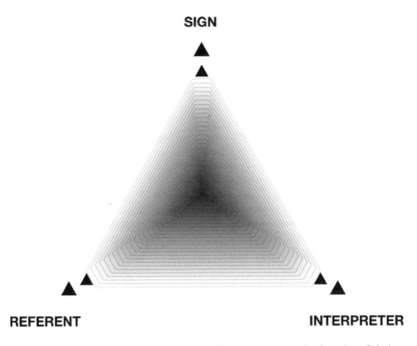

Figure 8.4. The Semiotic Triad, by Charles Peirce. Illustration by Amethyst Saludo.

could be interpreted as a well-designed seating experience, a symbol of .com success, a true innovation, etc. These interpretants will be different for the designers, the manufacturers, users, and so forth.

Peirce did not perceive the world of signs as being limited to humans. "The action of a sign generally takes place between two parties, the *utterer* and the *interpreter*. They need not be persons; for a chameleon and many kinds of insects and even plants make their living by uttering signs" (Peirce 1907: 205–6, in Deely 1990: 83). Further, Peirce created an extensive and complex classification of signs, of which three types have relevance for design—symbols, icons and indexes. A symbol is a sign that does not have any direct resemblance to the object but is accepted to stand for it by convention. Punctuation marks, flags and Morse Code are examples of symbols. An icon is a sign that closely and possibly literally reproduces the idea of an object or event. Cartoons and portraits are examples of icons. Indexes do not derive their meaning through cultural codes but through experience and observation of the material world. Lightning and thunder form an index, the meaning of which is storm. Peirce's classification broadens the scope of semiotics beyond Saussure's focus on language, making it more suitable to the analysis of a wider range of cultural artifacts. Scholars generally find Peirce's system to be grounded in the object world and therefore less idealistic than Saussure's, which was based primarily in language and human communication. The work of Saussure and Peirce set in motion international interest in the science of signs, with scholars developing and building upon their ideas and finding newer applications for semiotic analysis.

DENOTATION AND CONNOTATION

One of the most important scholars to build upon Saussure's work was Roland Barthes, who extended the semiological system further, introduced concepts of the denotative and connotative meanings of signs, and developed a theory of myth to decode hidden and often manipulative meanings of everyday cultural phenomena. As signs always refer to something, they *denote* a certain accepted meaning. However, Barthes suggested that signs also *connote* additional meanings that are often not plainly visible. The terms denotative and connotative have themselves evolved in meaning over time. Initially, the term denotative referred to the more obvious, common or literal meanings of signs, and the connotative to the socio-cultural, ideological ones that often necessitate deeper analysis to decode. However, it became clear that it is not always easy or even possible to distinguish between these kinds of meanings. The denotative meaning of a single-use water bottle is exactly that—a bottle of water that is to be used once. However, as one interprets advertising, patterns of use, bottle designs and its engineering, such meanings as convenient access to water, affluence or distaste of tap water, start to emerge. The BlingH$_2$O, Ethos and Arrowhead bottles all share the denotative meaning. Some of the connotative signifieds, on the other hand, refer to the fact that these bottles are signifiers of affluent consumption, environmental pollution and non-degradable waste. More specifically, BlingH$_2$O signifies, at the connotative level, excessively conspicuous consumption, ostentatious display of wealth, celebrity, status and blatant references to some of the more materialistic aspects of hip-hop culture. In case of Ethos water, the connotative meanings may be perceived to stand in opposition to the denotative meanings. Though sold in small, personal containers as water for the individual, the bottles carry the caption "Water for the World" as a reference to the company's humanitarian mission of donating 2.77 percent of the price of the bottle to water-based developmental projects for poorer parts of the world. The Ethos water bottle carries the message of humanitarian aid, societal benefit and ethical consumption. The name "Ethos" conjures a set of meanings as well. Yet another example, Fiji water connotes environmental responsibility. The company's website promises that "every drop is green" and has decided to become carbon negative (removing more greenhouse gases from the atmosphere than those released in production) by reducing packaging, using renewable energy in manufacturing and investing in forestation. (Fijiwater.com 2008). In 2007, Nestlé Waters, North America's largest bottled water company with over 31 percent of total sales spread over all its labels, introduced the Eco-Shape˚ bottle for Arrowhead, which is advertised as using 30 percent less plastic. However, Nestlé Waters performed very poorly when evaluated against other major companies according to a recycling scorecard by the Container Recycling Institute.[2] It is clear that corporations choose names and marketing campaigns carefully to steer the meanings of their product offerings in specific, desired directions.

BARTHES' MYTHOLOGIES

In suggesting that "the world of signifieds is none other than that of language," Barthes (1968: 10) casts the net of language over all of semiotics. In *Elements of Semiology*, a critical examination and extension of Saussure's *Course in General Linguistics*, he posits that instead of considering the science of signs (semiotics or semiology) to be a part of language, it should be the other way around. Barthes also conceives of an expansive definition of language that is not limited to words, sounds and their grammatical structures. From this point of view, products, graphics, movies, advertising and many other forms of communication can be considered to be a form of language. "Such language is not quite that of the linguist: it is a second-order language, with its unities no longer monemes or phonemes, but larger fragments of discourse referring to objects or episodes whose meaning *underlies* language, but can never exist independently of it" (Barthes 1968: 11). Language therefore becomes not just a mechanism for verbal communication but a system of signification for a variety of discourses, linguistic and non-linguistic. It provides a structure by which to critique ordinary products, images and rituals. "Semiology … aims to take in any system of signs, whatever their substance and limits; images, gestures, musical sounds, objects, and the complex associations of all these, which form the content of ritual, convention or public entertainment: these constitute, if not *languages*, at least systems of signification" (Barthes 1968: 9). In *Mythologies*, he develops a theory of the myth as a second order meaning that is often hidden and requires analysis to decipher. "Myth is a system of communication

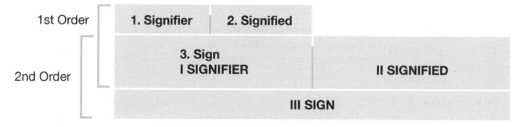

Figure 8.5. Barthes' Diagram of Myth and the Second Order Semiological System.

... it is a message" (Barthes 1972: 109). *Mythologies*, one of the most influential books in semiotics which presents theoretical concepts along with analyses of the common images, objects and rituals of everyday life, too was built upon the semiology of Saussure. We know from Saussure that the sign is composed of two inseparable elements: the signifier and the signified. This sign, which Barthes refers to as the first order semiological system, becomes the signifier for the second order semiological system, and in that process creates a myth. Figure 8.5 illustrates the first and second order systems of signification.

Barthes demonstrated his system of myth by analyzing a cover of the 1954 edition of a popular French magazine called *Paris Match*, which, as he suggested, one may encounter in a barbershop, a mundane meeting place in the city. This particular magazine cover, which included a full-page photograph of a young African soldier saluting, serves as the signifier, and its first-order signification (leading to the signifier) is the presence of an African soldier in the French army. The image and this meaning may seem rather innocuous if not analyzed within the historical context of France's colonization of North Africa. When the magazine was published, there was increasing resistance from the African continent, the public opinion at home of France's war was suffering and several colonized nations all over the world were either fighting for or had recently gained independence. The photograph of an obedient and willing African saluting to the French flag creates the myth of normalcy and acceptance, and in this process stifles the story of subjugation and colonization.

In his analysis of the Citroën D.S. which was introduced in the 1950s, Barthes compared it to a Gothic cathedral and referred to it as a "magical object" consumed by a vast majority if not through acquisition and use, certainly through advertising (it too appeared on the cover of *Paris Match*). Barthes starts his analysis with the name of the automobile D.S. which reads *Déesse* in French and translates as goddess. The first myth therefore arises in its comparisons to such divine entities as cathedrals and goddesses, "objects from another universe," which transform the car into a heavenly body (Barthes 1972: 88). He interprets its organic, streamlined form as depicting perfection. The Citroën's smooth form does not expose ungainly connections and joints between components, and therefore hides its own process of assembly. Its seamless body suggests that no human hands were involved in its assembly. This smoothness is accompanied by a lightness achieved through its organic form

1. Signifier	2. Signified
	'A young Negro in French uniform is saluting, with eyes uplifted, probably fixed on a fold of tricolour.'

3. Sign	
I SIGNIFIER 'A black soldier is giving the French salute'	**II SIGNIFIED** 'Purposeful mixture of Frenchness and militariness.'

III SIGN (MYTH)
'France is a great Empire, that all her sons, without any colour discrimination, faithfully serve under her flag, and that there is no better answer to the detractors of an alleged colonialism than the zeal shown by this Negro in serving his so-called oppressors.'

Figure 8.6.   Barthes' Semiological Analysis of the Cover of *Paris Match*.

and the use of glass. Barthes compares the interior (especially the dashboard) to a domestic appliance, more homely than industrial, designed for comfort rather than performance. The car is the "very essence of petit-bourgeois advancement" (Barthes 1972: 90). In this analysis, Barthes reveals several layers of meaning (literal, technological, material, formal, graphic and sociological) as seen in Figure 8.7.

Using Barthes' model, we can perform an analysis of General Motors' vehicle, the Hummer, to reveal its first-order signification through denotative meanings, connotative meanings, and also the myths that it perpetrates. According to its denotative meaning, the Hummer is essentially a mode of individual and/or family transportation. At the connotative level, this expensive car (which was modeled after an army vehicle) signifies status, adventure and affluence. Another range of connotative meanings arises from the critique this vehicle has attracted due to its low fuel efficiency. The car has come to signify environmental disregard, wastefulness, pointless male bravado and shameless American consumerism. On the other hand, the Hummer is also surrounded by several myths that refer to notions of personal safety, outdoor adventure and solidarity with the U.S. Army. As a high-profile vehicle with significant weight, size, ground clearance and an armor-like body, it looms over other vehicles creating a sense of domination, advertising the potential damage it could cause other vehicles in an accident. It provides fortification in the name of safety, separating the driver from other car owners physically, economically and by class. Climbing into the Hummer is scaling up the ladder of exclusivity.

However, these meanings of the General Motors' vehicle are vastly different from the original H.M.M.W.V. (High Mobility Multi-purpose Wheeled Vehicle) designed and man-ufactured for the U.S. Army by A.M. General, located in South Bend, Indiana. The original

ANALYSIS	MEANING
Literal	As goddess, derived from the name D.S. (*Déesse*)
Technological	As the perfect object, not assembled by humans
Material	As the light object, made of glass (like soap bubbles)
Formal	As a smooth and streamlined perfect form
Graphic	Citroën logo as representing organism rather than engine
Sociological	As the emblem of lower middle class advancement

Figure 8.7. The Multiple Meanings of the Citroën. Illustration by Amethyst Saludo.

vehicle was designed to operate in desert conditions and extremely rough terrain. According to A.M. General's website, "no one would ever accuse the H.M.M.W.V. of being cute. When American soldiers first began using the vehicle in the mid-1980s, they often referred to it as a 'Jeep on steroids.' The vehicle was designed for the world's toughest environment—war. Its looks are a result of its requirements. It is a pure example of form following function" (A.M. General 2009). The H.M.M.W.V., although first manufactured in 1985, gained publicity when seen the world over during the Persian Gulf War of 1991. This heavily televised war broadcast several images of soldiers in their H.M.M.W.V.s driving in the Iraqi desert making it "visually" available to the public. While at this time it was not a civilian vehicle, interest from Arnold Schwarzenegger, recognition by A.M. General of a potential market, and·GM's acquisition of the brand names Hummer, H1 and H2, eventually completed its transformation from a military vehicle to a domestic S.U.V.[3]

THE SIGN AS STIMULUS

In the 1930s, the field of semiotics in the U.S. took a turn away from linguistics, partly inspired by Russian physiologist Pavlov's work on human and animal behavior. Pavlov, who won the Nobel Prize in 1904, is best known for his classic experiments with conditioned reflexes in dogs and the development of the stimulus-response theory. In a simple experiment, Pavlov set up two stimuli (food and the sound of a bell) and measured the response (secretion of saliva) in dogs. Initially, both stimuli were presented to the dog simultaneously and the response observed; eventually the stimulus of food was removed. Yet, the dog salivated simply at the sound of the bell. This type of behavior came to be referred to as conditioned reflex. The bell therefore becomes the sign that stands for something else (food), and in Eco's words, is a lie. Charles Morris developed a behavioral theory of signs based upon publicly observable stimuli and responses. He explained the sign as "something that directs behaviour with respect to something that is not at the moment a stimulus" (Cobley and Jansz 1999: 111). He referred to the sign as a "preparatory stimulus," something that anticipates a response that may or may not occur. It was important to Morris to associate

Figure 8.8.   The Original H.M.M.W.V., by A.M. General. Image courtesy of Lee Woodward, A.M. General.

signs with goal-seeking behavior, which in the case of the dog would be satisfying hunger. He therefore sets up the following conditions under which something may be referred to as a sign. "If something, A, controls behavior towards a goal in a way similar to (but not necessarily identical with) the way something else, B, would control behavior with respect to that goal in a situation in which it were observed, then A is a sign" (Morris 1946: 7). Designers observe people through ethnographic studies, so that they may understand and document behavioral patterns, identify problems, list unmet needs and design products that satisfy those needs. From a behavioral semiotic perspective, designers look for situations where the goal-seeking behaviors are hindered by poorly designed products or the lack of products altogether. Morris identifies four key terms in behavioral semiotics that resonate with design praxis. We can think of advertising as a preparatory stimulus, because it signifies potential action. Our world is full of such stimuli that incite a "disposition to respond." A logo or a billboard prepares the audience and makes it more disposed to buying the product being advertised. When a person acts on this disposition, it may lead to a response-sequence—a series of actions set in motion by the stimulus. In order to account for the variety of responses, Morris introduced the notion of a "behavior family" that represents all potential response sequences. One of the primary tasks of ethnography in design research is to identify all possible behavior families of individuals and groups.

The application of behavioral semiotics to design can serve the purpose of shifting its focus from actions to behavior. Ethnographic methods help with the observation of visible actions, which may not always indicate why people behave in certain ways. If in the design process one takes into account all potential behavior-families that account for all possible actions that someone may be disposed to perform in a given situation, the design solutions might be better suited not only physiologically, but cognitively as well.

SOCIO-SEMIOTICS

In addition to explaining the sign, social semiotics, (also referred to as socio-semiotics) focuses on the process of sign-making within a social context. "The premise of socio-semiotics is that any cultural object is both an object of use in a social system with a generative history and social context, and also a component in a system of signification" (Gottdiener 1995: 29). This form of semiotics steps away from purely textual or linguistic analyses, or from purely behavioral explanations and includes political and economic structures in laying the foundation for a new meaning of the sign. One of the hallmarks of socio-semiotics is the inclusion of human beings in the process of semiosis; it considers people and social groups to be the "bearers of meaning" (Gottdiener 1995: 172). Socio-semiotics is particularly suited for a critical, cultural analysis of things for several reasons. First, it

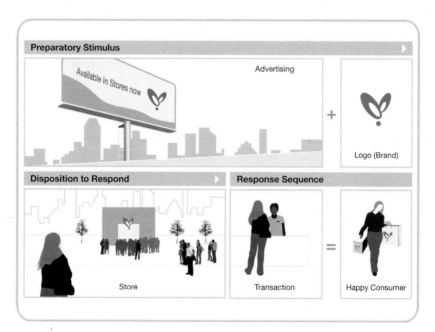

Figure 8.9.   Behavioral Semiotics in the Purchase of Products. Illustration by Amethyst Saludo.

takes into account not only the perspective of the analyst or the structure of language but also the role of people and society. For example, "a socio-semiotic analysis of Disneyland would try and uncover the production codes used by the designers of the park (mainly Walt Disney) and the social context of the park experience itself (within the context of everyday life in Los Angeles)" (Gottdiener 1995: 29). A second reason for the appropriateness of socio-semiotics is that it embraces the notion that things have multiple meanings—they are polysemic. All cultural phenomena and artifacts have a range of meanings determined by the ever-changing interpreters and contexts. A third reason why socio-semiotics is useful is because in its analysis it considers the agency of the producer along with that of the user; it is neither production-centric nor consumption-centric. It is both. And in order to recognize and incorporate both points of view, socio-semiotics utilizes ethnographic methods like interviews and observations in addition to textual analysis and interpretation.

Such approaches are also found in media and cultural studies. Michael Bull, in his examination of the Sony Walkman, draws "critical theory together with a more ethnographic approach tied to an empirically orientated phenomenological methodology" (2000: 10). In other words, his study of the Walkman is grounded in theoretical concepts but is also informed by how people use it in everyday life.

POLYSEMY

Polysemy, or the notion that signifiers are ambiguous and may have multiple signifieds, is scantly covered in semiotic literature. Barthes makes it clear that a signifier may have multiple signifieds, and therefore several meanings defined by context. Barthes, who discussed the polysemous nature of the sign in explaining the fashion system (1983), examined what causes the multiplicity of meaning and also what leads to their regulation. Though signs have multiple meanings, some of these are kept in check by social institutions through carefully managed power structures. For example, if traffic signs were interpreted differently by different people it could lead to utter chaos. Their meanings, therefore, are kept stable and are controlled by governmental organizations. In spite of these controls, it is impossible to tightly regulate the process of meaning-making, and at times people will make sense of things in ways that are individually determined. Therefore, there is no one-to-one relationship between the signifier and the signified. Individual interpreters are, within limits, free to choose their own meanings of signs. Like Barthes, Mikhail Bakhtin too recognized meanings were polysemic, and referred to them as multivocal. Bakhtin's term "multivocality" is equivalent to the notion of polysemy of the sign.

SEMIOTICS AND THE PRACTICE OF DESIGN

Design theoreticians were naturally attracted to principles of semiotics because it provided a convenient and simple mechanism by which to understand and explain the signaling or communicative properties of images, objects and spaces. As an analytical tool, semiotics offers a new way to critique the built environment. However, it was in industrial design where its development progressed farther than in many other design disciplines. Termed product semantics in the 1980s, this area of study attracted significant interest and scholarship from around the world.[4] One of the earliest publications that assembled some of this scholarship was the Spring 1989 volume of *Design Issues*, guest edited by Klaus Krippendorff and Reinhart Butter. The editors defined product semantics as "the study of the symbolic qualities of man-made forms in the cognitive and social contexts of their use and the application of the knowledge gained to objects of industrial design" (Krippendorff 1989: 10). While acknowledging its roots in historical semiotics (especially in ideas developed by Saussure), product semantics clearly charted its own epistemological direction in theory and application. It concerned itself with the meanings of mass-produced things, the meaning of design, the semiotics of spaces and buildings, the changing role of design in a post-industrial age, the role of perception in the cognition of meaning, and the significance of mythologies in design. The fundamental goal of product semantics was to explain the mechanism by which objects acquire meaning (or how humans assign meanings to things) and to generate a better comprehension of the role that design plays in this process.

Krippendorff distinguishes and distances the product semantics effort from semiotics, though the roots of the term lead back to Charles Morris's division of semiotics into syntactics, pragmatics and semantics. Morris explained syntactics as the division of semiotics that focuses on the relationship between signs, pragmatics as the branch that examines the relationship between signs and interpreters and finally semantics as the relationship between signs and the objects they refer to. Krippendorff makes it clear that "product semantics should not be tied to traditional semiotics" (1989: 10). He argues that the triadic relationship when a sign stands for something else does not function for objects, which "can hardly be viewed as substitutes for something else" (1989: 11). However, this denotational quality of signs does not necessarily mean that objects are substitutes; it may very simply be understood in the words of Phaedrus as *non semper ea sunt quae videntur* (things are not always what they seem). Eco has famously said that a sign is a lie; Barthes has pointed out that signs can be based on myths and it is indeed possible (though not desirable) for objects to represent what may not be true. Examples discussed earlier about bottled water attest to this notion. Krippendorff who has been prolific in this field, illustrates the relationship between meaning, artifacts and people (users and designers) lucidly in Figure 8.10. He explains: "Form and meaning are intricately related ... and their relationship is a fundamental concern of product semantics. Something must have form to be seen, but must make sense to be understood and used" (Krippendorff 1989: 14).

It is important to note—and this is evident in Figure 8.10—that product semantics avoids a deterministic position by clarifying that designers do not create meanings—they create form; it is users who create meanings. The network within which things exist serves as a location where designers in the process of design and users in the process of use construct meanings. Each actor—designer, user, thing, environment—in the context of the network and in interaction plays its agentic role of making meaning. And by selecting certain forms,

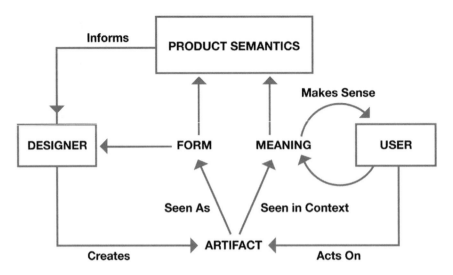

Figure 8.10.   The Role of Users and Designers in Product Semantics (Krippendorff 1989).

materials, colors and textures, designers nudge users to construct meanings in certain ways. Once the thing is made, it too nudges users in certain ways. As we have seen earlier, people and things configure each other. When a designer specifies gold and diamonds on a product like the Vertu mobile phone, she or he is pre-configuring the object for a set of potential meanings of luxury, affluence and exclusivity. When the product enters the market, it does so at a certain price point and in certain locations, pre-configuring the type of user it will attract. Meaning is generated in this material-semiotic web, with active participation of all actors. "Actor-network theory is a disparate family of material-semiotic tools, sensibilities and methods of analysis that treat everything in the social and natural worlds as a continuously generated effect of the webs of relations within which they are located. It assumes that nothing has reality or form outside the enactment of those relations" (Law 2007). Meaning is generated in interaction; it is a relation, not a static entity. In its design of the Prius hybrid vehicle, Toyota seeded a network where meanings of environmentally responsible transportation could be negotiated. This does not, in any way, dictate the meanings people will construct. In their own cognitive realms and contexts of use, people will make sense of the objects in the world based upon their past and present experiences and their location in the network. It is, however, possible to conceive a comprehensive range of meanings that is likely to emerge in use and imagine some that will probably not. The Vertu phone with its price tag of several thousand U.S. dollars *cannot* possibly signify cheap and disposable for most of the human population. Its design says otherwise. However, meanings are entirely context dependent and for the extraordinarily affluent—people, for instance, with invest-able assets of 30 million or more U.S. dollars who are referred to as the U.H.N.W.I.s (Ultra High Net Worth Individuals)—the Vertu may not be perceived as too exorbitant.

A credit card is not cash; it is debt. It serves as a sign for money and it is able to give users a taste for the power of consumption, ownership and status. The American Express charge card is not quite a credit card. It is, in fact, a very short-term (approximately a month) loan for a purchase. When the first American Express card was introduced in 1958, it was purple—the color of their Traveler's Cheque. "It wasn't until 1969 that the Green Card appeared. American Express decided that year to make the cards 'money green' based on the U.S. dollar color of money," writes Ira Galtman, American Express Corporate Archivist (personal communication, 31 July 2009). According to Deyan Sudjic, Director of the Design Museum in London, the company pulled off "a really intelligent coup when they facelifted their plastic credit card... It was only when the American Express card took on the look of real currency that it took off in a big way" (Sudjic 1985: 23). The design decision to change the color transformed the sign-value of the card.

Suggesting that "form follows meaning" rather than function, Krippendorff and Butter (1989) recommend that designers focus on contexts and use scenarios to help people make sense of the things in their world. An emphasis on context-dependent meanings automatically leads product semantics to embrace the notion of polysemy. A tennis ball, originally designed for the obvious purpose of play has several contexts of use and therefore has several meanings. For instance, it is frequently used in India for street cricket; it is often found attached to walkers used by older adults who need ambulatory assistance; it has appeared in interesting instances of furniture design; and, it has been discovered to be a tool in opening car door locks. In Indian urban environments, where street cricket is

Figure 8.11. The First American Express Card from 1958. Image courtesy of American Express Corporate Archives.

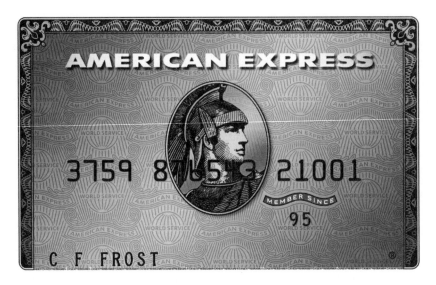

Figure 8.12. The American Express Card (Green). Image courtesy of American Express Corporate Archives.

enormously popular and played wherever possible, the traditional cricket ball is not always available, affordable or feasible. Made of hard leather and stuffed with cork, it is unwise to use the cricket ball without significant protection. As an inexpensive and safer substitute, the tennis ball "stands for" the cricket ball and is widely used across India and Pakistan. (However, "purists," find tennis-ball cricket an aberration of the "real" sport.) In the second context of use, tennis balls have been rigged to serve as smooth glides for wheel-less walkers. In this case, they take on the meaning of soft supports, an application far removed from its original intent. In fact, this user-driven innovation has now been converted into a mass manufactured object by corporations and sold for 22 U.S. dollars.

The Ball Boy Stool designed in 2004 by Charles O'Toole is manufactured "in a limited run of just 10 signed and numbered pieces" (O'Toole, personal interview 2009). The Ball Boy has meanings that are not visible at first glance. The tennis balls used in the design of the seat are the last few to be manufactured in Ireland. O'Toole's design is political commentary on the massive changes affecting manufacturing industries all over the world. With global pressures of reducing costs, the making of things is moving to nations where labor is plentiful and much cheaper. This stool captures the last few material manifestations of this industry into its form, which is simple in appearance but complex in meaning.

In a third devious and ingenious application, the tennis ball has apparently served as an illicit key to open car doors. Though the claim has been denied by many, it is believed that if one punctures a small hole in a tennis ball, lines it up against certain car locks and gives it a hearty whack, it can release a puff of air generating just enough force to realign the tumblers in the lock of a car door to pop it open. The tennis ball, as these examples show, serves

Figure 8.13. Tennis Balls as Walker Glides, by Golden Violin. Image courtesy of Golden Violin, www.goldenviolin.com.

purposes other than those for which it was designed and thus has multiple meanings that have been constructed in use. "*What something is* (the totality of what it means) *to someone corresponds to the sum total of its imaginable contexts*" (Krippendorff 1989: 13).

DESIGN METHODOLOGIES FOR SEMANTICS

Scholars involved in the exploration of product semantics were also interested in the application of the theories and analytical tools of semiotics in the design of new products, graphics and spaces. In most cases, the process involved transfer of verbal meanings into formal physical manifestations. The goal in these explorations was not to create a specific semantic iconography or a repertoire of symbols to be used by designers. The aim, instead, was to use semiotic principles in generating meaningful experiences for people. A methodology developed by Butter (1989: 52), outlines an eight step process that assists in the "systematic generation of semantically relevant design concepts":

- Step 1. Establishment of general objectives and constraints for the product or system.
- Step 2. Identification of the product's projected context of use covering user groups and the system's semantic performance characteristics.
- Step 3. Generation of a list of desired attributes expressing the projected semantic performance characteristics.

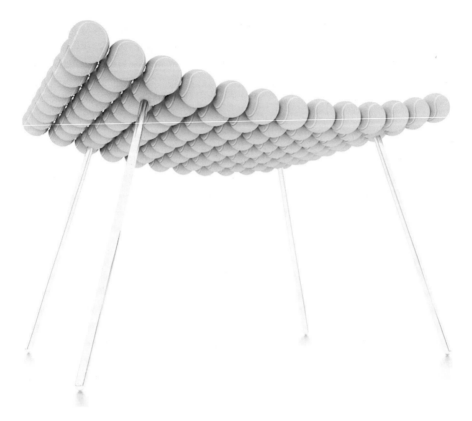

Figure 8.14. Tennis Ball Stool, by Charles O'Toole. Image courtesy of Charles O'Toole.

- Step 4. Generation of a list of undesired attributes expressing those semantic characteristics to be definitely avoided.
- Step 5. Analysis, grouping, and ranking of all attributes.
- Step 6. Search for concrete manifestations capable of supporting desired attributes and contrasting with undesirable attributes.
- Step 7. Assessing, selecting, and integrating semantically feasible manifestations into expressive wholes.
- Step 8. Evaluation of compatibilities and technical feasibilities of the ideas.[5]

Crucial in this process is the systematic methodology and the emphasis on translating verbal attributes into physical manifestations. Step 6, which is identified as one of the most critical steps in the process, relies on the designers' ability to successfully convert verbal/ textual information (linguistic skills) into product form using metaphors and the standard design elements of form, color, textures, etc. (form-based skills). It is expected that the process will yield designs that are easier to make sense of so that users may have meaningful experiences with the object.

In this process, the translation of verbal attributes into formal characteristics is achieved with the use of metaphors. For example, in order to create a new product design that is hi-tech in appearance, a designer would use as a metaphor something else that has already been identified as hi-tech. This could be an object like the B-2 Spirit aircraft, the Nintendo Playstation PS3 or the Sony TDM-NC1 Wi-Fi client. The visual elements of these products that make them appear hi-tech, such as rectilinear, sharp forms and materials such as stainless steel or black plastic are then identified and applied to the new product. Metaphors, in this case, can be defined as mental operations that transform meanings from a familiar domain to a relatively unknown or new domain. Traditionally known as linguistic devices, metaphors are themselves signs that stand for something else. If appropriately used, metaphoric devices can lead to understandable and recognizable products with features that are legible and self-evident. For example, in the design of the viewphone seen in Figure 8.15, the hand mirror serves as a metaphor standing in for the familiar notion of a reflection. Designed by Philip White, then a graduate student at the Cranbrook Academy of Art, the videophone is meant to be at once familiar yet fresh, recognizable yet innovative. Some of the more interesting experiments in the application of principles and theories of semiotics were carried out at the Cranbrook Academy of Art in Michigan under the direction of Katherine and Michael McCoy. In addition to making product-user experiences more meaningful, the McCoys also took on the challenge of making products more communicative. In the 1980s, designers often lamented the tyranny and ubiquity of beige and black boxes inspired by a form of design asceticism masquerading as good product design. Described by some as clean, simple and universal, many thought these forms were inexpressive, non-communicative and culturally insensate. Designers called for objects that communicated their purpose and the cultural milieu within which they would be used. Product semantics was seen as a new philosophy and methodology that could change this. "Objects informed by semantics have tended toward making visual connections between the technological object and other aspects of life through metaphor, analogy, simile and allegory in their form" (Krohn and McCoy 1989: 115).

In the earlier experimental designs, students at the Cranbrook Academy of Art used semiotics in the creation of product forms that were metaphorical in nature and expressed their meanings in unique ways. Later work was concerned with the "essences or archetypal qualities of objects, looking for the spirit of the artifact" (McCoy and McCoy 1989: 18), and the designs placed a heavier emphasis on the experience that the thing affords. This change was inspired by a theoretical shift in focus to phenomenology and post-structuralism, which involved a closer examination of ritual, myth and everyday life. For example, "the morning ritual of making toast is celebrated in this toaster with 'friendly waves of heat' molded into the cast-aluminum housing" in a design by Van Hong Tsai, a student at Cranbrook (Aldersey-Williams 1990: 93).

These experiments in melding theories of semiotics, post-structuralism and phenomenology questioned the very role of design in human life and society. A good design, it is generally

Figure 8.15.   Viewphone Design by Philip White, Cranbrook Academy of Art.
Image courtesy of Philip White and Michael McCoy.

expected, adds value to the product, improves the user experience, increases consumer desire and enhances the bottom line for the corporation. This is no secret. However, when anti-consumerist writing of Baudrillard and Barthes become driving forces for new design, it creates conundrums that may be irreconcilable. Students at Cranbrook were encouraged to grapple with such paradoxes and make sense of where and how theoretical positions could be balanced with design production. The McCoys also actively sought out such critiques as a means to update their design methodologies:

It has been fashionable among some at Cranbrook to quote Jean Baudrillard on "object culture" and the "sign function" of objects in an attempt to explain how their designs abet the creation of their eventual owners' domestic myths. Cranbrook thinking soon parts company with Baudrillard, however. His philosophy rejects the whole capitalist manufacturing system. Most designers can't afford to do that and wouldn't want to. Their future success lies in alliance with the forces of commerce. Cranbrook graduates should recognize (and accept?) that they are using "object culture" to fulfill new capitalist fantasies. (Aldersey-Williams 1990: 22)

Perhaps there is no resolution to the incongruity inherent in a Baudrillard-inspired profit-making product. Perhaps that is the wrong question to ask. The designs inspired by these ideas are provocative, whimsical, exploratory, evocative and a bit strange. They are a form of research; they are experiments in design theory, design methodology and design education.

AFFORDANCES AND ABILITIES

In the discussion of meaning, another concept that took hold was that of affordance, a term coined by American psychologist James Gibson (1966), who proposed that human beings perceive affordances rather than objects. Affordance may be described as the quality of a thing that communicates the action that may be performed on or with it. For example, a bell

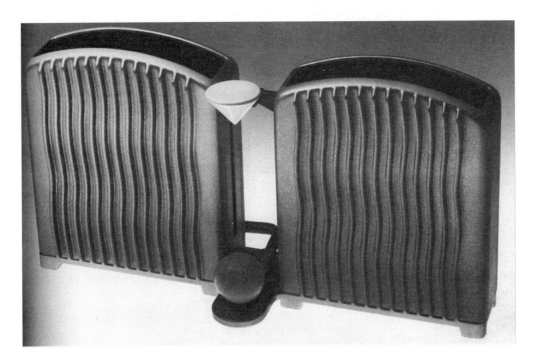

Figure 8.16.   Toaster Design by Vang Hong Tsai, Cranbrook Academy of Art. Image courtesy of Vang Hong Tsai and Michael McCoy.

affords ringing, book affords reading, a pen affords writing, and so on. However, affordance is not entirely a function of the object; it has a behavioral component that depends upon people and their condition/state of being. For instance, the more tired someone is, the more objects appear chair-like; in such cases even a box or a window ledge or the floor can serve as a chair. Gibson's notion of affordance brings into play yet another context that defines meaning—behavior. This concept bears a resemblance to Von Uexküll's notion of counter-ability, or the property of objects to accommodate human ability:

> We find all over an ability [*Leistung*] of man which the object sustains by its counter-ability [*Gegenleistung*]. The chair serves seating, the stair climbing, the vehicle riding, etc… In the counter-ability lies the meaning of the object for our existence. This counter-ability is what the constructor of the vehicle has in mind, what the architect thinks of when designing the plan of the house, what the butcher thinks of who slaughters the ox, as also the writer writing the book, the watchmaker fabricating the watch. (Krampen 1994: 516)

The affordance or counter-ability is that quality of a thing that makes it what it is; it defines its essence. It is what gives a cup its "cupness", a chair its "chairness", and so on. As designers design new cups and new chairs, they gradually change what a generic cup or a common chair looks like. In this process, they slowly change the accepted meanings of these objects.

In spite of the immeasurable varieties of chairs that exist, human beings have no trouble in recognizing them or being able to use them. "The process of categorization is one of the ways by which the mind develops order out of the chaotic variations that occur in everyday life" (Athavankar 1989: 102). The human mind creates concept categories and groups them by visual identifiers to aid in object recognition. Athavankar illustrates this point through an experiment conducted by linguist William Labov, in which subjects were asked to label cups, bowls, and vases as a means of examining the relationship between variations in product form and their conceptual meanings. The experiment suggests that identification of meaning (recognition of the object) depends upon a socially agreed upon archetype or typical example. It is assumed that majority of people can recognize a quintessential chair based upon familiarity, history, memory, etc. "Typical instances or the prototype represents the core meaning of the linguistic term" (Athavankar 1989: 103). This object, the archetypal prototype, becomes the sign for all products in that category, by standing in for them. Athavankar also points out that the boundaries between these product categories are not tidy with several peripheral objects that defy tight definitions or strict taxonomic rules. Such ambiguity is accounted for in semiotics through polysemy.

TYPES OF SIGNS

For Peirce, signs did not exist independently but were manifestations of real phenomena. He classified these phenomena into three categories by their firstness, secondness and thirdness (Cobley and Jansz 1999: 27). Peirce was referring to the kinds of feelings that one experiences while listening to music, or seeing a certain color. These are qualities of signs. Secondness refers to the causal relationships or the interconnectedness among things, described as the "brute facts which arise from a relationship" (Cobley and Jansz 1999: 27). Thirdness is the "realm of general laws" (Cobley and Jansz 1999: 27) or conventions that guide actions. Mapping the triad of representamen, object and interpretant against the triad of firstness, secondness and thirdness, Morris described a matrix that defines nine types of signs.

A qualisign is a representamen that refers to a certain quality of the object (color, material, texture, etc.). These are the elements that designers work with in the creation of new products. A sinsign is a representamen that points out a particular object. Pointing fingers, highlighted text, the words "here" and "there" are all examples of sinsigns. A lexisign is a representamen that refers to laws or conventions that guide behavior. Sporting events are replete with such lexisigns as whistles, cards, hand gestures, etc. Peirce called "signs resulting from resemblance *icons*, those from relations *indexes*, and those from convention *symbols*" (Danesi 2007: 41). An icon, widely used in graphic design, is a sign that bears some direct resemblance to its object. Photographs, literal illustrations, digital images of such things as trashcans and folders are all examples of icons. Such icons are widely used as graphics on products, on packaging (fragile = broken wine glass), and in user manuals. Most assembly instructions for flat pack furniture include several iconic illustrations of components and tools. One of the biggest advantages of icons is that, if well designed and culturally accepted, they can have universal legibility and cross–contextual application, which can minimize the use for language. Several Braun products designed in the 1950s by Hans Gugelot and Dieter Rams used icons exclusively instead of text to allow for universal application. An index is a sign that expresses a causal relationship to the object. The sound of the bell used in conditioning is an index, as is lightning an index for thunder. In visual terms, timelines, flowcharts and bubble diagrams that show connections between components are examples of indexes. Symbols rely on convention and cultural codes in order to be interpreted. All words are symbols for ideas, flags are symbols for nations, the cross a symbol for Christianity, the Swastika a symbol of the Nazis and of goodness in Hindu mythology, logos symbols for corporations. On products, symbols—like the one seen on an on/off button—are often used to represent conditions, and in graphics, they may be used in company logos. Colors too are symbols as they carry specific culturally-dependant connotations. "A symbol … cannot indicate any particular thing, it denotes a kind of thing" (Clarke 1990: 76) . The last three classifications of signs—rhemes, dicents and arguments—exist at the third level of interpretants. The rheme is a sign that is interpreted as a possibility; it refers to a possible object. A dicent for the interpretant is a sign of actual existence; here the object is a fact. The argument is a sign of law for its interpretant; it is interpreted as a reason. Cobley and Jansz provide an example of a football (soccer) player and demonstrate the use of these signs. "A football referee shows a red card to a football player who has committed a blatant

	Quality Firstness	Brute facts Secondness	Law Thirdness
Representamen Firstness	Qualisign	Sinsign	Legisign
Object Secondness	Icon	Index	Symbol
Interpretant Thirdness	Rheme	Dicent	Argument

Figure 8.17.   Nine Types of Signs. Illustration by Amethyst Saludo.

professional foul. As the red card invokes rules (professional fouls are illegal and lead to penalties against the perpetrator), it is an argument. It is also symbolic (the red card signifies the professional foul by convention), and therefore also a legisign (a general law)" (Cobley and Jansz 1999: 35).

Automated teller machines (A.T.M.s) in banks and self-checkout systems in supermarkets use a broad range of signs in their operation. Most of them are equipped with graphic user interfaces and touch screen monitors. The user interface of a drive-through A.T.M., for instance, has a series of icons to represent physical objects like cash, checks, envelopes and debit cards. Buttons that say "Press Here to Start" are indexical signs. The materials, colors and textures of the device are qualisigns. Logos of the bank and the A.T.M. manufacturer, or graphics of $ and ¢ (dollars and cents) or € (Euros) to represent money are symbols, while lane lines and arrows painted on the ground that denote directional and spatial rules for cars are lexisigns. Pointed index fingers guiding traffic to the A.T.M. lanes (environmental signage) serve as sinsigns. Someone driving down a road looking for an A.T.M. might see a street corner or a strip mall from a distance, and see the possibility of finding a bank there. In this case, the strip mall acts as a rheme. If indeed a bank exists and it has a drive-through A.T.M., it becomes an actuality and therefore a dicent. Banks often do exist in such common urban American environments by convention, and for the interpreter, this knowledge represents an argument. It seems clear, as Peirce suggested, that our environment is "perfused with signs."

Thomas Sebeok, prominent philosopher and semiotician, has suggested six types of signs, which include symptoms, signals and names in addition to Peirce's indexes, icons and symbols. Symptoms are generally physiological signs of the body that indicate a certain condition; examples include swellings, rash, etc. A collection of symptoms that suggests an illness is referred to as a syndrome. Signals are mechanisms seen in organisms (humans and other animals) in the form of winking, changing color, making sounds, etc. Names—

important signifiers of individuality—are words used to identify specific things or people. First names for individuals and second names for families are common; but people often name their products to connote personalization and an emotional connection. For a corporation, the naming a product is itself a design process; it is complicated, involved and time consuming. The name has to embody the design and it has to distinguish itself in the market. It has to appeal to all the target user groups, it has to suggest the essence of the brand and it should be a name that can be legally protected. Convia, a Herman Miller product, is a smart building platform that allows quick installation and change of entire electrical systems within a building. It integrates power delivery and computer technology within its system. The name Convia was conceived by design consultancy SHR Perceptual Management. According to graphic designer Brad Jones who worked on the Convia naming project, the key criteria used in naming included distinction, attribute relevance, pronunciation, spelling and availability. Distinction compares the uniqueness of the potential product name with those of competitor products. Naming specialists list the product's defining features in order to ensure that the name reflects the key attributes of the product. The criterion of attribute relevance measures this specific quality of the potential name. However, they also pick names that allow flexibility so that the product line has room to grow. Here, a name that has more room for polysemic interpretation offers more room for design development. Retention refers to the level of memorability and ease of recall of the name in the consumer's mind; and higher retention and memorability are desired qualities. A fourth criterion ensures that names are easy to pronounce and difficult to mispronounce in any language. Lastly, legal availability of the name is critical, because a name is intellectual property and it cannot be used if already owned by another individual or corporation. Naming is an essential component of brand design, and names are chosen with serious deliberation and extreme care because of their potential impact. The naming process, in some ways, deconstructs the mechanism by which audience members may make sense of it.

When in design development, products generally have a code name that stands in for the final name; in case of Convia, it was Purple. The naming process starts with a series of questions about the key attributes and features of the product, the characteristics of the users/audience, the markets it will enter, the competition it will have to face, and the types of opportunities and challenges available to the corporation.

Designers, brand specialists and marketing experts generate multiple name ideas based upon the themes identified and attributes selected. These name alternatives developed by the naming strategists are interpretants suggested by the object. According to Jones (personal interview 2007), "Convia was conceived as a metaphoric (coined) word created as a result of combining **conv**ergence and **via** (the Latin root word for pathway) meaning "converging pathways" which is symbolic of the convergence of technologies, building infrastructural systems, ideas and methodologies inherent with the Purple product. Pathway is also symbolic of the "transmission channel" of electricity, data and control information".

When the sign (name) exits the design studio and makes its way into the world, it has the potential of generating a host of additional interpretants in the minds of users. Brand strategists strive to foresee as many variations of interpretants as they possibly can and manipulate the sign to lead the users to a specific set of interpretants. As one may imagine, and as polysemy makes clear, signs in the world lead to a host of signifieds determined by contexts and the interpreters/users.

SEMANTICS, SYNTACTICS, PRAGMATICS: THE STRUCTURE OF SIGNS

As discussed earlier, Morris divided the semiotic method into three components: "the study of sign assemblages, which he called *syntactics*; the analysis of the relations that are forged between signs and their meanings, which he called *semantics*; and the investigation of the relations between signs and their users, which he called *pragmatics*" (Danesi 2007: 10). The Aeron chair, which signifies high-tech, modern furniture with new materials and new suspension technologies, operates within a network of signs in an environment that includes a desk, a computer, books, a keyboard, lighting and other accessories of a contemporary office. A syntactic study of the network of signs within which the Aeron chair exists would shed light on how it's meaning is influenced by other signs in its environment. Semantics, the relation between the sign and its meaning has substantial significance for design and is the fundamental question that guides product semantics. The knowledge of what an Aeron chair means to its user can help designers improve the existing design and it can also assist in the development of future seating solutions. Pragmatics focuses on the relationship between signs and their interpreters. Pragmatic studies examine how people respond to the signs in their environment. It deals with the processes of communication between objects and people. How effective is the Aeron chair in communicating its features and functions to its users? Do the form and graphic treatment serve the purpose they are designed for? These questions can help designers minimize miscommunication and therefore minimize errors in operation.

It is evident in the discussion of syntactics, semantics and pragmatics that it is not sufficient to think of signs alone; one needs to consider relations as well. Saussure, too, was convinced that language should be considered in terms of the relationship between its parts. This view, supported and adopted by several semioticians, came to be formally referred to as structuralism. It endorses a relational or structural view of language and culture rather than a fragmented or individual view. In other words, all signs exist within a structure, and meanings depend not on the individual signs but their relations. "In order to recognize something as a sign, one must (1) be able to differentiate it from other signs; and (2) know how its component parts fit together. More technically, a sign is a sign if it has both *paradigmatic* (differential) and *syntagmatic* (combinatory) structure" (Danesi 2007: 53). In language, the reason we understand what words mean is because of the difference between their sounds and the way they are written. In other words, what gives the words "book" and "cook" their different meanings is the difference in the first sound in both words. This

1 ANALYZE CURRENT SITUATION	2 DEFINE ISSUES	3 CHARACTERIZE AUDIENCE
• Understand company's existing portfolio • Recommend a naming model	• Key product attributes and benefits • Audience • Markets • Competition • Opportunities • Challenges	• Define personality traits • Define 'must have' and 'would like to have' • Understand points of resistance • List alternatives
4 DEFINE MARKETS & INDUSTRIES	5 DEFINE BENEFITS & VALUE KEYWORDS	6 DEFINE COMPETITION
• List appropriate industry sectors • Identify appropriate language	• List adjectives to define the product • Create a hierarchy of keywords	• List competitor product names • Analyze value keywords for competitor names
7 CREATE THEMATIC DIRECTIONS	8 GENERATE NAME ALTERNATIVES (brainstorming)	9 EVALUATE NAME ALTERNATIVES AGAINST CRITERIA
• List possible themes to drive name • Write brief descriptions and justifications for themes	• Option A • Option B • Option C	• Attribute relevance • Distinction • Retention • Pronunciation • Spelling
10 TEST NAMES WITH USERS	11 NARROW DOWN ALTERNATIVE NAMES	12 SELECT FINAL NAME
• Conduct tests to gather user opinions	• Analyze user responses • Rank order names • Select top three for further analysis	• Pick top name from rank order

Figure 8.18.   The Naming Process. Illustration by Amethyst Saludo.

refers to the paradigmatic structure of language. In addition, meanings are constructed on the basis of how signs come together. In a sentence, the words have to be structured along grammatical rules for them to make sense. The sentence "When I am done with this book, I will become a cook" has meaning because it follows the principles of English grammar. In the design of complex products with multiple moving and removable parts, it is critical that the components are designed to be visually different from one another to avoid confusion, and yet they need to be bound together with the appropriate formal characteristics that clearly signify how they do fit together. Poorly designed kit furniture often causes tremendous frustration during assembly because it does not do either of these things well.

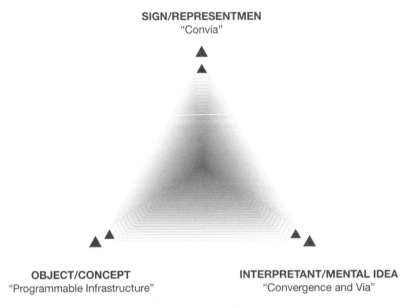

SIGN/REPRESENTMEN
"Convia"

OBJECT/CONCEPT
"Programmable Infrastructure"

INTERPRETANT/MENTAL IDEA
"Convergence and Via"

Figure 8.19.   Convia: The Semiotic Triangle. Illustration by Amethyst Saludo.

Concepts of structuralism were developed in anthropology and in linguistics. Noted anthropologist Claude Levi-Strauss believed that not only can society be studied with methods used in linguistics, but also that culture itself could be conceived of as a language. And just as linguists such as Saussure have pointed out the significance of relations over individual signs, Levi-Strauss showed how social phenomena such as kinship, rituals, gift-giving, cooking, marriage, etc. were elements of larger cultural structures. Design operates within a world of creativity and commerce, production and consumption, manufacture and craft; and these oppositions create structure. But above all, design exists within networks of human relationships between the producers and consumers, structured around artifacts that are continuously being created and consumed. Just as the universe can be composed of signs, by tenets of structuralism, it can also be conceived as a structure.

SIGN AS VALUE

In his study of consumption, French sociologist Jean Baudrillard locates objects simult-aneously within semiotics and political economy. He overlays Marx's commodity system of use-value (utility) and exchange-value (tradability), with structural semiotics by adding symbolic and sign value. The meanings of things, to him, depend entirely upon the process of signification—a table, for example, exists only if it is designated. Baudrillard's analyses of objects and of consumption have had a significant impact on several areas of study. He posited that things needed to be examined less as material entities or results of processes of production and more as signs. And while Saussure had imagined the signifier and signified as inseparable (like two sides of a coin), Baudrillard suggests that "the signifier is detached

Figure 8.20. Aeron Chair. Image courtesy of Herman Miller, Inc.

from the signified just as exchange value is detached from use value. Like the price, the signifier floats in the social space of consumer capitalism" (Poster 1979: 282). It is indeed true that prices of goods are not determined by their utility. For several products on the market, low utility does not necessarily mean a low price, and a high price does not always signify high utility. Similarly, their meanings are not determined by a specific relation to price or any other attribute; they are detached from the object and set afloat, to be determined in context. Baudrillard's key argument states that the symbolic meanings of commodities have overtaken their utilitarian and commercial meanings in late capitalist societies. "If use value is the quality of the good (i.e. the product that is outside of the market economy), and the exchange value is the price set on the market of a commodity, then sign value is that value that gives status when it is consumed or spent" (Bolin 2005: 292). Sign values for Baudrillard can produce status and create social difference. Goods with high exchange values such as expensive cars possess high sign values and produce a sense of distinction for the owners.

SEMIOTICS AND SEMANTICS: A CRITIQUE

Though semiotics has been tremendously influential in a variety of disciplines including cultural studies and design, it has also been critiqued as being an analytical practice rather than a method or theory, and as being imperialist because of the belief that it is applicable to all cultural phenomena. The critique centers around the fact that the meanings of objects cannot simply be read using linguistic structures without understanding how the objects themselves are produced, distributed, shared, and consumed in society.

Product semantics, too, had its critics. Though the proponents explicitly stated that product semantics was not an aesthetic movement, some labeled it as style rather than a generative/interpretive method, and it lost some of the global attention it had initially attracted. Some of the critiques of the design methodology espoused by product semantics suggested that designers "confine themselves to communicating function and method of use, both of which are undoubtedly important, but only constitute part of the meaning and impact of products" (Richardson 1993: 36). Richardson suggests that the approach adopted by these experiments with product semantics was based upon the assumption that the user desires "singular, logical meaning" of the product. He adds "the commutability of meaning that an abstract form permits means that the designer has no way of conveying a singular meaning and that precise meaning only. Products can only communicate messages within boundaries of probability; there always remains a degree of uncertainty as to how the symbolisms will be decoded by their users" (Richardson 1993: 37). However, product semantics recognizes that designers cannot control meaning; it accepts the polysemic nature of objects, and suggests that *"what something is* (the totality of what it means) *to someone corresponds to the sum total of its imaginable contexts"* (Krippendorff 1989: 13). Designers generate forms that pre-configure certain functional and social meanings; but there is never any certainty to what meanings eventually will emerge in interaction. Meanings emerge in acts of negotiation.

Krippendorff distances the field of product semantics from semiotics, suggesting that "semiotic theories divert attention from the meaning of artifacts to the relations between signs and their referents, between signifiers and the signified, a move that unwittingly imports epistemological assumptions into discussions of meaning, which are alien to design and generally untenable" (Krippendorff 2006: 273). Krippendorff raises five key issues regarding the semiotic approach that disassociates it from product semantics. Krippendorff's first critique deals with the structural nature of semiotics, especially its dyadic nature. He argues that the "two–world ontology" of signifier–signified cannot be effectively used for objects as it leads to accounts of "artifacts as representations." Second, he notes that semioticians fail to factor in the role played by people in sign production, and neither do they recognize their own agency in this process. Third, he suggests that semiotics is not structurally able to deal with the multiplicity of meaning. He criticizes semiotics for creating and limiting signs to rigid categories and taxonomies, and expecting people to follow them. And finally, he disagrees with "semiotics' belief in a rational consensus" (Krippendorff 2006: 227) or its suggestion that all signs operate similarly (for example, in a triadic fashion). Krippendorff's critique, valid in some ways, seems to be directed largely towards the scholarship of Saussure, Peirce and Morris and does not refer to some of the newer variations of the discipline.

THE ROLE OF PEOPLE AND SOCIETY IN MAKING MEANING

Social semiotics (Hodge and Kress 1988, Van Leeuwen 2005) or postmodern semiotics (Gottdiener 1995) takes on and addresses some of Krippendorff's concerns of human agency. Social semioticians assert that signs cannot be separated from social intercourse or from users. They prefer to use the term "semiotic resources" instead of signifiers, which are

> observable actions and the objects that have been drawn into the domain of social communication and that have a *theoretical* semiotic potential constituted by all their past uses and all their potential uses and an *actual* semiotic potential constituted by these past uses that are known and considered relevant by the users of the resource, and by such potential uses as might be uncovered by the users on the basis of their special needs and interests. (Van Leeuwen 2005: 4)

By the tenets of socio-semiotics, meanings of things develop upon their past uses, which history can reveal, and their potential future uses which users will determine based upon their needs. Van Leeuwen's definition, though rather unwieldy, should be recognized for its emphasis on users—a term widely adopted in design—and the potential uses they may uncover. Meanings are socially constructed by individuals and groups operating singly or as subcultures and organizations. Social semiotics has folded this knowledge into its functional structure.

THE SEMIOGENESIS OF THINGS

Semiogenesis of things is the process of the evolution of meanings of objects over their lives. From design through manufacturing, use and disposal, objects signify different things to different people. Gottdiener (1995) identifies three key stages in the production of meaning of commodities of mass consumption. In the first stage, corporations create exchange-value as well as a sign-value for products through manufacturing and advertising. The structure of production and its agents control this stage of the creation of meaning. Once individuals buy these things, they create their own meanings by incorporating the objects into their lives. They may modify them, redesign them, repurpose them, and generate their own sign values in this second stage of meaning-making. In the third stage, producers who carefully observe and document how people make sense of the things they buy, reappropriate these

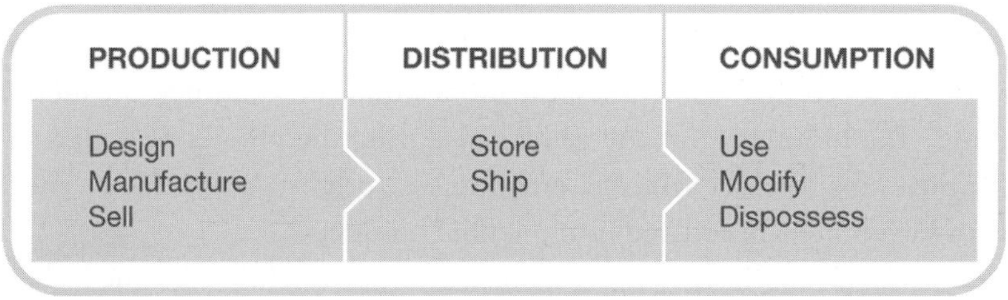

PRODUCTION	DISTRIBUTION	CONSUMPTION
Design Manufacture Sell	Store Ship	Use Modify Dispossess

Figure 8.21. Semiogenesis of Things. Illustration by Amethyst Saludo.

objects for mass production and introduce them as new commodities. This formulation of meaning can be divided into three key phases through its life: production, distribution and consumption. The object, in its journey through these phases, mutates in form as well as in meaning. The clean linearity suggested by the diagram is not necessarily an accurate representation of the process, which is full of repetitions, breaks, cyclicity, and so on.

During processes of production, meanings of things are constructed largely by the manufacturers. We can refer to this as pre-configuration. This stage includes processes of research, design, material selection, technological development, prototyping, manufacturing, testing, advertising, marketing and selling. Of late, processes of participatory design and co-creation have involved users actively in the earlier stages of the design process, thereby allowing consumers to shape the product before it reaches the market. At this stage, objects exist as ideas, sketches, renderings, control drawings, surveys, questionnaires, verbal descriptions, computer models, presentations, rough prototypes, appearance models, and so on. They are works in progress that signify designers' and engineers' visions, the process of innovation, projected corporate profit, satisfiers of people's needs, potential revenue streams for the company, and so on. Meanings at this stage are often regulated and controlled by a select few involved in the process of new product development. Depending upon the complexity of the project, it may involve designers, engineers, marketing professionals, advertising agencies, ergonomists, materials experts, anthropologists, researchers, lead users, etc.

Often, the meanings that arise in one realm of the life of the object (production, for example) are completely unavailable to another (consumption). Herman Miller's Executive Vice President for Research, Design and Development Don Goeman, who oversees a range of product development projects at the company, believes that he has a "tainted" view of what things mean, because he gets a very close view of the process of their evolution. He explained this in a conversation:

> I have this unique perch in the company that allows me to see projects from start to finish... I observe the evolution of these things, and I get to know them from their *dark side*. When I see our product somewhere, I first think of the journey that we went through to get it to that finished stage and how arduous that sometimes is. I know what the designers and project teams go through... And that is what taints my view. The perception of a product is different when you do not know that journey. (Goeman, personal interview 2009)

For Goeman, the "dark side" signifies all the challenges that emerge in the design process. However, he also added that "sometimes, the more arduous the journey, the more authentic the outcome." The meanings that are generated during the process of design as multiple actors (designers, managers, engineers, ergonomists, prototypes, sketches, and so forth) interact with each other, are codified into the final product.

Distribution involves the moving of goods through carefully designed channels and supply chains. At this stage, products are fully manufactured, packed and labeled. They are treated as inventory rather than individual products. Some of the graphic signs that play a crucial role in processes of distribution are packaging, bar codes, R.F.I.D. tags, shipping labels, packing slips and so on. These are the materials that take precedence over the actual products for the stakeholders involved in shipping and receiving. It is generally desirable to keep inventories low and transportation time to a minimum. This is particularly true with goods with limited shelf life. Large inventories and slow transportation times signify lost revenue and financial liability.

The consumption stage of the product involves purchase, use, maintenance, repair, storage, and disposal. The things in stores and shop windows, on glamorous posters and television commercials, on billboards and on websites are signs produced by manufacturers and designers and consumed by users. This is the arena of consumption; this is where things are lusted after and fetishized. It is in this realm that manufacturers vie for people's attention. As the things are bought, taken home and assimilated into daily rituals (or new routines), each individual consumer generates additional meanings unique to their situation in the network. The thing at this stage is being configured; it is being subjected to the user's agency. The formal and graphic techniques used by designers, the functionality introduced by the engineers, the history users have with similar products, the affordances built into the system are all factors that guide the generation of meaning. The exchange-value, which played a role when the object was bought, is now at least partially shadowed by the use-value and sign-value. Meanings of comfort, convenience, pride, status, etc. arise in use, and as the things age (with the owners) these meanings change. As the paint chips, as parts are replaced, as they are dropped, as newer products appear on the market, the objects move from the living room to the garage, and from there to the rubbish bin or the recycling plant. Meanings change as we divest ourselves of things; they become garage junk never to be looked at again, rummage sale items worth a little change, landfill tenants and environmental problems, or fodder for disassembly and raw material for something else. Through this process, things too configure the users. As the product assimilates itself into its new home, it configures the user and his or her environment. It may also shape the user's habits, relationships to friends, methods of communication, and so forth. The reciprocity of agency between people and things is at play here.

In this process of semiogenesis—the evolution of the meanings of things—people and objects take on multiple, fluid meanings as they traverse the journey from production to consumption and back, configuring each other in the process.

THINGS AS SIGNS

Things can indeed be considered as signs. The property of signifying—the process of representing a set of meanings—certainly applies to them. They possess agency. But the discipline of semiotics needs to be supplemented with the recognition that people's interactions with things are fundamental to how meanings are formed. As social semiotics suggests, theoretical examinations of things (central to semiotics) should be accompanied by empirical observations (central to design research), so that narratives of meaning are more holistic and comprehensive. Pure semiotic analyses run the danger of individual, subjective interpretations of objects that may not have much value for design. As the water bottles demonstrate, meanings are polysemic or multivocal, i.e. objects have multiple, not singular meanings, determined by the contexts within which they exist and shaped by their journeys through the entire lifecycle of production, distribution and consumption. In addition, there is no fixity to meanings of things; meanings are fluid and they change over time in their genesis from ideas to raw materials to finished product to rubbish and perhaps back to raw materials. The multiple signfieds of a signifying thing are constantly in a state of flux, changing with time, context, patterns of use and individuals involved. Signs should not be considered only individually or in isolation of each other. The world of signs should also be examined in terms of relations in a network. The relations between signs and people, signs and meanings, and signs themselves create a structure that guides the generation of meanings. Myths, found in all cultures, form a part of this structure, and play a significant role in how individuals, groups and institutions create meanings. As signs, things can extend folklores, recreate urban legends, distort and suppress facts, or tell lies.

Meanings do not exist within people's minds, and neither are they embedded within things. Meanings exist in a non-physical, non-psychical network that includes people and all of the material world. Meanings should not be thought of as entities, but rather as structures in motion, constantly evolving, heavily context-dependent and generated by individuals, social groups and things themselves. People and things generate meanings as they configure each other in specific contexts. Producers (designers, manufacturers, advertisers) can pre-configure networks so as to guide or encourage the construction of certain kinds of meanings. However, they cannot control or regulate the process of meaning-making; that is the privilege of the consumer and of the thing itself.

9 THE OBSESSION OF POSSESSION: FETISH OBJECTS

> Possessions are regarded not only as a part of self, but also as instrumental to the development of self.
>
> Russell Belk, *Collecting in a Consumer Society*

When things turn into possessions, they become signifiers of a whole new range of meanings. We buy things to satisfy needs and desires, to acquire status, to express our identity, to impress others, to identify with specific social groups, and perhaps, to complete a collection. If things are, at least partially, expressions of our material lust, their transformation from things into possessions signals realization of that longing. On a store shelf, a thing might be an object of desire beyond reach that beckons consumers with its seductive qualities. But once acquired, it becomes a domestic possession that signifies ownership. The product enters a stage in its lifecycle that Attfield (2000) refers to as its post-commodity phase:

> The post-commodity phase refers to an object once it has been personalised and thus transformed to mediate certain social transactions related to identity formation which do not necessarily have anything to do with the acquisition process, thus acknowledging that objects change meaning with the passing of time as a result of being incorporated into the life of an individual world together with all the changes that take place in the life cycle. (Attfield 2000: 145)

The attachment between people and their possessions can be organized on a spectrum of possibilities that ranges from fetishistic attachment to extreme antipathy. This chapter will focus on those relationships that involve collecting behavior and fetishistic behavior. While a collection has been described as an organized obsession, fetishism is often referred to as overvaluation of a thing. These two forms of relations demonstrate the agency of things, and the power they can exercise on people. Design, by imparting some of the agentic quality to things, plays a role in the process of converting objects into collectibles and fetish items. This chapter also includes an examination of the role of branding to demonstrate how the sign values of things can construct a series of meanings that lead to the fetishistic overvaluation of things.

The act of owning marks a transformation in the relationship between the possessed and the possessor, between the object and the subject. In some cases (and with certain kinds of objects), this relationship can become immensely powerful as well as overpowering. Fetishism refers to a process by which things take on unexpected religious, economic or erotic meanings. "A fetish is created through the veneration or worship of an object that is attributed some power or capacity, independently of its manifestation of that capacity... The fetish object will, for example, influence the lives of its human worshippers, determining some of their actions and modifying their beliefs" (Dant 1999: 43).

POSSESSING/BEING POSSESSED BY THINGS

In possessing things also lies the condition of being possessed by things. Ownership often signals dependence; once acquired, products become critical to the operation of everyday life. This applies not only to utilitarian objects that serve essential physiological functions, but also to a host of things that are often described as luxury goods, impulse buys, or unnecessary purchases. At spendster.org, consumers are invited to submit their stories of "impulse buying, over-spending or just plain wasting money on the stuff you don't need" (Spendster.org 2008). Many of the stories are tales of woe submitted by consumers who describe themselves as being obsessed with things and addicted to shopping. What is evident in these narratives is a form of helplessness in face of the powerful urge to consume. It is the desire to acquire more possessions like records, shoes, books and a range of other things that possess these consumers, converting them into addicted collectors. And it is this drive to collect (sometimes at any cost) that converts the thing into a fetish item. For Aristides, a collection is "an obsession organized" into an order determined by the collector (1988). "One of the distinctions between possessing and collecting is that the latter implies order, system, perhaps completion. The pure collector's interest is not bounded by the intrinsic worth of the objects of his desire; whatever they cost, he must have them. Except in the case of the rare and exciting find that turns out to be a bargain, he generally knows that he is paying more than he probably ought to for the items in his collection, but he cannot help himself. If he has any introspection, he begins at some point to sense that his collection possesses him" (Aristides 1988: 330). The agency of things reaches its zenith when they transform into fetish items; their means to configure us is at maximum potency. "When someone invests psychic energy in an object—a thing, another person, or an idea—that object becomes charged with the energy of the agent" (Csikszentmihalyi and Rochberg-Halton 1981: 8). If we imagine this to be a scalable process, the more energy one invests in a thing, the more "charged" it gets. A fetishized thing possesses not only its own agency, but is made more potent with the psychic energy of the fetishist. The more possessive we become of our things, the more possessed we are.

In consumer behavior studies, possessions have often been described as extensions of the self (Sirgy 1982, Belk 1988). An object possessed becomes (at least partially) an expression of the owner; it takes on the role of representing the owner's self. In their landmark study of over 300 Chicago households and their possessions, Csikszentmihalyi and Rochberg-Halton (1981), discovered that in their middle to late years, people tended to define themselves more in terms of their possessions. Belk explains three strategies (initially developed by Sartre) that people use to make an object an extension of the self. The first is by appropriating or controlling the object, the second is by creating it, and the third is by knowing it (Belk 1988). In other words, people invest their energy and their self into these things through these strategies of control, creation and knowledge. And in this process, they blur the distinction between the self and the thing. People and their possessions are generally conceived as two independent entities (subjects and objects); however, the more accurately things represent the self the more they act as subjects rather than objects. If it is our possessions that define us, consumption effaces and blurs the boundaries between subject and object.

FORMS OF POSSESSION

Our relationship to things can be situated on a continuum defined by the habit of obsessive collecting (possessive behaviors) at one end and utter disdain (dispossessive behaviors) at the other. Possessive behaviors, at one end of the spectrum include functional use, conserving, fetishistic use and obsessive collecting, while dispossessive behaviors include the practice of neglect, divestiture and extreme antipathy. Detachment from materiality is a condition of neutrality (often talked about in religion and spirituality) that signifies neither extreme.

Along the scale of possessive behaviors, *functional use* refers to situations in which the primary value of the object is its pure utility. For example, a car that is valued not as a status symbol but largely for its use as a means of transportation exemplifies functional use. There is no emotional attachment between the person and the object. *Interested engagement* signals either active use or the guarding and protection of objects. This state refers to things that one uses on a regular or occasional basis that have enough possessive value to be cared for and maintained. In this case, the relation between the person and the object displays a range of emotional values from high to low. *Obsessive collecting* refers to the fervent search and compulsive acquisition of goods, and most commonly includes such collectibles as stamps, records, books, shoes, etc. However, no boundaries can be drawn around what may or may not qualify as a collectible; people have been known to possess vast collections of utilitarian objects such as hammers, decorative things such as small porcelain pigs, fashion items such as purses and totally unexpected and non-utilitarian things such as air sickness bags and banana labels. The final element in the chain of possessive behaviors is *fetishistic*

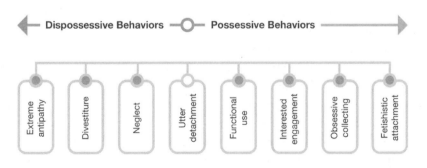

Figure 9.1.   Forms of Possession. Illustration by Amethyst Saludo.

attachment. In this form of possession, fetishists assign significant, additional values to the object that are not inherent to its "designed" properties. These wildly overvalued things therefore become fetish items.

Along the scale of dispossessive behaviors, neglect refers to situations where an object is left to the elements or carelessly tossed in a bin somewhere, often not in the house. An object that ends up in the garage and is almost never looked at but is never thrown out falls in this category. These things are generally discarded when people move. When an object reaches a stage in its life cycle where it is no longer desired in the house or attic or garage, it is discarded through a process of divestiture. In this case the object may be given to second-use stores or tossed out as rubbish to end up in a landfill. Finally, when a divested object has no further use for anyone in that form, it is destroyed through shredding, melting, compaction, etc. either by the user or by institutional systems such as recycling and take-back programs. Extreme antipathy occurs in situations where the user might have experienced a severe problem with the object and has developed an intense dislike towards it. Sometimes, this form of dispossession might include violent destruction of the device.

And finally, utter detachment—a neutral position between possessive and dispossessive behaviors—refers to an absolute lack of interest in the object. Such things have neither positive nor negative value to the dispassionate owner. This condition may be compared to the notion of choiceless awareness in Hindu spirituality. "Choiceless awareness implies to be aware, both objectively—outside—and inwardly, without any choice, just to be aware … not choose, not say, 'I like this, I don't like that,' or, 'I want this, I don't want that.' … And, in that observation, there is no decision, no will, no choice" (Krishnamurti 1992). This notion, borrowed to apply to things, results in a condition, not of valuelessness, but of neutral value.

These varied forms of possession, though visually depicted on the scale as discrete behaviors, are not necessarily so. The boundaries between fetish items and functional objects, for example, are not inflexible. It is contexts of use that define the meanings of objects and it is these contexts that determine their fetish quality.

COLLECTING THINGS

The desire to possess is acutely sensed by collectors, who often go to extreme lengths in acquiring specific objects for their collections. The habit of collecting focuses its keen eye on a wide range of things, natural and artificial, expensive and inexpensive, ordinary and extraordinary. Things do not necessarily possess a quality of collectability; it is the collector's desire that makes things collectible. According to Benjamin, "ownership is the most intimate relationship that one can have to objects. Not that they come alive in him; it is he who lives in them" (Benjamin 1968a: 67). As someone who "lives in" the collection, the collector instead of being the consumer of things, is consumed by them. "I would argue that there are five major reasons individuals collect things: to satisfy a sense of personal aesthetics, to gain a sense of control or completion, to connect themselves with history, for profit (real or imagined), and for, as one avid collector described it, the 'thrill of the chase'" (Akin 1996). Collectors are inspired by the unique characteristics of objects that meet a specific aesthetic sensibility, and the collected object could be an impressionist painting or a beer coaster. People often collect things that are markers of their own or someone else's history. For example, the collection of rare coins and seals often represents a fascination with the history of an empire, while the collection of refrigerator magnets from various cities are markers of a collector's travel history. A large number of collectors also expect their objects to have a certain market value and therefore may anticipate some form of profit, should they decide to sell their collection. Such value may be real or imagined. Once a collection is started (especially if it is a series with several related objects) the desire of a complete set becomes a very powerful consuming force. In such cases, the missing pieces constitute a challenge, they are voids that cannot be left empty.

COLLECTING CULTURES

In the anthropological and marketing scholarship on collecting (Belk 1995, Pearce 1998), earlier studies focused more on the objects collected but recent scholarship has directed its focus on the practice itself. For Belk *et al.*, collecting is "the selective, active, and longit-udinal acquisition, possession and disposition of an interrelated set of differentiated objets (material things, ideas, beings or experiences) that contribute to and derive extraordinary meaning from the entity (the collection) that this set is perceived to constitute" (1990: 8). This expansive definition foregrounds a few key components of the practice of collecting— selective acquisition, integrated set of objects and extraordinary meanings. Collectors are discriminating in their selection of the objects for the collection. The yearning for things is never satisfied by any thing; it has to be a specific object that either has the required aesthetic characteristics, brand name or uniqueness, and in many cases it is a desired miss-ing component of a larger set. The last piece of a set holds tremendous agentic power and can drive collectors to pay significant amounts of money for its acquisition. The collectible, though a thing by itself, is also incomplete by itself. In the collector's eye, it is destined to be joined with other incomplete items of a perfect set. A finished collection with all items in place signifies success, achievement and immense satisfaction for the collector.

The object of collection possesses symbolic meanings that replace or mask utilitarian meanings. For a collector of beer steins, a new specimen is not purchased because of its use-value; it most often immediately takes its position on a shelf with its predecessors in the set, to be exhibited as a "find" rather than used as a stein. Collectibles may or may not possess any financial value but in many cases, they do have exchange-value. The trading of baseball cards, coins, stamps and other collectibles in a barter system is common in the collecting community. The object of collection creates a world of commerce of its own; it exists in a financial system where value is defined by the community of collectors who know what's hot and what's not. "There is a continuing appeal in stamp collecting—where one may note, the stamps are preferably cancelled ones so that there is no doubt about their worthlessness in the circle of commodities for which they were originally intended" (Kopytoff 1986: 80). The cancelled stamp is more valued *because* it has no more use-value.

Pearce describes collecting in contemporary culture as a postmodern exercise because it "is an emblematic activity which ransacks the past to create a present idiosyncrasy of style" (1998: 14). She explains the postmodern situation as a "belief that the narratives which connect the past and present are merely the present viewing the past" (Pearce 1998: 14) and offers three premises that make collecting today a postmodern activity. One, collecting is much more common today than ever before; two, it includes a wider range of artifacts; and three, it is at once a part of and response to contemporary society. It is generally true that consumers have much better access to a much larger number and variety of commodities than any time in the past. In addition, online auctioning and sales services such as ebay and Craigslist have not only made millions of goods accessible to millions—they have also broadened the geography of availability. Belk explains collecting as a process of production *and* consumption. "Collectors create, combine, classify, and curate the objects they acquire in such a way that a new product, the collection, emerges. In the process they also produce meanings" (Belk 1995: 55). Collecting is not purely an activity of consumption or acquisition; it includes the creative fashioning of the collection itself, an activity of making or production. Although typically identified with leisure, a collection demands investment of passion, effort and financial resources. Belk draws parallels between collecting and consuming behavior; both are triggered by the economics of supply as well as practices of demand. However, collecting is often signified by a different value system:

> A collection is basically determined by the nature of the *value* assigned to the objects, or ideas possessed. If the *predominant* value of an object or idea for the person possessing it is intrinsic, i.e. if it is valued primarily for use, or purpose, or aesthetically pleasing quality, or other valued inherent in the object or accruing to it by whatever circumstances of custom, training, or habit, it is not a collection. If the predominant value is representative or representational, i.e. if said object or idea is valued chiefly for the relation it bears to some other object or idea, or objects, or ideas, such as being one of a series, part of a whole, a specimen of a class, then it is the subject of a collection. (Durost in Pearce 1998: 2)

Therefore, for a collectible to be truly valued as a collectible, it cannot be an individual item; it needs to belong to a larger idea. In addition, the hunt for the collectible generally involves a form of obsession that may not be visible in shopping for a thing. Though there is no doubt that the thrill of the chase (especially for bargain or sales shopping) excites consumers, the adventure involved in finding the collectible which will fill the empty spot in a series signifies a different set of emotional meanings.

The object of collection is no mere commodity. It inspires extraordinary emotions in the collecting individual. Though an individual object, it stands for an entire collection, and though negligible in use-value, it has significant exchange-value and sign-value. The collectible draws its value from its unique and indispensable place in the collection.

THE MULTIPLE FORMS AND MEANINGS OF FETISHISM

Discussed by scholars in anthropology, political economy, cultural studies and psychology, the term "fetishism" has been employed to refer to everything from witchcraft and the use of objects in primitive religious practices to sexual obsession with such things as leather and latex (Ellen 1988, Apter and Pietz 1993, Spyer 1998, Dant 1999). And it generally refers to the additional meanings consumers assign to mundane objects. "For Marx, Freud and Baudrillard, fetishism is a conceptual tool used to critique the overvaluation of goods as against their real value as inert, inanimate objects" (Dant 1999: 40). The root of fetish is *feitiço*, a Portuguese word that was used by early explorers of Africa's west coast in the sixteenth and seventeenth centuries, who found hand-crafted totems, amulets and idols that were deemed to have magical powers. "[T]he word *fetisso* came into parlance as a Portuguese trading term associated with "small wares" and "magic charms" used for barter between blacks and whites. White merchants, compromising both their religion and their "rational" economic principles, took oaths on fetishes in order to seal commercial agreements" (Apter and Pietz 1993: 5). These fetish items, charged with religious, cultural, social and sign value, and full of magical powers, became symbols of guarantees between trading partners. The meaning and application of the term fetish has since evolved significantly and is often used to refer to objects that are imparted special qualities through use. Following the work of Ellen (1988) and Dant (1999), we can classify fetishism into four primary categories: religious fetishism, commodity fetishism, sexual fetishism and semiotic fetishism.

RELIGIOUS FETISHISM

In anthropology, the term "fetishism" has traditionally been used to refer to certain religious and ritualistic practices of the so-called "primitive" peoples, or remote and unindustrialized cultures of the world. Charles de Brosses, an eighteenth-century French anthropologist and politician is credited with first use of the term fetishism, explained as "the direct worship of particular earthly material objects as themselves endowed with quasi-personal intentionality and divine powers capable of ratifying mundane desires" (Nelson and Shiff 2003: 307). De Brosses believed that the "savage mind" needed these tangible, inanimate things as the focus of its attention before it could contemplate the abstract and animate entities of this world. For the early anthropological elitist, the fetish object became a signifier for the "savageness" of unknown cultures. Following de Brosses, the concept was further developed by Auguste Comte as necessary in the development of religion from an individualistic to an organized form. He saw fetishism as the first step in the evolution of the religious ideas of polytheism and monotheism. He too, like de Brosses, described fetishism as the process by which "human mental qualities were attributed to non-human bodies" (Ellen 1988: 213). In these cases, fetishism was perceived as a somewhat aberrant and uncivilized practice of an uncultured mind. However, there is little conceptual clarity or agreement on the precise meaning of religious fetishism.

COMMODITY FETISHISM

Though the term "fetishism" had existed prior to Marx, he was the first to connect it to the economic lives of objects through the notion of commodity fetishism. Marx differentiated things from commodities on the basis of their role in economic and social circulation. Only when things enter commerce and are exchanged for money do they become commodities. This form of trade is possible because commodities possess use-value and exchange-value, and when things emerge as commodities in exchange, they acquire a mysterious value. Marx explained the source of this mysterious value through the concept of alienation—the estrangement between workers and the product of their labor. As we have discussed before, exploitative labor alienated workers from the people who paid them wages (the factory owners) and those who bought their goods (consumers). As a consequence, workers were alienated not only from the products and processes of their labor but also from other human beings and from human nature. Labor itself became commoditized and exchanged on the market, rather like the goods that it created. Its exchangeability (that it could be bought on the market in return for wages) situated it within a social system (in addition to an economic one) and reflected social relations. "To the latter [the producers], therefore, the relations connecting the labour of one individual with that of the rest appear, not as direct social relations between individuals at work, but as what they really are, material relations between persons and social relations between things" (Marx 1990: 165). This, to Marx, gave commodities their mysterious quality, and their fetishism.

Although Marx traced the origin of commodity fetishism to the labor expended in its production, the fetish value of products is also generated in consumption. Stratton (1996) recognizes these two forms of fetishization and categorizes them as passive and active fetishism:

> In passive commodity fetishism the commodity disguises from the consumer its origin in the process of capitalist production, appearing only as an object to the gaze of the consumer... Active commodity fetishism describes a qualitatively more dynamic relation between the commodity and the consumer in which the commodity appears to entice the consumer into buying it. Passive commodity fetishism describes the objectification of the commodity in capitalism; active commodity fetishism describes a further process of incorporating the consumer in the process of commodification (Stratton 1996: 32–3).

Both forms of fetishism, active and passive, determine the nature of the relationship between people and things; while one masks the commodity's labor origins, the other gives the commodity its seductive qualities. And the product's form, a key feature with which the consumer interacts, plays a significant role in the substantiation of these fetishes. The product's journey starts for the consumer not in production but in consumption. It appears in retail outlets seemingly magically; its form reveals nothing about its material journey from raw substance to finished good, and neither does it tell the human story of the labor that is expended in its making. The object is hermetically sealed and in the act of passive fetishism it holds within its form the mystery of its genesis and its evolution. The form, along with advertising, serves yet another function—that of seduction. In an act of active fetishism, the product's shape, color, texture and material—visible and tangible manifestations of its design—tempt the individual into becoming a consumer. Similarly, techniques of marketing designed to promote consumption endorse active fetishism through slick advertising. Commodity fetishism therefore operates both in realms of production and consumption.

SEXUAL FETISHISM

Fetishism has also appeared in the literature in psychology since the late 1800s, and has typically been used to describe a strong erotic attraction to things (such as shoes, stockings, leather) or to a non-genital part of the body (legs, feet, etc.). Freud, in *Three Essays on Sexuality* published in 1905, introduces his notion of fetishism as "after-effect of some sexual impression, received as a rule in early childhood." According to him, fetishism starts when the male child discovers the absence of a penis on the woman's body, assumes that the mother has been castrated and is afraid that he might be too. Shocked by this "lack," he finds objects to replace his anxiety and restore his erotic attachment to the woman's body. So the fetishized objects become substitutes for the penis that the male child expects to see on the woman. "Thus, foot and shoe fetishism reflects the inquisitive desire of young boys to approach a woman's genitals from below-from her feet upwards-whereas fur and velvet fetishism becomes a fixation on pubic hair" (Ellen 1988: 218). Sexual fetishism is based in the idea of association or metonymy, where one object stands in for another. In Freud's case, the fetish object stands in for the mother's (castrated) penis, and therefore it acts as a sign. Freud's critics note that his concepts of sexual fetishism are highly phallocentric and heteronormative, i.e. the fetishist is always a young heterosexual male. Recent scholarship, however, has expanded the concept of sexual fetishism by reframing it in terms of human desire rather than genital obsession.

SEMIOTIC FETISHISM

Dant (1999) offers semiotic fetishism as a means to incorporate Baudrillard's semiotic analysis of commodities and consumer culture. Baudrillard questions Marx's emphasis on exchange-value, not use-value, as the driver for fetishism. "For use value—indeed, utility itself—is a fetishised social relation, just like the abstract equivalence of commodities. Use value is an abstraction. It is an abstraction of the system of needs cloaked in the false evidence of a concrete destination and purpose, an intrinsic finality of goods and products" (Baudrillard 1981: 131). In other words, the utility of things is not a value intrinsic to them, and it does not exist to satisfy real needs. Baudrillard suggests instead, that (fake) needs are socially constructed by the system of production (which includes design, manufacturing, marketing, sales and distribution). For him, consumption is not an economic exchange of goods but a social exchange of signs. "Objects ... that have a sign value in excess of their functional capabilities" can be said to be demonstrative of semiotic fetishism (Dant 1999:

51). The fetishistic overvaluation of the object occurs as it is converted into a sign. In an interesting amalgamation of commodity fetishism and sexual fetishism, Baudrillard explains the sign value of make-up and fashion. "The significatory adornment of the modern body fetishizes it, creating a seductive sexuality that is no more than a sign or a simulacrum transforming the subject body into a fetishized object" (Dant 1999: 51). Body piercings, lipstick and other forms of body decoration convert the body into a sign, conflating subject and object. The body that performs the labor of production also becomes a site for fetishized consumption.

THE MAKING OF THE FETISH OBJECT

The four forms of fetishism, though different in several ways, also share certain commonalities, the primary one being that they overvalue the object. Religious fetishism bestows socially shared magical properties to objects; commodity fetishism imparts mystery and seductive qualities to objects while hiding their labor function; in sexual fetishism, an object stands in for some form of sexual desire; and finally semiotic fetishism gives the commodity a sign value which is higher than its functional capabilities. Ellen identifies four key cognitive mechanisms below that convert objects into fetishes.

1. A concrete existence or the concretisation of abstractions;
2. The attribution of qualities of living organisms, often (though not exclusively) human;
3. Conflation of signifier and signified;
4. An ambiguous relationship between control of object by people and of people by object. (Ellen 1988: 219).

Concretization refers to the conversion of ideas into physical form, a process also labeled objectification. These concertized ideas, as things, are individually and socially meaningful and they determine relations between people. For instance, products such as expensive cars convey the abstract concepts of status, power, affluence, etc. through their physical form. It is also common for fetish items to be personified and bestowed with qualities of such living things as plants, animals and people. Referred to as phytomorphism, zoomorhphism and anthropomorhpism, these processes are visible during activities of production and consumption. During the process of form development, designers may use biological forms as metaphors in order to give them personalities such as cuteness or humanness. Luigi Colani, recognized for aerodynamic designs of cars, trucks, cameras and other products, refers to the organic forms of his products as biodynamic. Inspired by sharks, birds and other creatures, these fantastic forms signify a form of high tech, natural design that is singular in its aesthetic. Franco Lodato's design for Camp's Woodpecker ice axe has an aluminum alloy and dual-density neoprene handle that is shaped like a woodpecker's spine, and the titanium/stainless head also mimics the woodpecker's head and beak.

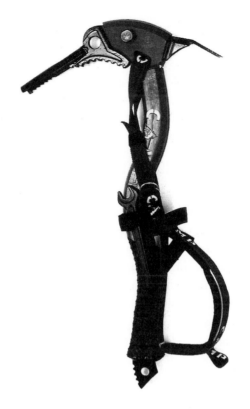

Figure 9.2. Camp Woodpecker Ice Axe. Image courtesy of Franco Lodato.

Other examples include icons on computers (happy and sad Macs), cars (such as the Mini or Neon) and robots (like Sony's Asimo) (DiSalvo and Gemperle 2003). Several products by Alessi Corporation are consciously designed to evoke humor through the use of human forms, and are also personified by names. Designer Mattia Di Rosa's products for Alessi have such names as "Luca, a little monster eating a napkin" (a napkin holder), and "Carlo, a little ghost on top of a bottle" (a bottle cap). Consumers often see human or animal characteristics in products, even though they may not necessarily be designed to possess features of living organisms.

Ellen's third mechanism of conflation of signifier and signified refers to situations where the fact that a signifier only stands in for something else that is forgotten: "Where 'fetishisation' has occurred, therefore, the material object itself may be regarded as an active causative agent as much as anything it might stand for" (Ellen 1988: 227). For the fetish objects therefore, the signifier and the signified are no more perceived as clearly separate entities. A credit card is no longer seen as a representative of the promise of a future financial transaction between two institutions; instead it is perceived as a cache of available funds. The fourth mechanism of power relations between the fetish objects and people raises the question of whether people control the fetish objects or whether they are in turn controlled by them. Indeed, an ambiguity of power is central to fetish objects. The owner of an expensive car is able to exercise the power that is available through affluence and status, both signifiers of the object. The owner is aware of the manipulation that is possible through this fetish object but also recognizes that maintaining its fetish quality requires a form of subservience to it. One is required to be in as much awe of the object as one expects to inspire in society with it; the fetish object gives as much power as it exacts from its owner.

THE ROLE OF DESIGN IN FETISHISM AND POSSESSION

One of design's central objectives is to create things that have sufficient use- and exchange-value so as to meet consumer needs and encourage consumption. In this process, it also imparts sign- and fetish-value to these things. These values, however, are only partially created during design, manufacturing and marketing; consumers, as they acquire and use the goods, generate their own sets of meanings and values. A product's form and its advertising can pre-configure a specific set of meanings which may be entirely accepted, rejected or modified in contexts of use. Though the genesis of use-, exchange- and to a certain extent sign-value can be traced back to the process of design when user needs as well as product features and functions are being configured, that is not the case with fetish-value, which is largely reliant on the life of objects in the post-commodity phase. Once an object enters individual and social use it acquires fetishistic meanings that transform its character. These fetishistic meanings may also be promoted and amplified through media outlets where objects are often popularized and propagandized. In their fetishized state, things become powerful agents, gain significant value and appear magical.

"The industrial commodity . . . becomes a fetish precisely because it has managed to remove itself from the concrete contexts of human need and human labor and has thus contributed to a 'separation of man from things,' which now confront each other as objectified realms of social experience" (Schmidgen 2001: 31). Schmidgen argues that the fetish object no longer addresses human need and in this process distances itself from people. Haug (1986) posited that use-value is fetishized into an "appearance of use-value" through design and advertising. According to Haug, therefore, instead of adding meaning (or value to the object for the consumer), processes of design disconnect the product from its true meaning and replace it with a fetishistic meaning. By these analyses, the form of the object, which lies in the realm of design's expertise, itself is a fetishization of utility, which tricks the user into buying things for the benefit of the capitalist. It is clear that Haug's Marxist critique of commodity aesthetics does not take into account any of the pleasure afforded in the beauty of things or the developmental potential of consumption.

BRAND FETISHISM

Every year, Interbrand, a branding agency, compiles a report titled *Best Global Brands*.[1] According to this report, Coca-Cola's brand (which has been on the top of the list for several years) is valued at 66,667 million U.S. dollars, I.B.M. at 59, 031 million U.S. dollars and Microsoft at 59,007 million U.S. dollars. These staggering sums reflect not only the size of these multinational corporations but also the level of overvaluation and therefore fetishization of the brands. Haug argues that the process of design subordinates the use-value of the commodity to a brand name, thereby assuring consumer loyalty and a position in the market. When the image of the corporation has established itself with conviction in the buyer's mind, when brand loyalty is ascertained, use-value is eclipsed entirely and may not even be missed. The promise of use-value is replaced by the promise of brand ownership which fulfils the consumer's need for status and recognition. The ownership of a brand is a paradoxical situation because while it is indeed the consumer who possesses the branded item, it is also the consumer who is possessed by the corporation; and as Ellen (1988) explains, this form of ambiguous power sharing is one of the conditions for fetishism. The sign-value of the brand, a highly visual signifier, is exaggerated into fetish-value, and leads to obsessive conspicuous consumption.

Nike's 1982 Air Force 1 basketball shoe was the first to incorporate a cushioning air pocket in its heel. Though used by a few celebrity basketball players when it was first re-leased, it quickly became popular on the street and has become one of Nike's top selling shoes. When released, it was priced at 89.95 U.S. dollars, and in 2007, "a crocodile-skin 25th anniversary edition cost more than $2,000 at Flight Club New York, a consignment sneaker store in Lower Manhattan" (Bierman 2007). These shoes entered popular culture through the entertainment industry in a significant way in 2002 when hip-hop artist Nelly released a song dedicated entirely to the shoe called *Air Force Ones*. In the music video, throngs of people are seen flocking at a store and leaving with multiple boxes of shoes. Nelly sings "I said give me two pair, cause I need two pair" suggesting in rather unsubtle terms that one pair is certainly not enough. According to a New York Times article, "Few people buy Air Force 1s to wear on a basketball court, and many collectors keep several pairs in pristine condition to protect their value" (Bierman 2007). Though originally designed to function as a basketball shoe, its primary meaning has shifted remarkably as it is has taken on signifiers of urban fashion and hip-hop culture. Nike regularly releases limited editions (a few hundred) of the shoes in unique styles in specialty stores that are bought up in minutes after they hit the market. Such techniques of marketing build an aura of mystery and exclusivity around the Air Force 1 brand and instantly fetishize them.

The obsessive collection of things conflates processes of fetishization and consumption. Fetish objects—collectibles and possessions—while mundane things of everyday life, also stand in as signifiers of obsessive consumption.

CONCLUSION

At every moment, the world is a geography of objects, whether they are made of the latest plastics or were born at the dawn of time.

Graham Harman, *Tool-Being*

One of the very early titles for this book, prior to settling upon *Designing Things*, was *A Very Strange Thing*—a title inspired by a piece of intriguing and somewhat confounding writing in Marx's *Capital Vol. 1*. "A commodity appears at first sight an extremely obvious, trivial thing. But its analysis brings out that it is *a very strange thing*, abounding in metaphysical subtleties and theological niceties" (Marx 1990: 163). In addition to "metaphysical" and "theological" Marx uses the terms enigmatical, mystical, peculiar, fantastic, wonderful and transcendent to describe properties of the commodity. To Marx, these philosophical, religious and magical qualities of things were expressions of commodity fetishism, the origins of which he traced back to the economic power of exchange-value and the social character of the labor of production. Regardless of whether or not one considers things to be replete with such power and magic, there is no question that mundane, inanimate objects are repositories of many untold stories. These are stories of the scores of people who have touched the objects through their journeys from raw material to post-consumer waste, and these are the stories that critical analysis seeks to lay bare. The interactions among people, products and institutions occur within large, dynamic, intricate networks, and therefore narratives of production and consumption can be neither comprehensive nor complete. In spite of their unfinished form, the stories of value, labor, beauty, need, durability, symbolism and fetishism in these pages are written to suggest that things are not always what they seem; they are, as Marx suggests, very strange.

These stories reveal that there are significant issues of contention surrounding the concepts of value, labor, beauty, etc. For instance, the study of value shows that the primacy of shareholder value can often compromise those things that are valuable to employees, society and the environment. Similarly, a critique of labor practices reveals gender inequities, lack of success with flexible manufacturing, and the difficulty of abolishing child labor outright. However, individuals, corporations and institutions have also developed new concepts and practices such as stakeholder value (which takes into account the needs of all those affected by the design of a new product) and fair trade (which mitigates labor exploitation) as a means of finding solutions to some of these concerns. Implementing these solutions will require, as Bruce Mau would say, "massive change." Things are deeply embedded within large "webs of significance" (Geertz 1973). These webs consist of several actors, and their participation is essential to institute significant change.

Can these contentious issues of value, labor, aesthetics, need, obsolescence, semiotics and fetishism be resolved with new design paradigms of the future? In *Design for Society*, Nigel Whiteley suggests that "we have entered an age in design in which the memorable and seductive slogan (and its three-dimensional equivalent) has to be replaced by informed and intelligent thought and action" (1993: 170). He recommends green design, responsible design and feminist design (as alternatives to consumer-led design) as new paradigms for the future. Thackara (2005) believes that the world needs a "transition from mindless development to design mindfulness," and offers the following points of sound, critical advice:

- think about the consequences of design actions before we take them and pay close attention to the natural, industrial, and cultural systems that are the context of our design actions;
- consider material and energy flows in all the systems we design;
- give priority to human agency and not treat humans as a "factor" in some bigger picture;
- deliver value to people—not deliver people to systems;
- treat "content" as something we do, not something we are sold;
- treat place, time, and cultural difference as positive values, not as obstacles;
- focus on services, not on things, and refrain from flooding the world with pointless devices. (Thackara 2005: 8)

Thackara's recommendations are a call to designers to entirely re-imagine the relationship between people and things. Orchestrating an effort of this kind (as Thackara recognizes and warns) will undoubtedly be a long, difficult journey that will involve rethinking of the social, economic, political and environmental issues surrounding the production, distribution and consumption of things.

DESIGN EDUCATION

This book has sought to make theoretical analyses of things more accessible to readers of design. In this process, it has explored literature in a variety of disciplines, with the eagerness and hope of discovering new ideas and new ways of looking at old ideas. Interdisciplinary approaches hold the promise of this kind of discovery. "Critical interdisciplinarity seeks to take the effort involved in mastering or going deep into anyone discipline and spread it over a number of disciplines, going just as deep in a discipline as is necessary or appropriate to grasp the essentials" (Frodeman and Mitcham 2005: 513). In this process of engaging other disciplines, design can be enriched by new points of view and more holistic conceptions of things. Armed with a broader understanding of what things are, designers might be better equipped to create products appropriate to their cultural contexts of use. Design education can benefit by bringing allied and not-so-allied disciplines into the studio. Students, if exposed to socially and culturally informed analyses of things, might rethink the role of design. A recognition that things have agency might make a designer a careful observer/ listener of the world of goods. The knowledge that things, people, institutions, plants, animals and all else in this world are actors in a network might encourage a student to fully map out the impacts of design activity. Critical examinations of the notions of value, production, form, need, durability, symbolism and fetishism, inspired by the scholarship from other disciplines like anthropology or philosophy can greatly assist students in developing a more holistic conception of design as an activity with considerable cultural and ethical dimensions.

FROM VALUE TO VALUES

In business terms, design is often construed as a value-adding activity, and if that is the case, what kind of value should it bring to things? Though certain kinds of value (such as economic and aesthetic value, for instance) may be more dependent on processes of production, most value creation (symbolic and emotional value) occurs during consumption. For design to have positive, societal impact, it is critical to ascertain that the "value aggregate" considers needs of all stakeholders. During production, focusing purely on shareholder value or financial value creates situations in which value is created for one group (a corporation and a few users, for instance) at the expense of another (the environment and the majority in the world, for instance). If value is price and values are priceless (Miller 2008), societal benefits can best be achieved if objects are designed to further universal human *values*, and not conceived as mechanisms that provide individual value. Rokeach defines the concept of human values as "an enduring belief that a specific mode of conduct or end-state of existence is personally or socially preferable to an opposite or converse mode of conduct or end-state of existence" (1973: 5). He classifies these values into two major categories: terminal values, which represent the end-states we hope to achieve in life, and instrumental values, which are means by which we can achieve these terminal values. Terminal values include such things as a comfortable life, an exciting life, a sense of accomplishment, a world at peace, a world of beauty, equality, family security, freedom, happiness, inner harmony, mature love, national security, pleasure, salvation, self-respect, social recognition, true friendship and wisdom (Rokeach 1974: 226). Rokeach lists instrumental values as qualities that make people "ambitious, broad-minded, capable, cheerful, clean, courageous, forgiving, helpful, honest, imaginative, independent, intellectual, logical, loving, obedient, polite, responsible and self-controlled" (1974: 229).[1] Some of the human values, like world at peace or equality, have a universal dimension; their pursuit benefits many. Some of the other values such as recognition and wisdom operate at a personal level. The prioritization of these values may vary by social, cultural and economic situations, but they have to strike a balance between the two. Design should strive to expand its focus from *things of value* to *things with values*. While the former category of goods focuses on providing benefit primarily at the individual level, the latter can assist human populations universally to achieve their human values. While the former category is defined more in material, financial and immediate terms, the latter emphasizes long-term, ethical and moral concerns. The transition from *value* to *values* will highlight design's role as a positive, transformative agent for all humanity.

FAIR PRACTICES IN LABOR

Labor is human capital. The manufacturing of products involves significant amounts of blue and white-collar labor, most of which is invisible in the finished goods. The perfect product often perpetuates a myth that it arrives magically on store shelves as a shiny, innovative thing to behold and enjoy, while masking all stories of its journey. Very few companies chronicle and make their supply chains visible. Patagonia, a clothing and sports gear manufacturer, recently launched The Footprint Chronicles™ website "that allows you to track the impact of a specific Patagonia product from design to delivery" (Patagonia.com 2008). Their goal, through this unusually transparent policy, is to examine each stage of the product's journey from raw material to the consumer's home, and minimize environmental impact at every stage possible. A down sweater, for instance, involves processes of design, raw material collection (down, recycled polyester fabric), processing (design, material cleaning and processing, sewing) and distribution. The sweater is designed in Ventura, California; the down feathers are collected from geese in Godollo, Hungary; they are cleaned and processed in Los Angeles, California; the recycled polyester fabric is manufactured in Nobeoka, Japan; the sewing is done in factories in Qingdao, China; and the finished product is distributed through a facility in Reno, Nevada. It is clear that a large number of workers across the globe are involved in the manufacture of a single item. Patagonia is a founding member as well as a fully accredited member of the Fair Labor Association (F.L.A.), a non-profit organization that combines "the efforts of industry, civil society organizations, and colleges and universities to protect workers" rights and improve working conditions worldwide by promoting adherence to international labor standards" (Fla.org 2008). All F.L.A. accredited members abide by a code of conduct regarding labor practices that address issues of forced labor, child labor, harassment and abuse, nondiscrimination, health and safety, freedom of association and collective bargaining, wages and benefits, hours of work and overtime compensation. Adherence to F.L.A. codes of conduct is voluntary but such companies as Nike, Puma, Adidas and others have established their codes of conducts in alliance with F.L.A. and are now affiliate members. The goal of these fair labor practices is to educate corporations and consumers about labor exploitation and minimize worker alienation in factories.

Supporters of low-cost outsourced labor emphasize the economic benefits provided by multinational corporations to regional economies that also reduces prices of finished goods in affluent countries. Critics of this practice stress the individual, societal and environmental damage caused by sweatshop like conditions often seen in the factories where these goods are produced. Labor, as the A.F.L.-C.I.O. explains, should not be considered purely in financial terms. "Labor is more than just a cost of production. Labor involves human dignity; it involves another whole dimension than does capital or interest or the other factors of production, and therefore it has to be treated very differently from them" (Leebron 1996: 101, note 67). Most things today are global goods that rely on supply chains stretched across several continents. Products emerging from these networks of multinational corporations and their suppliers are repositories of an infinite number of stories of labor, most of which are inaccessible to consumers. The story of labor is too often the story of social inequity, exploitation, and pointless human toil. But it can also be the story of equity, dignity and enrichment. Through fair trade, labor regulations, better corporate codes of conduct and worker empowerment, labor's dignity can be restored. When the narratives of labor embedded in our soccer balls and T-shirts are those of equity and justice, it will be to the benefit of all. "The process that has come to be called "globalization" is exposing a deep fault line between groups who have the skills and mobility to flourish in global markets and those who either don't have these advantages or perceive the expansion of unregulated markets as inimical to social stability and deeply held norms. The result is severe tension between the market and social groups such as workers, pensioners, and environmentalists, with governments stuck in the middle" (Rodick 1997: 2). Things, which sit right in the middle of this fault line, are signifiers of the dynamic tensions between social and financial dimensions of outsourcing, between multinational corporations and labor organizations, and between free market economists and Marxist socialists.

THE POLITICS OF BEAUTY

> "Style, more and more, has become the official idiom of the marketplace. In advertising, packaging, product design, and corporate *identity*, the power of provocative surfaces speaks to the eye's mind, over-shadowing matters of quality or substance. Style, moreover, is an intimate component of subjectivity, intertwined with people's aspirations and anxieties. Increasingly, style has emerged as a decisive component of politics; political issues and politicians are regularly subjected to the cosmetic sorcery of image managers, providing the public with a telegenic commodity. Democratic choice, like grocery shopping, has become a question of which product is most attractively packaged, which product is most imaginatively merchandised. (Ewen 1999: 22)

Ewen's analysis demonstrates how global commerce, public politics and individual aspirations have become arenas of consumption driven by aesthetic manipulation. Style, a central area of concern for design, should not be imagined purely as an exercise in form, color, texture and material; it has political dimensions that determine what appearance signifies and how it is used to achieve certain means. Style plays a critical role in the creation of class distinction, definition of subcultural identity, seduction of consumers, development of corporate image, etc. But it also is a tool that consumers use to define identity, express creativity, and ritualize resistance.

The skin of the product becomes the vehicle for a range of meanings: those constructed in production and those developed during consumption. Aesthetics is often called on to generate the appropriate meanings in the retail outlet so as to lead to purchase. In marketing and packaging, this is sometimes referred to as the first moment of truth—the situation when a potential consumer looks at the packaging of a product and makes the decision whether or not to buy. A packaging manager at Procter & Gamble explains the significance of aesthetics at this instant of initial contact with the product:

> First moment of truth is aesthetics. Are you going to make a big difference versus the competition? ... If you look at the "Ariel" box it's green and [the text] is red. If you look around, a lot of boxes are green. We own the brand "Ariel" [and] we own the colour, but competition is very aggressive. The colour is not enough nowadays. So we need a different shape. The carton can be higher, smaller, or wider; that's the 3D aspect... We want repurchase. We want them to test, to be pleased, and then to repurchase. That's the business. (Löfgren 2005: 210)

Beauty cannot be entirely explained as a manipulative practice. The pleasure that beautiful things afford do play a significant role in people's sense of well-being. As Herman Miller's products often demonstrate, beauty can emerge organically from the vision that a company sets for itself. If the intangible vision is to create timeless, sustainable, useful, human things, the activity of design will reveal tangible beauty. In the complex network that links production to consumption and the designer to the user, beauty plays a critical financial, social and cultural role.

OPTIMAL LIFE

Just as the acquisition of things is a socially and economically embedded practice, so is their divestment. Collectors, hoarders and packrats often tend to fetishize things and are therefore unable to part with them easily. People might keep things for extended periods of time for reasons of emotional, symbolic or financial value. In other words, objects with high personal or communal value carry significant meanings and therefore are not easily divested, while things with little or no emotional or symbolic meaning are easy to dispose quickly. Design often sets out to create things that people can develop meaningful relationships with, thereby lengthening their life spans. However, at times, design and engineering do make a concerted effort to deliberately assign a death date to things, artificially shortening their life spans. Haug refers to this as "product senility" or "artificial obsolescence" and decries the practice as manipulative (1986: 40).

"If you look hard enough, you'll find that many of the products we use every day—chewing gums, skin moisturizers, disinfecting wipes, air fresheners, water purifiers, health snacks, antiperspirants, colognes, teeth whiteners, fabric softeners, vitamins—are results of manufactured habits" (Duhigg 2008). All of these products are short-lived but are likely to be packaged in materials that might last forever. The discussion of obsolescence and durability raises the question of the optimum life spans of things. On one hand, Irv Gordon's Volvo is pushing close to 3 million miles and is still running without showing any signs of breakdown. On the other hand, such things as paper cups have the life span of less than a few minutes. Certainly, heavier, complex, multi-use, expensive things tend to and should have longer life spans. However, an eternal life for things may not always be the right solution. As newer technologies lead to better solutions (such as higher energy efficiency or benign materials), design will have to grapple with the question of whether it makes environmental sense to retire existing products. From an environmental perspective, the life span of things is not the entire issue, though; it is waste that presents the problem. In natural ecosystems, the life spans of organisms range from a few minutes up to a few hundred years. However, despite short lives, the waste these organisms leave behind provides life for others. The closed loop of natural systems does not create unusable, toxic waste that needs to be isolated in refuse dumps. Design effort should be directed towards the creation of objects with optimal life spans within closed loop systems. The optimality should allow some user control in determining the life of the product while stressing the minimization of waste. In fact, mathematical models that allow the calculation of optimal life spans exist (Chalkley *et al.* 2003) in engineering literature. The cultural life spans (and therefore the physical life spans) of these goods will be determined predominantly on the basis of all the dimensions of their value aggregate (economic, symbolic, historical, aesthetic, etc.). The goal of design is then to optimize these values of things as a means of optimizing their lives. Management of product life and the handling of waste are both practices with significant personal, social, aesthetic, cultural, environmental, political and economic dimensions that need careful consideration by design and designers.

POSITIVE FETISHISM AND ITS AURA

Most critiques of fetishism tend to view the practice in a negative light. However, fetishism has also been explained as a form of meaning-making and equated to design.

> *Fetishism is the action of investing objects with meanings not inherent to their nature.* The different types of fetishism each attribute a symbolic value—respectively spiritual, ideological and psychological—to the concrete existence of material artefacts. Simply put, they bring things to life. This is to say, in other words, that fetishism as a concept describes the way in which we human beings attempt to include non-human things in our humanity while, at the same time, connecting ourselves to their essential nature and to what we sometimes suppose to be their divine essence. Taking fetishism in a broader sense than any of the three existing denotations of the word, it becomes a useful tool for thinking about the way in which people endow things with meaning. (Cardoso 2004: 10–11)

Cardoso explains fetishism in terms of divine essence/magical value, depleting the concept of its connotations of deviance, and reimagining it as process of semiosis—the act of production of meaning. Having defined it thus, it is clear that fetishism and design share the primary task of investing objects with meaning. And as all things come into being by (some form of) design and as it is rather difficult to circumscribe those meanings that are "inherent to their nature" from those that are not, Cardoso's explanation suggests that every object could therefore be a fetish object. Indeed, as meaning is constructed not only in the process of design but also in use, all things could be fetishized.

The fetishism of things can also be explained as an aura that gives them extra value and power that far exceeds their utility. In his seminal essay, *The Work of Art in the Age of Mechanical Reproduction*, Walter Benjamin explains the "aura" of a work of art as a unique and irreproducible quality that a copy can never possess; "it is that which withers in the age of mechanical reproduction" (1968b: 221). The products of industrial design practice are manufactured in large quantities, and therefore the notion of an original from which the copies emerge does not exist. In the world of identical goods, the authenticity of an individual product can only exist in the unique stories it collects through its journey from design to delivery. These stories become the object's aura, its overvaluation and its fetish.

THE NEED FOR THINGS (AND FOR HAPPINESS)

The classification of needs into categories of primary, secondary and tertiary, or real and fake, or basic and luxury, or actual and pseudo, do not really assist in better comprehension of which needs might be considered to be more genuine and appropriate, and which ones might be considered frivolous and wasteful. In an attempt to reach broader and broader swaths of consumers, corporations are focusing on customer requirements; in order to generate the most appropriate features and functions engineers are listening to the voice of the customer; and designers, in their attempt to be more empathic, are advocating human-centered methods to truly understand user needs. This has led to a stunning diversity in product offerings, the result of which is an infinite choice of goods, products tailored for individual users, enhanced profits for the corporation, etc. However, it has also led to consumer confusion, environmental degradation, waste generation, needs escalation and social distinction.

The paradigm shift from individual value to universal values discussed earlier can be employed towards reforming the notion of needs as well. If, as Max-Neef *et al.* suggest, we adopt the notion that human needs are a system and that all human needs are inter-related and interactive, a similar shift from individual *need* to universal *needs* is possible (Max-Neef *et al.* 1989: 19). This does not suggest that we ignore the individual; instead, it recommends that we respond to a much broader network of needs. Recognition of each need as a force in a network links all needs in a complex, causal chain, urging us to carefully consider the long-term and long-distance impacts of our need-satisfying decisions.

IN THE END…

If our culture is becoming increasingly more material, critical examinations of the things that fill our everyday life serve as mechanisms by which to understand human culture. Design, in its role as a creator of things, is an agent of cultural production. In its study of the material world, this book has attempted to foreground the multiple meanings of things, the social significance of their manufacture and the cultural implications of their use. While we should be wary of the politics of power inherent in systems of production, we should also recognize the developmental and aesthetic power of consumption. It is clear that the presence of things in our life has positive as well as negative impacts. Through its emphasis on sustainable development and human-centered thinking, design has already taken on the responsibility of maximizing its positive societal potential. If design's immediate task is the creation of things, its true value is in its ability to improve the human condition.

> As a general matter, subjective well-being varies directly with income and inversely with material aspirations. At the start of the life cycle those with higher income are happier, because material aspirations are fairly similar throughout the population, and those with more income are better able to fulfill their aspirations. Income growth does not, however, cause well-being to rise, either for higher or lower income persons, because it generates equivalent growth in material aspirations, and the negative effect of the latter on subjective well-being undercuts the positive effect of the former. Even though rising income means that people can have more goods, the favorable effect of this on welfare is erased by the fact that people want more as they progress through the life cycle. It seems as though Emerson (1860) had it right when he said 'Want is a growing giant whom the coat of Have was never large enough to cover' (Easterlin 2001: 481).

This suggests that the income-generated escalation of the need for things can derail the human quest for well-being. The conflation of material desire with human happiness, if unchecked, can become the vice of systems of production and rituals of consumption. Nations across the world use volumes of production and consumption as a means by which to evaluate their economic well-being. The gross domestic product (G.D.P.), the total market value of goods and services produced, generally serves as an index of socio-economic development. However, the G.D.P. is not a reliable measure of the standard of living and does not help account for such human needs as happiness, physical and mental health, social connection, etc. The beautiful and sleepy Himalayan nation of Bhutan has recognized this limitation and instead uses gross national happiness (G.N.H.), a concept first articulated by the fourth king His Majesty Jigme Singye Wangchuck, as an alternative. "GNH seeks to maximize the happiness of all Bhutanese to enable them to achieve their full and innate potential as human beings and forges an alternative path that goes beyond the conventional income-based measures of development. The GNH approach seeks to integrate the basic human aspiration of happiness and the largely intangible and non-material aspects of spiritual and cultural needs of people into the development equation."[2] The G.N.H. is developed on a complex set of subjective and objective indicators to measure "national happiness" in various domains (living standards, health, education, eco-system diversity and resilience, cultural vitality and diversity, time use and balance, good governance, community vitality and psychological well-being).

What the world needs today more than anything else is an inspired vision for design that adopts as its essential obligation the production of global human happiness.

NOTES

INTRODUCTION

1. The reference to "burden of comprehension" is found in Klein J. (1990) *Interdisciplinarity: History, Theory, and Practice*, Detroit: Wayne State University Press. Note 20 in Chapter 6: "Janice M. Lauer used this term in 'Studies of Written Discourse: Dappled Discipline.' Address to the Rhetoric Society of America at the thirty-fourth meeting of the Conference on College Composition and Communication in Detroit, Mich., 17 March 1983."

CHAPTER 1

1. In *Material Culture and Mass Consumption*, Miller (1994) asked whether material culture qualified as a discipline. Since then there has been an explosion of academic programs and courses, the establishment of the *Journal of Material Culture* and an abundance of books on the topic, leading to the firm establishment of material culture as a discipline in its own right.
2. See, for example, publications by Buchanan and Margolin (1995), Doordan (1995), Forty (1992), Margolin (1989), Meikle (1995), Sparke (1990), Walker (1989) and Woodham (1997).
3. The teaching of design skills is critical for students to be able to perform well in their jobs as designers. However, there is a dire need for courses that critique the cultural significance and impact of products and provide students the tools to do so on their own. It should be recognized that university programs are constrained by a limited number of credit hours in which to teach a large number of courses on design and general studies. There is no lack of interest in developing and teaching such coursework dealing with critical and cultural aspects of design and designed things.
4. In response to the suggestion in the U.S. that evolution is a theory, not fact and should be removed from school science curricula, or taught along with intelligent design/creationism, the National Academy of Sciences established the Steering Committee Science and Creationism. This quotation is from the report *Science and Creationism: A View from the National Academy of Sciences*, written by the committee and published by the National Academies Press, Washington in 1999. This free PDF was downloaded from: http://www.nap.edu/catalog/6024.html, accessed 23 July 2008.
5. This quotation is extracted from the report *The Role of Theory in Advancing 21st Century Biology: Catalyzing Transformative Research* written by the Committee on Defining and Advancing the Conceptual Basis of Biological Sciences in the 21st Century. Printed by the National Academies Press, Washington, 2007.
6. Grounded theory (GT) is a qualitative research method often used in the social sciences for theory construction in which data are collected, coded and grouped to identify repeating patterns. These patterns are then generalized to formulate theories. The codes allow significant features and details of the data to be isolated. They are then grouped by similarity to form concepts, which then become the building blocks of a new theory.
7. Meanings and etymologies of terms are derived from two primary sources, including *The Concise Oxford Dictionary of Current English*, (Oxford: Clarendon Press, 1995) and http://www.etymonline.com, accessed 21–9 July 2008.

8. Polysemy is a concept in semiotics that refers to the ambiguous nature of the signifier. This led to the proposition that things possess multiple meanings. This will be discussed in greater detail in Chapter 8 on semiotics.

9. See http://www.therai.org.uk/pubs/resguide/discovering_contents.html, accessed 21 July 2008.

10. Definitions from the University of California, Los Angeles, Department of Anthropology website, http://www.sscnet.ucla.edu/anthro/academic.htm, accessed 15 September 2004. Also from Wikipedia http://en.wikipedia.org/wiki/Anthropology#cite_ref-27, accessed 21 July 2008.

11. Attfield (2000), Cockburn (1985), Schwartz-Cowan (1983), Sparke (1990) and Wajcman (1991) are some scholars who have analyzed products from feminist perspectives.

CHAPTER 2

1. Several other approaches have been developed to better understand customer value. See Woodruff and Gardial (1996) for additional models.

2. See the special issue of *Economy and Society* Volume 29 Number 1 February 2000, for a detailed discussion of the impact of shareholder value and financialization on present-day capitalism.

3. The division of value into qualitative and quantitative is a rather simplistic division of a much more complex explanation of value in Marx. However, this distinction does foreground the difference between use- and exchange-value. See http://www.marxists.org/glossary/terms/e/x.htm, accessed 26 September 2008.

4. These phases are loosely based upon the five generally accepted phases of Life Cycle Assessment: raw material, manufacture, transportation, lifetime use, and end-of-life.

5. This data was extracted from a 2008 Fact Sheet published by the Self Storage Association (SSA) at their website http://www.selfstorage.org/, accessed 12 August 2008.

CHAPTER 3

1. The term "poorer nations" is preferable to the terms "the third world" or "developing countries" as it is a more accurate representation of the differences between nations that are more and less industrialized. All countries are constantly developing, and industrialization does not necessarily mean development or progress. Hence the terms "developing countries" is an inaccurate description. Similarly, classification of the world into first, second and third tiers, developed by Alfred Sauvy in 1952 too does not accurately represent the differences between these nations, and is no longer relevant in today's world, making that term unsuitable.

CHAPTER 4

1. However, it is important not to limit the craft potential of a machine. A skilled craftsperson on a milling machine can produce wonderfully crafted goods, just as easily as an unskilled worker can create rubbish with the best tools. In industrial situations, it is the system of production that defines what is a tool and what is a machine.

2. If this study is to be taken for its word (and the evidence is rather compelling), not only is Taylorism a misnomer, but it also casts Frederick Taylor as an unscrupulous individual. In addition to borrowing large sections of *Principles of Scientific Management* from a manuscript written by Cooke, some of the "observations" were fictitious and his references to newspaper articles written about Taylorism were false (Wrege and Hodgetts 2000).

3. For a detailed discussion, see Piore and Sabel, *The Second Industrial Divide* (1984). The authors offer an in-depth examination of the socioeconomic crisis of this time.

CHAPTER 5

1. The term "significant form" was introduced by Clive Bell in his book *Art*, published in 1914. "When I speak of significant form, I mean a combination of lines and colours (counting white and black as colours) that moves me aesthetically" (Bell 1914: 20).
2. Designers and authors such as Dreyfuss (1957), Papanek (1971), Stumpf (1998), Whiteley (1993) and countless others have cast design as an activity that has the means of making positive societal impact. While affording people fulfilling, aesthetic experiences by design certainly qualifies as improvement of the human condition, there is critical urgency in solving a range of other problems of energy, healthcare, education, etc. Some of these issues will be discussed further in Chapter 6 on needs.
3. The Smartskins phone did not make it to market, the Kyocera-Wildseed partnership collapsed and the Smartskins website is no longer active.

CHAPTER 6

1. Aristotle also defines a fifth sense of necessity—one that is absolute and independent. He includes god and eternal cyclical motion as these absolute necessities. However, they are less relevant in the discussion of our need for things.
2. The *PDMA Handbook of New Product Development* edited by Milton D. Rosenau, Jr. *et al.,* provides an excellent overview of many of these methods and tools.
3. These words were included in the brochure designed for the Design for Need conference organized at the Royal College of Art in London in 1976. Select papers were compiled into a book edited by Julian Bicknell and Liz McQuiston (1977).
4. Whiteley's *Design for Society* is written in the tradition of *Design for the Real World* by Victor Papanek and *Design for Business* by J. Gordon Lippincott. Whiteley offers a comprehensive critique of the morality and ethics of market-led design, suggesting green design, responsible design and feminist design as alternatives. Green design is generally defined as design through such techniques as material selection, energy consumption, etc. and it minimizes impact on the environment. Responsible design focuses on the development of products that are socially useful. And finally, a feminist critique of design reveals the stereotype femininity, gender biases and lack of consideration of women as users rampant in design practice.
5. According to the United Nations Development Programme, the world's poor are disproportionately affected by environmental degradation and lack of access to clean, affordable energy services. Climate change, loss of biodiversity and depletion of natural resources are both national and global issues requiring cooperation among all countries. http://www.undp.org/publications/annualreport2008/poverty.shtml, accessed 19 November 2008.

CHAPTER 7

1. Steve Jobs on Brian Williams, Nightly Report, 26 May 2006, http://www.msnbc.msn.com/id/12974884, accessed 5 January 2008.
2. From the Milwaukee Art Museum web archive, http://www.mam.org/collection/archives/brooks/faq2.asp, accessed 4 January 2008.
3. According to Swivel, a data compilation and visualization company 344,000,000 LPs were sold in the U.S. market in 1977 and 1,000,000 in 2005. See www.swivel.com, accessed 21 January 2006, for more information. The data for music statistics was gathered from The World Almanac and the R.I.A.A..
4. The Natural Marketing Institute creates periodic LOHAS reports, which are available for purchase at www.lohas.com/about.html, accessed 24 February 2008.

5. The Volvo Club of America maintains a running log of the mileage on Irv Gordon's car. See www.vcoa. org/irv-o-meter/ for the latest update, accessed 26 February 2008. In an article in Auto Channel, Gordon discussed his record-breaking, 2.7 Million Mile Volvo P1800, as he celebrated the fortieth anniversary of his purchase www.theautochannel.com/news/2006/06/20/011973.html, accessed 26 February 2008.

6. Cannibalization refers to a situation where the company's bottom line suffers because the sales of one product negatively impact the sales of another, resulting in loss of revenue. In situations where Model B has an entirely new market, cannibalization does not occur.

7. A monopoly involves a single company controlling an industry or refers to a situation in which it is the sole provider of a product or service. An oligopoly occurs when there are so few suppliers of a product that the actions of one supplier actions can have an important effect on prices and on competitors.

8. As is true with most economic analyses, several assumptions limit massive generalizations of these findings. Bulow writes, "perhaps the greatest weakness of this paper is that it follows in the tradition of durability as a proxy for obsolescence. This assumption, combined with the perfect second-hand market assumption, permits the model to regard goods produced at different times as homogenous, and greatly simplifies the analysis" (Bulow 1986: 747).

9. See Susan Strasser (1999: 177) for a detailed analysis of the common drinking cup and its paper replacement.

10. The L.C.A. calculates mineral resource depletion, global warming potential, ozone depletion potential, human toxicity potential, fresh water aquatic eco-toxicity potential, marine aquatic eco-toxicity potential, fresh water aquatic eco-toxicity potential, terrestrial eco-toxicity potential, photochemical ozone creation potential, eutrophication potential and acidification potential.

11. Several life cycle assessments comparing plastic and paper bags have shown that plastic bags have significantly lower impact than paper grocery bags. Peer-reviewed L.C.A.s comparing reusable cloth to single use bags are unavailable.

12. For a detailed analysis of the Pop movement, work of the IG and its impact on design, see Nigel Whiteley's *Pop Design: Modernism to Mod-Pop Theory and Design, 1952–72* (1987).

CHAPTER 8

1. By certain accounts (Deely 1990), St. Augustine, rather than any of the ancient Greek philosophers, is considered the first thinker to have proposed a general semiotic theory or doctrine of signs.

2. The claim of 30 percent reduction needs some clarification. See Wall Street Journal article at http://blogs. wsj.com/numbersguy/category/advertising/page/2/, accessed 24 May 2008. For the Recycling Scorecard, the Container Recycling Institute used three core criteria in their evaluation: inclusion of recycled content in beverage containers, involvement in beverage container recovery and recycling, and involvement in source reduction of plastics, aluminum and glass. By their scorecard, Nestlé Waters North America received a failing grade for all three criteria (Bakshi 2006).

3. See *The Hummer: Myths and Consumer Culture* (2007) by Elaine Cardenas and Ellen Gorman (Editors) for a series of essays on the cultural meanings of both AM General's H.M.M.W.V. and the later versions Hummer, H1 and H2 by General Motors.

4. In *The Semantic Turn*, Krippendorff (2006) provides a comprehensive historical overview of product semantics.

5. This methodology was developed by Reinhart Butter at The Ohio State University along with graduate student Edward A. Dorsa. Dorsa's master's thesis was titled "A Methodology for the Generation of Visual Metaphors to be Used in the Design of Three-Dimensional Objects," and was completed in 1986.

CHAPTER 9

1. See http://www.interbrand.com/best_global_brands.aspx for Interbrand's report on the Best Global Brands of 2008, accessed 12 June 2008. According to Interbrand, "our approach to valuation starts by forecasting the current and future revenue specifically attributable to the branded products. We subtract operating costs from revenue to calculate branded operating profit. We then apply a charge to the branded profit for capital employed. This gives us economic earnings. All financial analysis is based on publicly available company information. Interbrand culls from a range of analysts" reports to build a consensus estimate for financial reporting."

CONCLUSION

1. Rokeach lists instrumental values as qualities that make people ambitious, broad-minded, capable, cheerful, clean, courageous, forgiving, helpful, honest, imaginative, independent, intellectual, logical, loving, obedient, polite, responsible and self-controlled (Rokeach 1974: 229). However, for this discussion, it is terminal values that are more critical to design practice.
2. This quote is part of a report titled "Bhutan's Progress: Midway to the Millennium Development Goals" and was prepared for the U.N.D.P. (United Nations Development Programme) by Karma Tshiteem, Secretary, GNH Commission, Royal Government of Bhutan and Nicholas Rosellini, UN Resident Coordinator of Bhutan, http://www.undp.org.bt/mdg/MDG_Midway.pdf, accessed 3 April 2008.

BIBLIOGRAPHY

Adler, P. and Cole, R. (1993), "Designed For Learning: A Tale Of Two Autoplants," *Sloan Management Review*, Vol. 34, No. 3: 85–94.

Adler, P. and Cole. R. (2007), "Designed For Learning: A Tale Of Two Auto Plants," in Å. Sandberg (ed.), *Enriching Production: Perspectives On Volvo's Uddevalla Plant as an Alternative to Lean Production*, digital edition, Avebury: Aldershot.

Adorno, T. (1991), *The Culture Industry: Selected Essays on Mass Culture*, London: Routledge.

Aglietta, M. (1979), *A Theory of Capitalist Regulation: The U.S. Experience*, London: New Left Books.

Aitken, H. (1960), *Taylorism at Watertown Arsenal; Scientific Management in Action, 1908–1915*, Cambridge: Harvard University Press.

Akao, Y. (2004), *Quality Function Deployment: Integrating Customer Requirements into Product Design*, Cambridge: Productivity Press.

Akin, M. (1996), "Passionate Possession: The Formation of Private Collections," in D. Kingery (ed.), *Learning from Things: Method and Theory of Material Culture Studies,* Washington, D.C.: Smithsonian Institution Press.

Aldersey-Williams, H. (1990), *Cranbrook Design: The New Discourse*. London: Rizzoli.

AM General, www.amgeneral.com/vehicles/hmmwv/features.php, accessed 12 July 2009.

Amin, A. (1994), *Post-Fordism: A Reader*, Oxford: Blackwell.

Antipodes (2007), www.antipodes.co.nz/ourwater.html, accessed 22 June 2007.

Antonelli, P. (1995), *Mutant Materials in Contemporary Design: The Museum of Modern Art*, New York: Museum of Modern Art.

Anzieu, D. (1989), *The Skin Ego*, New Haven: Yale University Press.

Appadurai, A. (1988) (ed.), *The Social Life of Things: Commodities in Cultural Perspective*, New York: Cambridge University Press.

Apter, E. and Pietz, W. (1993), *Fetishism as Cultural Discourse*, New York: Cornell University Press.

Aristides, N. (1988), "Calm and Uncollected," *American Scholar*, Vol. 57, No. 3: 327–36.

Arthur, C. (2003), "Mr. iMac Winds Design Prize for Banishing Beige," *Independent*, 3 June.

Asher, R. and Edsforth, R. (1995), *Autowork*, Albany: The State University of New York Press.

Athavankar, U. (1989), "Categorization... Natural Language and Design," *Design Issues*, Vol. 5, No. 2: 100–11.

Attfield, J. (2000), *Wild Things: The Material Culture of Everyday Life*, Oxford: Berg.

Bakshi, N. (2006), "U.S. Beverage Container Recycling: Scorecard and Report Waste and Opportunity," report by As You Sow and Container Recycling Institute, www.asyousow.org/sustainability/bev_survey.shtm, accessed 24 June 2009.

Barnes, J. (1984), *The Complete Works of Aristotle: The Revised Oxford Translation,* Princeton: Princeton University Press.

Barthes, R. (1968), *Elements of Semiology*, New York: Hill & Wang.

Barthes, R. (1972), *Mythologies*, New York: Hill & Wang.

Baudrillard, J. (1981), *For A Critique of the Political Economy of the Sign*. St. Louis: Telos Press.

Baudrillard, J. (1996), *The System of Objects*, London: Verso.

Baudrillard, J. (1998), *The Consumer Society: Myths and Structures*, London: Sage, London.

Baudrillard, J. (2001), *Selected Writings*, Stanford, CA: Stanford University Press.

Bayazit, N. (2004), "Investigating Design: A Review of Forty Years of Design Research," *Design Issues*, Vol. 20, No. 1: 16–29.

Beardsley, M. (1958), *Aesthetics: Essays in the Philosophy of Criticism*, New York: Harcourt, Brace.

Belk, R. (1988), "Possessions and the Extended Self," *The Journal of Consumer Research*, Vol. 15, No. 2: 139–68.

Belk, R. (1995), *Collecting in a Consumer Society*, London: Routledge.

Belk, R., Wallendorf, M., Sherry, J., Holbrook, M. (1990), "Collecting in a Consumer Culture," *Highways and Buyways: Naturalistic Research from the Consumer Behavior Odyssey*, Provo, UT: Association for Consumer Research, 178–215.

Bell, C. (1914), *Art*, New York: Stokes.

Bell, M. and Carolan, M. (2004), *An Invitation to Environmental Sociology*, Thousand Oaks: Pine Forge Press.

Benjamin, W. (1968a), *Illuminations*, New York: Schocken Books.

Benjamin, W. (1968b), "The Work of Art in the Age of Mechanical Reproduction," in *Illuminations: Essays and Reflections,* New York: Schocken Books.

Benjamin, W. (1973), *Charles Baudelaire: A Lyric Poet in the Era of High Capitalism*. London: NLB.

Berger, A. (1992), *Reading Matter: Multicultural Perspectives on Material Culture*, New Brunswick, Transaction.

Berggren, C., (1992), *Alternatives to Lean Production. Work Organisation in the Swedish Auto Industry*, Ithaca: Cornell ILR Press.

Betsky, A. (1997), *Icons: Magnets of Meaning*, San Francisco: Chronicle Books.

Bhagwati, J. (1999), "Globalization: Who Gains Who Loses," in Horst, S. (ed.), *Globalization and Labor*, Tübingen, Germany: Mohr Siebeck.

Bhamra, T. and Lofthouse, V. (2007), *Design for Sustainability: A Practical Approach*, Burlington, VT: Ashgate Publishing Company.

Bicknell, J. and McQuiston L. (1977), *Design for Need: The Social Contribution of Design*, Oxford: Pergamon Press.

Bierman, F. (2007), "The Nike Air Force 1 Sneaker Turns 25 Years Old," *The New York Times*, December 23, 2007.

Biggs, L. (1995), "Building for Mass Production: Factory Design and Work Process at the Ford Motor Company", in R. Asher and R. Edsforth (eds), *Autowork*, Albany: The State University of New York Press.

Bijker, W. (1985), *Of Bicycles, Bakelite, and Bulbs: Toward a Theory of Sociotechnical Change*, Cambridge: MIT Press.

Blackburn, P., Coombs, R. and Green, K. (1985), *Technology, Economic Growth, and the Labour Process*, Basingstoke: Macmillan.

Bling H_2O (2007), bling H_2O.com, accessed 21 June 2007.

Boddewyn, J. (1961), "Galbraith's Wicked Wants," *Journal of Marketing*, Vol. 25, No. 6: 14–18.

Bolin G. (2005), "Notes From Inside the Factory: The Production and Consumption of Signs and Sign Value in Media Industries," *Social Semiotics*, Vol. 15, No. 3: 289–306.

Boradkar, P. (2001), "A Very Strange Thing: Commodity Discourse in Design and Cultural Studies," in D. Durling and J. Shackleton, J. (eds), *Common Ground, The Design Research Society International Conference* [CD-ROM], Staffordshire: Staffordshire University Press.

Borgmann, A. (1987), *Technology and the Character of Contemporary Life: A Philosophical Inquiry*, Chicago: University of Chicago Press.

Bourdieu, P. (1984), *Distinction: A Social Critique of the Judgement of Taste,* Cambridge: Harvard University Press.

Braverman, H. (1974), *Labour and Monopoly Capital: The Degradation of Work in the Twentieth Century*, New York: Monthly Review Press.

Bridge, G. and Smith, A. (2003), "Intimate Encounters: Culture-Economy-Commodity," *Environment and Planning D: Society and Space*, Vol. 21: 257–68.

Brown, B. (2001), "Thing Theory," *Critical Inquiry*, Vol. 28, No. 1: 1–22.

Brown, J. (1954), *The Social Psychology of Industry*, Harmondsworth: Penguin Book.

Buchanan, R. and Margolin, V. (1995), *Discovering Design: Explorations in Design Studies*, Chicago: University of Chicago Press.

Buchli, V. (2002), *The Material Culture Reader*, Oxford: Berg.

Bull, M. (2000), *Sounding Out the City: Personal Stereos and the Management of Everyday Life,* Oxford: Berg.

Bulow, J. (1986), "An Economic Theory of Planned Obsolescence," *The Quarterly Journal of Economics*, Vol. 101, No. 4: 729–50.

Burawoy, M. (1979), *Manufacturing Consent: Changes in the Labor Process under Monopoly Capitalism*, Chicago: University of Chicago Press.

Butter, R. (1989), "Putting Theory into Practice: An Application of Product Semantics to Transportation Design," *Design Issues*, Vol. 5, No. 2: 51–67.

Cagan, J. and Vogel, C. (2002), *Creating Breakthrough Products*, Upper Saddle River: Prentice Hall.

Calkins, E. (1932), "Introduction: What Consumer Engineering Really Is," in R. Sheldon R. and E. Arens, *Consumer Engineering*, New York: Harper & Brothers.

Callon, M. (1986), "Some Elements of a Sociology of Translation: Domestication of the Scallops and the Fishermen of St. Brieuc Bay," in J. Law (ed.) (1986), *Power, Action and Belief: A New Sociology of Knowledge*, London: Routledge & Kegan Paul.

Canabou, C. (2004), *Fast Talk: Better by Design*, Fast Company, www.fastcompany.com/magazine/83/fasttalk.html, accessed 12 October 2008.

Cardoso, R. (2004), "Putting the Magic Back into Design: from Object Fetishism to Product Semantics and Beyond," *Art on the Line*, Vol. 1, No. 2: 1–21.

Cavallaro, D. (2001), *Critical and Cultural Theory: Thematic Variations,* London: Athlone Press.

Chalkley, A., Billett, E., Harrison, D. and Simpson, G. (2003), "Development Of A Method For Calculating The Environmentally Optimum Lifespan Of Electrical Household Products," *Proceedings of the Institution of Mechanical Engineers, Vol. 217, Part B: Journal of Engineering Manufacture*: 1521–31.

Chandler, D. (2002), *Semiotics: The Basics*, London: Routledge.

Chandler, D. (2008), *Semiotics for Beginners*, www.aber.ac.uk/media/Documents/S4B/sem11.html, accessed 12 October 2009.

Chao, E. and Utgoff, K. (2005), *Women in the Labor Force: A Databook*, U.S. Department of Labor and U.S. Bureau of Labor Statistics, Report 985, stats.bls.gov/cps/wlf-databook-2007.pdf, accessed 17 February 2006.

Chapman, A. (2005), *Emotionally Durable Design: Objects, Experiences and Empathy*, London: Earthscan Publications.

Christian Science Monitor (2008), www.csmonitor.com/2006/1222/p01s03-wosc.html, accessed 30 June 2008.

Cipolla, C. (1965), *Guns, Sails and Empires: Technological Innovation and the Early Phases of European Expansion, 1400–1700*, New York: Pantheon Books.

Clarke, A. (2005), *Situational Analysis: Grounded Theory after the Postmodern Turn*, Thousand Oaks, CA: Sage.

Clarke, D. (1990), *Sources of Semiotic: Readings with Commentary from Antiquity to the Present*, Carbondale: Southern Illinois University Press.

Clarke, J., Hall, S., T. Jefferson and B. Roberts, (1993), *Resistance Through Rituals: Youth Subcultures in Post-War Britain*, in S. Hall (ed.), London: Routledge.

Clean Clothes Campaign (2002), www.cleanclothes.org/component/content/article/7-resources/1156-executive-summary-of-the-global-march-report-on-the-football-stitching-industry-of-pakistan, accessed 2 January 2007.

Clegg, S. (1990), *Modern Organizations: Organization Studies in the Postmodern World*, London: Sage Publications.

Cobley, P. and Jansz, L. (1999), *Introducing Semiotics*, Cambridge: Icon Books.

Cockburn, C. (1985), *Machinery of Dominance: Women, Men and Technical Know-How*, London: Pluto.

Connor, S. (2004), A Skin that Walks, www.bbk.ac.uk/eh/skc/skinwalks, accessed 30 March 2004.

Constanze, C. (2005), *Automotive Production Systems and Standardisation: From Ford to the Case of Mercedes-Benz*, New York: Physica-Verlag.

Cook, P. (1972), *Archigram*, Basel: Birkhauser.

Copeland, T., Koller, T., Murrin, J. (1995), *Valuation: Measuring and Managing the Value of Companies*, New York: John Wiley & Sons Inc..

Cosgrove, S. (1984), "The Zoot-Suit and Style Warfare," *History Workshop Journal*, No. 18, Autumn 1984, 77–91.

Crawford, D. (1974), *Kant's Aesthetic Theory*, Madison, Wisconsin: The University of Wisconsin Press.

Cross, N. (2006), *Designerly Ways of Knowing*. London: Springer.

Csikszentmihalyi M. and Rochberg-Halton, E. (1981), *The Meaning of Things: Domestic Symbols and the Self*, Cambridge: Cambridge University Press.

Danesi, M. (2007), *The Quest For Meaning: A Guide To Semiotic Theory And Practice*, Toronto: University of Toronto Press.

Dant, T. (1999), *Material Culture in the Social World: Values, Activities, Lifestyles*, Buckingham: Open University Press.

Dant, T. (2005), *Materiality And Society*, Maidenhead, England: Open University Press.

Daston, L. (2004), *Things that Talk: Object Lessons from Art and Science*, New York: Zone Books.

Davis F. (1985), "Clothing and Fashion as Communication" in M. Solomon (ed.), *The Psychology of Fashion*, Lexington, MA: Heath.

Davis, F. (1989), "Of Maids' Uniforms and Blue Jeans: The Drama of Status Ambivalence in Clothing and Fashion," *Qualitative Sociology*, Vol. 12, No. 4, Winter: 337–355.

Davis, F. (2005), *Fashion, Culture, and Identity*, Chicago: University of Chicago Press.

Davis, S. (1987), *Future Perfect*, Reading, MA: Addison-Wesley.

Debord, G. (2006), *Society of the Spectacle*, London: Rebel Press.

Deely, J. (1990), *Basics of Semiotics*, Bloomington, IA: Indiana University Press.

Deleuze, G. and Foucault, M. (1977), "Intellectuals and Power," in D. Bouchard (ed.) and S. Simon (trans.), *Language, Counter-Memory, Practice*. Ithaca, NY: Cornell University Press.

Dell, K. (2008), "Vinyl Gets Its Groove Back," *Time Magazine*, www.time.com/time/magazine/article/0,9171,1702369,00.html, accessed 5 February 2008.

Dewey, J. (2005), *Art as Experience*, New York: Perigee Books.

Dilnot, C. (1984), "The State of Design History Part II: Problems and Possibilities," *Design Issues*, Vol. I, No. 2: 3–20.

Dilnot, C. (2001), "Beauty: The Promise of Happiness," *Innovation*, Winter: 42–4.

DiSalvo, C. and Gemperle, F. (2003), "From Seduction To Fulfillment: The Use Of Anthropomorphic Form In Design," *DPPI '03: Proceedings of the 2003 International Conference On Designing Pleasurable Products And Interfaces*.

Doblin, J. (1987), "A Short, Grandiose Theory of Design," *STA Design Journal*: 6–16.

Doblin, J. (1988), "Discrimination," *STA Design Journal*: 22–9.

Doordan, D. (1995), *Design History: An Anthology*, Cambridge: MIT Press.

Doordan, D. (2003), "On Materials," *Design Issues*, Vol. 19, No. 4: 3–8.

Doyal L. and Gough, I. (1991), *A Theory of Human Need*, Basingstoke: Macmillan Education.

Draut, T. and Silva, J. (2003), *Borrowing to Make Ends Meet: The Growth of Credit Card Debt in the '90s*, www.demos-usa.org/page19.cfm, accessed 12 January 2009, New York, NY: Demos: A Network for Ideas and Action.

Dreyfuss, H. (2003), *Designing for People*, New York: Allworth Press.

Duening T. and Click, R., (2005), *Essentials of Business Process Outsourcing*, Hoboken, NJ: John Wiley.

du Gay, P., Hall, S., Janes, L., Mackay, H. and Negus, K. (1997), *Doing Cultural Studies: Story of the Sony Walkman*, Thousand Oaks: Sage.

Duhigg, C. (2008), "Warning: Habits May Be Good For You," *The New York Times*, Sunday July 13, 2008.

Durant, W. (1961), *The Story of Philosophy: The Lives and Opinions of the Greater Philosophers*, New York: Simon & Schuster.

Dziersk, M. (2001), "Beauty+Desire," *Innovation*, Winter: 36–7.

Eagleton, T. (2000), The *Idea of Culture*, Oxford: Blackwell.

Earth Policy Institute (2006), www.earth-policy.org/Updates/2007/Update68_data.htm#fig6, accessed 12 July 2009.

Earth Policy Institute (2007), Data and diagram from the Earth Policy Institute, www.earth-policy.org/Updates/2007/Update68_data.htm#fig3, accessed 23 May 2008.

Easterlin, R. (2001), "Income And Happiness: Towards A Unified Theory," *The Economic Journal*, 111 (July), 465–84.

Eco, U. (1979), *A Theory of Semiotics*, Bloomington: University of Indiana Press.

Economides, L. (2007), "Blake, Heidegger, Buddhism, and Deep Ecology: A Fourfold Perspective on Humanity's Relationship to Nature," in Lussier, M. (ed.), *Romanticism and Buddhism*, Montana: Praxis, www.rc.umd.edu/praxis/buddhism/economides/economides.html/, accessed 1 July 2009.

Edgar, A. and Sedgwick, P. (2008), *Cultural Theory: The Key Concepts*. London: Routledge.

Edelberg, W. (2003), "Risk-Based Pricing of Interest Rates in Household Loan Markets," *Finance and Economics Discussion Series 2003– 62*. Washington: Board of Governors of the Federal Reserve System, December 2003.

Elkington, J. (1997), *Cannibals with Forks: The Triple Bottom Line of 21ˢᵗ Century Business*, Gabriola Island, BC; Stony Creek, CT: New Society Publishers.

Ellen, R. (1988), "Fetishism," *Man*, New Series, Vol. 23, No. 2., Jun., 1988: 213–35.

Elson, D. and Pearson, R. (1989), *Women's Employment and Multinationals in Europe,* Basingstroke: Macmillan.

Emerson, R. (1860), "Wealth," in R. W. Emerson, *The Conduct of Life*, Boston: Ticknor & Fields.

Engels, F. (1973), *The Condition of the Working Class in England from Personal Observations and Authentic Sources*, Moscow: Progress Publishers.

Esslinger, H. (2006), "Getting Emotional with Hartmut Esslinger," Design and Emotion Society, www.design-emotion.com/2006/08/15/getting-emotional-with-hartmut-esslinger/, accessed 12 February 2009.

Eternally Yours (2009), web.archive.org/web/20031122232556/http://www.eternally-yours.org/, accessed 24 May 2009.

Ethos.cos (2008), www.ethoswater.com/, accessed 24 May 2008.

Evans, J. (2004), *Marketing in the 21ˢᵗ Century*. Mason, OH: Atomic Dog Publishing.

Ewen, S. (1999), *All Consuming Images: The Politics of Style in Contemporary Culture,* New York: Basic Books.

Fairtrade.net (2008), www.fairtrade.net/about_fairtrade.html accessed 14 July 2008.

Federal Reserve Statistical Release (2008), www.federalreserve.gov/Releases/g17/20080416, accessed 6 June 2008.

Fijiwater.com (2008), www.fijiwater.com/Default.aspx, accessed 23 May 2008.

Fishman A., Gandall N. and Shy, O. (1993), "Planned Obsolescence as an Engine of Technological Progress", *Journal of Industrial Economics*, Volume XLI, No. 4: 361–70.

FLA.org, (2008), www.fairlabor.org/about_us_fla_mission_b1.html, accessed 18 January 2009.

Flatpak (2009), www.flatpak.com, accessed 12 January 2009.

Flusser, V. (2000), *Towards a Philosophy of Photography*, London: Reaktion.

Ford, H. (1922), *My Life and Work*, New York: Doubleday, Page & Company.

Forty, A. (1992), *Objects of Desire: Design and Society, 1750–1980*, London: Thames & Hudson.

Fox, J. and Johnston, W. (1978), *Understanding Capital: A Guide to Volume I*, Toronto: Progress Books.

Fraser, I. (1998), *Hegel and Marx: The Concept of Need*, Edinburgh: Edinburgh University Press.

Frederick, C. (1929), *Selling Mrs. Consumer*, New York: Business Bourse.

Frederick, G. (1928), "Is Progressive Obsolescence the Path Towards Increased Consumption?" *Advertising and Selling*, Vol. 11, No.10: 19–20, 44–46.

Friedman, K. (2000), "Toward an Integrative Design Discipline," in S. Squires and B. Byrne (eds), *Creating Breakthrough Ideas: The Collaboration of Anthropologists and Designers in the Product Development Industry*, New York: Bergin & Garvey.

Friedman, K. (2003), "Theory Construction in Design Research: Criteria, Approaches and Methods," *Design Studies* 24: 507–22.

Frodeman, R. and Mitcham, C. (2005), "New Directions in Interdisciplinarity: Broad, Deep, and Critical", *Bulletin of Science, Technology and Society*, Vol. 27, No. 6: 506–14.

Frondizi, R. (1971), *What Is Value? An Introduction To Axiology*, LaSalle, IL: Open Court Publishing.

Frondizi, R. (1972), "Value as a Gestalt Quality," *Journal of Value Inquiry*, Vol. 6, No. 3 (Fall): 163.

Fry, T. (2008), *Design Futuring: Sustainability, Ethics and New Practice*, Oxford: Berg Publishers.

Galbraith, J. (1998), *The Affluent Society*, London: Penguin Book.

Galway, K. (2001), "On the Scent of Product Lust," *Innovation*, Winter: 50–3.

Gans, H. (1974), *Popular Culture and High Culture*, New York: Basic.

Garrido N. and Alvarez del Castillo, M. (2007), "Environmental Evaluation of Single-Use and Reusable Cups," *International Journal of Life Cycle Assessment*, Vol. 12, No. 4: 252–6.

Gartman, D. (1986), *Autoslavery; The Labor Process in the American Automobile Industry, 1897–1950*, New Brunswick and London: Rutgers University Press.

Gaut, B. and McIver Lopes, D. (2005), *The Routledge Companion to Aesthetics*, New York: Routledge.

Geertz, C. (1973), *The Interpretation of Cultures*, New York: Basic Books.

Gibson, J. (1966), *The Senses Considered As Perceptual Systems*, Boston: Houghton Mifflin.

Goldman, A. (2005), "The Aesthetic" in B. Gaut and D. McIver Lopes, D. (eds), *The Routledge Companion to Aesthetics*, New York: Routledge.

Goldthorpe, J. (1966), "Attitudes and Behaviour of Car Assembly Workers: A Deviant Case and a Theoretical Critique," *British Journal of Sociology*, Vol. 17, No. 3: 227–44.

Gottdiener, M. (1995), *Postmodern Semiotics: Material Culture and the Forms of Postmodern Life*, Cambridge: Blackwell Publishing.

Graeber, D. (2001), *Toward an Anthropological Theory of Value: The False Coin of Our Own Dreams*, New York, NY: Palgrave Macmillan.

Greenhalgh, P. (1993), *Quotations and Sources on Design and the Decorative Arts*, Manchester: Manchester University Press.

Griffin, A. and Hauser, J. (1993), "The Voice of the Customer," *Marketing Science*, Vol. 12, No. 1: 1–27.

Grossman, E. (2006), *High Tech Trash: Digital Devices, Hidden Toxics and Human Health*, Washington, DC: Island Press.

Grout P. and Park, I. (2005), "Competitive Planned Obsolescence," *The RAND Journal of Economics*, Vol. 36, No. 3: 596–612.

Grünberg, L. (2000), *Mystery of Values: Studies in Axiology*, Grünberg, Ludwig, Atlanta, GA: Rodopi.

Gscheidle, G., Stumpf, W. and Weber, J. (2008), *Promoting Healthy Movement And Natural Alignment" The Research And Design Behind The Embody™ Tilt*, Herman Miller Solutions Essays, www.hermanmiller.com, accessed 21 November 2009.

Gutman, J. (1982), "A Means–End Chain Model Based on Consumer Categorization Processes", *Journal of Marketing*, Vol. 46, Spring: 60–72.

Hamilton, R. (1985), *Collected Works*, London: Thames & Hudson.

Hampton, M. (2006), "How Nike Conquered Skateboard Culture," *Adbusters*, 65(2).

Harman, G. (2002), *Tool-being: Heidegger and the Metaphyics of Objects*, Chicago: Open Court.

Harman, G. (2005), *Guerrilla Metaphysics : Phenomenology and the Carpentry of Things*, Chicago: Open Court.

Haug, W. (1986), *Critique of Commodity Aesthetics: Appearance, Sexuality and Advertising in Capitalist Society*. Cambridge: Polity Press.

Hausman, A. and Haytko, D. (2003), "Cross-Border Supply Chain Relationships: Interpretive Research of Maquiladora Realized Strategies," *The Journal of Business and Industrial Marketing*, Vol 18, No. 6/7: 545–63.

Hebdige, D. (1988), *Hiding in the Light: On Image and Things*, London: Routledge.

Hebdige, D. (1991), *Subculture: The Meaning of Style*, London: Routledge.

Hegel, G. (2009), Encyclopedia of the Philosophical Sciences, www.marxists.org/reference/archive/hegel/index.htm, accessed 14 May 2009.

Heidegger, M. (1967), *What Is a Thing?*, trans. W. B. Barton, Jr., and V. Deutsch, Chicago: Henry Regnery.

Heidegger, M. (1971), *Poetry, Language, Thought*, New York: Harper & Row.

Heidegger, M. (1996), *Being and Time*, New York: State University of New York Press.

Heller, A. (1976), *The Theory of Need in Marx*, New York: St. Martins Press.

Herman Miller (2008), *Embody Chairs: For Your Body and Your Mind* [Product Brochure], Zeeland, MI: Herman Miller, Inc.

Herman Miller Materials Program (2009), http://www.hermanmiller.com/MarketFacingTech/hmc/designResources/materialsDetail/Materials_Learn_More/learnmore.html, accessed 12 March 2009.

Herrnstein Smith, B. (1988), *Contingencies of Value: Alternative Perspectives for Critical Theory*, Cambridge, MA: Harvard University Press.

Heskett, J. www.johnheskett.net/BetterbyDesign.pdf, accessed 5 October 2008.

Heskett, J. (2003), "The Desire for the New: The Context of Brooks Stevens' Career", in C. Adamson (ed.), *Industrial Strength Design: How Brooks Stevens Shaped Your World*, Cambridge; MIT Press.

Heskett, J. (2005), "Design as an Economical Function?" *Designmatters*, Vol. 74: 76.

Hocking, M. (1991), "Paper Versus Polystyrene: A Complex Choice", *Science*, New Series, Vol. 251, No. 4993: 504–5.

Hodge, R. and Kress, G. (1988), *Social Semiotics*, New York: Cornell University Press.

Holbrook, M. (1999), *Consumer Value: A Framework for Analysis and Research*, London: Routledge.

Horkheimer, M. (1972), *Critical Theory: Selected Essays*, New York: Herder & Herder: 188.

Hounshell, D. (1985), *From the American System to Mass Production, 1800–1932: The Development Of Manufacturing Technology in the United States*, Baltimore: Johns Hopkins University Press.

Howard, A. (2007), "Labor, History, and Sweatshops in the New Global Economy," in J. Livingston and J. Ploof (eds), *The Object of Labor: Art, Cloth, and Cultural Production*, Cambridge MA: MIT Press.

Hughes, T. (1999), "Edison and Electric Light," in D. MacKenzie and J. Wajcman, (eds), *The Social Shaping of Technology*, Philadelphia, PA: Open University Press.

Human Rights World Report (2008), Human Rights World Report website, http://hwr.org/, accessed 20 June 2008.

Hussain-Khaliq, S. (2004), "Eliminating Child Labour from the Sialkot Soccer Ball Industry," *Journal of Corporate Citizenship*, Vol. 13, Spring: 101–7.

International Labour Organisation (2008), *The International Labour Organisation* website, www.ilo.org/public/english/bureau/stat/isco/index.htm, accessed 11 July 2008.

International Fair Trade Association (2008), www.ifat.org/index.php?option=com_content&task=view&id=2&Itemid=14, accessed 16 July 2008.

International Valuation Standards (2003), *Market Value Basis of Valuation*, www.romacor.ro/legislatie/07-ivs1.pdf, accessed 12 June 2008.

Investor Responsibility Research Center (2008), The Investor Responsibility Research Center website, http://ircc.org/, accessed 30 June 2008.

Inwood, M. (1983), *Hegel*, London: Routledge & Kegan Paul.

Ireland, C. (2003), "Qualitative Methods: From Boring to Brilliant," in B. Laurel, (ed.), *Design Research: Methods and Perspectives*, Cambridge: MIT Press.

Johnson K. (2005), "Recent Developments in the Credit Card Market and the Financial Obligations Ratio," *Federal Reserve Bulletin,* Autumn: 475.

Johnson, W. and Weinstein A. (2004), *Superior Customer Value in the New Economy: Concepts and Cases, Second Edition*, www.myilibrary.com/Browse/open.asp?ID=21725&loc=9, accessed 3 June 2007.

Kahney, L. (2004), *The Cult of Mac*, San Francisco: No Starch Press, Inc.

Kamrani, A. and Salhieh, S. (2002), *Product Design for Modularity*, Boston: Kluwer Academic Publishers.

Kant, I. (1902), *The Critique of Pure Reason*, New York: American Home Library Company.

Kant, I. (1951), *The Critique of Judgment*, translated by John Henry Bernard, Charleston, SC: Forgotten Books.

Keith, R. (1960), "The Marketing Revolution," *Journal of Marketing*, Vol 24, No. 3, pp. 35–8.

Kellner, D. (1989a), *Critical Theory, Marxism and Modernity.* Baltimore: John Hopkins University Press.

Kellner, D. (1989b), *Jean Baudrillard: From Marxism to Postmodernism And Beyond.* Stanford, CA: Stanford University Press.

Kellner, D. (2001), *Jean Baudrillard: From Marxism to Postmodernism and Beyond,* second edition. Stanford, CA: Stanford University Press.

Kemnitzer, R. and Grillo, A., "The Mathematics of Beauty," *Innovation*, Winter: 45–9.

Kennedy, G. (2007), *An Ontology of Trash: The Disposable and its Problematic Nature*, Albany: State University of New York Press.

Kenny, A. (2006), *An Illustrated Brief History of Western Philosophy*, Malden, MA: Blackwell.

Kivy, P. (2004), *The Blackwell Guide to Aesthetics*, Oxford: Blackwell.

Klein, J. (1990), *Interdisciplinarity: History, Theory, and Practice.* Detroit, MI: Wayne State University Press.

Kolano, F., et al. (2007), *Value Standard and Body of Knowledge*, SAVE International, The Value Society, http://www.value-eng.org/, accessed December 12, 2008.

Kopytoff, I. (1986), "The Cultural Biography of Things: Commoditization as Process", in A. Appadurai (ed.) *The Social Life of Things: Commodities in Cultural Perspective*, Cambridge: Cambridge University Press.

Krall, F. (1994), *Ecotone: Wayfaring on the Margins*, New York: State University of New York Press.

Kramer, K. (2006), Jeans, *Historical Materialism*, Vol. 14, No. 4: 289–94.

Krampen, M. (1994), "The Semiotics of Objects Revisited", in T. Sebeok and J. Umiker-Sebeok, (eds), *Advances in Visual Semiotics: The Semiotic Web 1992–93*, Berlin: Mouton de Gruyer.

Krippendorff, K. (2006), *The Semantic Turn: A New Foundation for Design*, Boca Raton: Taylor & Francis.

Krippendorff, K. (1989), "On the Essential Contexts of Artifacts or on the Proposition that Design is Making Sense (of Things)," *Design Issues*, Vol. 5, No. 2: 9–39.

Krippendorff, K. and Butter, R. (1989), Editorial, *Design Issues*, Vol. 5, No. 2.

Krishnamurti, J. (1992), *Choiceless Awareness: A Selection of Passages from the Teachings of J. Krishnamurti*, Ojai, CA: Krishnamurti Foundation of America.

Krohn, L. and McCoy, M. (1989), "Beyond Beige: Interpretive Design for the Post-Industrial Age," *Design Issues*, Vol. 5, No. 2 (Spring, 1989): 112–23.

Kurtgözü, A. (2002), "Deciphering Myths in Design: Towards Restoring the Materiality of the Object through the Technique of Re-sketching," in D. Durling and J. Shackleton, (eds), *Common Ground, The Design Research Society International Conference* [CD-ROM], Staffordshire: Staffordshire University Press.

Laszlo, C. (2008), *Sustainable Value: How the World's Leading Companies are Doing Well by Doing Good*, Stanford, CA: Stanford University Press.

Latour, B. (1993), *We Have Never Been Modern*, (trans.) C. Porter, New York: Harvester Wheatsheaf.

Latour, B. (2004), "Why Has Critique Run Out of Steam? From Matters of Fact to Matters of Concern," *Critical Inquiry* 30, Winter: 225–48.

Latour, B. (2005), *Reassembling the Social: An Introduction to Actor-Network Theory*, Oxford: Oxford University Press.

Laurel, B. (2003), *Design Research: Methods and Perspectives*. Cambridge, MA: MIT Press.

Law, J. (2003), "Notes on the Theory of the Actor Network: Ordering, Strategy and Heterogeneity," Centre for Science Studies, Lancaster University, Lancaster LA1 4YN, at www.comp.lancs.ac.uk/sociology/papers/Law-Notes-on-ANT.pdf, accessed 19 July 2009.

Law, J. (2007), John Law, "Actor Network Theory and Material Semiotics," version of 25 April 2007, www.heterogeneities.net/publications/Law-ANTandMaterialSemiotics.pdf, accessed 13 May 2009.

Law, J. and Hassard, J. (1999), *Actor Network Theory and After*, Malden, MA: Blackwell.

Leborgne D. and Lipietz A. (1988), "New Technologies, New Modes of Regulation: Some Spatial Implications," *Environment and Planning D: Society and Space,* Vol. 6, No. 3: 263–80.

Leebron, D. (1996), "Lying with the Procrustes", in J. Bhagwati and R. Hudec, *Fair Trade and Harmonization: Prerequisites for Free Trade?* Cambridge, MA: MIT Press.

Leiss, W. (1978), *The Limits to Satisfaction: An Essay on the Problem of Needs and Commodities*, Kingston, Ontario: McGill-Queen's University Press.

Levinson, J. (2003), "Philosophical Aesthetics: An Overview" in J. Levinson (ed.), *The Oxford Handbook of Aesthetics*, New York: Oxford University Press.

Levinthal, D. and Purohit, D. (1989), "Durable Goods and Product Obsolescence", *Marketing Science*, Vol 8, No. 1: 35–56.

Lidgus, S. (2003), "Custom Jeans for Every Butt", Salon.com, http://dir.salon.com/story/tech/feature/2003/03/05/levis/index.html, accessed 3 May 2008.

Ligthart, T. and Ansems, A. (2007), *Single Use Cups or Reusable (Coffee) Drinking Systems: An Environmental Comparison*, Appeldoorn, The Netherlands: Netherlands Organisation for Applied Scientific Research.

Lipietz, A. (1987), *Miracles and Mirages: The Crisis of Global Fordism*, London: Verso.

Littler, C. (1978), "Understanding Taylorism," *British Journal of Sociology*, Vol. 29, No. 2: 188.

Lloyd-Jones, P. (1991), *Taste Today: The Role of Appreciation in Consumerism and Design,* New York: Pergamon Press.

Loewy, R. (2002), *Never Leave Well Enough Alone*, Baltimore: Johns Hopkins University Press.

Löfgren, M. (2005), *Winning At The First And Second Moments Of Truth: An Exploratory Study, Managing Service Quality:* 102–15.

LOHAS.com (2009), www.lohas.com/, 24 accessed May 2009.

Lupton, E. (2002), *Skin: Surface, Substance + Design*, New York: Princeton Architectural Press.

Lynes, R. (1954), *The Tastemakers*, New York: Harper.

MacKenzie, D. (1990), *Inventing Accuracy: A Historical Sociology of Nuclear Missile Guidance.* Cambridge: MIT Press.

MacKenzie D. and Wajcman, J. (1999), *The Social Shaping of Technology,* Philadelphia: Open University Press.

Manzini, E. (1989), *The Material of Invention*, London: Design Council Books.

Margolin, V. (ed.) (1989), *Design Discourse: History, Theory, Criticism*, Chicago: University of Chicago Press.

Margolin, V. (2002), *The Politics of the Artificial: Essays in Design and Design Studies.* Chicago: University of Chicago Press.

Markoff, J. (2007), "Fever Builds for iPhone, Anxiety Too", *New York Times,* 29 June 2007.

Marx, K. (1964), *Capital: A Critique of Political Economy, Volume 1,* New York: International Publishers Co., Inc.

Marx, K. (1968), *Economic and Philosophic Manuscripts of 1844,* New York: International Publishers.

Marx, K. (1990), *Capital: A Critique of Political Economy, Vol. 1*, London: Penguin.

Marx, K. (2001), *Capital, Volume I.* London: GBR: ElecBook, http://site.ebrary.com.ezproxy1.lib.asu.edu/lib/asulib/Doc?id=2001687, accessed 5 January 2010.

Marx, K., Fermbach, D. and Fowkes, B. (1981), *Capital: A Critique of Political Economy, Volume Three*, London: Penguin Classics.

Mascha, M. (2007), *Fine Waters: A Connoisseur's Guide to the World's Most Distinctive Bottled Waters*, Philadelphia, PA: Quirk Books.

Maslow A. (1943), "A Theory of Human Motivation," *Psychological Review*, Vol. 50: 370–96.

Mauss, M. (2005), *The Gift: The Form and Reason for Exchange in Archaic Societies,* London: Routledge.

Mayer, N. (2007), March 4. "Rich Man, pour man: Bling H_2O sells \$tatus by the bottle", SignOnSanDiego.com.

Max-Neef, M., Elizalde, A. and Hopenhayn, M. (1989), "Human Scale Development: An Option for the Future," *Development Dialogue* (1): 1–80.

McCoy, M. (1998), Eternally Yours, Lecture in The Hague, Netherlands, HighGround Design, www.2011_highgrounddesign.com, accessed 3 June 2009.

McDonough, W. and Braungart, M. (2002), *Cradle to Cradle: Remaking the Way We Make Things*, New York: North Point Press.

Mehri, D. (2005), *Notes from Toyota-Land: An American Engineer in Japan*, Ithaca, NY: Cornell University Press.

Meikle, J. (1979), *Twentieth Century Limited: Industrial Design in America, 1925–1939*. Philadelphia, PA: Temple University Press.

Meikle, J. (1995), *American Plastic: A Cultural History*, New Brunswick, NJ: Rutgers University Press.

Menzel, P. and Mann, C. (1994), *Material World: A Global Family Portrait*, San Francisco: Sierra Club Books.

Middleton, T. and Giles, J. (1999), *Studying Culture: A Practical Introduction*, Oxford: Blackwell.

Miller, D. (1994), *Material Culture and Mass Consumption,* Oxford: Blackwell.

Miller, D. (1998), *Material Cultures: Why Some Things Matter*, Chicago: University of Chicago Press.

Miller, D. (2001), *Car Cultures*. Oxford: Berg.

Miller, D. (2005), *Materiality*, Durham, N.C.: Duke University Press.

Miller, D. (2008), "The Uses of Value," *Geoforum,* 39: 1122–32.

Miller, P. and Rose, N. (1997), "Mobilizing the Consumer: Assembling the Subject of Consumption", *Theory, Culture and Society,* 14: 1–36.

Mills, C. (1951), *White Collar: The American Middle Classes*, New York, Oxford University Press.

Minh-Ha, T. (1989), *Woman, Native, Other: Writing Postcoloniality and Feminism*, Bloomington: Indiana University Press.

Mintel.com (2008), Jeans-U.S.-February 2006, http://oxygen.mintel.com/sinatra/reports/display/id=295910/display/id=165031, accessed 21 May 2008.

Mitcham, C. (1994), *Thinking Through Technology: The Path Between Engineering and Philosophy*, Chicago: University of Chicago Press.

Miklitsch, R. (1998), *From Hegel to Madonna: Towards a General Economy of "Commodity Fetishism,"* Albany: State University of New York Press.

Mitcham, C. (2005), *Encyclopedia of Science, Technology and Ethics*, Detroit, MI: Macmillan.

Mithen, S. (2003), "Handaxes: The First Aesthetic Artefacts," in E. Voland and K. Grammer (eds), *Evolutionary Aesthetics*, Berlin: Springer-Verlag.

MoMA (2008), Museum of Modern Art, (moma.org), www.moma.org/collection/browse_results.php?criteria=O%3AAD%3AE%3A22559&page_number=6&template_id=1&sort_order=1, accessed 20 November 2008.

Montagu, A. (1986), *Touching: The Human Significance of the Skin*, New York: Harper & Row.

Moran, D. (2000), *Introduction to Phenomenology*, London: Routledge.

Morris, C. (1946), *Signs, Language, and Behavior*, New York: Prentice Hall.

Moyal, G. (1991), *René Descartes: Critical Assessments, Volume 1*, London: Routledge.

Muniz, A. and Schau, H. (2005), "Religiosity in the Abandoned Apple Newton Brand Community," *Journal of Consumer Research,* Vol. 31, No. 4: 737–47.

Nelson, G. (1967), "Obsolescence", *Perspecta*, Vol. 11: 170–6.

Nelson, R. and Shiff, R. (2003), *Critical Terms in Art History*, Chicago: University of Chicago Press.

Noori, H. (1990), *Managing the Dynamics of New Technology: Issues in Manufacturing Management*, Englewood Cliffs, NJ: Prentice Hall.

Nöth, W. (1990), *Handbook of Semiotics*. Bloomington: Indiana University Press.

Oleson, J. (1998), *Pathways to Agility: Mass Customization in Action*, Hoboken: Wiley.

Orbach B. (2004), *The Durapolist Puzzle: Monopoly Power in Durable-Goods Market*, University of Michigan Law School, The John M. Olin Center for Law and Economics Working Paper Series Year 2004, Paper I, Berkeley Electronic Press.

Packard, V. (1960), *The Waste Makers*, London: Longman.

Padgett, B. (2007), *Marx and Alienation in Contemporary Society*, New York: Continuum.

Papanek, V. (1971), *Design for the Real World: Human Ecology and Social Change,* New York: Pantheon Press.

Papanek, V. (1995), *The Green Imperative: Natural Design for the Real World,* New York: Thames & Hudson.

Patagonia.com (2008), www.patagonia.com/web/us/footprint/index.jsp, accessed 18 January 2009.

Patton, P. (1999), For the Tech Hungry, Shops Full of Candy, www.philpatton.com accessed 4 April 2004.

PBS.org (2004), The Secret History of the Credit Card, www.pbs.org/wgbh/pages/frontline/shows/credit/, accessed 29 May 2009.

Pearce, S. (1998), *Collecting in Contemporary Practice*, London: Sage Publications.

Peirce, C. (1963), *The Charles S. Peirce Papers*, [Microform], Cambridge: Harvard University Library.

Peirce, C. (1992), *The Essential Peirce: Selected Philosophical Writings, Volume 1 (1863–1893)*, N. Houser and C. Kloesel (eds), Bloomington: Indiana University Press.

Peirce, C. (1998), *The Essential Peirce: Selected Philosophical Writings, Volume 2 (1893–1913)*, N. Houser (ed.), Bloomington: Indiana University Press.

Penner, T. and Rowe, C. (2005), *Plato's Lysis*, Massachusetts: Cambridge University Press.

People (2007), Country Special, 19.

Pevsner, N. (1936), *Pioneers of the Modern Movement: From William Morris to Walter Gropius.* Harmondsworth: Penguin Books, Ltd.

Pine, J. (1993), *Mass Customization: The New Frontier in Business Competition*, Boston, MA: Harvard Business School Press.

Piore, M. and Sabel, C. (1984), *The Second Industrial Divide*, New York: Basic Books.

Porter, M. (1998), *Competitive Advantage: Creating and Sustaining Superior Performance*, New York: Simon & Schuster.

Poster, M. (1979), "Semiology and Critical Theory: From Marx to Baudrillard," *Boundary 2*, Vol. 8, No. 1, 'The Problems of Reading in Contemporary American Criticism: A Symposium', Autumn, 1979: 275–88.

Poster, M. (1988), *Jean Baudrillard: Selected Writings*, Stanford: Stanford University Press.

Postrel, V. (2003), *The Substance of Style: How the Rise of Aesthetic Value is Remaking Commerce, Culture, and Consciousness*, New York: HarperCollins.

Postrel, V. (2004), "Why Buy What You Don't Need: The Marginal Appeal of Aesthetics," *Innovation*, Spring: 30–6.

Prahalad, C. (1994), "Corporate Governance or Corporate Value Added?: Rethinking the Primacy of Shareholder Value," *Journal of Applied Corporate Finance*, Vol. 6, No. 4: 40–50.

Ramsay, M. (1992), *Human Needs and the Market*, Brookfield, VT: Avebury.

Rathje, W. and Murphy, C. (2001), *Rubbish! The Archaeology of Garbage*, Tucson: University of Arizona Press.

Ravallion, M. and Datt, G. (2003), *Is India's Economic Growth Leaving the Poor Behind?*, World Bank Policy Research Working Paper No 2846, Washington, DC: World Bank.

Reader, S. (2005), *The Philosophy of Need*, New York: Cambridge University Press.

R.I.A.A. Recording Industry of America, www.riaa.com/keystatistics.php, accessed 5 February 2008.

Richardson, A. (1993), "The Death of the Designer," *Design Issues*, Vol. 9, No. 2: 34–43.

Rodick, D. (1997), *Has Globalization Gone Too Far?*, Washington, DC: Peterson Institute.

Rokeach, M. (1973), *The Nature of Human Values*, New York: Free Press.

Rokeach, M. (1974), "Change and Stability in American Value Systems, 1968–1971," *The Public Opinion Quarterly*, Vol. 38, No. 2: 222–38.

Rosenau, M. (1996), *The PDMA Handbook Of New Product Development*, New York: Wiley.

Rosenthal, E. (2008), "With Irish Tax, Plastic Bags Go the Way of the Snakes," *New York Times*, 2 February.

Roth, S. (1999), "The State of Design Research", *Design Issues*, Vol 15. No. 2: 18–27.

Rowe, C. (2005), "Needs and Ethics in Ancient Philosophy," in S. Reader (ed.), *The Philosophy of Need*, New York: Cambridge University Press.

Salzinger, L. (2003), *Genders in Production: Making Workers in Mexico's Global Factories*, Berkeley: University of California Press.

Sandberg, Å. (2007), *Enriching Production: Perspectives On Volvo's Uddevalla Plant As An Alternative To Lean Production*, digital edition, Avebury: Aldershot.

Sargant, P. (1953), *The Logic of British and American Industry*, Chapel Hill: The University of North Carolina Press.

Saussure, F. (1959), *Course in General Linguistics*, C. Bally and A. Sechehaye (eds), New York: McGraw Hill, New York.

Scanlan, J. (2005), *On Garbage*, London: Reaktion Books.

Schanberg, S. (1996), http://query.nytimes.com/gst/fullpage.html?res=9905EFD9143FF937A2575 1C0A961958260, accessed 12 March 2008.

Schmidgen, W. (2001), "Robinson Crusoe, Enumeration, and the Mercantile Fetish," *Eighteenth-Century Studies*, Vol. 35, No. 1: 19–39.

Schmitt, B. and Simonson, A. (1997), *Marketing Aesthetics: The Strategic Management of Brands, Identity, and Image*, New York: Free Press.

Schmittel, W. (1975), *Design Concept Realisation*. Zurich: ABC Verlag.

Schneider, M. (2006), *The Theory Primer: A Sociological Guide*, Maryland: Rowman and Littlefield Publishers.

Schoenberger, E. (1988), "From Fordism to Flexible Accumulation: Technology, Competitive Strategies, and International Location," *Environment and Planning D: Society and Space*, Vol 6: 245–62.

Schwartz-Cowan, R. (1983), *More Work for Mother: The Ironies of Household Technology from the Open Hearth to the Microwave*, New York: Basic Books.

Sebeok, T. (1974), "Semiotics: A Survey of the State of the Art," in T. Sebeok (ed.), *Current Trends in Linguistics*, Vol. 12, The Hague: Mouton.

Shand, J. (1993), *Philosophy and Philosophers: An Introduction to Western Philosophy*, London: UCL Press.

Sheldon, R. and Arens, E. (1932), *Consumer Engineering*, New York: Harper & Brothers.

Sherman, H. (1987), *Foundations of Radical Political Economy*, New York: M.E. Sharpe.

Shils, E. (1978), "Mass Society and its Culture," in P. Davidson, R. Myersohn and Shils, E. (eds), *Literary Taste, Culture and Mass Communication, Volume 1*, Cambridge: Chadwyck Healey.

Shorris, E. (2004), *The Life and Times of Mexico*, New York: W.W. Norton & Co., Inc.

Shusterman, R. (1997), "The End of Aesthetic Experience," *Journal of Aesthetics and Art Criticism*, Vol. 55, No. 1: 29–41.

Simmel, G. (1978), *The Philosophy of Money*, Boston, MA: Routledge & Kegan Paul.

Simmel, G. (2001), *The Philosophy of Money*, Second Edition, London: Routledge.

Sirgy, J. (1982), "Self-Concept in Consumer Behavior: A Critical Review," *The Journal of Consumer Research*, Vol. 9, No. 3: 287–300.

Slade G. (2006), *Made to Break: Technology and Obsolescence in America*, Cambridge: Harvard University Press.

Smartskins (2006), www.smartskins.com, accessed 19 September 2006.

Smith, P. (2001), *Cultural Theory: An Introduction*. Malden, MA.: Blackwell Publishers.

Social Technologies, (2009), *12 Consumer Values to Drive Technology-Related Product and Service Innovations*, Press Release, www.socialtechnologies.com/FileView.aspx?fileName=4-24-06_12 ConsumerValues_Josh.pdf, accessed 12 November 2006.

Solomon, R. and Higgins, K. (1996*), A Short History of Philosophy*, New York : Oxford University Press.

Sparke, P. (1987), *Design in Context*, Secaucus: Chartwell Books.

Sparke, P. (1990), *The Plastics Age: From Modernity To Post-Modernity*, London: Victoria and Albert Museum.

Sparke, P. (1995), *As Long as it's Pink: The Sexual Politics of Taste*, San Francisco: Pandora.

Sparke, P. (1998), *A Century of Design: Design Pioneers of the 20ᵗʰ Century*, Hauppauge, NY: Barron's Educational Series.

Spendster.org (2008), http://spendster.org, accessed 29 November 2008.

Spreng, S., MacKenzie, S., Olshaysky, R. (1996), "A Reexamination of the Determinants of Consumer Satisfaction," *Journal of Marketing*, Vol. 60, No. 3: 15–32.

Spyer, P. (1998), *Border Fetishisms: Material Culture in Unstable Spaces*, New York: Routledge.

Strasser, S. (1999), *Waste and Want: A Social History of Trash*, Metropolitan Books, New York.

Stratton, J. (1996), *The Desirable Body: Cultural Fetishism and the Erotics of Consumption*, New York: St. Martin's Press.

Sudjic, D. (1985), *Cult Objects: The Guide to Having it All*, London: Paladin.

Suri, N. (2007), "Offshore Outsourcing of Services as a Catalyst of Economic Development: the Case of India," in P. Eva (ed.), *Global Capitalism Unbound: Winners and Losers from Offshore Outsourcing*, New York: Palgrave.

Target (2008), Target Corporation Website, accessed 16 November 2008, http://sites.target.com/site/en/company/page.jsp;jsessionid=TKBI15W1HAPKRLARAAVPYAA?contentId=WCMP04-031806, accessed 23 August 2008.

Tasmanian Rain (2007), www.tasmanianrain.com/product.html, accessed 21 June 2007.

Taylor, F. (1947), *Scientific Management, Comprising Shop Management and the Principles of Scientific Management*, New York: Harper.

Thackara, J. (2005), *In the Bubble: Designing in a Complex World*, Cambridge: MIT Press.

Thomson, G. (2005), "Fundamental Needs", in S. Reader (ed.), *The Philosophy of Need*, New York: Cambridge University Press.

Tilley, C., Keane, W., Küchler, S., Rowlands, M. and Spryer, P. (eds) (2006), *Handbook of Material Culture,* London: Sage.

Toyota.co.jp (2009), www2.toyota.co.jp/en/vision/production-system/index.html, accessed 6 February 2009.

Tucker, R. (1972), *The Marx-Engels Reader*, New York: W. W. Norton & Company, Inc.

U.S. Census Bureau (2009), www.census.gov/ipc/www/idb/region.php, accessed 21 July 2009.

Van Hinte, E. (2004), *Eternally Yours: Time In Design : Product Value Sustenance,* Rotterdam: 010 Publishers.

Van Leeuwen, T. (2005), *Introducing Social Semiotics*, London: Routledge.

Varley, P. (1998), *The Sweatshop Quandary: Corporate Responsibility on the Global Frontier*, International Labor Project Profiles, Washington.

Veblen, T. (1973), *Theory of The Leisure Class*, Boston: Houghton Mifflin.

Venturi, R. (1977), *Complexity and Contradiction in Architecture*, New York: Museum of Modern Art.

Verbeek, P. (2005), *What Things Do: Philosophical Reflections on Technology, Agency, and Design*, University Park, PA: Pennsylvania State University Press.

Verbeek, P. and Kockelkoren, P. (1998), "The Things that Matter," *Design Issues*, Vol.14, No. 3: 28–42.

Verbeek, P. and Kockelkoren, P. (2004), "Matter Matters," in Van Hinte (ed.), *Eternally Yours,* Rotterdam: 010 Publishers: 101–15.

Viemeister, T. (2001), "Beautility," *Innovation*, Winter 2001: 38–41.

Vigon, B., Tolle, D., Cornaby, B., Lathan, H, Harrison, C., Boguski, T., Hunt, R. and Sellers, J. (1994), *Life-Cycle Assessment: Inventory Guidelines and Principles*, Boca Raton, FL: CRC Press.

Wajcman, J. (1991), *Feminism Confronts Technology*, Cambridge, UK: Polity Press.

Waldman, M. (1993), "A New Perspective on Planned Obsolescence", *Quarterly Journal of Economics*, Vol. 108, No. 1: 273–83.

Walker, J. (1989), *Design History and the History of Design*, London: Pluto.

Walker, R. (2006), "Consumed: Big Gulp". *New York Times*, 26 February 2006.

Walker, S. and Marr, J. (2001), *Stakeholder Power: A Winning Strategy for Building Stakeholder Commitment and Driving Corporate Growth*, New York: Basic Books.

Wasson, C. (2000), "Ethnography in the Field Of Design," *Human Organization*, Vol. 59, No. 4: 377–88.

Wedberg, A. (1982), *A History of Philosophy*, Oxford: Clarendon Press.

Weiner, A. (1992), *Inalienable Possessions: The Paradox of Giving-while-keeping*, Berkeley: University of California Press.

Weisman, A. (2007), *The World Without Us*, New York: Thomas Dunne Books/St. Martin's Press.

White, P., St. Pierre. L. and Belletire, S. (2007), *The Okala Design Guide*, Dulles: Industrial Designers Society of America.

Whiteley, N. (1987), "Toward a Throw-Away Culture: Consumerism, 'Style Obsolescence' and Cultural Theory in the 1950s and 1960s," *Oxford Art Journal*, Vol. 10, No. 2: 3–27.

Whiteley, N. (1993), *Design for Society*, London: Reaktion Books.

Whitston, K. (2002), "Worker Resistance and Taylorism in Britain", in J. Wood and M. Wood (eds), *F. W. Taylor: Critical Evaluations in Business and Management, Volume 4*, London: Routledge.

Wigfield, A. (2001), *Post-Fordism, Gender and Work*, Aldershot: Ashgate.

Williams, R. (1975), *Television: Technology and Cultural Form.* New York: Schocken Books.

Williams, R. (1976), *Keywords: A Vocabulary of Culture and Society*, Oxford University Press: New York.

Williams, R. (2001), *The Raymond Williams Reader*, J. Higgins (ed.), Oxford: Blackwell Publishing.

Wilson, E. (1984), *Biophilia: The Human Bond with Other Species*, Cambridge, MA: Harvard University Press.

Winner, L. (1980), "Do Artifacts Have Politics," *Daedalus*, Vol. 109, No. 1: 121–36.

Wittgenstein, L. (1998), *Tractatus Logico-Philosophicus*, New York: Dover.

Womack, J., Jones, D. and Roos, D. (1990), *The Machine that Changed the World: Based on the Massachusetts Institute of Technology 5-Million Dollar, 5-Year Study on the Future of the Automobile*, New York: Rawson Associates.

Woodham, J. (1997), *Twentieth Century Design*, Oxford: Oxford University Press.

Woodruff, R. and Gardial, S. (1996), *Know Your Customer: New Approaches to Understanding Customer Value and Satisfaction*, Cambridge, MA: Blackwell.

World in Balance.net (2009), www.worldinbalance.net/agreements/1987-brundtland.php, accessed 24 May 2009.

Wrege, C. and Hodgetts, R. (2000), "Frederick W. Taylor's 1899 Pig Iron Observations: Examining Fact, Fiction, and Lessons for the New Millennium," *The Academy of Management Journal*, Vol. 43, No. 6, Dec., 2000: 1283–91.

Wrege, C. and Stotka, A. (1978), "Cooke Creates a Classic: The Story behind F. W. Taylor's Principles of Scientific Management," *The Academy of Management Review*, Vol. 3, No. 4: 736–49.

Wright, M. (2006), *Disposable Women and other Myths of Global Capitalism*, London: Routledge.

Yale Law Journal (1971), "Annual Style Change in the Automobile Industry as an Unfair Method of Competition", *The Yale Law Journal*, Vol. 80, No. 3: 567–613.

Younker, D. (2003), *Value Engineering: Analysis and Methodology*, New York: CRC Press.

Zemach, E. (1997), *Real Beauty*, University Park, PA: Pennsylvania State University Press.

Zinn, H. (2004), *The People Speak: American Voices, Some Famous, Some Little Known: Dramatic Readings Celebrating the Enduring Spirit of Dissent*, New York: HarperCollins.

ACKNOWLEDGMENTS

The contract for *Designing Things* arrived in the mail the day before my dearest friend Paul Rothstein died unexpectedly in the middle of the night. As soon as I opened the envelope, I called Paul to tell him about it. He had been waiting for it with as much eagerness as I had. But, in his usual fashion of caring deeply but deliberately not showing it, he said, "big deal." This book is dedicated to Paul. He would have been truly delighted to see it in print. This book is also dedicated to my parents, who unfortunately never got to meet Paul. They too, have been waiting eagerly to see it in print. My father's patience, usually rather limitless, has been wearing thin. My mother, as she is wont to do, is already planning the parties she intends to throw simply because I have completed it. I want to thank them for all they have done for me. They are both truly remarkable and incredibly special to me. My gratitude also extends to my sister Manisha, my friend Debashis and my nephew Binbin, who at the young age of seven asked me why in the world would I spend so much time at my desk working on it (instead of playing with him), when no one in particular (especially my teachers or my parents) had "told me" to write this book.

Books cannot be written without the love, nurturing and often invisible labor of friends. These pages can only partially express my sincere thanks to all of them. Heidi Fischer, Paul's wife and dear friend, has been a source of endless strength, spirit and support. Her kindness knows no limits. Amethyst Saludo, who designed the cover for this book and its website, as well as all the illustrations in these pages, has spent countless hours on this project. Her creativity, eye for detail and her friendship mean a lot to me. Dan Brouwer and I have spent countless hours together in cafés working on our respective writing projects, and his presence in my life has been invaluable. Many friends, though not in my immediate environment in Arizona have played a crucial role in helping me through this journey. Donna Chavez, my dear friend of many years, has had an unshakeable faith in me and has been urging me with patience and insistence to "just get it done!" And so has my friend Abhay Sharma. Farther away, in India, Rashmi Ranade and Unmesh Kulkarni, my close friends since design school, have helped with ideas and concepts for the book. A shout out to Shuchi Kothari and Nabeel Zuberi for all their encouragement.

Several colleagues at Arizona State University have supported me through this process and I owe much to them all: Mookesh Patel, Lauren McDermott, Dosun Shin, Philip White, Jordan Meyers, Jacques Giard, John Takamura, Peter Wolf, Don Herring Aisling Kelliher and Pepe Velasquez. Other ASU faculty and friends who have been wonderfully helpful include Jennifer Brungart, Nancy Levinson, Brad Jones, Jim Hershauer, Andy Weed,

Jose Bernardi, Craig Hedges and Bill Verdini. For their support and friendship, thanks to Renata Hejduk and Darren Petrucci. To my friend Tom Duening, who inspires by example, thank you, you writing fiend. Sue Elliott, Kelly Slania and Joni Escobedo at ASU have been marvelous with their reliable assistance. Other friends who have lent a hand in many ways include Leigh Flayton, Marilu Knode, Duke Reiter and Pattie Moore. Thanks also to Ted Leeson and Betty Campbell, both writers of exquisite skill. I am deeply indebted to all my students, undergraduate and graduate, past and present, who have shaped me as a teacher. Emily Callaghan, Tamara Christensen, Lisa Broome, Greg Burkett, Dan Wandrey, Tejas Dhadphale, Liqing Zhou, Qian Yang, Altay Sendil, Nate Morehouse and Adrian Smith, thanks to you all.

At Berg, I am deeply indebted to Tristan Palmer, who guided me through several stages of this long process with trust and encouragement. A big thanks to Jonathan Mazliah for his incredible patience and also to Anna Wright, Emily Medcalf and David Michael. I am also grateful to the anonymous reviewers whose critical recommendations helped improve the text tremendously.

The case studies would not have been possible without the assistance of several corporations. At Herman Miller Inc., I would like to extend my gratitude to Brian Walker, Don Goeman, Doug Bazuin, Gretchen Gschiedle, Mark Schurman, Joe Schwartz, Janet Barnes, Bob Nyhuis and Kris Farrugia. Thanks also to designer Jeff Weber. For their assistance with several Numark products, I owe a great deal to Jonathan Hayes and Roy Thompson. Similarly, thanks to Gavin Ivester and Benoit Duverger at Puma. For their assistance with the case studies, many thanks to Steve McCallion and Pierre Harper of Ziba Design, Yani Deros of ATOMDesign, Bruce Fitzpatrick of Abernathy Auto Parts and Charles O'Toole of Charles Furniture. To Irv Gordon, the very embodiment of autodurability with his 2.79 million mile Volvo, thanks for your help. I wish the rest of the world would keep living with their products as long as you have been able to live with yours.

At the peaceful Desert House of Prayer, a retreat where one is invited into silence with open arms, I wish to extend my deepest gratitude to Father Ricardo, Sister Rita, Sister Genny, Brother Bill and Jacqueline.

Chapter 2, "Theorizing Things: Disciplinary Diversity in Thinking About Objects" borrows from an article titled "Theorizing Things: Status, Problems and Benefits of the Critical Interpretation of Objects" that appeared in 2006 in *The Design Journal*, Vol.9, Issue 2, pp. 3–15.

My gratitude extends also to all the women and men I will never know who, once I am done writing this, will labor over typesetting, printing, packing, shipping, transporting, shelving, inventorying and storing copies of the book. Thank you.

INDEX